POINTS...

Interviews,

1974–1994

MERIDIAN

Crossing Aesthetics

Werner Hamacher
& David E. Wellbery
Editors

Edited by
Elisabeth Weber

Translated by
Peggy Kamuf
& others

*Stanford
University
Press*

*Stanford
California
1995*

POINTS...

Interviews, 1974–1994

Jacques Derrida

Originally published in French in 1992
as *Points de suspension, Entretiens*
by Editions Galilée,
© 1992 by Editions Galilée.

Assistance for this translation
was provided by the French
Ministry of Culture.

Stanford University Press
Stanford, California
© 1995 by the Board of Trustees of the
Leland Stanford Junior University

Printed in the United States of America

CIP data appear at the end of the book

Stanford University Press publications
are distributed exclusively by
Stanford University Press within
the United States, Canada, and Mexico;
they are distributed exclusively by
Cambridge University Press
throughout the rest of the world.

Foreword to the English Translation

by Peggy Kamuf

Fourteen of the twenty-three interviews collected in this volume appear here for the first time translated into English. Of the remaining interviews, one, "Heidegger, the Philosophers' Hell," has been retranslated for this edition. The interview titled "The Work of Intellectuals and the Press (The Bad Example: How the *New York Review of Books* and Company Do Business)" was specially commissioned for this volume, and one other previously translated interview, "*Honoris Causa*: 'This is *also* extremely funny,'" has been added to those collected in the original French edition. The circumstances in which the interviews were given and the dates and places of their first publication (or their broadcast, in the case of radio interviews) are described by the initial note accompanying each text.

Besides this initial note, other notes have been added to many of the interviews, either by the editor of the collection, Elisabeth Weber, or by the translator. Translator's notes are identified by "—Trans." at the end of the note; author's notes are identified by "—J.D." All other notes are the editor's. In the text and notes, square brackets indicate an insertion made by the editor or translator, except in "Between Brackets I" and "*Ja*, or the *faux-bond* II," where square brackets are used by Derrida and curly brackets by the editor or translator. Complete bibliographical information for works by Derrida frequently referred to in the text of the interviews or in the notes is listed at the end of the volume.

A word about the translation of the original title, *Points de suspension*. This expression commonly refers to the punctuation mark called suspension points in English. But as Elisabeth Weber explains in her introduction, the expression, in its position as title of a collection of interviews, gets overwritten or re-marked by a more "literal" sense of points of suspension, punctual interventions suspended from, for example, the other's discourse and often interrupted by an interlocutor. Hence the graphic solution chosen to translate, for the eye and the ear, this double title. The three dots (set close together: ...) will also frequently punctuate the suspended remarks of Derrida and his interlocutors. An ellipsis, or three spaced dots (. . .) will be used to indicate any omissions.

Finally, a word of gratitude to the other translators whose work is reprinted here. It is often said that translation is a thankless task, which is true enough if one means that it is, by definition and in advance, doomed to a kind of failure since it can do no more than approximate the original. Translators of Derrida's writings have the additional awareness that this failure is often actively anticipated and aggravated by the language of the original and by a thinking that, at every turn, seeks something like its idiom. That added awareness, however, need not be counted as a negative or a handicap when figured into the experience; on the contrary, these texts, in their consideration of and for translation's impossibility (and therefore its necessity) can reconfigure "thanklessness" or "ingratitude" in a wholly different economy of meaning and experience. In any case, if it takes one translator to recognize and appreciate the work of others, then let that be the case here. Namely:

Christie V. McDonald, for "Choreographies," originally published in *Diacritics* 12, no. 2 (1982): 66–76, and reprinted by permission of Johns Hopkins University Press.

Verena Andermatt Conley, for "Voice II," originally published in *boundary 2*, 19:2. Translation © 1984 by Verena Conley. Reprinted by permission of Duke University Press.

John P. Leavey, Jr., for "*Comment donner raison?* 'How to Concede, with Reasons?'" originally published in *Diacritics* 19, nos. 3–4 (1989): 4–9, and reprinted by permission of Johns Hopkins University Press.

Michael Israel, for "The Rhetoric of Drugs," originally published in *differences: A Journal of Feminist Cultural Studies* 5.1 (1993): 1–24.

Peter Connor and Avital Ronell, for "'Eating Well,' or the Calculation of the Subject," originally published in *Topoi* 7, no. 2 (1988): 113–21, and reprinted by permission of Kluwer Academic Publishers.

Marian Hobson and Christopher Johnson, for "*Honoris Causa*: 'This is *also* extremely funny,'" originally published in the *Cambridge Review* 113, no. 2318 (October 1992), and reprinted by permission of Cambridge University Press.

All other translations are mine. The translation of *Che cos'è la poesia?* first appeared in *A Derrida Reader: Between the Blinds*, Peggy Kamuf, ed., 1991 © Columbia University Press, New York. Reprinted with permission of the publisher.

We thank the publishers for their kind permission to reprint. Whatever modifications may have been made occasionally to these translations were adopted to regularize usage and vocabulary across the volume.

Contents

Introduction: Upside-Down Writing
by Elisabeth Weber   1

Between Brackets I   5

Ja, or the *faux-bond* II   30

"The Almost Nothing of the Unpresentable"   78

Choreographies   89

Of a Certain Collège International de
Philosophie Still to Come   109

Unsealing ("the old new language")   115

"Dialanguages"   132

Voice II   156

Language (*Le Monde* on the Telephone)   171

Heidegger, the Philosophers' Hell   181
followed by

Comment donner raison? "How to Concede,
with Reasons?"   191

"There is No *One* Narcissism"
(Autobiophotographies)   196

Is There a Philosophical Language?   216

The Rhetoric of Drugs   228

"Eating Well," or the Calculation of
the Subject   255

Che cos'è la poesia?   288

Istrice 2: Ick bünn all hier   300

Once Again from the Top: Of the Right
to Philosophy   327

"A 'Madness' Must Watch Over Thinking"   339

Counter-Signatures   365

Passages—from Traumatism to Promise   372

TWO "AFFAIRS"

Honoris Causa: "This is *also* extremely funny"   399

The Work of Intellectuals and the Press
(The Bad Example: How the *New York Review
of Books* and Company Do Business)   422

Notes   457

Works Cited   489

Bibliography of Other Interviews with
Jacques Derrida   495

POINTS...

Interviews,
1974–1994

Introduction:
Upside-Down Writing

by Elisabeth Weber

Why can't I avoid speaking, unless it is because a
promise has committed me even before I begin the
briefest speech. . . . From the moment I open my
mouth, I have already promised; or rather, and
sooner, the promise has seized the *I* which promises to speak to the other, to say something, at the
extreme limit to affirm or to confirm by speech at
least this: that it is necessary to be silent; and to be
silent concerning that about which one cannot
speak. . . . Even if I decide to be silent, even if I decide to promise nothing, not to commit myself to
saying something that would confirm once again
the destination *of* speech, and the destination *to-*
ward speech, this silence yet remains a modality of
speech: a memory of promise and a promise of
memory.[1]

Number of yes, again, the twenty[2] interviews collected here
represent as many variations on this modality of speech. Each one
of them—and the commitment is each time unique—remains
faithful to the memory of a promise and to some promise of
memory: here and there in the interview, an "I" is indeed "seized,"
conscripted, held to the pledge. It is in fact a matter of an always
singular address. It begins, one could say, by responding (to the
other as well as for itself). Like the "yes," it is "originally in its very
structure, a response"[3]: in a dated situation and, as one says, in a
"context" that the interview, as one will often notice, does not fail
to remark, plying itself and pleasing itself sometimes by analyzing
it—right away and along the way, in a more or less explicit fashion.

Each time a speech is addressed or answers, it listens—to the other, itself, the law, I mean that agreement that holds them to its law, even when it is a matter of debate, discussion, dispute, or separation. This speech sometimes gives itself over to improvisation, sometimes mimics it or plays with it, and for that reason one might be tempted to call it by an old name that Derrida is said to have made into a target: *living* speech. One could just as well say *written word* or *given word*, and the three most often intersect in the same sentence, I will even dare to say the same voice. For I often have the impression also of a written improvisation that finds once again, upside down in some way, a spontaneity that the aforementioned living speech would have in reality already lost. We know that especially when readers are in a hurry, Jacques Derrida often passes for someone who has taken the *side of writing*—and against speech! He would have thus opposed the one to the other, then reversed the order or the hierarchy, and so forth and so on. Now, just a little attention, for example to the first move of *Grammatology*, is enough to discredit the simplism of such a *siding with writing*. Without going back over here the theoretical demonstrations that make of this thinking of writing something altogether other than a war against speech, but rather a problematic of *address* and *destination*, which is to say, in effect an *experience of the interview*, I would suggest that one reread for example, in the margins of this collection, a chapter of *Mémoires for Paul de Man* ("Acts: The Meaning of a Given Word") or certain confidential remarks in *The Post Card*: "writing horrifies me more than at any other moment in the past" (December 9, 1977), claims the signatory of the "Envois." Elsewhere he at least pretends, out of irony or melancholy, to present himself also as a "man of speech" who writes "upside down." A card dated May 1979: "What cannot be said above all must not be silenced but written. Myself, I am a man of speech, I have never had anything to write. When I have something to say I say it or say it to myself, basta. You are the only one to understand why it really was necessary that I write exactly the opposite, as concerns axiomatics, of what I desire, what I know my desire to be, in other words you: living speech, presence itself, proximity, the proper, the guard,

etc. I have necessarily written upside down—and in order to surrender to Necessity.

and 'fort de toi."[4]

Is it enough to recall that this thinking of writing, address, and
destination is also an experience of the interview, that is, of the
plurality of voices ("The call of the other is the call to come, and
that happens only in multiple voices"[5])? One must also specify that
it is marked, sometimes in a suspensive way, sometimes clearly, by
sexual difference. Still more specifically, and certain interviews here
make it their theme, it is marked by that which in sexual difference
carries beyond the one and the two, dual or oppositional difference.[6] During the whole period covered by the twenty interviews
collected here, long before and after *The Post Card* that I have just
cited, the texts in several voices proliferated in fact. In each case, a
woman's voice can be heard there, even an indeterminate number
of women's voices. Of themselves they come to *engage* the discussion: to apostrophize, resonate, argue, respond, correspond, contest, provoke, affirm, give—to give one to think or to give, period.[7]

The several exchanges in which Jacques Derrida will have participated over these last twenty years were dispersed in journals,
newspapers, or collections, in many countries and in more than
one language. Isn't it necessary, I asked myself, and hasn't the time
come to suspend for a moment dissemination—the time of a few
suspension points[8]—and to present a selection of them bound
together in a book? At the risk, of course, of arresting them by
marking them out, but thereby also underscoring their traits, this
time of suspension points can also determine, in order to situate it
better, the configuration of the other writings, I mean those that
were published elsewhere and simultaneously. In a recent publication, Derrida specified in a note concerning that which "*gives rise
and place* . . . throws into relief the place and the age": "The dotted
lines of a suspended writing *situate* with a formidable precision."[9]

Faced with the number and variety, certain selections remained
indispensable, but their criteria were difficult.[10] What needed to be

privileged first? I believed I had to let myself be guided above all by diversity, by the greatest diversity possible in the limits and the coherence of a single volume: twenty interviews, twenty years.

First of all, the *diversity of subjects*, to be sure: the collected interviews treat the question of women, but also of poetry and teaching, the media, drugs, AIDS, sacrifice and anthropophagy, the relation to tradition, language—national or other—and therefore translation, philosophy and nationalism, politics and philosophers, and so forth.

Next, *diversity of style* and *variation in tone* (Derrida has often insisted, in particular in *The Post Card*, on the *Wechsel der Töne*). Playful, strategic, impassioned, analytic, militant, "autobiographical": the difference in these modulations can sometimes be heard within one and the same dialogue.

These tonalities vibrate, of course, with the interlocutors, which is to say, also with the addressees of the interviews, many of which were published in France, but also sometimes in several European countries, and in the United States: another *diversity, that of others*.

For reasons that have to do also with a certain *logical* linking of the different contents, notably as concerns that which relates them to the sequence thus punctuated of Jacques Derrida's other publications, *chronological* order had to prevail, almost always, over the presentation of the interviews. As for the titles, it seemed advisable at times to change them, especially when they were chosen by newspaper editors and not by the interlocutors themselves. In each of these cases, the original title has been noted. I also thought it useful to add here or there some clarifications—in notes.

Between Brackets

I

Q.: Jacques Derrida, your work for some time now (let us say since the publication of *Glas*) seems to have taken shape according to a novel division. You have been publishing concurrently: theoretical or critical texts of a relatively classical form (*Le facteur de la verité*, on Lacan[1]); interventions on certain political or institutional questions (your articles on the teaching of philosophy and the Haby reform[2]); and more wide-ranging texts which are unclassifiable according to normal standards—*Glas* (on Hegel and Genet), "+ R (Into the Bargain)" (on Adami and Benjamin)[3]—in which you implicate yourself, along with your "body," your "desire," your "phantasms," in a way that perhaps no philosopher has ever done until now.

To what does this diversification or multiple unfolding of your activity correspond for you? To the extent that this multiplicity was already readable in both your mode of writing and in the theses which you put forward, what has determined its extension "here" and "now"? How do you conceive the relations among and the necessity of the different forms of your activity?

J.D.: You make me cling {*vous me cramponnez*}[4] to the idiom. *Cramponnement* {clinging, cramping, clamping, holding, hooking or hanging onto}: it's quite a word, don't you think? Be forewarned, that's all I have on my mind today: the hook {*le crampon*}, clinging, what Imre Hermann calls the "clinging instinct." The "word" no less than the "thing," to be sure.

In part because, in a certain way, I missed the *cramponnement* in *Glas*, even though I indicated its place, its necessity, its contour and even though everything called out for it—everything that is written there, for pages on end, about the fleece [beginning, for example, around page 68 somewhere], about the *erion*, the erianthus, the "fleecing text" or the cheating text, the theory of the clutching hook, of clutching in general and, throughout, about the return or the loss of either pubic or capital hair.

As you know, Hermann proposes a powerful deduction—one which is "archi-psychoanalytic" according to Nicolas Abraham— an articulated, differential, concrete deduction of all psychoana- lytic concepts (that are by the same token reelaborated) beginning from the theory of *cramponnement*, the clinging instinct, and a traumatic archi-event of *dé-cramponnement*, de-clinging, which constructs the human topical structure. This topical structure ini- tially knows no "triangulation," but is first played out, before the traumatic de-clinging, between the four "hands" of the baby ape and the hair of the female. But I should let this drop. Read the rest of the story and of this fantastic theory/fiction in *L'instinct filial*, which is prefaced by an admirable "Introduction to Hermann" by Nicolas Abraham.[5]

The word *crampon* will not let go its hold on me because it would have been absolutely necessary in *Glas*. I would like instead to show you the places where something like an active absence of the word *crampon* is at work—at least one of these places, as an example. Perhaps it is better—in any case it interests me more—to speak of what is not there and what should have been there in what I have written. All of this supposes, for the facility of the interview, that what is there is there and what is not is not. I am going to look for where it is to be found.

Here it is: in a passage that is talking about the thesis, as does your question. So I will not be too far off the subject, which I cling to.

It is a question of both the "bunch of grapes" pinned inside

Stilitano's trousers and the appearance on stage of Bataille, a disconcerted reader of Genet. First I will read the text in large type and then the "judas hole" in its right side:

> The text is clustered.
>
> Whence the permeable and seduced nervousness, on its knees, of someone who would like to take it, comprehend it, appropriate it.
>
> The text treats of *ersatz*, in a foreign tongue, of what is posed and added instead.
>
> The thesis (the position, the positing, the proposition, *Satz*) protects what it replaces, however (this hanging counterpart).
>
> Now here is a contemporary (the fact matters a great deal) who— everything, if not his own proper *glas*, should have prepared him for reading the scene—is unsettled, who no longer wishes to see, states the contrary of what he means (to say), mounts a campaign, gets on his high horse.
>
> The *ersatz*, he says, is not good.

And here is the judas hole. The whole book would lead back to it if there were such a thing here as a whole. Everything, thus, should have motivated the staging of the *crampon*. I read:

> everything comes down to living in the hook {*crochet*; also bracket} of the cripple; the cluster, the grapnel are a kind of hooked matrix. "*Grappe...* E. Picardy and env. *crape*; provenç. *grapa*, hook; Span. *grapo*, hook; Ital. *grappo*, hook; low Latin *grapa*, *grappa* in Quicherat's *Addenda*; from the old High-German *chrapfo*, hook, mod. German *Krappen*; cp. Cymric *crap*. The *grappe* {grape cluster} has been so called because it has a hooked or grappled quality" (Littré).[6]

The *crampon* should have imposed itself on the relation (a clinging/de-clinging dual unity, inhibited at the origin) between the two columns or colossi, as well as each time reference is made to the "rhythm" of the "little jerks, gripping and suctions, patchwork tacking {*placage*}—in every sense and direction—and gliding penetration. In the embouchure or along the column"[7]; or yet again to the "general sucker {*ventouse*}" ("The sucker is adoration. Adoration is always of the Holy Mother, of the Galilean mother, in whom one is conceived without a father . . ."[8]) or to the concept (*Begriff*) as a stricture of gripping or of the grip, or to the hairy body, golden fleeces or pubic fleeces, the "glabrous face" of effeminate "Pop-pop," and so forth. And especially in the passage from *gl,* to *gr,* and to *cr* that moves all throughout the last pages and the last scenes, and so on.

From Nicolas Abraham's Introduction, just after he has explained that "Yes, had it not been for 'the-shining-eyes-that-unhooked {*décramponné*}-the-child-too-soon-from-its-mother,' we would still be stuck in a simian poetics of the reassuring maternal fur," today I read this:

> . . . no need have we of a furry mother, whatever might have been the ardor of our vows for her fur—which, by the way, is nonexistent... A glabrous mother of oneself, that is what it means to be human. And how sad it is, a sadness unto death... from laughter.
>
> The analyst, who knows, does not laugh. No more, by the way, than he dies because of what he knows.[9]

You make me cling to the idiom.

But what if there were no idiom? What if it, the idiom, had the structure of fur, and were as labile as fur? One would have to let go right away. Here and now. You ask me what is happening here and now. I quote: "what has determined its extension 'here' and 'now'?" The response I give you ought to be idiomatic, concerning very precisely this and not that, here-now, and should even make of my response an idiomatic event. I ought to avoid any recourse to this or that readable argumentation—more elaborated, more involved, and thus more protected—in the texts to which you have just referred. I ought to tell you here and now, along with the delay, the losses, the degradation (but also with the benefits, for the other, of a didactic simplification that grants a greater role to the symptom), with all the risks of exhibition and within the constraints set by the scene of the tape recorder, I ought to tell you, in a few sentences, what I think of this "extension here and now." The question about this "here-now" that you ask...

Q.: ... in quotation marks...

J.D.: ... yes, exactly, in quotation marks. What happens when "here-now" is put in quotation marks? or in parentheses? or between brackets {*entre crochets*}?

It/Id gets unhooked.[10] Like hooks that unhook. Like pliers or cranes (somewhere, I think, I have compared quotation marks to cranes) that grab in order to loosen the grasp. But how is one to efface or lift the brackets once one begins *writing* [here and now] anything whatsoever? Writing—already in the tongue—would operate, with regard to immediate adherence, somewhat like the red-eyed father who shames the young ape, like "his gaze which, like fire, unhooks the child from the mother, unhooks the mother from the child, the child that has become her tree. ." I have just quoted Nicolas Abraham again and his "parenthemes" [by which are meant: "hooking" themes].[11] But written hooks—dashes, "parentheses," (quotation marks)—also hook up, by the same redoubled token, with the mother. Such is the crafty logic of this "topical structure" at work, I think, in *Glas*.

Do you know what German word translates the Hungarian *kapaszkodas* (clutching) or *kapaszkodni* (to clutch)? It is *Anklammerung* or *sich anklammern*. *Klammer*, hook, cramp, anchor, or clothespin, is also the word for bracket, parenthesis, embrace. *Klammerband* (is a) bracket in the architectural sense. And *klamm* means *close together, narrow, strict*. I now hear the *stricture*, the essential false matrix of *Glas*, reasoning {resounding} like this *Klammer*.

What happens when "here-now" is put in quotation marks? And when one says that one is using quotation marks even though no one can read them here and now, and when a tape recorder records that which—such is the implicit contract of this interview—I will certainly reread, which I may even transform here and there, perhaps even from beginning to end, before publication?

Here and now an "interview" is taking place, what is called an "interview," and it implies all kinds of codes, demands, contracts, investments, and surplus values. What is expected from an interview? Who requests interviews from whom? Who gets what out of them? Who avoids what? Who avoids whom? There are all sorts of questions and programs that we should not run away from, here and now. "Political" questions (economic, editorial, academic institutional, theoretical, and so forth) which, it seems to me, were on the agenda for *Digraphe* (*Le moment venu*[12]). Perhaps we should have begun there. I wonder if it is not necessary to begin with these kinds of questions. They are, finally, the ones that have always interested me the most and the most consistently (even though I don't speak of them directly), since I began taking part for better or worse in this theater (somewhere between the book fair and the medieval tournament) in which one signs books, manages courses and discourses, attacks and assails names, properties, clienteles with all kinds of weapons (from every period in history), according to all sorts of trajectories and motivations and alliances that are so terribly sophisticated, overdetermined, but finally so simple, plain, and derisory.

Here, for example—and to limit myself to just this one feature— is there anyone who does not expect me to defend, justify, consolidate things that I have done these last years and about which you have asked me certain questions, having yourselves an interest (a legitimate one, you think, and so do I, which is why we are doing this together) in our gaining some ground when the whole thing is over? And even if I were to indicate, in an autocritical mode, such and such a limit, or negative aspect, or strategic weakness, would anyone be duped by the maneuver of reappropriation?

The fact that I have accepted—for the second time[13]—to expose myself to the risks of this tape-recorded surprise, that I have agreed to pay the price (simplification, impoverishment, distortion, displacement of argument by symptom, and so forth), now here is right away a singularity which I would like to insist on, rather than on what I have written and which is a little bit somewhere else, somewhere else for me, somewhere else for others. Okay, you are going to think I am piling up the protocols in order to run away from an impossible question. So running away is a bad thing? And why is that? Does one have to be noble and brave? What if all the questions put to me about what I write came down to fleeing what I write? Okay. I give in and return to your highly differentiated question about differentiation...

Q.: diversification...

J.D.: ... yes, diversification, the "novel division." Is it so new? I have the impression that the same divisions, the same crossings (which can also be taken in the genetic sense) were at work in the earlier publications.

As you mention, it is a matter only of an "extension" of this gap. In fact, it is as if, from the initial premises, the possibility of such an extension, with its attendant capitalization and risks (which are, of course, always limited, necessarily finite), it is as if this very possibility had been put in place, wagered upon. On the other hand, several of these books, *Glas* or *Dissemination* for example, *explicitly* open onto the concrete question of the *this, here-now*. All of them do so *implicitly*. They do not ask the question; they stage it or overflow this stage in the direction of that element of the scene which exceeds representation.

What is it that writing de-clings of a here-now?

And how could a here-now pass through writing unscathed? Perhaps we interpret today more effectively, with or without Hegel, the intervention of a written trace (in the ordinary sense) in the chapter of the *Phenomenology of Spirit* on sense certainty and its here-now. In 1967, I believe it was, we fit a whole seminar within this question, and the "first" line of *Glas* is divided on it or cuts across it as well.

I do not want to leave your question behind, but I have trouble responding to it. Not only for this reason of principle (the recited, the recitation that sweeps every here-now up into a fable without content), but also because the *topos* of the continuity *or* discontinuity of a writing trajectory always seems up in the air. Demonstrations of the most contradictory sort on this subject are always equally pertinent, thus equally impertinent. No doubt another logic is necessary to account for what must have in fact taken place between one text and another, between a group of texts and another, augmenting in an at least regular fashion (this economic difference is quite clear but it cannot be homogeneous and a matter of degree) the gap between simultaneously engaged types of writing. It is difficult for me to *talk* about it first of all because these texts explain themselves, in a mode that does not allow for the kind of verbal overview you have invited me to give here. They explain themselves on the necessity of this gap by which each of them is already placed in relation to itself. *Glas*, for example, is also nothing other than a long explanation of itself as... as that which you say about it in your question as well as that which your question says about "other" texts ("theoretical or critical texts of a relatively classical form; interventions on certain political or institutional questions [your articles on the teaching of philosophy]"): all the questions and all the themes addressed in *Glas* are explicitly political and the teaching of philosophy is treated at length (see for example around the Cousin-Hegel exchange and their political relation to the academic institution;[14] the fragments I selected from it were the most relevant ones in 1975[15]). There is another reason it is difficult for me to *talk* about this off the cuff: what happened in this "gap" did not happen only through me, could not have depended on me alone. It depended as well on a history, the laws of a certain "market" that are very difficult to delimit: the relations between what I have already written and what I am writing on a scene in transformation that constantly exceeds me, the structure of capitalization, of ellipsis, of filtering, the more or less virtual relations with those who read me or those who do not, the more or less distorted perception that I have of this, the system of exchange with a very complex socio-political or ideological field. All of this depends on more or less conscious, more or less imaginary calculations, on daily mini-X-rays, on a whole chemistry of information largely under the sway of unconscious drives, as well as affects and phantasms that were already in place before any calculation. In any case, my representation cannot possibly master them; it sheds no more light on them than a flashlight in a prehistoric cave. This is true even when one endeavors—as I would like to do—to illuminate at each moment the widest surface area and to avoid getting taken in by the constraints of such a "market." Yet, while it is necessary to break with the persistent and politically coded illusion of a "textual production," as the phrase goes, that escapes the laws of such a market, while it is necessary, it seems to me, to expose everything one can about this "market" *in* the product itself (and here errors of taste today constitute taste itself), while it is sinister to foster a forgetting of the subtle and more or less spontaneous *marketing* that controls even the most sensational ruptures with the marketplace (literary or philosophical, for example), it remains the case that the delimitation of what I have just called, for the sake of convenience, the *market*, does not seem to me to be masterable by any discourse, method, or scientific program presently in use. This does not necessarily disqualify them, on the contrary; I believe we are in a period of great effervescence and renewal in this regard. Now, precisely (here I return to your question about "diversification"), in order to begin to analyze the "field" or the "market," to analyze it practically, thus to transform it really, effectively, must one not *produce* (and you know how much I mistrust this word) "instruments" able to measure up to everything which, *in the market*, *in* the field of production and reproduction, claims to master the field, its law of saturation or unsaturability? The competition is not between finite forces (whether discursive or non-discursive) but between hegemonic claims which each have a regulated potential to exceed the bounds, a super-regional scope whose internal logic one must also understand. If, just so as to go more quickly, I only indicate some proper names, well, what is needed is to "produce" some "concepts" of the field able to measure up, from within and from without, to those various logics of the field (which are also part of it) that are referred to with the names "Marx," "Nietzsche," "Freud," "Heidegger," and so forth. And not only to "produce" these new "concepts," but to transform the mode of their production: to write differently (no more courses or no more literature, for example, from the moment one treats these questions; in any case, nothing whose norms would be set by what is submitted to a deconstructive analysis). Parody is here the least one can do. And diversification, removed each time from the authority of a local program, of a singular claim to hegemony, beginning with that of the so-called signatory.

Well, I'll cut it off there. If the analysis of what might have been going on "with me" cannot be dissociated from the rest, nevertheless I do not want to skip over it. Between what I was calling the "market" (do not rush to fix its meaning; it is also a matter of a certain *pas* [I note here in brackets that by means of this angled stumbling block, that will no doubt appear in parentheses, I am not just trying to incite you to read a text by that title (*pas*) that will soon appear,[16] I also call your attention to the fact that the structure, logic, and scene that this text develops, following in Blanchot's footsteps {*pas*}, have what it takes, in my view, to unseat all the hegemonic discourses on the market]), between the "market" and "me" (a certain montage of forces, drives, affects, phantasms, representations, let's say of "inhibited de-clingings" and I'll let you complete the list), something must have happened in the last few years that allowed me, at the same time as it constrained me, to expose something that, probably, I had had good reason to keep under wraps, something that protected itself.

And that still protects itself, no doubt, but by exposing itself in another manner.

For example—it's easier to talk about it and it has a somewhat more general interest—my belonging to the institution of the university. It has never been a comfortable relation of identification, quite to the contrary, and for reasons that must also have to do with my "idiosyncratic" history. Yet it is true that the critique, let us call it the political critique, that I have on occasion undertaken of this institution remained either "private," empirical, more or less spontaneous, tied to evaluations, allergies, unhesitating rejections, or else it was ready to conform to programmatic or stereotypical critiques of the educational system. In the latter case, and in fact whenever I become aware of this mechanical hum, that is, each time I begin to get bored, I head for the door and I turn off. That is always the ultimate motivation, as it is no doubt for everyone. Naturally, one ought to investigate what is behind the boredom. But however long I might ruminate on the good reasons for leaving, it is always at the moment when *it bores me*, when whatever has held my attention up until then starts putting me to sleep, that the decision is taken. Basically, up until the last few years, the only critical operations that have been effective against the dominant educational system (and they have indeed been effective—I am not talking now of certain anti-academic tics that characterize a whole tradition of literary avant-gardism, which is complicitous in this regard with a power base in the university that the avant-garde tradition has never disturbed, one whose mechanisms have maintained a close resemblance to that tradition, even as they remain unrecognized, while the power of publishers and their very specialized agents provide a shuttle service between them) have seemed to me to be tributaries of the very "philosophies" that I was elsewhere attempting to read deconstructively. This did not prevent me from considering certain of these critiques to be necessary and effective, or even from taking part in them to a certain degree. But if anything has changed for me from this point of view, it is that at a certain stage in the trajectory, it began to seem possible for me to join certain, let us call them theoretical, premises that I had tried to elaborate, with this or that public and political position as concerns teaching, and to do this especially within the ongoing work of teaching (for the articles to which you refer are only reference points to this work). As long as this joining did not seem possible or *coherent* enough to me, then there was no choice but to adjust one's positions to discourses that, in relation, let us say, to a given deconstructive advance, remained outmoded or regressive (I dismiss the "progressivist" connotation of all these words, but you see what I mean). It is not a matter here of "delays" or uneven development. The heterogeneity of the field of struggle requires that one make alliances, in a given situation, with forces that one opposes or will oppose in another place, at another time. I tried to say or do something specific—and no longer just align my criticism—only from the moment I thought it possible to articulate together, in a more or less coherent fashion, a certain deconstruction, which had arrived at a certain state, a certain critique, and the project of a certain political transformation of the educational and university apparatus. This transformation appeared to me possible and effective (and by effective I mean beginning to transform the scene, the frame, and the relations of forces) only on the condition of this coherence; finally, if possible, it would no longer pour discourses that stem from the revolutionary code or stereotype into the intact forms of teaching, its rhetoric, and its programs. These forms often force one, both within the educational system and outside of it (for example, in corporatist organizations, unions, and parties) to challenge educational reproduction. The difficulty—which needs to be constantly reevaluated—is in marking a distance from these programmatic forms (those of unions and of the parties on the left) without giving comfort to the common enemy. This is a well-known schema, but it is more implacable than ever.

The "multiple unfolding," to use your term, is a strategic necessity. It does not designate any willful representation, any ruse of battle, but rather a calculation that is made (which is not anyone's in particular) in order to make appear (no, not to make appear, but rather because there can then appear, at a determined stage in a process), through displacements, grafts, parodies, and multiplications, some elements of a code, some unnoticed conventions, some laws of property, and so forth, that are regulating markets and institutions, reassuring productive agents and consumers (who are very often one and the same). For example, take a text that is received as philosophical, which lends itself to that appearance, is signed by someone situated in a certain place within philosophical commerce, by some philosophical agent respecting the demands whose norms are the rules of exchange in the philosophical university. People read it. Suppose then that (after the period of relevance, confidence, and credibility has done its work, a necessary period that explains why what we are talking about does not happen in some abstract *hic et nunc*) heterogeneous (almost inadmissible) forces are introduced into the text with a more or less surreptitious violence (this more or less makes for all the difficulty of the economic calculation). One cannot resist these forces, or rather one resists them, but in such a way that the resistance creates a symptom and is set to work on the body, transforming, deforming it and the corpus from head to toe—down to its very name. Then, perhaps, a forced entry will have taken place. But it is never assured, nor given, nor done: it may always let itself be reappropriated. What I have just called forced entry designates, beyond the stage effects, an effraction and an operation of force, of the difference of force. Of course, this supposes a "maximum" risk (which is limited, thus, to the maximum possible risk) for whoever commits his or her forces and strength. But the incalculable has to be part of the game. The inadmissible {*irrecevable*}—that which at a determined moment takes the formless form of the inadmissible—can, it should even, at a determined moment, find no reception whatsoever; it can and it should escape from the criteria of receivability, be totally excluded, and this may occur in broad daylight, even as the inadmissible product circulates from hand to hand like Notre-Dame-des-Fleurs's tie in *Glas*. And it/id may even never find a reception. This is the risk one has to take if there is to be any chance of attaining or altering anything whatsoever. The inadmissible (as well as the ungraspable) is also that which may never be taken, that can be dropped, that, even, can only be dropped. Like the rest.

This incalculable remainder would be the "subject" of *Glas* if there were one ("[Ah!] you're ungraspable [very well] remain[s]," and so forth),[17] and when it is explained in its undecidable economy. The syntax of the word *reste* as well.[18] The ungraspable—remain(s) ("the skidding that forces a certain letting go" ["Dissemination"], a certain de-clinging of the dual or dialectical unity) is the relation without relation of the two columns or colossi or bands; it is what sets the gap, to which you were referring, in motion.

One might mention—but there is no point in insisting on it since it is not the object of our discussion—that in the texts you classify as "theoretical" (*Le facteur de la vérité* for example), the demonstration inasmuch as it is effective in classical terms, is constantly overrun, carried beyond itself by a scene of language, of counter-signature set adrift, of smuggled-in fiction (generally either unreadable or neglected) which affiliated it with texts that you have classified differently, with *Glas* for example. The "division" you are talking about falls within each text, but always according to *another* trajectory or *another* place of insistence. In *Glas*, the pieces [you know that it is an organ score in pieces {*morceaux*} (bits or bites {*mors*} detached either by the teeth, coated in saliva, and then half swallowed and half thrown up, or by the fingernails and then left in hairy shreds)] that could be called "theoretical," the "theses," the "dissertations" (on dialectics and galactics, on absolute knowledge, the *Sa*[19] and the Immaculate Conception, the *IC*, on the stricture of the general economy, on the appeal of the proper name or nomenclature in the class struggle, on the limits of the Freudian or Marxist theory of fetishism, phallogocentrism, or the logic of the signifier, on the logic of antherection or obsequence, on the anthoedipus and castration, on the arbitrariness of the sign and the so-called proper name, on mimesis and the so-called impulsional bases of phonation, on the faceless figure of the mother, on language, sublimation, the family, the State, religion, mourning-work, feminine sexuality, the colossos, the double bind—the double band—and schizophrenia, and so forth) all of these "theoretical" morsels are processions tattooed, incised, inlaid into the bodies of the two colossi or the two bands which are stuck on and woven into each other, at the same time clinging to each other and sliding one over the other in a dual unity without any relation to self. In the same way, "+ R (Into the Bargain)," where I play at reading the drawings I baptized *Chimère* (*Ich* and *Chi*) or the one titled *Ritratto di Walter Benjamin*, a theoretical argumentation about the surplus value of the signature in the market, about the "mighty gallery" (Maeght), as well as about the operation in which I was participating ("what happens when a surplus value places itself *en abyme?*"[20]), marks an event in the unique course of a super-fiction that is intolerant of any metalanguage about itself. This argumentation also dismantles, as you perhaps recall, "fingernails" {*ongles*} (like Stilitano's in *Glas*) and "brackets," detaches them, like hooks, in representation ("supple flexion of an erect phallus or of the fish between life and death, still hanging on the hook [a sort of bit too]"), "hooked signature," "harpoons, arraigns," "and since there is the angle and the wave {*onde*}, the indefatigable and worrying insistence of fingernails {*ongles*} in all Adami's drawings (except, well well, in the three congeneric *Glas* drawings; for once they are setups without hands)," de-clung, and so forth.[21]

Discursive utterances about closure are necessary, but they are insufficient if one seeks to deform closure, as well as displace it. Not just this or that but the form "closure," the enclosing structure. In this sense, there is no closure of a set (for example *the* metaphysical as such) that can be related to its other or its opposing term. The schema of this oppositional closure is precisely that by which metaphysics and phallogocentrism vainly try to recenter themselves; it is their logic. Their relation to the other cannot therefore follow the same logic. It must have another structure.

In the course of each closure, it is perhaps a matter of setting a trap for this form "closure." It is a matter {*il s'agit, s'agit*}: I have often deliberately privileged that expression; it avoids the ethico-pedagogico-professorial prescription of the "one must" {*il faut*} and redirects the effect of law back to an agency that no subject can master. So, a matter always of a trap: to trap closure to the point where one can no longer rely on the circumprescription of a code. One thinks one is reading a "thesis," while in fact a prosthesis has been fobbed off that forces one to transform the code, to upset the translation in order to flush slumbering investments out of their cover. One thinks one is reading literature (possibly avant-garde literature), while in fact one is swallowing a demonstration of the staleness of the avant-garde. And vice versa: one thinks one can grab onto a manageable conclusion, and one sees oneself (or does not see oneself) shaken off by the inflexible force of a simulacrum. Neither the initiative nor the end of this practice of contraband, which I try to theorize and accelerate in *Glas*, can be signed. It matters, it acts itself out {*elle s'agit*}: our little historical episode has its specificity perhaps in being able to exhibit better or faster (some little progress in the machine) this impossibility of signing or reappropriating to oneself the profits of contraband. What I "sign" concerns finally this small acceleration, and I say this not out of politeness in order to minimize it for I also think that this little acceleration can make a space for all sorts of deviations, for some skidding off the track from which one cannot recover...

Q.: In other words, in an earlier moment you used a type of discourse of a rather classic form—or what is called thus—that is, a thetic or demonstrative discourse, even as you accompanied the thesis with something altogether other. In *Speech and Phenomena*, the "I am" as in "I am dead" appears in its phantasmatic dimension, and it is this dimension that is exposed as such in your later writings.

J.D.: A thesis is a position one sets out and which the other grabs onto. One holds onto the other {*On tient à l'autre*}. And then it starts moving, as in Hermann's primeval forest. But this time a prosthesis was needed to supplement the de-clinging with which everything began. In *Speech and Phenomena*, the philosophical shaking up of phenomenology gets moving within Poe's tales, somewhat like a fragmentary oscillation within the hors d'oeuvre, the epigraph. I quote from memory: "Mr. Valdemar was speaking: 'Yes;—no;—I *have been* sleeping—and now—now—*I am already dead.'* "[22] I no longer remember if he says *already*; in any case I hear always already. Husserl inside the epigraph. But "inside" does not mean that a so-called fantastic tale borders or exceeds the borders, frames a philosophical critique (since it was already no longer a commentary of Husserl, unlike the *Introduction to "The Origin of Geometry,"* which is much more insistent in this regard). The fantastic epigraph makes an angle from the edge toward the inside; it also "analyzes" philosophical power in its domestic regime, first penetrating it by effraction and then grinding it down to the point that the epigraph alone can render an account—in a philosophical or quasi-philosophical manner, both with and without philosophy—of certain utterances that control everything: the "I am dead," for example, implied by the Husserlian and Cartesian cogito in the last chapter on "The Supplement of (the) Origin." There, the epigraph returns, this time within and against philosophical argumentation.[23]

This does not get closed off in a book. To follow just this one thread, one could say that the explanation *with* Poe's fantastic goes on for a long time. *With*: it is not a reading *of Poe*, but other texts read with the aid of Poe, based on this reading operator or this head of a magnetic reading device which is, in its turn, *Poe's* reading, Poe reading Husserl or Lacan. There was the stage of the *Logical Investigations*, the episode of the *Seminar on the Purloined Letter*, and then *Glas*. Of course, it is essential for this that one read Poe and read him according to some determined rules. In *Glas*, as you know, Mallarmé's translation of *The Bells* (*Les cloches*) is put to what I call there an essential *use* within the economy of a "judas hole" on *mimesis*, on what are supposed to be the "impulsional bases of phonation" and the + 1 effect.[24] As for the *déjà* {already} of the "I am already dead," which is something like the general siglum or acronym of the book, it is set moving again, reinterpreted (with reference to *Speech and Phenomena*, and to Hegel and Genet), particularly, at least, on pages 76–86. ("How is one to decipher this strange anteriority of an *already* that is always shouldering you with a cadaver?"[25] Before that, on page 19: "read the *déjà* {already} as an abbreviation. When I sign, I am already dead [. . .] hence the siglum . . .") Naturally, the siglum supports the hypothesis of the *gl-* as well as signifying my initials in the margins, and so forth.

The scene of "I am dead"—with all of its investments—maintains for a long time a very general value. Universal structures are interpreted through it. But somewhere—and hence the signature effect—they "shift gears" not just into my readable proper name (that is easy to decipher), but into a particular, if not absolutely singular phantasmatic organization. Even if I had many things of an idiomatic sort to say about the "I am dead" that manipulate me, or which I try to outsmart, something of them remains absolutely hidden, unreadable, on the side of what I call timbre or style in "Qual Quelle": accessible only from the place of the other.[26] I imply this in *Glas*: this text can only *interest* the reader if, beyond all the cunning and all the impregnable calculations, he or she is certain that after a certain point I don't know what I am doing and cannot see what is staring me in the face. I am looking for the page

on "the title DOUBLE BAND(s)" and the "you are ungraspable, etc."
Here it is: "It is not enough to be crafty, a general theory of the ruse
that would be part of it must be available. Which comes down to
making a confession, unconscious, to be sure. The unconscious is
something very theoretical. If I write two texts at once . . ." (p. 65).

On the other hand (and this is just an example of an argument,
there are others), whereas "thesis" as a value qualifies an instituting
discourse (philosophical or political: the thesis in the strict sense is
found neither in science nor in literature), *Glas* operates on *theses*,
on *positions*, a word which the book by that title ended up exposing
or diverting (first of all *in view* of my interlocutors at that moment)
in its Hegeliano-sexual modes: *Setzung* + "scenes, acts, figures of
dissemination."[27] This Hegeliano-sexual scene ends up being unfolded, carried off-course, amplified (along with a long list of
partners: Hegel, Genet, but also Bataille, Freud, Marx, Poe, Mallarmé, Nietzsche, and a few others) in *Glas* which overturns the
question: "What is a thesis?" In its own way.

But I still have not answered your questions. I cannot, for
reasons of principle, have answered your questions. Because of the
impossible or inaccessible idiom (what the other has access to that
remains hidden from me is still not purely idiomatic), but also
because of the difficulty there is in speaking about texts that were
done in view of such a difficulty.

Q.: The body of the question concerned more exactly the relation between the different types of discourse that one can, at least
schematically, distinguish: the one that works on theses, the other
on phantasms (although neither thesis nor phantasm constitutes
units that can be rigorously isolated from the text in which they are
caught up).

A so-called philosophical discourse always repeats something of
the phantasm, of the phantasmatic space, and vice versa. How is
one to evaluate this relation and what is to be done with it?

J.D.: I wonder if one can still be satisfied here with the common definitions of phantasm, either in the increasingly common
and confused sense in which they are used, or even according to

the psychoanalytic definitions which are anything but clear and unambiguous.

One possible entry into this question would be precisely at that point where philosophical discourse is not only governed by the phantasmatic (either originary or derived) but, more seriously, can no longer be assured of possessing a philosophical concept of the phantasm, a knowledge that would control what is at issue in this word. *Glas* attempts a practical analysis of the phantasm at the very point where it eludes the philosophical grasp, where it is no longer a term in a conceptual opposition that arises from philosophy (originary/derived, real/imaginary, material reality/psychic reality, and so forth). What happens if the absolute phantasm is coextensive with absolute knowledge? It should be possible to demonstrate, by means of a philosophically correct technique (that is, a technique which, on one of its planes, is irrefutable in philosophic terms), that the philosophic is the phantasmatic. There follows on both sides a certain number of consequences that I attempt to draw, in the name of "homosexual enantiosis," particularly in those pages of *Glas* (pp. 223 ff.) where the other scene of the *Sa* is x-rayed and read over the radio—as Ponge would say of the Sun placed *en abyme*—at the point where the IC disqualifies the logic of the "only" {*ne-que*}. On the other side, in the other column, it is organography, the systematic description (nomenclature and history) of the organ which "would be as it were the absolute knowledge of *glas*," if absolute knowledge was not, like "jealousy," but "a piece of the machinery, a running effect"; it is also the argument of the girdle, the folding of the Freudian theory of fetishism over the "double band" logic, the "*sanglant de gaine*" {the blood-red glanslessness of the sheath} of *Pour un funambule*, and so forth. This elliptical reminder is only meant to point out that the philosophical demonstration is necessary but insufficient. That demonstration must itself be dragged onto the stage, into the play of forces where it no longer holds the power to decide, where *no one ever holds that power*, where the undecidable forces one to release one's hold, where one can't even hold onto it—the undecidable. To make of the undecidable (as some might now be tempted to do) a certain value, an instrument worth more than the particular situation in which it has a necessary place (for example, against binary logic, dialectics, or philosophy) is to double band oneself to the point of paralysis or tetanus—I would say, rather, to the point of cramping.

The double band: when it is tightened to the limit, there is indeed the danger of a cramp; it cadaverizes and empties out between the two incompatible desires. This is the condition of possibility [and] of impossibility of erection. Play is then paralyzed by the undecidable itself which, nevertheless, also opens up the space of play. There is also in Hermann a theory of the "doubly cited movement" (N. Abraham's term) of anxiety. [See as well what Abraham says about anxiety and, in a note on the same page, about mourning as concerns the loss of clinging ("the lost mother weeps, along with the mourning child, her own loss," and so forth).] Everything Hermann says about the "dual unity" also leads to a topical logic of the "whirlpool {*tourbillon*}" provoked by a system of "double induction" which both constructs and threatens the topical structure at the edge of the "chasm," the "abyss," the "maelstrom," the "whirlpool." This double induction accounts for effects of the abyss, for aspiration and defense, for the relation between the abyss and desire. Nicolas Abraham speaks of the "whirlpool-like character" that belongs to all the instincts and of a "couple of forces always ready to set off the whirlwind-like discharge." But, once again, read Nicolas Abraham's "glossary." This is how it ends: " 'Oh! But that is something I've always known... How could I have forgotten it?' If we have our way, this is what the reader will now refer to with a single word: to hermannize."[28]

Where were we? Oh yes, the cramp. The article from the Von Wartburg {etymological dictionary} is really beautiful:

> *Crampe*, 11th cent., in addition, adj. 13th cent., notably in the locution *goutte crampe*, still in dictionaries; *crampon*, 13th cent. Frankish **kramp* "curved" (cf. High German *kramph*, id.). The two nouns, which surely come from a same root, very probably already existed in Frankish. The Middle Dutch *cramp*, Ger. *krampf,* Eng. *cramp* allow one to restore the Frankish word **krampa* id.; likewise the Anglo-Saxon *krampo*

"crochet" {bracket, hook} and the Eng. *cramp* render the existence of a Frankish *krampo*, masc., probable. Der.: cramponner, 15th cent.

Q.: What strategic and critical importance do you attribute to the question, which is so prominent in your latest writings: that of the proper name and the signature?

J.D.: You are right, it is a question that traverses most of the latest texts or that in any case has become more precise since "Signature Event Context," the last essay in *Margins*, which ends, as does therefore the whole work, with *my* handwritten, reproduced, and translated signature. It is a forgery, of course; the possibility of the forgery always defines the very structure of the event called signature, its location (on the border, neither in the text nor outside of it, and yet both at the same time, defying therefore all the presumptions about the limit of a corpus: these presumptions construct both "formalisms" and classical "biographisms") and its logic which is no more that of the signified than that of the signifier, and so forth. I think the elaboration of these questions can transform or displace the problematic of the "event," of the place of the "subject," of its inscription in language, of literature and of the simulacrum—which is to say, many other things as well which I cannot go into here. There are two essential "strategic" values, as you just put it, that I will mention briefly: (1) Work on the proper name and the signature must be scientific (recognize or elaborate laws, universally valid propositions, and so forth), but this scientificity must each time take into account singularities which are not just cases or examples. Here, the aleatory is no longer accidental or accessory; it intervenes in the law of the corpus. It is difficult to be more specific here. What I have to say about it is perhaps clearer in *Glas* or in texts that will be appearing on the signatures of Ponge and Blanchot.[29] It is a matter of another scientificity. (2) For this very reason, such a "scientificity," if that is what it is, requires a signatory that is neither an empirical subject that the scientific corpus as such can let drop nor the transcendental holder of a metalinguistic power. He has to put in play, with his so-called proper name and his signature, everything that is invested there and that is part of the exposed corpus, according to that other logic that I was talking about a moment ago. In the course of such an operation, properness can be dealt with in all its states and worked up into quite a state. Its fragmentation and its recomposition are not limited to work on the whole name *in language* (Genet's name, or Hegel's, Ponge's, Blanchot's, but as well, for reasons I have just mentioned, and at the same time, "my" name [at least according to "*déjà*," *Ja, Da, débris, derrière khi, dérision*, and so forth]); it does not only enrich the aleatory ("the glue of chance makes sense"[30]) of a whole semantic necessity (the work of the *da* and the *déjà*, for example, does not at all depend, for its demonstrative value, on the fortuitous connection to my name) and one which is not just semantic (the relation of the *déjà* to the absolute ancestor, to the past that has never been present, and so forth, ends up breaking through the semantic limit which is always constructed by the affinity of meaning and presence); it is also working on the non-linguistic corpus of writing.

And this passes through not only the spectacle of the proper name or the signature as the insertion of the whole proper name in language. The signature of the proper name can also play the role of the hiding place (sheath or fleece) that dissimulates another signature, the signature of an other—man or woman—which is wilier, older, ready for anything and for any name.

This (let's call it a *decelebration*: it desacralizes by taking it out on the head, by going after the head; it slows down or blocks the capitalizing acceleration of a well-oiled program that is in a rush to confuse absolute knowledge with the avant-garde so as to accumulate all of the surplus values. The decelebration of a great-philosopher, for example, must deal rigorously with his great-philosophemes in their most forceful internal arrangement—other-wise, one has no effective leverage and destroys all the effects of the analysis, leaving the mechanism intact, which is no doubt the result that was obscurely sought after. One must also reinscribe this most powerful internal mechanism in a general functioning or agonis-tics. For example, Hegel's *Sa* and his political philosophy, his philosophy of religion or of the family reinscribed in Hegel's family, the academic institution, editorial haggling, the bargaining over awards, the fascination with political power, and so forth. All of this, as far as possible, in a parody that eschews the facileness of collage, of empirical juxtaposition, as gaily and as scientifically as possible, determining the necessary relation between some so-called internal system and its outside, or rather an outside which it fails to make *its* outside. The precise topical structure of this *failure* or of this disappropriation, that is what interests me. It is not that I find it "interesting"; let us say rather that it concerns me and surrounds me like an element in which I struggle. Right now I do so in the precise form which you indicated in your question with the reference to certain publications), this, then, could only happen, in this form, at a very determined moment in the history of "my signature," of the texts I have published, of their reception or non-reception, of their socio-political "market," and of a few other effects that I would prefer not to leave out of the picture for the reasons of modesty, ignorance, or disavowal which are so often the rule. Without neglecting, of course (pardon me for referring to it in order to save time), a certain argument-of-the-girdle, the analytical and political exposure of this "market" seems to me more necessary than ever. I also believe that, despite a few sensational infractions that have been muffled, made profitable, and reinvested in an outmoded form of marketing, this exposure is still powerfully forbidden (the sensational always works by presenting its proclamation in a very submissive and frightened homage to the system of the interdiction). More and more and each time as much as possible, to render this exposure contemporary and in solidarity with what is produced on the market or as market—even when what is produced there does not leave the concept of "production" or "market" intact—that is what would interest me most, would bore me the least today.

First of all because it is always difficult and I do not know how to go about it: there is no ready-made program, one has to establish or recognize the program with every gesture and it can always go wrong—to a certain degree, even, it goes wrong every time. For example, I can no longer teach without trying, at least, to make the content and the process of teaching, even down to its details, dislocate, displace, analyze the apparatus in which I am involved. This is to be done not only according to the order of a recognizable political code, but by politicizing the places that the code of politics leaves out of the picture and leaves out for reasons, in view of interests and relations of force that one can try to analyze. But what then interests me the most is to attempt to limit a certain delay: for example, the delay that occurs between this work on and against the institution (let us give it that name in order to go quickly) and, on the other hand, what I see to be the most advanced position of (let us give it this name in order to go quickly) "deconstruction" of a philosophical or theoretical type. A deconstruction cannot be "theoretical," beginning with its very principle. It is not limited to concepts, to thought content, or to discourses. That has been clear since the beginning. If the deconstruction of institutional structures [for example, those that *contain* the academic discourse, or rather discours*es* wherever they set the norm and the rules—and it goes without saying that this occurs not only in the university, but most often outside the university, given the nature of the university or the educational apparatus: they set the rules therefore, sometimes in an all-powerful fashion, for those who occasionally represent themselves as anti-university; but this representation does not prevent them from dreaming of an index, theses, archives, and other academic celebrations of yesterday's avant-gardes; here and there this dream becomes (is there anything more comical today?) compulsive, feverish, hyperactive management], if, then, this political deconstruction is indispensable, one must not overlook certain gaps but attempt to reduce them even though it is, for essential reasons, impossible to erase them: for example, the gap between the discourses and practices of this immediately political deconstruction, on the one hand, and a deconstruction of a theoretical or philosophical kind, on the other. At times these gaps are so great that they hide the links or render them unrecognizable for many people.

What is valid for the educational apparatus is also valid for the editorial apparatus. Here the link is internal: of a system, a marketplace, and so forth. How can anyone who publishes today accept to leave out of the picture, in the non-text, or rather in the non-published, the whole complex functioning of the editorial machine: its mechanisms of selection, control, sanctioning, recruitment, internal promotion, elimination, censorship, and so on? How can one accept to "publish" without putting on the "published" stage the forces, conditions, agents of the editorial machine? Without at least trying (I do not kid myself about the difficulties of this operation, the wily complexity of the obstacle, the cunning of the adversaries both within and without) to put this machine on stage and, if possible, to transform it?

Decelebration which, patiently, goes after the head—I will stop here, I can tell it's time to change the tape. It would be a good idea, for the other questions, to change the rhythm as well.

Ja, or the *faux-bond*

II

Q.: Another question on *Glas*. Any somewhat attentive reading has to follow, even if unbeknownst to itself, the motifs that you trace in Hegel, in Genet, between Hegel and Genet. But these are also your own motives: your phantasmatic, your style, what makes you write and speak.

How do you conceive this coincidence (if that is what it is)? What is at stake, for you personally, in such an activity? How does it pay off? By what rights do the effects of this activity concern philosophical discourse?

Why exactly Hegel and Genet?

How do you analyze the reading effects that such a device has already produced?

J.D.: Yes. Well, the tape {*bande*}[1] does not wait for us. I mean the recording tape, the second one. It's making a little noise, no time to look for the right words.

The last time, two months ago, when we did the first interview, I was reading Hermann, you remember. And the great history of clinging, a kind of science of utopia, *occupied* us constantly like a magnetic field, like the real magnetic power of what we were recording.

Right now, I am rereading *Gulliver's Travels*, another science of utopia. More precisely, Book Four, the "Voyage to the Land of the

Houyhnhnms" (how is that pronounced?). Since I feel that this is
going to imprint, over-imprint itself on everything I might improvise, I would like to read a few lines of it; in that way, you can
put them in epigraph in order to set the tone, if you don't mind,
and then perhaps entitle this second interview "Return of the
Houyhnhnms."

> I plainly observed, that their language expressed the passions very well,
> and the words might with little pains be resolved into an alphabet
> more easily than the Chinese.
>   I could frequently distinguish the word *Yahoo*, which was repeated
> by each of them several times; and although it was impossible for me
> to conjecture what it meant, yet while the two horses were busy in
> conversation, I endeavoured to practice this word upon my tongue;
> and as soon as they were silent, I boldly pronounced *Yahoo* in a loud
> voice, imitating, at the same time, as near as I could, the neighing of a
> horse. . . . Then the bay tried me with a second word, much harder to
> be pronounced; but reducing it to English orthography, may be spelt
> thus, *Houyhnhnm*. . . . I heard the word *Yahoo* often repeated betwixt
> them; the meaning of which word I could not then comprehend,
> although it were the first I had learned to pronounce. . . . In about ten
> weeks time I was able to understand most of his questions, and in three
> months could give him some tolerable answers. He was extremely
> curious to know . . . how I was taught to imitate a rational creature,
> because the Yahoos (whom he saw I exactly resembled in my head,
> hands and face, that were only visible), with some appearance of
> cunning, and the strongest disposition to mischief, were observed to
> be the most unteachable of all brutes. . . . It was with some difficulty,
> and by the help of many signs, that I brought him to understand me.
> He replied, that I must needs be mistaken, or that I "said the thing
> which was not." (For they have no words in their language to express
> lying or falsehood.) . . . For he argued thus; that the use of speech was
> to make us understand one another, and to receive information of
> facts; now if any one *said the thing which was not*, these ends were
> defeated. . . . When I asserted that the Yahoos were the only governing
> animals in my country, which my master said was altogether past his
> conception, he desired to know, whether we had Houyhnhnms among
> us. . . . I had explained the use of castrating horses among us . . . to

render them more servile. . . . The Houyhnhnms have no written texts; all their knowledge is based on oral tradition. . . . Neither has their language any more than a general appellation for those maladies, which is borrowed from the name of the beast, and called *hnea-yahoo,* or the yahoo's evil, and the cure prescribed is a mixture of their own dung and urine forcibly put down the Yahoo's throat. . . . Another thing he wondered at in the Yahoos was their strange disposition to nastiness and dirt; whereas there appears to be a natural love of cleanliness in all other animals. . . . [One should also read all the passages on "emetics" but that would take too long; just this, then, to conclude:] . . . the Houyhnhnms have no word in their language to express any thing that is evil, except what they borrow from the deformities or ill qualities of the Yahoos. Thus they denote the folly of a servant, an omission of a child, a stone that cuts their feet, a continuance of foul or unseasonable weather, and the like, by adding to each the epithet yahoo. For instance *hhnm yahoo, whnaholm yahoo, ynhnmawihlma yahoo.* . . . I could with great pleasure enlarge farther upon the manners and virtues of this excellent people; but intending in a short time to publish a volume by itself expressly upon that subject, I refer the reader thither. And in the mean time, proceed to relate my own sad catastrophe.[2]

Yes, but as I was saying, the tape does not wait and there is no time to look for the right words.

Exactly how long does one have the right to look for the right words? This is the beginning of a limitless question. If I say, if I rush to say that this question is also a political one, if I say that politics is always allied with whatever regulates the time to look for one's words, or the words of others, I will have allowed myself to be hurried along by a determined urgency of our "epoch" (determined does not mean unjustified, but belonging to a set of determinations that some would like to have the time to interrogate, analyze, define, name before answering).

The "epoch" is perhaps just that, a certain suspensive relation to the tape: *epochē.*

Is it always politically harmful to take the time to look for the right words? To make the tape wait? It goes on turning all the time, at least for as long as one can afford to let it. This is not at all clear or certain. Political analysis must be begun again, adjusted, refined in each situation, taking into account its greatest complexity, the forces or the current that one is plugging into, or attempting to plug into, immediately or through some media [as far as possible don't mistake one's interlocutors, don't believe, for example, that one is speaking to the "masses"—in just the right manner, of course—when one is walled up inside an enclosure of cultural super-capitalization; or don't believe that it then suffices to accelerate, to popularize or simplify, to weaken, in function of what one imagines is being understood outside the walls, in order immediately to plug back into the main current—this produces comic signs of what one believes to be the language of the outside and confirms in a spectacular manner the belonging that has been denied], or vice versa.

The effect of the band, I mean the tape recorder band, in its impatience, is no doubt to *hasten*: one is afraid of the loss—the virgin tape, force expended for nothing, unproductive time.

But it/id[3] hastens, it/id prevents one from looking for the right words, up to a certain point, as soon as the other is there.

As soon as some other is there, there is a band.

And one must learn to make it wait, and as far as possible, *just what it takes* {juste ce qu'il faut}. And because today it is necessary, as you know, to talk of the political-sexual scope, dimension, implication of everything, and without delay, I am going to do so but at my own rhythm, of course, or rather at a rhythm that compromises between the other-band and what seems to me to be mine, and I hasten, but not too much, to point out that this "just what it takes" is politico-sexual through and through. This remains tautological, as is frequently the case, if one troubles to remember that the politico-sexual defines itself with this relation to the other-band. To stay within your question, that {*ça*} could be one of the "reading effects" of *Glas.*

The magnetophonic band can be distinguished from other bands, and even from other recording bands, in that, as a differentiated apparatus or system interposed between an emission and a reception—as, therefore, an intervention of a whole battery of relays, delays, late-maturing investments—it nevertheless incites an urgency, it hounds the emitter so as to flush him out from behind any protective mediation, forcing him to expose himself without any defenses, in his naked voice. It has thus a double and contradictory effect. In this sense as well the double-band is an effect of differance. Now, you will say perhaps that the same is true for the cinematographic band: it is also an apparatus that catches one off-guard, and you will add that, inversely, once outside of the allegedly improvised "interview" situation, one can dispel the urgency and master the machinery to the benefit of... of what? (let's just leave this "what"). The difference, perhaps, with the cinematographic band is that what it records—which is also always a signifying apparatus and thus capable of manipulating urgency—has less delaying power, in its rigorous (optical) specificity, than discourse. Language, in the strict sense, oral discourse is already, *almost* in its totality, a machine for undoing urgency, an apparatus that also has its band, which is working here against the recording band and trying to appropriate it, to exploit it (band-contra-band). Voice itself perhaps plays this contraband within the body, beginning with the cry. One generally attributes to it, to the cry, an inarticulated immediacy; it is opposed to discourse just as complete, uncoded urgency is opposed to an apparatus of coded relays. Yet, I wonder whether, always already encoded, the "first" cry does not act to suspend (by displacing it for a time upwards and toward an auto-affective inside) some intense pleasure that, for one reason or other (but it always comes down to the same reason), one wants to put off. As much as possible, and, if possible, *just what it takes.*

If the cry is contraband, then there is never a response to any urgent request without the skip of a missed encounter {*un faux-bond*}.[4] One always responds off the beat and off to one side, off-balance, even over the head.

How can one love a *faux-bond*? Or even just the word? What a word! How many different spellings—count them—are stood up by its phonemes! How many orthodoxies taken at their word it has to default on, numerous defaults![5]

Well, let's drop the word. But the *faux-bond* betrays himself, gives himself away, *he stands himself up*, which comes down to saying that he lacks truth, he leaves his truth behind when, betraying himself and becoming, in spite of everything—in spite of the consciousness or representation of the respondent or the listener— exact, punctual, true response, he shows up at the rendezvous. Even if I decided not to answer your questions, for one reason or another or for a whole bundle of reasons, even if I were sure that I was not capable of it or that I had to delay the deadline, I *will have* responded in any case.

This is another way of saying that the cry already gives what it delays. By delaying, it maneuvers to hold onto longer the very thing it delays, the pleasure or pain that it causes to pass one into the other by a temporal economy—to save time.

One only undoes the urgency of a striction by compressing the other side of it. This law might sound rather simple, but since it governs solely effects of over- and counter-determination, it concerns only differences (of force), economic differences, and nothing there is ever simple, monotonous, selfsame.

It/Id always amortizes itself: the band used up to no good end, apparently to say nothing, is reinvested elsewhere, otherwise. But it's difficult to calculate and to control the profits. When nothing gets recorded on this band, or nothing that one expected, asked for, demanded, it may still get recorded elsewhere, on an invisible band that doesn't miss a trick. When one can't manage to write on an electric typewriter (I know someone who plugs in the machine so as to receive the order to write: the slight whirring sound reminds him, like an unconscious, that he has to get his money's worth), one can always presume that it/id is working and getting written elsewhere. It is not the case that nothing happens when one has to pay the analyst for a session in which nothing was said, or even one in which the analyst gets stood up by the patient. I don't mean to say that something always happens, that it/id always gets inscribed. On the contrary, I believe there is always a place, or if you prefer a non-place, where it/id is not working, not inscribing itself, even when the text is overloaded, continually saturated (and no doubt more often in that case). I mean that an economic evaluation of what is inscribed, at work, recorded, and producing writing or—as in your question—reading effects, such an evaluation is beyond our reach, at least in the neutral and objective form that one might expect. And this for at least three types of reasons that can always let us catch our breath in a burst of laughter when faced with evaluating self-assurance [even and especially when it rages out of control in utterances such as: this writing is worth more, or less, it counts or signifies more, or less, and so forth]. The first reason is that it is difficult to know and to keep a rigorous account of all the "bands," their type, their number, their quantity, their duration, all the types of *sciences* that treat them (the technology, the political economy, the sociology of the band, and so forth); the second typical reason is that, in relation to all these sciences in their classic form (representation, consciousness, objectivity), this classic form that is already so necessary and so difficult, the unconscious constitutes a heterogeneous band that requires one to redo all the calculations including even the principle of the previous calculations. Contraband for a burst of laughter that breathes ever easier, unless, of course, the knowledge of the unconscious models itself again on the old bands and launches again the evaluating self-assurance which is all the rage. Thirdly, then, and here there is no more recourse for those assurances that are insured by an insurance more powerful than themselves... [it/id all ends up at an international firm—*firma*, signature—that has its headquarters in a large metropolis], it so happens that the evaluation is also recorded and constitutes a band effect. It is a part. It cannot stand apart and face to face. The evaluated is always stood up by the evaluable.

So, here one has to improvise. But I can no more improvise than escape improvisation. Because of all the apparatuses that we have been talking about, the putative "improvisation" is "elaborated" in advance (this is a little piece of *Glas*: the many-sided striction of the word *elaborated*), but it/id improvises behind the back of the most controlled and masterful elaboration: it/id undoes the work.

Thus I remain in your questions rather than facing up to them. I'm dragging them out a little, the time of a tape and then we can cut it anywhere.

"Produced," you say. "Reading effects produced."

If I am arrested by this word, the last one of your question, then backing up, by each of the others, more and more arrested (if one could say that), you will suspect me of doing everything to bog down the interview, to paralyze it—or rather, in view of its *paralyse*. *Paralyse* is a new *name* I make use of (elsewhere, in *Pas*) to announce a certain movement of fascination (fascinating fascinated) that itself analyzes what prevents and provokes at the same time the step of desire/no desire[6] in the labyrinth which it, *pas*, is—not.

Produced, you say.

To produce, that is the big verb today.

And production is the all-purpose concept, just indeterminate enough around the edges to move in everywhere where other notions have been disqualified: notions like "creation," "causality," "genesis," "constitution," "formation," "information" (of a material or of a content), "fabrication," "composition," and many more still. It is not a question of fleeing or criticizing this word (production) and there is no doubt a necessity behind its installation. It does not merely let in the back door that which it claims to have thrown out the front door (in the final analysis, the metaphysical determination of truth). But no more than any concept, it cannot escape from this determination purely and simply. In certain conditions it can cause it to return in full force. When its installation becomes so powerful, assured, dominant, almost saturating, one can always suspect some return of a dogmatism that, naturally, would be in the service of determined interests.

To be sure, like you, I use the word and how could one do otherwise? But shouldn't we be using it now, during this phase of its installation, as if we had lost the use of it? As if a selective aphasia suspended its availability, submitted it to the order of the false encounter or *faux-bond*, forbade it or at least did not allow it to proffer itself beyond the time of a precarious, uncertain, critical (yes, critical), almost inaudible articulation? This is for me at any rate the heading of a problem, a practical problem, in the practical interpretation of (for example) Marx, Nietzsche, Heidegger, and all discourses on "production."

I am not saying this to reject your question nor to make it rebound off a word or some picky partition. It is just that I really no longer know what one "means to say" today with the word "produce," in general and *a fortiori* for this type of "product" or "produced effect" that is called a book, all the more so for a writing that is no longer altogether a book, that is, *Glas.* Because before producing—or not—"reading effects," it is itself, is it not, a product and an effect of reading.

And then you say "already produced."

The "already" {*déjà*} which *Glas* touches on, by its "form" (the form of the word *déjà* which we will leave aside for the moment) and by its meaning, is a past that is more than past and more than present-past. You know that the two columns of the text return incessantly to this "already." The least one can say about it here is that this "already" exceeds the thinking of production toward an "unproduction" that would not be its negative either, but rather an "oblivion" that no economy, including that of repression, at least insofar as it still holds onto something, can get the better of. The "already" with which one would here be put in relation, a relation that only relates by removing itself, would be a stranger to the time, memory, logic, or economy of production.

But that is not sufficient; even if we were to develop its consequences more patiently than I can do here, we would not have acquitted ourselves of your question about "*the reading effects that such a device*" would have "*already produced.*" I agree with you that we must force these questions as long and as far as possible, until reaching the productivity or unproductivity that is "unconscious" or inaccessible to current instruments of analysis.

This is perhaps less difficult for what you call the "device" {*dispositif*} (of *Glas*) than for that which is constantly working to upset or *indispose.* For the "device"—that which is instituted, posed, given a regular form and function (the "dispositif" is also the *object* in *Glas*, it is treated by the text in the form of the spatial disposition of two instituted columns, in the process of erection and *antherection*,[7] relating to each other in a relation that only relates by removing itself, deposing itself, and so forth)—this "device," as such, is a machine for reproducing, for producing reading effects in the form of a reproduction. The device is the easiest thing to reproduce (for example the play of the two typographic columns, the break with linearity, the inscription of the judas holes, and so forth). From this point of view, we could perhaps speak of reading effects already produced with discouraging, worrisome speed—but this is easy and not very interesting.

The indisposition within the "dispositif" or as another "dispositif," as that which does not show up at the appointed rendezvous with the device—this is perhaps more *interesting*, more inevitable. If there are sought-after reading effects, they are here: what must one do in order to indispose?

Am I in a situation, would I accept to put myself in a situation to talk about such reading effects? Because of the privileged perspective that could be mine here, I am also in the worst position from which to accede to such effects and especially to evaluate them. All the same, I would like to talk about them, if only so as to break with—and make into an object—the code of modesty, the polite manners common in belles lettres which forbid the presumed "author" of a book from talking about it in such or such a way. Naturally, I have all sorts of clues, impressions, hypotheses, even before publication, concerning such reading effects, or such non-reading or non-effects. What makes me hesitate to talk about them is rather the mass of preliminaries that would have to be clarified before starting. What is a reading effect? Where can it be found? Where does it show up? Where does it come (back) from? Only in other texts? Surely not, and yet some would be tempted to think that a text that transforms the writing of just one other person (I mean what is superficially identified as the unity of *a* text signed by *an* author) may, if that other deploys X amount of power, have "produced" a greater "reading effect" than if it reaches a million readers without an equivalent transformation, and so forth. This economy is very complex, but its analysis is essential for any sociopolitics of reading and writing that would get beyond the evaluations—that are apparently spontaneous but in fact prescribed by all sorts of hidden programs—that everyone who reads or writes pro-

ceeds to do. It is an essential task if one wants to reach the forces
(here "represented," one would say, by those who read or write)
that a specific socio-political machinery marginalizes, dissociates,
dislocates. In general, those who "represent" the dominant forces
in the cultural field in which are produced those texts called philosophy, literature, theater have a very common tendency (which is
just as common to the world of literary "prizes"—all the prizes,
because there are many more than one realizes being awarded all
the time—as it is to the world of the prize-less, priceless "avant-
gardes"), like the bourgeois or petit-bourgeois that they (we) are,
almost all of them, almost all of us, a tendency to consider that in
order to reach, attract, or assemble the excluded forces (which one
imagines therefore as "masses," "popular masses," *less* prepared,
informed, and so forth, less this or that), it is necessary or it suffices
to "simplify," "popularize," even trivialize, get rid of the attributes
of the intellectual cast, regress, which is sometimes indeed done but
then, of course, to no good purpose given the simplistic premises.
Etc. In fact, it is probably still too simple, *today,* to define as
"bourgeoisie" or "petite-bourgeoisie" the affiliation of those who
"do" literature or philosophy and who easily recognize—it's become a commonplace—this affiliation, its constraints and its limits.
I think that the analysis—all of which remains to be done—should
be more differentiated and pass by way of new studies, in particular, of the educational and editorial apparatuses, a mapping of new
locations. Where does a "reading effect" take place, if it takes place?
And in the latter case, how does it manifest itself, through which
reading or writing devices, which systems of promotion and censorship (publishing and publications, the university and universities, the school and schools, clubs—whether institutionalized or
not—clans, "cliques," in the sense that a certain sociology gives to
the latter term, claques [and since you ask me about *Glas,* I put in
brackets the fact that "claque," the word and the thing, as one says,
is one of the objects of the book—it makes its appearance on the
second page—as are "clientele," "class," classes from one end to the
other])? Through which *scribbles*? (This word, the economy of this
word [critical discrimination, sifting {*criblante*} like the psycho-

political operation of the scribe], was imposed on me by a reading of Warburton's *Essay on Hieroglyphs*.[8] The *Essay* concerns, among other things, the powers—in particular, the political powers—that belong to the sacerdotal caste of the priests-scholars-scribes. The latter "produce," sift, discriminate and overdetermine, encrypt and over-encrypt codes so as to guarantee a hegemony of the forces they serve and make use of. The logic of these operations of overcoding scrift {*scriblage*} is obviously very complex, too cunning to be put back together here.) And then, to the question about the "place" for a reading effect, one would have to add or rather identify the question of the "rhythm," the rhythmed delays, and so forth. So you see, the least response to your question would have to be preceded by such a long methodological procession that I prefer here to give up. And to say to you once again, not in order to sidestep your question but because that's the way it is, that *Glas* also proposes, in its fashion, a program, a problematic ensemble, a system, if you like, of anticipation as concerns these "reading effects," and its reception or non-reception. I can only refer to it while adding this: the most *surprising* question and thus the only one that, here at least, remains new and novel and thus necessary, would perhaps be the following: what type of effect (of reading or non-reading) is absolutely *unanticipable*, out of sight, structurally out of sight, I won't say for me or for the presumed signatory/ signatories of such a text, but for the (galactic and/or dialectic) logic of the scenes where *Glas foresees*, advances at every turn as the foresight, the foreseeing organism of its reading and its non-reading (on occasion they can be the same thing), where *Glas* reads or over-reads itself in itself and outside of itself? By definition, I cannot answer these questions; I can only ask them blindly, mutely, deprived of a language in which to say "the thing which is not."

One more point on this subject, a point of principle concerning the paradox of the "reading effect." When I say that *Glas* is also working on the "reading effect," what I mean in particular is that it has as one of its principal themes reception (assimilation, digestion, absorption, introjection, *incorporation*), or non-reception (exclusion, foreclosure, rejection, and once again, but this time as internal expulsion, *incorporation*), thus the theme of internal or external vomiting, of mourning-work and everything that gets around to or comes down to *throwing up*. But *Glas* does not only treat these themes; in a certain way, it offers itself up to all these operations. To do that, it will have been necessary to calculate, as deliberately as possible, with all the forces of rejection that are active in the field of production (whether immediate or not), to accumulate all the conditions of non-receivability, or in any case the greatest number possible, the greatest number that is (for example, for *Glas* or for me) tolerable or worth the trouble. The point is not to be rejected for the sake of being rejected (although... but I am not sure of anything here and I like to write precisely at that point where calculation gets absolutely lost), but to make all (or the greatest number) of the "field" 's forces of exclusion appear (which are, precisely, what define it as a field) and—who knows—to be received elsewhere (an elsewhere that can be either cultural or unconscious, another place where, by definition, "I" am not, *I* do[es] not return to me). Naturally, it is not a question of accumulating these conditions of non-receivability in any manner whatsoever. One must, as far as possible, take precise aim at what it is *precisely forbidden to aim at* {*viser* juste où il faut pas}. The device for "indisposing" must approach a weld, the place toward which defensive and reproductive apparatuses are drawn to try to reach a provisional welding together, like one machine with another: these apparatuses might be, for example, the machine-machine, machine of being, the socio-political machine, the editorial machine (with its techno-economic norms of fabrication, distribution, stockpiling, and so forth), the university machine (with its types of discourse, transmission, decoding, reapplication), the journalistic machine (apparently the most important within the processes of marketing, reception or rejection, but whose power is today, I believe, more spectacular than effective), the theoretical machine (the systematic arrangement of discourses, procedures of selection and exclusion of concepts or of conceptual chains), all of these reading (or non-reading) machines producing, around the center of greatest concentration (sometimes an individual, a name, a

group, a school, an editorial consortium, a movement), an ag-
glomeration of "clienteles." Naturally, within each of the categories
I have just enumerated (but I am going quickly—there are others
and one should refine the analysis), there are several more or less
anonymous societies whose responsibility is more or less limited[9]
and they are in competition, even in conflict with each other. All
the possible combinations of provisional alliances among these
societies and these machines form a very complex and shifting field
of play. But in order to accede to what makes for the unity of the
field (of combinations), or at least (because I think the field cannot
finally be unified) the unity toward which the field tends to gather
itself together so as to furnish its whole clientele with the-beautiful-
life or the-beautiful-death, one must move toward whatever it is
that all the belligerent parties, at the height of the war now raging
in the public arena, *agree to exclude together.* What does the unanimity of clienteles want to have nothing to do with? In other
words, out of what exclusion is it constructed? What does it desire
to vomit? I say "desire" because the unanimity already *feels* (in itself
but elsewhere) what it vomits, and what it protects itself from it
also loves in its own way; the non-receivable is received [which is
why it is not a matter here of the non-receivable for its own sake],
received at the wrong time, as an assimilated *faux-bond*—which is
to say, one which has been destroyed. The neither-swallowed-nor-
rejected, that which remains stuck in the throat as other, neither-
received-nor-expulsed (the two finally coming down to the same
thing): that is perhaps the desire of what has been (more or less)
calculated in *Glas.* Naturally, the important thing (for me in any
case) is not to succeed with this calculation. I am not altogether
responsible for it, the "I" is not altogether responsible for it, and *the
calculation only succeeds in/by failing.* What is more, I have few
illusions or expectations on this score. But I would like to get closer
to what urges me to do this. And from where. That {*ça*} I don't
know. I know a lot of things, I mean about what I write, but that I
don't know and it's that that interests me and works on me.

You say *unbeknownst,* "*a reading that has to follow, even if unbeknownst to itself.*" The question becomes even more difficult.

Which "unbeknownst" is in question here? Ignorance, misprision, unconscious? In any case, it seems to me that what comes to pass (or gets passed over) "unbeknownst" always leaves the most, let's say, marks, is always the most effective. What is more, it/id does not return to the presumed "father" of the text, which is indeed the effect—the only effective one—of a dissemination. The perceptible influences, the declared references, the assumed debts, the borrowings that are either obvious or easily decipherable, the manifest criticisms or dissociations—these are always secondary. They are the most "tied-down" phenomena and they remain rather superficial with little transforming effect. These are weak effects because they point to a mastery or a reappropriation. If the history and the analyses of "reading effects" remain always so difficult, it is because the most effective current passes by way of assimilations or rejections that, by analogy, I would name "primary," the most "unconscious." And by way of rejection (for example, internal, incorporative vomiting) even more than assimilation. This rejection leaves marks (more or less deferred) which it would be hasty, I believe, to think of as simply negative or unproductive.

And then mustn't one take into account a certain absolute unproductivity? The one that, at the point of writing's internal collapse, opens onto the mass (enormous, impassive, indifferent—the figure of the sea in *Glas*, p. 204) of non-reading, non-inscribability, at that zero point of reading that no longer has even the unproductivity of the non-reading of avoidance, resistance, disavowal, or rejection. There is perhaps too often the tendency, even in the most subtle economic evaluations, to forget this outside. It recalls one to the right measure, in particular to the political measure, the only one on the basis of which a transformation can become effective. The standard measure gets lost because the more it/id over-encodes or over-encrypts itself, the more it/id accumulates virtual power and the more it/id tends, by the same path, toward the degree zero of what is called in *Glas*—which is a discussion somewhat of it—the *potence*.[10]

The only interesting, novel, to-be-produced "reading effect" would thus be another reader, a still inexistent reader who cannot be predicted merely by the combination of the possibilities of reading that are given by any determined historical situation. Such a reader is thus no longer, simply, what is called a reader in the common and limited sense of the term: a receiver sitting in front of an archive in a library. To change (the) readers: this political necessity—and not only political—should not consist in looking for readers *constituted elsewhere,* for reading capacities encoded elsewhere, "another public," but in working for the "production," if you will, of something that is not yet encodable, in any class and that especially is not, I repeat, in the situation of "reader," in the still stereotyped sense given to this word. A reader adjusted to "the thing which is not."

Well, okay, I'll try now to retrace the thread of your first series of questions. To the questions *"why exactly Hegel and Genet,"* "how *does it pay off,"* and to the concern with *"philosophical discourse,"* I cannot respond here; I can only refer to *Glas* which is occupied with these questions throughout.

My "own motives": Once again the idiom, which is where we began. What "makes me," as you put it, "write and speak." That is precisely what I am looking for through all of this {ça}, even if I do not think there exists, in the strictest sense, a *pure* idiom. What I am looking for there remains in any case very far—it falls far short or falls outside—from what I say or write; or rather, it is connected, relayed by so many spaces, languages, apparatuses, histories, and so forth, by so many bands, that I am able to say at one and the same time: I am, to be sure, mobilized by the immediate stakes of these texts "produced" in my name, but I also live this relation with a disinterestedness that is more and more distracted, an accelerated forgetfulness that is more and more profound, and with the certainty that the essential thing, as it is called, is going on elsewhere. Elsewhere: not simply in general, outside of me, which goes without saying, but also for me, in "me," or if not totally elsewhere, then at least in a place whose paths are infinitely multiplied and confused by the "texts." Hence the attention and, at the same time, the distraction with which I relate to what I write. What interests me is going on elsewhere, is not taking place where I write (but) I have to write *by another route* {par ailleurs}.

What is going on here is a manner of hearing oneself make a false leap, of our agreeing to stand each other up {*c'est une manière de s'entendre* (*à*) *faire faux-bond*}.

There are those who would give everything to be on time at the rendezvous (with history, with the letter that supposedly always arrives at its destination, with the revolution) and who are afraid to miss it. That is not enough to be there on time, but it should give us a few ideas about what bad luck a rendezvous can have and what assurance it may signify.

As well as about the uneasy compulsion that, every season, calls up the mirage of a rendezvous.

I would like to render at least readable (and I hope it is somewhat for certain people) the distraction that characterizes my relation to the scene in which I write, or at least in which I publish. Distraction is perhaps not the right word. It is a kind of demotivation or disinvestment, as one says nowadays, that undermines one's attention, but that I also cultivate because I think they mean something that concerns me personally at a point where singular historical and historico-political conditions are crossing: the more or less clear awareness that the combinatory possibilities are exhausted or in any case that their combinatory character has become apparent. Can become apparent. If one wants to look elsewhere, for something else, or rejoin the place or the force(?) from which this combinatory grid has been cut off, if one wants to avoid the sinister repetition of possibilities that have been exhibited and recombined ad infinitum over the last fifteen or so years, if one wants most of all to limit the degree of precritical regression (in relation to what was critical about this last period, and for which it has of course paid the price; among all the prices to be paid, there will be—one can already see it coming—a powerful reaction, powerfully supported by old markets, old alliances and socio-political combinations which are trying either to efface critical culture beneath its waves {*vagues*}, or to recombine the same elements so as to form weaker and instantly consumable products, or else both simultaneously— in short, trying still to find a place and time in an oversaturated element), then one must perhaps recognize the reproductive exploitation of writing in order to make the symptomatic value of this general disinvestment more apparent as well as what is looking for its way there or what is at work, in an as yet unforeseen manner. Recognizing reproductive exploitation does not come down to stigmatizing reproduction or complaining about accelerated mimetic expropriation [that is precisely a precritical, scared reaction that continues to oppose production to reproduction, the copyright of original property to imitative misappropriation, progression to regression; this reaction is often perpetrated by so-called avant-gardes that continue to hold on tight to the old schemas according to which creators are plundered by imitators, plagiarizers, students, teachers, and so forth. The old myth of literature as something external to the apparatus of production, to any school or philosophy. We now know the resources and the politics of this myth; it is allied with that which it claims to oppose, and it is also, it has always been an effect of the same combinatory grid]; on the contrary, it needs to be analyzed practically in order to move it in another direction, elsewhere; or rather, since there is no room here for a voluntaristic activism, it needs to be to analyzed with the presumption of this elsewhere that is leading it and constraining it beneath its surprised rehashing, its uneasy swelling, or its jubilant manipulation.

My "own motives," that which makes me "write and speak": I could perhaps say many things of a general sort on this subject, the subject of this *other thing* that orders, commands (with a whip), where heteronomy is the rule, *the implacable* with which one tries to draw up a contract that it itself will finally sign, and so forth. I have already explained myself elsewhere in these general terms and you are right that one has to look for the most singular [but that {*ça*} is for you to find in what I believe I say in the form of a generality], the most *clinical*: before whom, before what do I lie down, with what and with whom—clinic, as you know, speaks of the *bed* {lit} and *clin* (in all its forms and in all its senses) makes *Glas* work from one end to the other.

All of a sudden, the word *implacable* comes to me. That cannot be appeased, assuaged, quenched {*désaltérer*} (and with good reason), but, for the same reason (following the drift of the derivation), that one can in no sense abandon or give up {*plaquer*}. The trace of the implacable: that is what I am following and what leads me by the nose to write. Thus, like everyone, I have a flair that is at once good and bad: at the right moment I go where one must not, and at the wrong moment I go where one must. Always the *faux-bond* where necessary, and where it fails (to fail).[11] Not "*where* one must/it fails {*il faut*}" but where either *one must/it fails* or *one must not/it fails not*: that is, in the vicinity where the *one must/it fails* or the *one must not/it fails not* gets elaborated. "Elaborated" {*S'élabore*} is a quotation from *Glas*.

If a motive becomes or appears "proper" only by putting in motion toward the *colossal*, the erected, overhanging, stony double of the dead phallus—the *colossos*—if I am thus (following) the desire of/for my double {*si je suis donc le désir de mon double*}, then I have (been) worked on (by) mourning. But do we already know what mourning is or, a sharper concept that we ought perhaps to make use of, *semi-mourning*? Mourning-work as the only motif or motive that would be proper to me, as the only drive tending to reappropriate me even to my death, but also a work *on* mourning, on the work of mourning in general and in all its modes (reappropriation, interiorization by introjection *or* incorporation,[12] or between the two—once again semi-mourning—idealization, nomination, and so forth).

To work on mourning, is also, yes, to enter into a practical, effective analysis of mourning, to elaborate the psychoanalytic concept and concepts of mourning. But it is first of all—and by that very token—the operation which would consist in working *on* mourning the way one says that something functions on such and such an energy source, or such and such a fuel—for example, to run on high octane. To the point of exhaustion.

And to do one's mourning for mourning.

Without them, beyond the philosophemes and post-philosophemes (so refined, polished, recombined, infinitely crafty) that treat all the states (which have worked themselves into a great state) of death, nothingness, negation, denegation, idealization, interiorization, and so forth (I am speaking here of a place and a moment of my self in which I know them *too well,* in which they know me *too well*), I am trying to experience *in my body* an altogether other relation to the unbelievable "thing which is not." It's probably not possible, especially if one wants to make of this experience something other than a consolation, a mourning, a new well-being, a reconciliation with death, although that's not something I sneer at. But this impossibility as regards "the thing which is not" is, finally, the only thing that interests me. It's what I call—awkwardly still— the mourning of mourning. It is a terrible thing that I do not love but that I want to love. You ask me what makes me write or speak, there it is. It's something like that—not what I love, but what I would like to love, what makes me run or wait, bestows and withdraws my idiom. And the *re-bon.*[13]

I do not know why I go off in this direction, while improvising, rather than others, so many other possible directions. What is important here is the improvisation—contrived like all so-called free association—well anyway, what is called improvisation. It is never absolute, it never has the purity of what one thinks one can require of a forced improvisation: the surprise of the person interrogated, the absolutely spontaneous, instantaneous, almost simultaneous response. A network of apparatuses and relays—and first of all language, the element of this finite interview I am speaking about—has to interrupt the impromptu, put it beside itself, set it aside from itself. A battery of anticipatory and delaying devices, of slowing-down procedures are already in place as soon as one opens one's mouth—even if there is no microphone or electric typewriter present—in order to protect against improvised exposition. And yet, even if it always already does this, it never succeeds. The delay of differance will have always precipitated the other, toward the other, the wholly different. The use one may make of all these apotropaic machines will always end up forming a place that is exposed, vulnerable, and invisible to whoever tries out all the clever ruses: it is a blind spot, but one which takes on a certain relief, that leaves behind a text, a little hill {*talus*} of a heel {*talon*} on which the clever one cannot turn around. There always remains improvisation, and that is what counts here. What counts is what limits the defenses, anticipation, or the time of writing—what he who defends himself *pays*, without realizing it, for his defense, the fence with which he divides himself in order to mount his defense and which remains as a trace of the payment. That is why I speak of the *talon* which is also a check stub (as well as a heel like Achilles') and with which he will one day have to balance his accounts upon receiving the debit notice. Someone is interrogated who has taken, who thinks he has taken (up to a certain point) the time to write and to elaborate coded, supercoded machines, and so forth. So as to capitalize the reading effects (effects of all sorts to which one can assign all sorts of attributes: socio-political, sexual, and so on), he has paradoxically rarefied the field of immediate efficacy, bringing it almost to absolute zero. Then he is asked some questions. These are a kind that, in any case, he will not be able to answer at leisure and in a manner as closely controlled as in a published text where he can correct galleys and page proofs. The interesting thing, then, or at least the pertinent thing is not *what* he says—the more or less novel or repetitive, clarifying or impoverished content of his re- sponses—but what he selects, what selects (discriminates, scribbles, chooses, excludes) itself in the rush as he clips out clichés from the more or less informed mass of possible discourses, letting himself be restricted by the situation, the interlocutors. This is what will betray his defenses in the end.

Betray his defenses: as much in one sense (the defenses caught off- guard) as in the other (the defensive structure all at once laid bare), which is what is happening right now, right here, on my part, because a protocol concerning the necessity of improvisation also provides a measure of protection, a rate of furtive protection. Do not expose yourself too quickly nor too much, make last pleasure's excitement by the recording tape (a question of tape, strip, stripe), do not translate too quickly into a symptom. But one can also see how (and here is a motif or a trait that would be more properly my own or that in any case would be relevant only to a single type) the speaker defends, confesses, betrays himself only by exposing his system of defense; at least (a new supplementary ruse), its principle or its form. This delays again or withholds the most vulnerable laying-bare, that for which one signs a blank check. It is another way of remaining an exhibitionist around the edges. But whoever decided that all of this deserved to be published or that anything deserved to be published, or rather that between a secret and its publication there has ever been any possibility of a code or a common rate in this place?

So, one has to, one fails to improvise {*Improviser il le faut, donc*}.

How did we get here? Ah, yes, the mourning for mourning, to the point of exhaustion. What one might dream of is the end of mourning. But this end is the normal finish of mourning's process. How to give *affirmation* to an *other end*?

The link of affirmation (yes, oui, *Ja, ungeheures unbegrenztes Ja*) in the end returns at the end of *Glas*. Some have said that the last words left hanging ("... pour avoir compté sans" or, in the other band, "... ici, maintenant, le débris de" {"... for it counted without" "... here, now, the debris of"}, because they seemed to pick up again the "first" phrases of the book, formed a Moebius strip. No, not at all: a caesura or hiatus prevents what in effect resembles such a band or strip from turning back on itself. The Moebius strip is a powerful figuration of the economy, of the law of reappropriation, or of successful mourning-work that can no longer, in the writing of *Glas*, toll a knell {*sonner un glas*} which is its own (its *glas*) without breakage {*bris*} and debris. The *debris* of this band is not even the last or the first; it repeats and scatters the debris of a *bris de verre* {glass breakage} or of a mirror {*glace*}, and it has a multiple occurrence in the book (impossible to count them: it is always, at least, once again a piece of the name of Jean Genet's mother: Ga*bri*elle, of my name, or of all the numerous brilliant objects and words, or of that which bridles and unbridles the horse and the "cavalier phantasm" of the *genet*, the Spanish horse that plays a very important role in all of this {*ça*}—the last words are "débris de," of all the *dé, dés* {die, dice, or sewing thimbles}, *dais* {dais, or canopy} [for example "dais de l'oeil révulsé" {canopy of the upturned eye}, but there are many others], the funerary dais or the bridal canopy with the bride or the fiancée the day of her wedding which is, *for me*, Genet's or Hegel's mother, as if these two were my bastards, that is those of an unknown woman who would have called herself in secret Marie-Gabrielle Derrida, and so forth); in short, before closing the book on a prefabricated Moebius strip, one has perhaps to let oneself be taken in a little longer by the words, the morsels of words or of dead bits {*mors*} in decomposition that let the writing go a bit more unbridled. And first of all with the word *débridé*. The Moebius strip is a detachable part in this treatise on detachment, an effect of partial simulacrum, a dead bit there where there is always more than one.

How to give affirmation to an other end? *Glas* tries to show ("class against class"[14]) that mourning-work is not just any kind of work but something like the "essence" of work. Perhaps one can then "speculate" (I am using Freud's term from *Beyond the Pleasure Principle*, a word whose reevaluation I am attempting this year in the course of a seminar on *Life Death*[15]), speculate then on an "end" of mourning-work which would not be the "normal" completion of mourning, but something like a beyond the mourning principle. This is almost unimaginable; it/id can always come down to aping in a rigid manner what it/id wants to exclude since the beyond of mourning can always put itself "at the service of" mourning-work. Very soon, then, one would find oneself back in the necessarily aporetic movement of the pleasure principle's beyond. It is the unimaginable, even unthinkable logic of this step/not {*pas*} beyond which interests me. Even if it is unthinkable, it/id lends at least a contour to the able-to-be-thought.

The "proper" motif, then, where is it to be found? How does *ex-appropriation* (a word that had to be forged in *Signsponge/Signéponge*[16]) intersect at a point of minimal adherence (you also call it coincidence) with the singularity of the "style," of the "phantasmatic," of the idiom in general? This question besieges the texts I have published recently. Even if I could, up to a certain point, elaborate such a question elsewhere, put it in the form of general propositions, something would remain inaccessible *to me*, inaccessible in any case to these approaches, eluding any becoming for itself—and that would be, precisely, "my" idiom. The fact that this singularity is always for the other does not mean that the latter accedes to something like its truth. What is more, the idiom is not an essence, merely a process, the effect of a process of exappropriation that "produces" only perspectives, readings without truth, differences, intersections of affect, a whole history whose very possibility has to be disinscribed or reinscribed. These limits are valid not only for the relation of someone to *his/her* idiom, but for any idiom or any signature. When I have tried to interrogate, in an altogether preliminary fashion, the singularity of such and such an idiom (the signature according to all the implications of this word—I explain what I mean in the first part of *Signsponge*), I marked each time the essential limit of such a reading, its preliminary character, to be sure, but also what doomed it to a kind of failure for structural reasons, especially if one attempted to link the signature to the name, and even more so to the father's name or the patronymic recognized by one's civil status.[17]

One can find an example—just an example—of the difficulty with the "proper" motive in the old debate labeled, if you like, "motivation vs. arbitrariness," and more generally within the vast field of *Mimesis.* I entered into this in "The Double Session."[18] The effort in *Glas* is at once systematic and practical (it does not take shelter in metalanguage, it works on a defined corpus and forms itself a corpus) to disengage, from the tenacious grasp of a foreclosure, the conditions for a return to the drawing board. Such a return is not limited to the several pages that have a more "theoretical" appearance, which is to say reassuring enough to be grabbed like the right end of the stick—the pages on Saussure and Fónagy. These pages themselves, moreover, remark that, by excluding the question of the signature, and more generally the question of borders of the proper inscribed within the text, along with the immense problematic represented there, by keeping to the presumed immanence of a linguistic system (of a system in general), within its "normal" and framed functioning that is strictly distinguished, by its margin, from its margins (as if such a thing existed), one misses what is at stake in phenomena of so-called motivation. One is forced to treat them as marginal accidents (employing for that purpose a knowledge that pretends to certainty about what a margin is), as daydreams that are childish, ludic, esthetic, or literary (that is, belles lettres whose margins are themselves immaculate), or even symptoms deemed pathological in the most naive sense of this word. Thus one manages to avoid having any effective recourse to psychoanalysis. I am not talking here about either the Bachelardian kind or even the Lacanian kind and still less some mixture of the two. There is a certain twist within the logic of doubles and *mimesis* that of itself deconstructs not only the vague Bachelardian imaginary but the more rigorous and therefore all the more tranquilizing Lacanian distinction of the symbolic from the imaginary. This distinction is one of the objects of *Le facteur de la vérité*.

To wish to contain "mimetic" effects within what is so calmly called the imaginary, to wish to contain there even literature or literary *mise en oeuvre*, literary work on these effects, constitutes the traditional limitation of this problematic. But the wish to contain is not only a theoretical gesture; it is the movement of a force that has always been at work and already within the so-called normal practice of language. *Glas* proposes a deconstruction (that as far as possible and as always—but it seems it is necessary to repeat this— would be *affirmative*) of the opposition arbitrary/motivated there where it remains entrenched in dogmatism and subjected to increasingly readable interests. That opposition can have, it has had *critical* and even scientific powers, and it retains them within certain limits. It is even essentially *critical* (but deconstruction is not a critical operation; it takes critique as its object; deconstruction, at one moment or another, always aims at the trust confided in the critical, critico-theoretical agency, that is, the deciding agency, the ultimate possibility of the decidable; deconstruction is a deconstruction of critical dogmatics); there is, however, a moment and a place where this critical value is designed to maintain the belief— no doubt salutary from a certain point of view—in the impenetrable, invulnerable, non-contaminable, immaculate interior of the linguistic system and in the strict purity of its limits. In the *Introduction to "The Origin of Geometry"* and then in *Speech and Phenomena*, I wanted to analyze the process of idealization and the structures of ideality (of the signified but also of the signifier) that support the effect of arbitrariness—and thus of rigorous identity,

closed on itself—of the linguistic system. *Of Grammatology* concerned the stakes and the interests engaged in this search (which is
at once credulous and, precisely, scientific, at a certain point in the
development of science), the search for the internal system of
language. This develops, finally in a fairly consistent manner, in the
interest I have had lately in the questions of the frame and the
signature ("The Parergon," "+R," or *Margins*).[19] In *Glas*, there is a
judas hole that puts these questions in play with reference to
Saussure's confused embarrassment concerning onomatopoeia and
the words *glas* and *fouet*. I cannot go back over this ground here
(and my answer is already too long, as if I wanted to prevent you
from posing other questions), but I will remark that this piece of a
judas hole, opening onto the "logic of the dead bit {*mors*} and of
antherection,"[20] embeds itself in a column at the precise point
where it is treating the generation of Christ, the Trinity, and
Absolute Knowledge in Hegel's logic. Since *mors*, antherection,
obsequence (are these words part of language?) can be understood
only within the lexical and syntactic system of *Glas*, which is in
neither this language nor another, I will not try to translate them.
We have to let things drop {*Il faut laisser tomber*}. But perhaps just a
few more words on the subject of the internal system of language
("and what if *mimesis* so arranged it that language's internal system
did not exist?"). I am not saying that it does not exist or at least that
the demand for such a system has no meaning or does not exist as
demand. The very meaning of such a system (meaning itself) and
its existence are constituted, like every value of arbitrary conven-
tionality, as guardrails. To keep within them is also to hang onto
what has made science possible or rather a science, a region, and an
epoch, or a model of linguistic science. But if the ideal effect of
such an internal system is constantly being overrun, if it has to
defend itself against what has always deconstructed it as if from
within and according to necessary laws, then this model of scientificity, *this* scientific project should be put back into question or at
least complicated—at the point where it poses an obstacle to a more
powerful, as well as a more transformative science, where it sustains
at the same time a scientism and an obscurantism (classic alliance).

Glas also deals with classicism (and class phenomena) at the

point where a theoretical argumentation is put forward against a
Saussurian Remark on the subject of occurrences "dangerous for
our thesis," for *the* thesis, the thesis on the thetic structure of
language and the arbitrariness of the sign.[21] It also forms a quasi-
corpus that a formalist, pre-psychoanalytic reading, a reading that
clings to the protective institution of arbitrariness, of the "repre-
sentativist" or hermeneutic interpretation of *mimesis* (I have nick-
named it mimetology), can only be eager to avoid. But of course
(and this introduces a complication that some may consider discouraging), *Glas* also takes aim at the current concept of "motivation," at "symbolism" (in the Hegelian-Saussurian sense of the
term), at its pre-psychoanalytic interpretations whether historicist
or simply semiotic. It is always a matter of recognizing the limits of
the sign's logic. There is an undue haste—let us call it *motivationist*
to save time—that *Glas* parodies, puts on stage and in trouble in
order to make way for a general reelaboration. Well, I will end here
this overly long and overly indirect response on the subject of
"reading effects" or non-effects.

Q.: On two occasions (in "+ R (Into the Bargain)" and in your
response to a questionnaire published in *Digraphe*[22]) you have
quoted this watchword of Benjamin's: that an author should "not
be content to take a position, through discourse, *on the subject* of
society, and that he [should] never, be it with revolutionary theses
or products, stock up an apparatus of production without transforming the very structure of that apparatus."[23]

How do you conceive the relation of your work to this imperative? How do you evaluate the political, social, ideological effects
produced by this work?

How is one to conceive, in a broad way, today, putting into
practice this imperative, for example in the academic institution
and in the publishing apparatus?

J.D.: It is not a literal quotation of Benjamin, but more like a
transposition, a somewhat active translation. But I do not think it
is an abusive one.

Yes, to transform the structure of the apparatus. But as the apparatus is always represented by very different agencies, that are quite distant from each other, according to a topology that has to be redefined, the transformation calls for a multiplicity of apparently heterogeneous gestures. Both individual and group gestures. What is more, it/id most often is done without gestures and without knowledge. It/Id happens just as well by means of ruptures and disruptions of the code in one's manner of writing, teaching, practicing, or trafficking in language or the instruments of logic and rhetoric, as by means of what are called "actions" intervening in or through the most recognizable form of the apparatuses. What seems necessary to me, in principle—and I can only give you the principle of an answer—is to try to avoid separations, to partition as little as possible, and never to engage in an action, a discourse, or a so-called revolutionary "force" within framing or coded forms that either cancel them out or absorb their shock right away. There are laws of production and receivability; they are very complex and overdetermined, but one can sometimes easily verify the constraints they impose. What appear to be the most revolutionary or subversive "contents" (whether of acts or discourses) are perfectly well received, neutralized, assimilated by the systems which they claim to oppose as long as certain rules of formal decency are respected. And decency can often assume the form of canonical and self-satisfied indecency (there are many of examples of this). It suffices that this decency knows enough to respect the thing which the dominant force forbids one to tamper with, and *voilà.* Inversely, without having revolution on one's lips nor wearing it on one's sleeve, one has only to graze "formally" the surface of whatever the guardian forms are guarding for the censorship machine to be engaged. In liberal regimes with formally "liberal" ethics (those in which we live, well, up to a certain point), this censorship does not always proceed by acts, decrees, or deliberate rejections, but by apparatus effects. Effectively, it/id does not reach this or that social force, it/id is not received, the media remain impervious, "people" do not buy, "they" do not understand, and so on. But of course, all of the scholarly, editorial, journalistic, and other sorts of apparatuses *and the forces they represent* produce and reproduce this situation. That is why I do not believe it is enough, given this state of things, to persist stubbornly to smuggle in super-refined avant-garde products without struggling for a massive transformation of the apparatuses. But neither is it useless. Still, to believe it is sufficient is to feed the dominant apparatuses with so many avant-gardist gadgets: and that is just what they need in their margins where they confine this avant-garde production. Yet to believe this is useless comes down to limiting the transformation in advance and in the name of a mild, reforming zeal. Thus, one must (you ask me about an "imperative"; we will not succeed in erasing the "one must" but must one? I will try to come back to this later) work in several directions, in several rhythms. The monorhythmic and the monocode always spell immediate reappropriation. One must, then, tamper with the code; in saying that, I refer as much to the monovalence, the unicity of the dominant code, as to its character as code. One must tamper with *the* code, its homogeneity and the singularity of the system that orders and regulates languages and actions. One must tamper with the fact that there is only one code. This does not imply (I have made use of the opposition form/content as a provisional convenience) that it suffices to dislocate rhetoric, "style," and frames for the rest to follow—even if, in "the final analysis" (an expression I would avoid using), one no longer accredits this limit between the framing and the framed. This limit is not itself a theoretical prejudice that can be snuffed out in a single breath or that goes away as soon as one has become critically conscious of it. It is a powerful, stratified *constructum* that calls for highly differentiated practical and critical interventions. Thus, analysis can lead one, in a specific, concrete situation, to advance "classical" discourses or actions and (recalling the phrase with which we began) can lead to "positions on the subject of"—in a simple, clear, univocal form, in a style I would call neo-classical. Once again: do several things at once and in several ways at once. This is never done alone, not even "within" a single gesture, a single discourse, a single text. The signature—and whether one likes it or not—is multiple, which means not only that it engages several patronymic names, but that it departs from itself, in advance of the proper name effect, onto different scenes, in different localities, into different spaced forces—an unconscious, a body whose topos and economy cannot be reassembled in the *vocabulary* of a nominal or a company signature.

For this reason as well (and on top of it all) I will not be able to improvise anything very satisfying on the subject of "my" relation, the relation of what you choose to call "my" work to all of this, to such an "imperative." I would be tempted at first to say: I work without "imperative," I work *on* the imperative (what is it? where does it come from? how is it formed? how does it disguise and insinuate itself? and so forth), but of course this is not true. I obey and it is even probable that I bow down {*je m'incline*[24]} before an "imperative" with which I am at the same time trying fiercely to negotiate; only this imperative does not have an ideological, moral, or political form that could serve as a representative relay of the one that has hold of my body and unconscious, like that other thing that watches me, that concerns me {*qui me regarde*}, heteronomizes or erotonomizes me. Having said that and while I mistrust political voluntarism, especially in its archaic forms of a logic of representation and of consciousness, I am no less wary of anti-voluntarism or the immobilist and comfortable exploitation of one's "good reasons," as well as of the meditating and suspensive exploitation that can be made of the motifs of differance or the undecidable (this can be at times a cunning war tactic with which to combat the necessity of these motifs and return to precritical and reactionary positions). This is naturally to understand nothing of these motifs, to have failed to read. In short, there is no political intervention without "voluntarism," "morality," "humanism," simplifying decision—all of which are subjected *on the other hand* to critical questions or to deconstructive analyses (and these are not finally exactly the same thing). In order to hold these two unequal necessities together and differentiate systematically a ("theoretical" and "political") practice, a general overturning is indispensable, *imposes itself*: not only as a theoretical or practical imperative, but already as a proceeding under way, one which invests, envelops, overflows us in an unequal fashion.

"My" relation to this proceeding is necessarily multiple and in transit. Its specificity, if it has one, concerns microscopic movements in a very marginal cultural space, very much of the minority; what is more, I cannot claim to be either alone or an initiator. Nor can I claim an overall analysis of the effects you speak of. I attempt such an analysis all the time, but at every moment it is a part of the space that it takes as its object. Since I just mentioned marginal minority, I will add that while the motifs of the "margin" and of "nomadism" are very insistent, as you know, beginning with the first texts I published, their insistence depended on certain conditions and certain protocols; these are, in large measure, foreign to the whole "ideology" being installed today, in a certain Parisian cultural forum, under the big top of nomadizing marginality. This effect—let's call it, if you will, "ideological"—is very convenient for the whole centralizing sedentariness which always prefers "nomads" to massive and organized oppositions. I do not mean to say that these ideological effects are accidental, having only an external relation with the words "margin" and "nomadism" which I used in another sense. None of this is fortuitous. It is these paradoxes within the law of ideologico-political effects that I work on or that work on me. You ask me how I evaluate the political, social, ideological effects produced by this work. What I have just said gives you a hint of the difficulty. The guiding thread for such an analysis might be the following fact: the work to which you refer (whether "mine" or that of others to which I feel close, whose necessity seems to me more obvious, more urgent, less repetitive) is not at present *well received* anywhere. No, I will not talk about censorship or misappropriation, and so forth (all of which are ill-adapted themes for this type of process, themes which are moreover reactive and in general manipulated in a way that, each time, generates a profit: look at how I am censored, which is obviously the sign that, etc.; or else look how well it sells, which is obviously the sign that, etc.); no, and yet *no* politico-syndicalist movement, *no* editorial organization (and you are aware of my effective "nomadism" in this domain[25]), *no* institution (academic, psychoanalytic, or both at the same time since we are witnessing today interesting concentrations in this regard, the editorial power being always present), *no* journalistic apparatus, *none* of the clienteles more or less visibly joined by the interests represented in these organizations—none of them accepts or can accept even to work with this work, still less receive it. This work is taken on or given a "home" in *none* of the places I have just named very quickly. It is not always a question of a deliberate rejection, or even of an argued critique, something that could merit our attention. This index interests me and also induces more work: where is the weld unifying the dominant code for this field? For such a "home"? What are the differentiated rhythms of development—theoretical and otherwise—in a given field? and so forth.

Among all these difficulties, the greatest one (if at least I want to try to answer your question quickly) would be: to render perceptible and effective the coherence between, on the one hand, what passes by way of published writings of a certain form, those to which you referred and that carry an individual signature, and, on the other hand, certain endeavors in which I participate more anonymously, knowingly or even without knowing it, in some more or less homogeneous group. All of this lends itself poorly to evaluation, is difficult to pin down in an analysis. Finally, analytical evaluation is useful, but it is not a categorical imperative and one must not look to it for a reappropriating reassurance. In any case, it takes off {*ça part*} and never comes back... All the more so since (such are the laws in this domain) when it/id works or goes down well, that means (sometimes) that it's easy, without importance, without interest (or at times serves the interests that one would wish to combat). And when it/id gets blocked, that means sometimes (but careful, not always) that it/id has hit effectively upon the veritable resistance. Outside *and* within oneself.

As for this resistance, I wish to add here, as I correct the proofs of our interview, a kind of apology for excess or for error when it takes the *form* of the more or less calculated blunder. Look at the Boutang affair:[26] a blunder, more or less calculated, in the declaration of the Collège de Philosophie precipitated onto the scene (with a spectacular movement of the whole, the entire right and up to a certain left, almost the entire left) the very thing that people especially wanted to avoid speaking of, that which it was imperative never to speak of again: Pétainism, anti-Semitism, racism, this enormous, tenacious repressed (hardly repressed or hard to repress) that works over the body, the memory, and the unconscious, the whole of French society, its institutions and organizations (see above) through an incredible, lively and living network. Suddenly, thanks to this blunder (more or less calculated), all of these forces could be seen rashly regrouping, attempting to make their *principal target* out of a text that exposed the thing that it was imperative not to speak of. In the name of liberalism, pluralism, tolerance (it should be said, in its more or less electoral, seasonal form), people confused racism with one of the legitimate currents of democracy in the great French family, they said anything whatsoever to drown out what must not be heard, they forbade anyone to ask questions or undertake struggles on the subject of the functioning of the university; and by attacking, as if in a single voice, the Collège de Philosophie, people tried to divert attention from the real problem that this vast consensus wanted to dissimulate or repress. And once again, it succeeded, up to a certain point, in repressing it, which is why I mention it again: if, after such a clarification, or rather such an uncovering of a certain reality of what is most unyielding about Boutang, and of the most indigestible and intolerable racism, of the very "worst taste," the one which the liberal bourgeoisie will not look at, cannot swallow, if at that point utterances (and more often distinguished silences) took on an embarrassed air (Oh, we didn't know, we didn't really realize, not to that degree...), then we have today to recognize that we are back almost to square one.

I come back to the academic institution and the publishing apparatus, those places that we are obliged to privilege in "ideological" work, and more and more in an advanced industrial society with such a high politico-economic concentration. I think one must (yes, once more) at the same time take into account the rigorous, refined, complex specificity of the functioning of such apparatuses, elaborate a problematic with regard to them, invent new, original forms of intervention (this task has hardly even been begun, it seems to me) *and simultaneously* avoid letting oneself be fascinated or closed in by the educational and publishing machines which are, in spite of everything, very dependent. The politicization of zones and processes that, in general, fall outside classical analysis, must not, even as it remains very specific, cut itself off from the massive political forces and the general political stakes that are represented there. A representation whose passages are not always "representable," precisely, not of a representative nature and even less like a conscious calculation or a reflection. This is where the recasting of the concept of what is called ideology, I mean its "theoretical" recasting, should be done *in* and *through* these new practices. Otherwise there would be nothing but alibis and reassurances for comfortable revolutionary eloquence. If an "ideologue" or "intellectual" does not attempt to transform effectively the cultural, academic, or editorial apparatuses in which he works, whether he is sleepily installed there or still claims to be free to "wander" within it (in the "secondary margins," of course, according to what a friend of mine calls official nomadism), then he is always in the process of maintaining the good working order of the most sinister of machines. Sometimes this is accompanied, as a confirmation, by an overt, disdainful, and moralizing lack of interest in matters having to do with teaching and publishing. In that case, one misjudges—and this misjudgment is traditional with literary people {*littéraires*}, it is the most direct legacy of literary avant-gardes, the most restrictive code in what may be called the world of letters—the theoretico-political stakes of the struggle that must be conducted in these areas. What is more, these stakes carry over into what *littéraires* naturally consider to be the autonomous process of "literary production." By *littéraire* here I mean someone who never fails to believe, want, claim himself or herself to be external, beside (in fact, above) the scholarly or academic apparatuses and does not see to what degree this phantasm itself is a product constantly reproduced in him or her by the academy. To fail to recognize the growing effects (which are in fact unlimited within the field of "ideology") of the academic apparatus within a certain type of society (ours), of the academic apparatus with its complex and widespread functioning, its internal struggles, its contradictions and heterogeneities, to consider this apparatus to be a closed system of simple reproduction, or else to cut it off from the publishing apparatus, for example literary publishing, all of this is an idealistic boast or a laughable illusion. It is always depoliticizing. Not surprising that this illusion should be common to all the adherents of literature as belles lettres whether they belong to the (eminently schoolish) academies or to what calls itself an avant-garde and thinks of itself as external to the University.

Inversely, to attack solely the scholarly or publishing appara-tuses, to believe that by beginning with them one can *immediately* get one's hands on everything, that an internal action suffices—this is also a comfortable alibi which resembles the other like a twin brother and belongs in fact to the same system. Without a general political transformation, the "agents" or partial and dependent functionings of either publishing or education can only be dis-placed to a practically insignificant degree.

As you see, what I am proposing here has once again and always the form of the double bind: neither simply this nor simply that, this and that being contradictory, *one must* have both this and that and go from this to that, and so forth. But have I invented this double band? Is it only my idiosyncrasy, the idiosyncrasy of what persecutes me and on the basis of which I would in turn persecute, ceaselessly foregrounding so many "one must"'s or "it is neces-sary"'s {*des "il faut"*} (what you were calling imperatives), but ones which are contradictory?

But if this double band is ineluctable (whether in me as an idiom and/or outside of me), *it is necessary*—a completely other *it is necessary*—that somewhere it not be the last word. Otherwise it/id would stop, become paralyzed, become medusa-ized immedi-ately—I mean even before it/id stops because, of course, it/id is going to stop in any case. It is necessary that, beyond the indefati-gable contradiction of the double bind, an affirmative difference—innocent, intact, gay—manage to give everyone the slip, escape with a single leap and come to sign in laughter what it allows to happen and unfold in the double band. All at once leaving the double band in the lurch {*lui faisant d'un coup faux-bond*}, suddenly no longer coming to terms with and explaining itself with the double band. That's what I love, this *faux-bond*, this one here (not to be confused with a missed rendezvous, nor with any logic of the rendezvous), the only thing I love is the moment of the "ungeheuren unbegrenzten Ja," of the "vast and boundless Yes" which comes at the end of *Glas* (system of the D.B.), of the "yes" that "we have in common" and on the basis of which "we are silent together, we smile our knowledge to each other," says Zarathustra.

It is the "come—yes" and the "desire to roll toward the sea" in "Pas."

You ask me about theory, politics, and so forth: let us say that when I do not hear there, even from a distance, this "yes, come" or one of its translations, I am very bored, very bored indeed.

Q.: You write, in *Glas*, p. 36: "Not to arrest the career of a Genet. For the first time I am afraid, while writing, as they say, 'on' someone, of being read by him. Not to arrest him, not to draw him back, not to bridle him. Yesterday he let me know that he was in Beirut, among the Palestinians at war, encircled outcasts. I know that what interests me always takes (its/his) place over there, but how to show that?"

To what degree does the category of exclusion (or of encirclement) seem to you pertinent in politics?

What form of interest are you talking about? For what reason do you consider it necessary to show it? What type of (de)monstration are you talking about and on what conditions do you think you can produce it?

Does the philosophical activity necessitate for you a political practice? What is it?

J.D.: I think we should shift gears, otherwise this is going to be too long for an interview. If you agree, I will try to limit myself to more aphoristic or elliptical responses.

The running of a Genet: *genet*, the common noun, is the name of a (Spanish) horse. The preceding page had recalled this fact as well as how "he rides horse(back) on his proper name" which "he holds

by the bit {*mors*}," and so forth. It also recalled the "cavalier
phantasm" which presides over the great "inner scene" and the "I
enter the lives of others on horseback like a Spanish grandee . . ."
and so on. This "horse" rides across the whole book and all of the
questions posed there, particularly those working on the proper
name. Well, I'll stop here with this contextual reminder which
could go on forever.

"I'm afraid": this is never me exactly, nor is the fear mine exactly.
These are also functions in the text, in the logic of the scene that is
being played out there. Fear because the horse I am straddling—the
text—the textual force on which I am mounted must be stronger
than me, must not let itself be dominated, broken, or mastered
by the bit that it has or that I put or that I take in its mouth.
Otherwise, it's not interesting. I am afraid because it/id concerns
me {*ça me regarde*}, because the other thing is watching what I do
and carries me off at the very moment I try all sorts of mastering
maneuvers. I try to explain the law governing this relation in *Glas*
and why, as I write, it is I who am being read first of all by what I
claim to write, by Genet and a few others, who may also be dead
and, for one reason or another, in no state to read or do damage.
"The first time": no, not really, not simply, but the first time to this
extent, which can be explained by the force of the texts that
"concern" *Glas*. Since then, there have been Ponge and Blanchot,
and that is no less scary. At least for a certain *I*, whom fortunately I
am able to leave in the lurch when I have to, like the friends or
other friendly texts that I have just named. Which is why they are
friends.

Not to bridle him: I have already explained why *bridle* (form and
meaning) was the necessary word and why one must not bridle. It
is also because, at the moment I am reading and working on some
text of Genet's, he is in an altogether other place, far from literature, and so forth, he leaves me in the lurch and I like that, admire
it and rejoice in it.

I also try to do the same thing.

Now, there was, it is true, a message transmitted by a Palestinian
friend. There are many "real" or so-called autobiographical events

encrypted, reinvested by the logic of the scene in *Glas*, but they are there only insofar as they fit this internal logic. In this specific passage, it was a question of situating the political schema of "encircled outcasts" and a few other things to which I will return in a moment. To answer your question very quickly, it seems to me that the category of encircling exclusion, of exclusion enclosing what it wants to neutralize or cast out, to put *out of commission* and to *exile* {hors d'état} (logic of the *pharmakos*) has *political* pertinence or efficacy only if one articulates these two things: *on the one hand*, a historical analysis or description of the elements traditionally filed under the category of the "political" (State, power, police, army, institutions, socio-economic power relations, and so forth) which in general has been done, up till now and so far as I know, following *pre-psychoanalytic* paths and conceptuality; and, *on the other hand*, an analysis that reckons, at least in principle, with the psychoanalytical problematic. I am not referring here to any particular doctrinal state of psychoanalysis, to this or that orthodox content, but to a problematic topos that psychoanalysis presents us with and that, in my opinion, remains unavoidable. As for me, I would look in the direction of the processes of mourning, of incorporative exclusion, of another topical structure of repression and suppression (this is what I began to do in *Glas*), without which one will never understand anything about the history of power, police, institutions, and so forth. The self-indulgent tendency of historians to neglect these questions, to keep psychoanalysis out of the picture comes along to repeat in a certain way the old encircling exclusion. But of course, one must also *politicize* the topical structure of mourning, not by means of artificial application or varnishing, but with the help of rigorous concepts and through a *psychoanalytical-and-political practice*.

When I write "what interests me," I am designating not only an *object* of interest, but the place that *I am in the middle of*, and precisely the place that I cannot exceed or that seems to me to supply even the movement by which to go beyond that place or outside of it. It is a matter there—for example—of the Palestinian struggle, insofar as it cannot be reduced to a local conflict, but deploys a war over *taking place*, and in a place that still gives place today to so much of our discourse, our history, our politics that we cannot be too assured of having any distance on it. Instead of glossing in this direction, I will simply point out that on the same page, below to the right and to the left, one may read something that defines the "interest" of this place—which thus finds itself in the middle, itself interested and overrun on all sides. Further down: "How right he is. This is what I want to show by deporting you as swiftly as possible to the limits of a basin, a sea, where there arrive for an interminable war the Greek, the Jew, the Arab, the Hispano-Moor. Which I am also (following), by the trace {*Que je suis aussi, à la trace*}." On the right: "Begin, then, to approach the unnameable crypt and the studio of Alberto Giacometti, where such a wound of the paraph takes on animal form. You will have already suspected that if the signature is all that at once, it is neither a thing, nor a flower, nor an animal. Remain(s) to (be) know(n) if there is any." To the left, the deportment of the Hegelian analysis of Christianity and Judaism (I give you a selection, for example: "Christianity itself is only completed by relieving itself {*se relevant*} into its philosophical truth." "... the upsurging of Christianity has been announced. There is family before the [Christian] family . . ." "The Christian thesis, the axial thesis that replaces the Jewish thesis by opposing it, overturns mastery..." "Here begins the legendary discourse on/of the eagle and the two columns. On castration and dissemination, a question going back to the flood." There follows the incredible Hegelian reading of the flood and the Middle East wars).

This value of "interest" is thus no longer an object for demonstration like any other (you ask me "what type of demonstration" I am thinking about). Once it envelops or exceeds (within the contextual opening we are considering here) our whole "history," "language," "practice," "desire," and so forth, the modes of demonstration should no longer be prescribed or coded by anything that belongs simply within these borders. And at the same time, all modes may be necessary here (autobiography, fictive narration, poem, theorem, and so on, as well as all the practical or theoretical movements that do not pass by way of "speech" or "writing," or what is ordinarily comprised by these words). To state this more clearly, here is a very partial, singular example of the trajectory I am thinking of. I refer to it because it is more on my mind today, that's all. Take the eighth *Thesis on Feuerbach* that speaks of the "rational solution" (by human practice and the concept of that practice) to the mystical effects of theory. To follow only this thread (but there are many others), one wonders what is this instance of rationality that is not yet or already no longer determined as theoretical *or* practical. From there, a philosopher could interrogate the historico-philosophical space in which such an instance of rationality could arise. Among others, the Kantian text, that defines an interest of reason even before its determination as speculative or practical (here I am simplifying drastically work that I am doing more patiently elsewhere), induces a question about an *interest* in reason in general, thus about the value of interest that no philosopheme other than that of reason can approach: the interest of philosophy itself, as reason. And the question: *What is reason, what is its interest,* its necessarily pre- or a-rational interest, the reason without reason of reason, and so forth, this question can no longer give rise to demonstrations of a philosophical type (the demonstration that Heidegger puts forward in *Der Satz vom Grund* on a very similar question, from a certain point of view, is already no longer strictly philosophical) or a traditional theoretico-scientific type. This does not mean that one has to back up or that one must still claim to have given a demonstration. Moreover, the trajectory that would lead from the *Theses on Feuerbach* back to Kant is only one possible trajectory, the one that resembles most closely the philosophical trajectory it parallels without reducing itself to that other trajectory. One could also attempt completely different operations (I am trying to do so elsewhere) by treating these theses otherwise than as philosophical or theoretical utterances, by redefining the context of their performance, the structure of their enunciation, and even by doing something besides "reading" them, by plugging them into altogether other circuits of the *interesting*. Well, I'll stop there. I merely wanted to anticipate an answer in principle to your last question: philosophical activity does not *require* a political practice; it is, in any case, a political practice. Once one has fought to get that recognized, other struggles begin that are both philosophical *and* political. What are they? I have no formula that could gather up the answer to such a question. Nothing to add, if you like. What is done or not done remains readable elsewhere for the interested parties. All I have wanted to do is go from the singular of your question to the plural (what is it, what are they) so as at least to emphasize what seems to me to be an axiom in this field: the front is always split, the paths double, the methods yet to be unfolded, the strategies intersected at angles.

Q.: To close or perhaps to open onto more work or another exchange, two more series of questions:

1. Last year, in the course of a seminar that you devoted, within the context of the GREPH,[27] to the teaching of philosophy, you were led to analyze a textual corpus that, up until then, had not been the object of any published work on your part. We refer, on the one hand, to a historical corpus (the history of the teaching of philosophy) and, on the other, to a set of Marxist texts (Marx-Engels, Gramsci, Althusser, Balibar) in which it is particularly a question of ideology and superstructures.

How does your relation to historical materialism and dialectical materialism stand today?

In what conditions and in what forms can the deconstructive activity have bearing on institutional apparatuses and on historical processes?

Do you think that Marxist texts can be the object of a deconstruction analogous in its modalities to the one that has been operated on metaphysical texts? How does one take into account the different stakes, scopes, and historical inscriptions?

Do you think that, provided there is a certain conceptual elaboration, one can utilize in a global fashion historical materialism in order to produce the analysis and transformation of a historical situation (ours)?

How do you evaluate the effects produced in the philosophical field by the construction of historical materialism and dialectical materialism?

2. You had announced, on the program of the same seminar, an analysis of the Marxist concept of ideology. On several occasions, you have expressed your reservations about a non-critical use of this concept. And yet you yourself have used it in limited ways.

Could you specify what it is, in the Marxist use of this term, that seems problematic to you? Under what conditions does this term seem usable to you?

How does your analysis of the sequence called "Western metaphysics" differ from Marxist theories of the "history of philosophy"?

How might one, in your opinion, think the relation of such a sequence to the history of social formations?

J.D.: I prefer to leave the last word here to your questions. They are necessary, vast, and fundamental, but for this very reason I cannot attempt a reply to them, especially given the limits which we must respect here. Let us say that I am trying or I will try to do it, here or elsewhere, in one way or another. Therefore, just a few words to go along with your questions.

1. For me, even less today than in the past, historical materialism, dialectical materialism do not exist in a manner that could be designated, for example, with a definite article: *the* historical materialism, and so forth. The first important difficulty is that of unity, the presumed unity, and then, if it exists somewhere, of the type of unity of *that* which, through these discourses and practices, claims to belong to dialectical and (or) historical "materialism." What is happening *right now today* has not given birth to this difficulty, but it confers on that difficulty an urgency that is, in my opinion, hitherto unknown. For this reason—and a few others—I do not have a relation, a single and simple relation to what is being asked by such a question. To situate what is important to me by means of schematic and negative indexes (which are insufficient, but that is the law of the genre that we are following here): You know to what extent I have remained unmoved in the face of various episodes of "Marxist" or pseudo-Marxist dogmatic eruptions, even when they

were attempting to be terroristic or intimidating, and sometimes
very close to places I was passing through; well, I find even more
ludicrous and reactive the hastiness of those who today think they
have finally landed on the continent of post-Marxism. They are
sometimes one and the same, but who would be surprised by that?
You are aware of the new Parisian consensus and all the interests
that are knotted together by it. These landings are happening right
here at an accelerated rhythm, and to the accompanying noise of
pages being turned at a furious rate. This compulsive amnesia
would be quite impressive—because, like a virginity that with-
stands all comers, it requires a certain strength—if one could ignore
all those drawn features in faces made tense by a daily panic before
the question: What if we landed too late to make our connection?
What if we got here after the dessert?

2. I have attempted to formulate this better elsewhere (for example in "Où commence et comment finit un corps enseignant"
{Where a teaching body begins and how it ends}): a deconstructive
practice that had no bearing on "institutional apparatuses and
historical processes" (I am using your terms), which was satisfied to
work on philosophemes or conceptual signifieds, discourses, and so
forth, would not be deconstructive; no matter how original it
might be, it would reproduce the auto-critical movement of philosophy in its internal tradition. This was clear from the beginning, as
soon as was put in place the minimal definition of deconstruction,
the one which concerns logocentrism, the last agency of meaning,
of the "transcendental signified," or of the transcendental signifier,
the last agency in general, and so forth.

3. I do not think that there are "the-Marxist-texts" and "the-
metaphysical-texts." The *unity* of metaphysics or of the "sequence
called 'Western metaphysics'" belongs to *a representation,* to an
auto-representation of something that one then continues to call
metaphysics only by invoking the name this thing calls itself and
the form of circular closure it wants to give itself. What has always
interested me (as I have said elsewhere) is the paradoxes of this
closure and its margins—a closure that does not *surround* a circular
field, but works on it *otherwise. Otherwise,* from then on, is posed

the question of whether or not one includes in this sequence Marxist texts or work whose unequal development, here and there, is made possible by these texts. These texts—which are themselves in constant transformation—are not limited to writings that have to be deciphered, even if, as writings, they assume a variety of forms, statuses, models of intervention (scientific or philosophical utterance, manifesto, declaration of position, watchword, "performatives," "imperatives," and so on) which should not be hastily reduced to homogeneity. And even supposing that Marxism presented itself as a "philosophical system" (a too-simple hypothesis), it would, *like any system,* carry with it possibilities of deconstruction that must be taken into account practically and politically.

You ask whether "Marxist texts can be the object of a deconstruction analogous, etc." If deconstruction were to find itself faced with some objects, or an *object* (I leave aside for the moment the question about this word and this concept, because I am not sure that deconstruction is concerned with something like an *object* or objects), it would not be simply a *constructum* or a structure that would have to be undone in order to uncover its archeological ground, its original foundation (or as someone recently put it, with a barely disguised and triumphant ingenuity, a *radical* beginning). On the contrary, it has been clear from the beginning that deconstructive questioning takes aim *at* and *against* such a fundamental mytho-radicology. At the same time, the question bears on the philosophical project insofar as it requires a foundation, an architectonics, and a systematics—and thus also an onto-encyclopedic *universitas,* what Kant rightly considers to be the *interest of reason.*[28] Does Marxism (insofar as it includes a system called dialectical materialism) present itself as a philosophy—already or yet to be elaborated—as a *founded* philosophical practice, as a "construction," to use a word from your question?

I know of no Marxist discourse—considered as such or calling itself such—that answers this question in the negative. Nor even, I will add, that poses this question or recognizes it.

That said, it has also always been clear and insistent that deconstruction is not an anti-philosophy or a critique of philosophy—of

Marxist philosophy still less than any other. But I would like to say this in a bit more patient, argued, and differentiated way, as I try to do elsewhere and especially in the work of teaching.

By way of anecdote and in order to emphasize the tangle, I might add that recently someone had the bright idea of translating "*aufgelöst werden können*" from *The German Ideology* by "peuvent être déconstruites" {can be deconstructed}. It is true that the declared Marxist who indulged in this operation against(?) the good translation of the Editions Sociales only ventured forth with such audacity and linguistico-theoretical frivolity in order to subordinate this "*Auflösung*"—that he wanted to pass off as *deconstruction* (by which is understood: *merely theoretical,* and so forth)—to "the practical subversion of real social relations." This has a double advantage: deconstruction is already in Marx, already in *The German Ideology,* and not just in a "practical state" but named as such; what is more, it is denounced there as insufficient, merely theoretical, or just on the level of ideas, the level below "practical subversion" (which is the very "in" and post-'68 translation of "*den praktischen Umsturz*"). But there would still be much to say about the fortunes and misfortunes of the word—notice I say the word—*deconstruction* today. The one just cited, besides its amusing linguistico-theoretical aspect, is interesting in my opinion because it constitutes a very significant political gesture. When the door is slammed too quickly, at least one knows there is a door.[29]

4. Ideology. Of course, I have had occasion (rarely) to use the term, in determined contexts where it seemed to me necessary to do so, even as I judge the concept, in a certain, equally determined state of the discourse that forms that concept, to be insufficient or rather unequal to the problematic corpus to which it is applied. But one is never obliged to reject a term because it names at a given moment a concept that still needs to be worked on. Nor need one constitute it as an untouchable fetish. I believe in the necessity of the problematic field *designated* by the Marxist concept of ideology, even if I find that in a particular historico-theoretical situation, the state of this concept, in the "Marxist" texts with which I am familiar, is unable to take the measure of the structure and com-

plexity of the field and the objects so designated. In the present
state of this concept (or rather I would say this *notion*, borrowing
from that code), such as it may be found dominating the Marxist
discourses I know, too many limits are still readable that come from
the initial conditions of such a notion's formation. These historical
and inevitable limitations (I say this from a point of view that I
think is Marxist), if one takes into account the theoretico-political
field in which this formation was inscribed, may be recognized by
several signs. I can only situate a few of them very schematically:
(1) The relation of the ideological to the scientific, about which the
very least one can say is that it remains a program for a Marxist
approach that is in constant displacement in this regard, that is,
regarding the most essential in this domain. What is more, this is a
dispersed displacement, not to say a contradictory one. (2) The
relation ideology/philosophy, that no Marxist discourse seems to
me to have as yet rigorously problematized, particularly insofar
as Marxists continue to take a detour around—this, at least, is
my hypothesis—the questions of a Nietzschean and/or Heideggerian sort on the subject of philosophy and the whole historico-
theoretical space which, to put it bluntly, has left its mark on the
notion of ideology (for example, a certain logic of representation,
of consciousness, of the subject, of the imaginary, of mimesis, a
precritical concept of illusion or of error—terms so often used to
define the ideological, and so forth). When I say that basically
"Nietzsche" and "Heidegger" (and quite a few others, I would even
include "Husserl" despite certain appearances) have not been *effectively* read and *situated*, have not been practically interpreted or
transformed by today's Marxist discourse, I am not referring to any
particular content, to some Nietzschean dogmatics and still less to
a Heideggerianism (for example). Rather, I refer both to a transformative irruption of certain modes and places of questioning, discourse, writing, intervention as well as to certain indissociable
historico-political events which Marxism, at least in France but
probably any Marxism, has so far been unable to take effectively
into account, which it has never rigorously confronted. It seems to
me. I think it would be, it will be necessary to do so for any

elaboration of the concept of ideology and for what is still called (but this title is itself a problem) a "theory of ideology." How can one pretend to such a theory so long as the relation of what is called the ideological to the "theoretical," the "scientific," the "philosophical" (for example) remains so inaccessible to a given conceptuality? (3) I would say, I have already said,[30] more or less the same thing concerning the problematics of the science of language, of writing, of semantics, of literature. I do not mean just science, but the problematics of scientificity in these domains. And most especially in "psychoanalysis." In its present state, the notion of ideology, such as it is currently used in statements that present themselves as Marxist, seems to me *either* massively pre-psychoanalytic *or* insufficiently articulated with a psychoanalytic problematic (here again I am speaking of a problematic and not a doctrinal content) *or else* totally dominated by *a* philosophy of psychoanalysis from which it imports this or that simplified notion, for example the Lacanian category of the imaginary (in the best of cases, and it sometimes happens that the "*imaginary,*" "phantasm," "reverie," and so forth—words commonly used to qualify the ideological— refer back to a very old psycho-philosophy). At that point, and *a fortiori* because of the above-mentioned simplification, one also imports in the raw state all of the effects of the Lacanian partition (imaginary/symbolic/real) in the form in which it manifested itself at a certain moment, along with all of the philosophical or phallogocentric guardrails that I have tried to identify elsewhere, notably in *Le facteur de la vérité.*

The work to come would not consist in articulating "theoretico-practical" fields that are *already given.* The fact that it has not yet been *done* in a dominantly Marxist discourse does not imply that it is all over with elsewhere. I do not believe that is at all the case. And it cannot be done *elsewhere alone,* it seems to me, outside of what I will call a *Marxist movement* to designate that which will have joined Marxist theory—the name of such a complex and such a problematic unity—to what that theory itself calls "revolutionary forces" or the "worker movement."

But the question is still open as to *what* these forces are (if they *are*) and what are/is their name(s).

Well, I am looking at the two bands out of the corner of my eye; they are going to stop very soon. Have to cut things off first, right. Naturally, there is nothing demonstrative in what I have just ventured here—I do not claim anything of the kind, this is neither the time nor the place. Only some hypotheses hastily delivered as provisional conclusions of some work that is supposed to be or that ought to be going on elsewhere.

Elsewhere, from a point of view—and in order to make visible the point of view—that situates *me* and what interests *me.* And perhaps will interest only me.

Who am perhaps deceived/who is perhaps deceiving me {*qui peut-être me trompe*}, letting myself/me expect too much from a *faux-bond.*

In that case, so much the worse, or the better, for "the thing which is not."

«The Almost Nothing of
the Unpresentable»

Q.: Your initial work indicated an interest for phenomenology;
you had published an introduction to Husserl's *Origin of Geometry*.

J.D.: At that period, phenomenology in France was more willing
to take up the problems of existence, of perceptive or pre-scientific
consciousness. Another reading of Husserl was also necessary, one
which would return to questions about truth, science, objectivity.
How does a mathematical object constitute itself on the grounds or
without the grounds of perception? What is the original historicity
of an object, a tradition, and a scientific community? For students
of my generation, the stakes of these questions were also political: I
see a sign of this in the fascination that some of us experienced for
the work of those like Tran-Duc-Thao (*Phénoménologie et maté-
rialisme dialectique*).[1]

But what was almost the last text of Husserl seduced me first of
all by what it has to say about writing, in a way that is at once novel
and confused, a little enigmatic: graphic notation is not an auxiliary moment in scientific formalization. Even as it poses a danger
for that formalization, it is indispensable to the very construction
of ideal objectivity, to idealization. This led to what seemed to me
to be the very limit of Husserlian axiomatics, of what Husserl calls
the "principle of principles," the intuitionist principle of phenomenology. I then continued to interpret other texts of Husserl in this

direction, most often while privileging the themes of the sign, language, writing, the relation to the other, as in *Speech and Phenomena*. Then I got away, so to speak, from phenomenology, no doubt unjustly and not without regrets...

Q.: At the time, philosophers hatched many dreams on the basis of the famous unpublished manuscripts of Husserl that could be consulted only in Louvain.

J.D.: I went there, intrigued as well by the mystery surrounding the unpublished works on temporality, "passive genesis," the "alter ego." Husserl's dogged attention to detail is exhausted in these zones where the "I" is dispossessed of its mastery, its consciousness, and even its activity.

Q.: Your philosophical work makes the problematic of writing into an essential bedrock. You break through the frontiers—which are moreover not well maintained—between literature and philosophy. To do this, you spend a lot of time with border texts like those of Mallarmé or Blanchot.

J.D.: My first desire was no doubt to go in the direction of the literary event, there where it crosses and even exceeds philosophy. Certain "operations," as Mallarmé would say, certain literary or poetic simulacra sometimes allow us to think what the philosophical theory of writing misapprehends, what it sometimes violently prohibits. To analyze the traditional interpretation of writing, its essential connection with the essence of Western philosophy, culture, and even political thought, it was necessary not to close oneself up in either philosophy as such or even in literature.

Beyond this division one may begin to see the promise or the profile of a singularity of the *trace* that is not yet language or speech or writing or sign or even something "proper to mankind." Neither presence nor absence, beyond binary, oppositional, or dialectical logic. At that point, it is no longer a question of opposing writing to speech, there is no protest against the voice; I merely analyzed the authority it has been given, the history of a hierarchy.

Q.: Certain American commentators have spoken of an influence of the Talmud.

J.D.: Yes, and it may be amusing to wonder how someone can be influenced by what he does not know. I don't rule it out. If I greatly regret not knowing the Talmud, for example, it's perhaps the case that it knows me, that it knows itself in me. A sort of unconscious, you see, and one can imagine some paradoxical trajectories. Unfortunately, I don't know Hebrew. The milieu of my Algerian childhood was too colonized, too uprooted. No doubt by my own fault in part, I received there no true Jewish education. But because I came to France, for the first time, only at the age of nineteen, something of this must remain in my relation to European and Parisian culture.

Q.: In the '60s, there was a lot of talk about the end of philosophy. For some, this meant that it was time to pass into action; for others, that philosophy was nothing but the myth of the Western ethnic group. Now, for you, one can only operate within the field of reason. There is no exteriority.

J.D.: I preferred to speak then of the "closure of metaphysics." The closure is not the end; it is rather, coming out of a certain Hegelianism, the constricted potential of a combinatory grid that is both exhausting and indefatigable. This closure would not have the form of a circle (the representation for philosophy of its own limit) or of a unilinear border over which one might leap toward the outside, for example, toward a "practice" that would finally be non-philosophical! The limit of the philosophical is singular; its apprehension is always accompanied, for me, by a certain unconditional reaffirmation. If one cannot call it directly ethical or political, it is nevertheless a matter of the conditions of an ethics or a politics, and of a responsibility of "thought," if you will, that is not strictly the same thing as philosophy, science, or literature as such...

Q.: You have just mentioned science. Marxism and psychoanalysis have in turn claimed to have a scientific vocation.

J.D.: The milieu in which I began to write was very marked, even "intimidated" by Marxism and by psychoanalysis whose scientific claims were all the more strenuous that their scientificity was not assured. They presented themselves a little like the anti-obscurantism, the "Enlightenment" of our century. Without ever going against "Enlightenment," I tried, discreetly, not to give in to the intimidation—by deciphering, for example, the metaphysics still at work in Marxism or in psychoanalysis, in a form that was not only logical or discursive, but at times terribly institutional and political.

Q.: Let us try to gauge your distance from Lacan.

J.D.: Psychoanalysis owes to Lacan some of its most original advances. It has been taken thereby to its limits, sometimes beyond itself, and it is especially in this way that it keeps fortunately that value of provocation also for what is most vital today in philosophy as well as in literature and the human sciences. But this is why it also requires the most vigilant reading. For it remains the case that, on the other hand, a whole systematic configuration of the Lacanian discourse (especially in the *Ecrits*, but also beyond) seemed to me to repeat or to assume a great philosophical tradition, the very tradition that called for deconstructive questions (about the signifier, *logos*, truth, presence, full speech, a certain use of Hegel and Heidegger...). I proposed a reading of this repetition of logocentrism and phallocentrism in *Le facteur de la vérité*.[2]

Lacan's seminar on Poe's "Purloined Letter" not only reproduces a common gesture of mastery in the interpretation of a literary writing taken up for illustrative purposes (effacement of the narrator's position, misapprehension of literary formality, careless cutting of the text), it does so in the manner of Freud and, to use a phrase of Freud's, in the name of a "sexual theory." The latter is always accompanied—and this is one of the things at stake here—by a precisely determined institution, practice, and politics.

Q.: You argue that to go against Hegel is once again to confirm Hegel. To head-on confrontations, renunciations, or pseudo-exits, you prefer minute but radical displacements. You practice a strategy of displacement.

J.D.: Frontal and simple critiques are always necessary; they are the law of rigor in a moral or political emergency, even if one may question the best formulation for this rigor. The opposition must be frontal and simple to what is happening today in Poland or the Middle East, in Afghanistan, El Salvador, Chile, or Turkey, to the manifestations of racism closer to home and to so many other more singular things that do not go by the name of a State or nation. But it is true—and these two logics must be understood in relation—that frontal critiques always let themselves be turned back and reappropriated into philosophy. Hegel's dialectical machine is this very machination. It is what is most terrifying about reason. To think the necessity of philosophy would perhaps be to move into places inaccessible to this program of reappropriation. I am not sure that this is simply possible and calculable; it is what escapes from any assurance, and desire in this regard can only affirm itself, enigmatic and endless.

Q.: What we have inherited under the names of Plato and Hegel would still be intact and provocative.

J.D.: Oh yes, I always have the feeling that, despite centuries of reading, these texts remain untouched, withdrawn into a reserve, still to come. This feeling cohabits in me with that of the closure and the combinatory exhaustion that I spoke of a moment ago. Contradictory feelings, or so it appears, but that's the way it is and I can only accept it. This is finally what I try to explain to myself. There is the "system" and there is the text, and in the text there are fissures or resources that cannot be dominated by the systematic discourse. At a certain moment, the latter can no longer answer for itself; it initiates its own deconstruction. Whence the necessity of an interminable, active interpretation that is engaged in a micrology of the scalpel, both violent and faithful...

Q.: You practice deconstruction, not destruction. This word signifies perhaps a way of undoing a structure in order to make its skeleton appear. Deconstruction—which was part of a chain of words—really caught on. It appeared in a context dominated by structuralism. It no doubt allowed some to escape from the sense that "it's all over."

J.D.: Yes, the word was able to succeed, which surprised me, only during the period of structuralism. To deconstruct is a structuralist and anti-structuralist gesture at the same time: an edification, an artifact is taken apart in order to make the structures, the nerves, or as you say the skeleton appear, but also, simultaneously, the ruinous precariousness of a formal structure that explained nothing, since it is neither a center, a principle, a force, nor even the law of events, in the most general sense of this word.

Deconstruction as such is reducible to neither a method nor an analysis (the reduction to simple elements); it goes beyond critical decision itself. That is why it is not negative, even though it has often been interpreted as such despite all sorts of warnings. For me, it always accompanies an affirmative exigency, I would even say that it never proceeds without love...

Q.: You have also invented the concept of differance. *Différer* is to be not the same, and it's also to put off until later. A large part of your work on differance puts in question again the illusion of presence to Being. You undo the figures of presence, objects, consciousness, self-presence, presence of speech.

J.D.: How could the desire for presence let itself be destroyed? It is desire itself. But what gives it, what gives it breath and necessity— what there is and what remains thus to be thought—is that which in the presence of the present does not present itself. Differance or the trace does not present itself, this almost nothing of the unpresentable is what philosophers always try to erase. It is this trace, however, that marks and relaunches all systems.

Q.: For you, every sign is graphic meaning, or rather every graphism is a sign. But this is not a reversal. It is not a matter of saying: up until now speech has dominated writing, so let's do the contrary.

J.D.: Of course, but the classical inversion or reversal, as I suggested a moment ago, is also unavoidable in the strategy of political struggles: for example, against capitalist, colonialist, sexist violence. We must not consider this to be a moment or just a phase; if from the beginning another logic or another space is not clearly heralded, then the reversal reproduces and confirms through inversion what it has struggled against.

As for the stakes of writing, they are not delimitable. Even while demonstrating that writing does not let itself be subjected to speech, one may open and generalize the concept of writing, extend it even to the voice and to all the traces of difference, all relations to the other. This operation is not at all arbitrary; it profoundly and concretely transforms all problems.

Q.: In *Of Grammatology*, you comment on the writing lesson in *Tristes Tropiques*.[3] Lévi-Strauss showed how writing was complicitous with a certain political violence. He described the arrival of this "evil" in a society "without writing."

J.D.: The possibility of this "evil" does not await the arrival of writing, in the common (alphabetic, Western) sense, and of the powers it guarantees. There is no society without writing (without genealogical mark, accounting, archivalization), not even any so-called animal society without territorial mark. To be convinced of this, one need merely give up privileging a certain model of writing. The paradise of societies without writing may nonetheless retain the very necessary function of myths and utopias. Its value is the value of innocence.

Q.: The extension of the concept of writing opens up numerous anthropological perspectives.

J.D.: And it goes beyond anthropology, for example into the domains of genetic information. We devoted the work of a seminar, from this point of view, to the analysis of *La logique du vivant* by François Jacob.[4]

Q.: You have foregrounded texts that are eccentric to the great philosophical tradition. Thus you comment on a text in which, on the subject of the critique of the judgment of taste, Kant speaks of vomit.

J.D.: Well in any case, he does everything necessary to speak of it without speaking of it.

The philosophical institution necessarily privileges what it comes to call the "great philosophers" and their "major texts." I also wanted to analyze this evaluation, its interests, its internal procedures, its implicit social contracts. By rooting out minor or marginalized texts, by reading them and writing in a certain way, one sometimes projects a stark light on the meaning and the history, on the interest of "majoration."

Such operations would remain impracticable and in fact unreadable for a sociology as such, I mean insofar as the latter does not gauge its competence against the internal rigor of the philosophical texts that are taken up and against the elementary, but very difficult demands of auto-analysis (philosophy or "sociology of sociology"); in short, this requires a completely different approach, a completely different attention to the codes of this writing and this scene.

Q.: You have also shed light on texts through contiguity. Thus you put together Genet and Hegel in *Glas*, Heidegger and Freud in *The Post Card*.

J.D.: By disturbing the norms and the etiquette of academic writing, one can hope to exhibit their finality, what they are protecting or excluding. The seriousness of the thing is sometimes measured, as you know, by the hatred and the resentment that a certain power in the university can no longer control. That is why it is important to tamper with what is mistakenly called the "form" and the code, to write otherwise even as one remains very strict as regards philosophical reading-knowledge and competence, simultaneously, which is something that, in my opinion, neither the protectionists of so-called internal analysis nor the positivists of the social sciences do, even when they appear to oppose each other. One could show that they agree altogether as regards the division of academic territory and they speak the same language.

You alluded to *Glas* and *The Post Card*. One may also consider them to be devices constructed for reading, without all the same claiming to dominate, their own reading or non-reading, the indignant evaluations or misapprehensions to which they are exposed. Why would it be illegitimate, forbidden (and who says so?) to cross several "genres," to write about sexuality at the same time as one writes about absolute knowledge and, in it, to couple Hegel with Genet, a post-card legend with a meditation (acted out, so to speak) on what "destining" means, between Freud and Heidegger, at a determined moment in the history of the post, of information technology, and of telecommunications?

Q.: You use undecidable words. Thus the hymen in Mallarmé is at once virginity and marriage, Plato's *pharmakon* cures and poisons.

J.D.: Words of this type situate perhaps better than others the places where discourses can no longer dominate, judge, decide: between the positive and the negative, the good and the bad, the true and the false. And thus the temptation to exclude them from language and from the city, so as to reconstitute the impossible homogeneity of a discourse, a text, a political body.

Q.: As regards the political field, you have never taken up noisy positions there; you have even practiced what you call a sort of withdrawal.

J.D.: Ah, the "political field"! But I could reply that I think of nothing else, however things might appear. Yes, of course, there are silences, and a certain withdrawal, but let's not exaggerate things. Provided that one has an interest in this, it is very easy to know where my choices and my allegiances are, without the least ambiguity. No doubt I don't manifest it enough, that's certain, but where is the measure here and is there one? It often seems to me that I have only typical and common things to say, in which case I join my voice or my vote to that of others, without claiming some authority, credit, or privilege reserved to what is so vaguely called an "intellectual" or a "philosopher."

I have always had trouble recognizing myself in the features of the intellectual (philosopher, writer, professor) playing his political role according to the screenplay that you are familiar with and whose heritage deserves to be questioned. Not that I disdain or critique it in itself; I think that, in certain situations, there is a classical function and responsibility there that must not be avoided, even if it is just to appeal to good sense and to what I consider to be the elementary political duty. But I am more and more aware of a transformation that renders this scene today somewhat tedious, sterile, and at times the crossroads of the worst procedures of intimidation (even when it is for the good cause), having no common measure with the structure of the political, with the new responsibilities required by the development of the media (when, that is, one is not trying to exploit the media for some small profit, a hypothesis not easily reconcilable with the classical typology of the intellectual).

This is one of the most serious problems today, this responsibility before the current forms of the mass media and especially before their monopolization, their framing, their axiomatics. For the withdrawal you spoke of does not at all mean in my view a protest against the media in general; on the contrary, I am resolutely for their development (there are never enough of them) and especially for their diversification, but also resolutely against their normalization, against the various takeovers to which the thing has given rise, which has in fact reduced to silence everything that does not conform to very determinate and very powerful frames or codes, or still yet to phantasms of what is "receivable." But the first problem of the "media" is posed by what does not get translated, or even published in the dominant political languages, the ones that dictate the laws of receivability, precisely, on the left as much as on the right.

It is for this reason that what is most specific and most acute in the research, the questions, or the undertakings that interest me (along with a few others) may appear politically silent. Perhaps it is a matter there of a political thinking, of a culture, or a counter-culture that are almost inaudible in the codes that I have just mentioned. Perhaps, who knows, for one can only speak here of the chances or the risks to be run, with or without hope, always in dispersion and in the minority.

Q.: This brings us back to your political activity with the group GREPH, the Research Group on the Teaching of Philosophy.

J.D.: GREPH brings together teachers, high school and university students who, precisely, want to analyze and change the educational system, and in particular the philosophical institution, first of all through the extension of the teaching of philosophy to all grades where the other so-called basic disciplines are taught. François Mitterrand has made very precise commitments in this direction. We were delighted by that and will do everything possible to see that they do not get shelved, as we have begun in the last few months to fear they might. In any case, these problems will not go away and neither will those who are fully aware of their seriousness and who have to deal with them.

All of this calls for a profound transformation of the relations between the State, research or teaching institutions, at the university level and elsewhere, science, technics, and culture. The models that are now collapsing are roughly those that, at the dawn of industrial society, were discussed by Germany's "great philosophers," from Kant to Heidegger, passing by way of Hegel, Schelling, Humboldt, Schleiermacher, Nietzsche, before and after the founding of the University of Berlin. Why not reread them, think with them and against them, but while taking philosophy into account? This is indispensable if one wishes to invent other relations between the rationalization of the State and knowledge, technics, and thinking, if one wants to draw up new contractual forms among them or even to dissociate radically their duties, powers, and responsibilities. Perhaps it would be necessary now to try to invent places for teaching and research outside the university institutions?

Choreographies

Q.:   Emma Goldman, a maverick feminist from the late nineteenth century, once said of the feminist movement: "If I can't dance I don't want to be part of your revolution." Jacques Derrida, you have written about the question of woman and what it is that constitutes "the feminine." In *Spurs*, a text devoted to Nietzsche, style and woman, you wrote that "that which will not be pinned down by truth [truth?] is, in truth, *feminine*." And you warned that such a proposition "should not . . . be hastily mistaken for a woman's femininity, for female sexuality, or for any other of those essentializing fetishes which might still tantalize the dogmatic philosopher, the impotent artist or the inexperienced seducer who has not yet escaped his foolish hopes of capture."[1]

What seems to be at play as you take up Heidegger's reading of Nietzsche is whether or not sexual difference is a "regional question in a larger order which would subordinate it first to the domain of general ontology, subsequently to that of a fundamental ontology and finally to the question of the truth [whose?] of being itself." You thereby question the status of the argument and at the same time the question itself. In this instance, if the question of sexual difference is not a regional one (in the sense of subsidiary), if indeed "it may no longer even be a question,"[2] as you suggest, how would you describe "woman's place"?

J.D.: Will I be able to write improvising my responses as I go along? It would be more worthwhile, wouldn't it? Too premeditated an interview would be without interest here. I do not see the particular finality of such an endeavor, its proper end. It would be interminable, or, rather, with respect to these questions—which are much too difficult—I would never have even dared to begin. There are other texts, other occasions for such very calculated premeditation. Let us play surprise. It will be our tribute to the dance [in French the word dance, *la danse*, is a feminine noun requiring the use of a feminine pronoun, *elle*]: it should happen only once, neither grow heavy nor ever plunge too deep; above all, it should not lag or trail behind its time. We will therefore not leave time to come back to what is behind us, nor to look attentively. We will only take a glimpse. [In French, to take a glimpse is to look into the spaces between things, *entrevoir*, that is, inter-view.]

It was a good idea to begin with a quotation, one by a feminist from the end of the nineteenth century maverick enough to ask of the feminist movement its questions and conditions. Already, already a sign of life, a sign of the dance.

One can question the repetition. Was the matrix of what was to be the future of feminism already there at the end of the last century? You smile, no doubt, as I do, at the mention of this word. [The word matrix in English like *matrice* in French comes from the Latin *matrix* meaning womb. In both languages it has taken on, among others, the following two meanings: (1) a situation or surrounding substance within which something originates, develops, or is contained; (2) in printing it means a metal plate used for casting typefaces.] Let us make use of this figure from anatomy or printing a bit longer to ask whether a program, or locus of begetting, was not already in place in the nineteenth century for all those configurations to which the feminist struggle of the second half of the twentieth century was to commit itself and then to develop. I refer here to their being in place at all levels—those of socio-political demands, alliances with other forces, the alternatives of compromise or various radicalisms, the strategies of discourses, various forms of writing, theory or literature, etc. One is often tempted to think of this program—and to arrive by way of conclusion at the stasis of a simple combinatory scheme—in terms of all that is interminable and exhausting in it. Yes, it is exhausting (because it always draws on the same fund of possibilities) and tedious because of the ensuing repetition.

This is only one of the paradoxes. The development of the present struggle (or struggles) is extraordinary not only in its quantitative extension within Europe—because of its progress and the masses that have been slowly aroused—but also, and this is a much more important phenomenon I believe, outside of Europe. And such progress brings with it new types of historical research, other forms of reading, the discovery of new bodies of material that have gone unrecognized or misunderstood up until now; that is to say, they have been excessively [*violemment*] concealed or marginalized. The history of different "feminisms" has often been, of course, a past "passed-over-in-silence." Now here is the paradox: having made possible the reawakening of this silent past, having reappropriated a history previously stifled, feminist movements will perhaps have to renounce an all too easy kind of progressivism in the evaluation of this history. Such progressivism is often taken as their axiomatic base: the inevitable or rather essential presupposition (*dans les luttes*, as we say in French) of what one might call the ideological consensus of feminists, perhaps also their "dogmatics" or what your "maverick feminist" suspects to be their sluggishness. It is the image of a continuously accelerated "liberation" at once punctuated by determinable stages and commanded by an ultimately thinkable *telos*, a truth of sexual difference and femininity, etc. And if there is no doubt that this theatre, upon which the progress of feminist struggles is staged, exists, it is a relatively short and very recent sequence within "extreme-Western" history. Certainly, it is not timely politically, nor in any case is it possible, to neglect or renounce such a view of "liberation." However, to credit this representation of progress and entrust everything to it would be to surrender to a sinister mystification: everything would collapse, flow, founder in this same homogenized, sterilized river of the history of mankind [man's kind in the locution *l'histoire des hommes*]. This history carries along with it the age-old dream of reappropriation, "liberation," autonomy, mastery, in short the *cortège* of metaphysics and the *technē*. The indications of this repetition are more and more numerous. The specular reversal of masculine "subjectivity," even in its most self-critical form—that is, where it is nervously jealous both of itself and of its "proper" objects—probably represents only one necessary phase. Yet it still belongs to the same program, a program whose exhaustion we were just talking about. It is true that this is valid for the whole of our culture, our scholastics, and the trouble may be found everywhere that this program is in command, or almost everywhere.

I have not begun as yet to answer your question, but, if you will forgive me, I am going to try to approach it slowly. It was necessary to recall the fact that this "silent past" (as that which was passed-over-in-silence) could still reserve some surprises, like the dance of your "maverick feminist."

q.: Yes, and in that respect, recognition of the paradox suggests that while nineteenth-century and late twentieth-century feminism do resemble each other, it is less because of their historical matrix than because of those characteristics which define them. True, the program was in place.[3] The resurgence in the United States during the nineteen sixties of anarchist-like attitudes, particularly within the feminist movement, attests to that. But Goldman was not before or behind the times. An admirer of Nietzsche as "rebel and innovator," she proclaimed that "revolution is but thought carried into action." She was an activist unable to support those forms of organized feminism that focused on merely contesting the institutionalizing of inequalities for women. Her stance was more radical—one that called for the restructuring of society as a whole. If she refused the vote, for example, it was because she deemed that behind standard forms of political action there lay coercion. As an anarchist-feminist she had no truck with statism.

j.d.: Perhaps woman does not have a history, not so much because of any notion of the "Eternal Feminine" but because all alone she can resist and step back from a certain history (precisely in order to dance) in which revolution, or at least the "concept" of revolution, is generally inscribed. That history is one of continuous progress, despite the revolutionary break—oriented in the case of the women's movement toward the reappropriation of woman's own essence, her own specific difference, oriented in short toward a notion of woman's "truth." Your "maverick feminist" showed herself ready to break with the most authorized, the most dogmatic form of consensus, one that claims (and this is the most serious aspect of it) to speak out in the name of revolution and history. Perhaps she was thinking of a completely other history: a history of paradoxical laws and non-dialectical discontinuities, a history of absolutely heterogeneous pockets, irreducible particularities, of unheard-of and incalculable sexual differences; a history of women who have—centuries ago—"gone further" by stepping back with their lone dance, or who are today inventing sexual idioms at a distance from the main forum of feminist activity with a kind of reserve that does not necessarily prevent them from subscribing to the movement and even, occasionally, from becoming a militant for it.

But I am speculating. It would be better to come back to your question. Having passed through several detours or stages you wonder how I would describe what is called "woman's place"; the expression recalls, if I am not mistaken, "in the home" or "in the kitchen." Frankly, I do not know. I believe that I would not describe that place. In fact, I would be wary of such a description. Do you not fear that having once become committed to the path of this topography, we would inevitably find ourselves back "at home" or "in the kitchen"? Or under house arrest, *assignation à résidence* as they say in French penitentiary language, which would amount to the same thing? Why must there be a place for woman? And why only one, a single, completely essential place?

This is a question that you could translate ironically by saying that in my view *there is no one place for woman*. That was indeed clearly set forth during the 1972 Cerisy Colloquium devoted to Nietzsche in the lecture to which you referred entitled *Spurs*. It is without a doubt risky to say that there is no place for woman, but this idea is not anti-feminist, far from it; true, it is not feminist either. But it appears to me to be faithful in its way both to a certain assertion of women and to what is most affirmative and "dancing," as the maverick feminist says, in the displacement of women. Can one not say, in Nietzsche's language, that there is a "reactive" feminism, and that a certain historical necessity often puts this form of feminism in power in today's organized struggles? It is this kind of "reactive" feminism that Nietzsche mocks, and not woman or women. Perhaps one should not so much combat it head on— other interests would be at stake in such a move—as prevent its occupying the entire terrain. And why for that matter should one rush into answering a *topological* question (what is *the* place of *woman* [*quelle est* la *place de la* femme])? Or an *economical* question (because it all comes back to the *oikos* as home, *maison, chez-soi* [at home in this sense also means in French within the self], the law of the proper place, etc., in the preoccupation with a woman's place)? Why should a new "idea" of woman or a new step taken by her necessarily be subjected to the urgency of this topo-economical concern (essential, it is true, and ineradicably philosophical)? This step only constitutes a step on the condition that it challenge a certain idea of the *locus* [*lieu*] and the place [*place*] (the entire history of the West and of its metaphysics) and that it dance otherwise. This is very rare, if it is not impossible, and presents itself only in the form of the most unforeseeable and most innocent of chances. The most innocent of dances would thwart the *assignation à résidence*, escape those residences under surveillance; the dance changes place and above all changes *places*. In its wake they can no longer be recognized. The joyous disturbance of certain women's movements, and of some women in particular, has actually brought with it the chance for a certain risky turbulence in the assigning of places within our small European space (I am not speaking of a more ample upheaval en route to worldwide application). Is one then going to start all over again making maps, topographics, etc.? distributing sexual identity cards?

The most serious part of the difficulty is the necessity to bring the dance and its tempo into tune with the "revolution." The lack of place for [*l'atopie*] or the madness of the dance—this bit of luck can also compromise the political chances of feminism and serve as an alibi for deserting organized, patient, laborious "feminist" struggles when brought into contact with all the forms of resistance that a dance movement cannot dispel, even though the dance is not synonymous with either powerlessness or fragility. I will not insist on this point, but you can surely see the kind of impossible and necessary compromise that I am alluding to: an incessant, daily negotiation—individual or not—sometimes microscopic, sometimes punctuated by a poker-like gamble; always deprived of insurance, whether it be in private life or within institutions. Each man and each woman must commit his or her own singularity, the untranslatable factor of his or her life and death.

Nietzsche makes a scene before women, feminists in particular— a spectacle which is overdetermined, divided, apparently contradictory. This is just what has interested me; this scene has interested me because of all the paradigms that it exhibits and multiplies, and insofar as it often struggles, sometimes dances, always takes chances in a historical space whose essential traits, those of the matrix, have perhaps not changed since then in Europe (I mean specifically in Europe, and that perhaps makes all the difference although we cannot separate worldwide feminism from a certain fundamental Europeanization of world culture; this is an enormous problem that I must leave aside here). In *Spurs* I have tried to formalize the movements and typical moments of the scene that Nietzsche creates throughout a very broad and diverse body of texts. I have done this up to a certain limit, one that I also indicate, where the decision to formalize fails for reasons that are absolutely structural. Since these typical features are and must be unstable, sometimes contradictory, and finally "undecidable," any break in the movement of the reading would settle in a counter-meaning, in *the meaning* which becomes counter-meaning. This counter-meaning can be more or less naive or complacent. One could cite countless examples of it. In the most perfunctory of cases, the simplification reverts to the isolation of Nietzsche's violently anti-feminist statements (directed first against reactive, specular feminism as a figure both of the dogmatic philosopher and a certain relationship of man to truth), pulling them out (and possibly attributing them to me though that is of little importance) of the movement and system that I try to reconstitute. Some have reacted at times even more perfunctorily, unable to see beyond the end of phallic forms projecting into the text; beginning with style, the spur or the umbrella, they take no account of what I have said about the difference between style and writing or the bisexual complication of those and other forms. Generally speaking, this cannot be considered reading, and I will go so far as to say that it is *to not read* the syntax and punctuation of a given sentence when one arrests the text in a certain position, thus settling on a thesis, meaning or truth. This mistake of hermeneutics, this mistaking of hermeneutics—it is this that the final message [*envoi*] of "I forgot my umbrella" should challenge. But let us leave that. The truth value (that is, Woman as the major allegory of truth in Western discourse) and its correlative, Femininity (the essence or truth of Woman), are there to assuage such hermeneutic anxiety. These are the places that one should acknowledge, at least that is if one is interested in doing so; they are the foundations or anchorings of Western rationality (of what I have called "phallogocentrism" [as the complicity of Western metaphysics with a notion of male firstness]). Such recognition should not make of either the truth value or femininity an object of knowledge (at stake are the norms of knowledge and knowledge as norm); still less should it make of them a place to inhabit, a home. It should rather permit the invention of an other inscription, one very old and very new, a displacement of bodies and places that is quite different.

You recalled the expression "essentializing fetishes" (truth, femininity, the essentiality of woman or feminine sexuality as fetishes). It is difficult to improvise briefly here. But I will point out that one can avoid a trap by being precise about the concept of fetishism and the context to which one refers, even if only to displace it. (On this point, I take the liberty of alluding to the discussions of fetishism and feminine sexuality in *Spurs*, *Glas* or *La carte postale*, specifically in *Le facteur de la vérité*.) Another trap is more political and can only be avoided by taking account of the *real* conditions in which women's struggles develop on all fronts (economic, ideological, political). These conditions often require the preservation (within longer or shorter phases) of metaphysical presuppositions that one must (and knows already that one must) question in a later phase— or an other place—because they belong to the dominant system that one is deconstructing on a *practical* level. This multiplicity of places, moments, forms and forces does not always mean giving way either to empiricism or to contradiction. How can one breathe without such punctuation and without the multiplicities of rhythm and steps? How can one dance, your "maverick feminist" might say?

Q.: This raises an important question that should not be overlooked, although we haven't the space to develop it to any extent here: the complicated relationship of a practical politics to the kinds of analysis that we have been considering (specifically the "deconstructive" analysis implicit in your discussion). That this relationship cannot simply be translated into an opposition between the empirical and the non-empirical has been touched on in an entirely different context.[4] Just how one is to deal with the interrelationship of these forces and necessities in the context of feminine struggles should be more fully explored on some other occasion. But let's go on to Heidegger's ontology.

J.D.: To answer your question about Heidegger, and without being able to review here the itinerary of a reading in *Spurs* clearly divided into two moments, I must limit myself to a piece of information, or rather to an open question. The question proceeds, so to speak, from the end; it proceeds from the point where the thought of the gift and that of "propriation" disturb without simply reversing the order of ontology, the authority of the question "what is it," the subordination of regional ontologies to one fundamental ontology. I am moving much too rapidly, but how can I do otherwise here? From this point, which is not a point, one wonders whether this extremely difficult, perhaps impossible idea of the gift can still maintain an essential relationship to sexual difference. One wonders whether sexual difference, femininity for example—however irreducible it may be—does not remain derived from and subordinated to either the question of destination or the thought of the gift (I say "thought" because one cannot say philosophy, theory, logic, structure, scene or anything else; when one can no longer use any word of this sort, when one can say almost nothing else, one says "thought," but one could show that this too is excessive). I do not know. Must one think "difference" "before" sexual difference or taking off "from" it? Has this question, if not a meaning (we are at the origin of meaning here, and the origin cannot "have meaning"), at least something of a chance of opening up anything at all, however im-pertinent it may appear?

Q.: You put into question the characteristic form of women's protest, namely, the subordination of woman to man. I shall attempt here to describe the direction of your argument, as I understand it, and then comment on it.

The new sense of writing (*écriture*) with which one associates the term deconstruction has emerged from the close readings that you have given to texts as divergent as those of Plato, Rousseau, Mallarmé and others. It is one in which traditional binary pairing (as in the opposition of spirit to matter or man to woman) no longer functions by the privilege given to the first term over the second. In a series of interviews published under the title *Positions* in 1972, you spoke of a two-phase program (phase being understood as a structural rather than a chronological term) necessary for the act of deconstruction.

In the first phase a reversal was to take place in which the opposed terms would be inverted. Thus woman, as a previously subordinate term, might become the dominant one in relation to man. Yet because such a scheme of reversal could only repeat the traditional scheme (in which the hierarchy of duality is always reconstituted), it alone could not effect any significant change. Change would only occur through the "second" and more radical phase of deconstruction in which a "new" concept would be forged simultaneously. The motif of differance, as neither a simple "con-

cept" nor a mere "word," has brought us the now familiar constellation of attendant terms: trace, supplement, *pharmakon* and others.
Among the others, two are marked sexually and in their most
widely recognized sense pertain to the woman's body: *hymen* (the
logic of which is developed in "The Double Session"[5]) and *double
invagination* (a leitmotif in "Living On/Borderlines").

Take only the term hymen in which there is a confusion or
continuation of the term coitus, and from which it gets its double
meaning: (1) "a membranous fold of tissue partly or completely
occluding the vaginal external orifice" [from the Greek for *mem-
brane*] and (2) marriage [from Greek mythology; the god of mar-
riage]. In the first sense the hymen is that which protects virginity,
and is in front of the uterus. That is, it lies between the inside and
the outside of the woman, between desire and its fulfillment. So
that although (male) desire dreams of violently piercing or breaking the hymen (consummation in the second sense of the term), if
that happens there is no hymen.

It seems to me that while the extensive play on etymologies (in
which unconscious motivations are traced through the transformations and historical excesses of usage) effects a displacement of
these terms, it also poses a problem for those who would seek to
define what is specifically feminine. That comes about not so much
because these terms are either under- or over-valued as parts belonging to woman's body. It is rather that, in the economy of a
movement of writing that is always elusive, one can never decide
properly whether the particular term implies complicity with or a
break from existent ideology. Perhaps this is because, as Adam says
of Eve in Mark Twain's satire, *The Diary of Adam and Eve*, not only
does the "new creature name . . . everything" because "it looks like
the thing," but—and this is the crux of the matter—"her mind is
disordered [or, if you like, Nietzschean]—everything shows it."

In this regard there comes to mind a footnote to p. 182 of "The
Double Session," concerning the displacement of writing, its transformation and generalization. The example cited is that of a sur-
geon who, upon learning of Freud's own difficulty in admitting to

the possibility of masculine hysteria, exclaims to him: "But, my dear colleague, how can you state such absurdities? *Hystera* means uterus. How therefore could a man be a hysteric?"

How can we change the representation of woman? Can we move from the rib where woman is wife ("She was called Woman because she was taken from man"—Genesis 2:23) to the womb where she is mother ("man is born of woman"—Job 14:1) without essential loss? Do we have in your view the beginning of phase two, a "new" concept of woman?

J.D.: No, I do not believe that we have one, if indeed it is possible to *have* such a thing or if such a thing could exist or show promise of existing. Personally, I am not sure that I feel the lack of it. Before having one that is new, are we certain of having had an old one? It is the word "concept" or "conception" that I would in turn question in its relationship to any essence which is rigorously or properly identifiable. This would bring us back to the preceding questions. The concept of the concept, along with the entire system that attends it, belongs to a prescriptive order. It is that order that a problematics of woman and a problematics of difference, as sexual difference, should disrupt along the way. Moreover, I am not sure that "phase two" marks a split with "phase one," a split whose form would be a cut along an indivisible line. The relationship between these two phases doubtless has another structure. I spoke of two distinct phases for the sake of clarity, but the relationship of one phase to another is marked less by conceptual determinations (that is, where a new concept follows an archaic one) than by a transformation or general deformation of logic; such transformations or deformations mark the "logical" element or environment itself by moving, for example, beyond the "positional" (difference determined as opposition, whether or not dialectically). This movement is of great consequence for the discussion here, even if my formulation is apparently abstract and disembodied. One could, I think, demonstrate this: when sexual difference is determined by *opposition* in the dialectical sense (according to the Hegelian movement of speculative dialectics which remains so powerful even beyond Hegel's text), one appears to set off "the war between the sexes"; but one precipitates the end with victory going to the masculine sex. The determination of sexual difference in opposition is destined, designed, in truth, for truth; it is so in order to erase sexual difference. The dialectical opposition neutralizes or supersedes [Hegel's term *Aufhebung* carries with it both the sense of conserving and negating. No adequate translation of the term in English has yet been found] the difference. However, according to a surreptitious operation that must be flushed out, one ensures phallocentric mastery under the cover of neutralization every time. These are now well-known paradoxes. And such phallocentrism adorns itself now and then, here and there, with an appendix: a certain kind of feminism. In the same manner, phallocentrism and homosexuality can go, so to speak, hand in hand, and I take these terms, whether it is a question of feminine or masculine homosexuality, in a very broad and radical sense.

And what if the "wife" or the "mother"—whom you seem sure of being able to dissociate—were figures for this homosexual dialectics? I am referring now to your question on the "representation" of woman and such "loss" as might occur in the passage from man's rib to the womb of woman, the passage from the spouse, you say, to the mother. Why is it necessary to choose, and why only these two possibilities, these two "places," assuming that one can really dissociate them?

Q.: The irony of my initial use of the cliché "woman's place" which in the old saw is followed by "in the home" or "in the kitchen" leaves the whole wide world for other places for the same intent. As for the "place" of woman in Genesis, and Job, as rib (spouse) or woman (mother), these are more basic functional differences. Nevertheless, within these two traditional roles, to choose one implies loss of the other. You are correct in observing that such a choice is not necessary; there could be juxtaposition, substitution or other possible combinations. But these biblical texts are not frivolous in seeing the functional distinction which also has distinguished "woman's place" in Western culture.

J.D.: Since you quote Genesis, I would like to evoke the marvelous reading that Levinas has proposed of it without being clear as to whether he assumes it as his own or what the actual status of the "commentary" that he devotes to it is.[6] There would, of course, be a certain *secondariness* of woman, Ischa. The man, Isch, would come first; he would be number one; he would be at the beginning. Secondariness, however, would not be that of woman or femininity, but the *division* between masculine and feminine. It is not feminine sexuality that would be second but only the relationship to sexual difference. At the origin, on this side of and therefore beyond any sexual mark, there was humanity in general, and this is what is important. Thus the possibility of ethics could be saved, if one takes ethics to mean that relationship to the other as other which accounts for no other determination or sexual characteristic in particular. What kind of an ethics would there be if belonging to one sex or another became its law or privilege? What if the universality of moral laws were modeled on or limited according to the sexes? What if their universality were not unconditional, without sexual condition in particular?

Whatever the force, seductiveness or necessity of this reading, does it not risk restoring—in the name of ethics as that which is irreproachable—a classical interpretation, and thereby enriching what I would call its panoply in a manner surely as subtle as it is sublime? Once again, the classical interpretation gives a masculine sexual marking to what is presented either as a neutral originariness or, at least, as prior and superior to all sexual markings. Levinas indeed senses the risk factor involved in the erasure of sexual difference. He therefore maintains sexual difference: the human in general remains a sexual being. But he can only do so, it would seem, by placing (differentiated) sexuality beneath humanity which sustains itself at the level of the Spirit. That is, he simultaneously places, and this is what is important, masculinity [*le masculin*] in command and at the beginning (the *archē*), on a par with the Spirit. This gesture carries with it the most self-interested of contradictions; it has repeated itself, let us say, since "Adam and Eve," and persists—in analogous form—into "modernity," despite all the differences of style and treatment. Isn't that a feature of the "matrix," as we were saying before? or the "*patrix*" if you prefer, but it amounts to the same thing, does it not? Whatever the complexity of the itinerary and whatever the knots of rhetoric, don't you think that the movement of Freudian thought repeats this "logic"? Is it not also the risk that Heidegger runs? One should perhaps say, rather, the risk that is *avoided* because phallogocentrism is insurance against the return of what certainly has been feared as the most agonizing risk of all. Since I have named Heidegger in a context where the reference is quite rare and may even appear strange, I would like to dwell on this for a moment, if you don't mind, concerned that I will be both too lengthy and too brief.

Heidegger seems almost never to speak about sexuality or sexual difference. And he seems almost never to speak about psychoanalysis, give or take an occasional negative allusion. This is neither negligence nor omission. The pauses coming from his silence on these questions punctuate or create the spacing out of a powerful discourse. And one of the strengths of this discourse may be stated (though I am going much too quickly and schematizing excessively) like this: it begins by denying itself all accepted forms of security, all the sedimented presuppositions of classical ontology, anthropology, the natural or human sciences, until it falls back this side of such values as the opposition between subject/object, conscious/unconscious, mind/body, and many others as well. The existential analytic of the *Dasein* opens the road, so to speak, leading to the question of being; the *Dasein* is neither the human being (a thought recalled earlier by Levinas) nor the subject, neither consciousness nor the self [*le moi*] (whether conscious or unconscious). These are all determinations that are derived from and occur after the *Dasein*. Now—and here is what I wanted to get to after this inadmissible acceleration—in a course given in 1928, Heidegger justifies to some degree the silence of *Sein und Zeit* on the question of sexuality.[7] In a paragraph from the course devoted to the "Problem of the *Sein und Zeit*," Heidegger reminds us that the analytic of the *Dasein* is neither an anthropology, an ethics nor a metaphysics. With respect to any definition, position or evaluation of these fields, the *Dasein* is *neuter*. Heidegger insists upon and makes clear this original and essential "neutrality" of the *Dasein*: "This neutrality means also that the *Dasein* is neither of the two sexes. But this a-sexuality (*Geschlechtlosigkeit*) is not the indifference of empty invalidity, the annulling negativity of an indifferent ontic nothingness. In its neutrality, the *Dasein* is not the indifferent person-and-everyone (*Niemand und Jeder*), but it is originary positivity and the power of being or of the essence, *Mächtigkeit des Wesens*." One would have to read the analysis that follows very closely; I will try to do that another time in relation to some of his later texts.[8] The analysis emphasizes the positive character, as it were, of this originary and powerful a-sexual neutrality which is not the *neither-nor* (*Weder-noch*) of ontic abstraction. It is originary and ontological. More precisely, the a-sexuality does not signify in this instance the absence of sexuality—one could call it the instinct, desire or even the libido—but the absence of any mark belonging to one of the two sexes. Not that the *Dasein* does not ontically or in fact belong to a sex; not that it is deprived of sexuality; but the *Dasein* as *Dasein* does not carry with it the mark of this opposition (or alternative) between the two sexes. Insofar as these marks are opposable and binary, they are not existential structures. Nor do they allude in this respect to any primitive or subsequent bisexuality. Such an allusion would fall once again into anatomical, biological or anthropological determinations. And the *Dasein*, in the structures and "power" that are originary to it, would come "prior" to these determinations. I am putting quotation marks around the word "prior" because it has no literal, chronological, historical or logical meaning. Now, as of 1928, the analytic of the *Dasein* was the thought of ontological difference and the repetition of the question of being; it opened up a problematics that subjected all the concepts of traditional Western philosophy to a radical elucidation and interpretation. This gives an idea of what stakes were involved in a neutralization that fell back this side of both sexual difference and its binary marking, if not this side of sexuality itself. This would be the title of the enormous problem that in this context I must limit myself to merely naming: ontological difference and sexual difference.

And since your question evoked the "motif of differance," I would say that it has moved, by displacement, in the vicinity of this very obscure area. What is also being sought in this zone is the passage between ontological difference and sexual difference; it is a passage that may no longer be thought, punctuated or opened up according to those polarities to which we have been referring for some time (originary/derived, ontological/ontic, ontology/anthropology, the thought of being/metaphysics or ethics, etc.). The constellation of terms that you have cited could *perhaps* be considered (for nothing is ever taken for granted or guaranteed in these matters) a kind of transformation or deformation of space; such a transformation would tend to extend beyond these poles and reinscribe them within it. Some of these terms, "hymen" or "invagination," you were saying, "pertain in their most widely recognized sense to the woman's body. . . ." Are you sure? I am grateful for your having used such a careful formulation. That these words signify "in their most widely recognized sense" had, of course, not escaped me, and the emphasis that I have put on re-sexualizing a philosophical or theoretical discourse, which has been too "neutralizing" in this respect, was dictated by those very reservations that I just mentioned concerning the strategy of neutralization (whether or not it is deliberate). Such re-sexualizing must be done without facileness of any kind and, above all, without regression in relation to what might justify, as we saw, the procedures—or necessary steps—of Levinas or Heidegger, for example. That being said, "hymen" and "invagination," at least in the context into which these words have been swept, no longer simply designate figures for the feminine body. They no longer do so, that is, assuming that one knows for certain what a feminine or masculine body is, and assuming that anatomy is in this instance the final recourse. What remains undecidable concerns not only but also the line of cleavage between the two sexes. As you recalled, such a movement reverts neither to words nor to concepts. And what remains of language within it cannot be abstracted from the "performativity" (which marks and is marked) that concerns us here, beginning—for the examples that you have chosen—with the texts of Mallarmé and

Blanchot, and with the labor of reading or writing which evoked them and which they in turn evoked. One could say quite accurately that the hymen *does not exist*. Anything constituting the value of existence is foreign to the "hymen." And if there were hymen—I am not saying if the hymen existed—property value would be no more appropriate to it for reasons that I have stressed in the texts to which you refer. How can one then attribute the *existence* of the hymen *properly* to woman? Not that it is any more the distinguishing feature of man or, for that matter, of the human creature. I would say the same for the term "invagination" which has, moreover, always been reinscribed in a chiasmus, one doubly folded, redoubled and inversed,[9] etc. From then on, is it not difficult to recognize in the movement of this term a "representation of woman"? Furthermore, I do not know if it is to a change in representation that we should entrust the future. As with all the questions that we are presently discussing, this one, and above all when it is put as a question of representation, seems at once too old and as yet to be born: a kind of old parchment crossed every which way, overloaded with hieroglyphs and still as virgin as the origin, like the early morning in the East from whence it comes. And you know that the word for parchment does not come from any "road" leading from Pergamus in Asia. I do not know how you will translate this last sentence.

Q.: It is a problem. In modern English usage the word for parchment no longer carries with it the sense of the French *parchemin*, on or by the road, as the Middle English *perchement* or *parchemin* did. The American Heritage Dictionary traces the etymology thus: "Parthian (leather) from *pergamina*, parchment, from Greek *pergamene*, from *Pergamenos*, or *Pergamun*, from *Pergamon*..." Lemprière's Classical Dictionary says further that the town of Pergamus was founded by Philaeterus, a eunuch, and that parchment has been called the *charta pergamena*.

J.D.: The Littré Dictionary which gives the etymology for French makes war responsible for the appearance of "pergamena" or "Pergamina." It is thereby a product of war: one began to write on bodies and animal skins because papyrus was becoming very rare. They say too that parchment was occasionally prepared from the skin of stillborn lambs. And according to Pliny, it was out of jealousy that Eumenes, king of Pergamus, turned to parchment. His rival, Ptolemy, the king of Egypt, was so proud of his library that he had only books written on paper. It was necessary to find new bodies of or for writing.

Q.: I would like to come back to the writing of the dance, the choreography that you mentioned a while back. If we do not yet have a "new" "concept" of woman, because the radicalization of the problem goes beyond the "thought" or the concept, what are our chances of "thinking 'difference' not so much before sexual difference, as you say, as taking off 'from' " it? What would you say is our chance and "who" are we sexually?

J.D.: At the approach of this shadowy area it has always seemed to me that the voice itself had to be divided in order to say that which is given to thought or speech. No monological discourse—and by that I mean here mono-sexual discourse—can dominate with a single voice, a single tone, the space of this half-light, even if the "proffered discourse" is then signed by a sexually marked patronymic. Thus, to limit myself to one account, and not to propose an example, I have felt the necessity for a chorus, for a choreographic text with polysexual signatures. I felt this every time that a legitimacy of the neuter, the apparently least suspect sexual neutrality of "phallocentric or gynocentric" mastery, threatened to immobilize (in silence), colonize, stop or unilateralize in a subtle or sublime manner what remains no doubt irreducibly dissymmetrical.[10] More directly: a certain dissymmetry is no doubt the law both of sexual difference and the relationship to the other in general (I say this in opposition to a certain kind of violence within the language of "democratic" platitudes, in any case in opposition to a certain democratic ideology), yet the dissymmetry to which I refer is still let us not say symmetrical in turn (which might seem absurd), but doubly unilaterally inordinate, like a kind of reciprocal, respective and respectful excessiveness. This double dissymmetry perhaps goes beyond known or coded marks, beyond the grammar and spelling, shall we say (metaphorically), of sexuality. This indeed revives the following question: what if we were to reach, what if we were to approach here (for one does not arrive at this as one would at a determined location) the area of a relationship to the other where the code of sexual marks would no longer be discriminating? The relationship would not be a-sexual, far from it, but would be sexual otherwise: beyond the binary difference that governs the decorum of all codes, beyond the opposition feminine/masculine, beyond bisexuality as well, beyond homosexuality and heterosexuality which come to the same thing. As I dream of saving the chance that this question offers I would like to believe in the multiplicity of sexually marked voices. I would like to believe in the masses, this indeterminable number of blended voices, this mobile of non-identified sexual marks whose choreography can carry, divide, multiply the body of each "individual," whether he be classified as "man" or as "woman" according to the criteria of usage. Of course, it is not impossible that desire for a sexuality without number can still protect us, like a dream, from an implacable destiny which immures everything for life in the number 2. And should this merciless closure arrest desire at the wall of opposition, we would struggle in vain: there will never be but two sexes, neither one more nor one less. Tragedy would leave this strange sense, a contingent one finally, that we must affirm and learn to love instead of dreaming of the innumerable. Yes, perhaps; why not? But where would the "dream" of the innumerable come from, if it is indeed a dream? Does the dream itself not prove that what is dreamt of must be there in order for it to provide the dream? Then too, I ask you, what kind of a dance would there be, or would there be one at all, if the sexes were not exchanged according to rhythms that vary considerably? In a quite rigorous sense, the *exchange* alone could not suffice either, however, because the desire to escape the combinatory itself, to invent incalculable choreographies, would remain.

TRANSLATED BY CHRISTIE V. MCDONALD

Of a Certain Collège International
de Philosophie Still to Come

Q.: Collège International de Philosophie: One thinks right away of Bataille's and Caillois's Collège de Sociologie, as well as Jean Wahl's Collège Philosophique. Is this a nod in their direction? A tribute? A chance encounter?

J.D.: There have been many colleges throughout history. Don't forget that the Collège Philosophique still exists; it has been given a new direction and we hope it will cooperate, as a completely independent body, with the Collège International. But let's not rush to call upon homonymous ancestors, however noble or reassuring they may be. The birth of an institution is always fascinating. It unleashes, not only passionate reactions, but also fabulous genealogies, rites of appropriation or exclusion. One can already see this happening. One day, someone should describe the process that *effectively* produced this present institution, that gave it its name and its first profile. These conditions were, as you may well imagine, complex, vertiginously overdetermined.

Q.: The definition of the Collège associates "sciences," "arts" and "inter-sciences" with philosophy. Will the latter play a traditional role (as critique or as legitimation of positive knowledge) and, if so, who will legitimate the legitimators?

J.D.: These questions will be addressed as such, no doubt at the center of the Collège. The concept of "critique," the concept of "legitimation," however useful and "legitimate," may also in turn call for new elucidations. Likewise for the concept of institution and so many others. But we cannot get into that here. You are right, it is indeed a question of philosophy, yesterday, today, and tomorrow. Is it limited to and can it survive a traditional representation such as, for example, the summit or the foundation of knowledge or the center of the encyclopedia? These representations were, moreover, inseparable from institutional and legal structures that we want to study. One could show that a certain hegemonic claim goes hand in hand with what could be called a history of the deaths of philosophy. That is one of the things we would like to help to analyze and to transform: more philosophy is still necessary, in less hierarchically organized spaces that are more exposed to the most irruptive provocations of the "sciences," of "technologies," of the "arts" (whether one is talking about the discourse on art or "practical," performative explorations). Beyond interdisciplinarity—a traditional concept for a necessary practice, to be sure—beyond cooperation among diverse specialties around an already identified object, the point is still to seek out new themes that are taking form and that call for new kinds of competence, and to this end, to make new passageways which other, more compartmentalized or necessarily specialized institutions have more difficulty doing, even if, this goes without saying and it is fortunately the case, they also do so.

Q.: I come back to the question of the "legitimators."

J.D.: It will be posed everywhere and always. In the end, and according to paths that are difficult to describe, it also passes by way of what is called work, creation, writing, and not only by way of legal forms. But we have foreseen original arrangements that ought to ensure a deontology that is as rigorous as possible. There will be, for example, no chairs, no permanent positions, only contracts of relatively brief duration. Thus, minimal structure, collegiality, mobility, opening, diversity, priority given to research that is, precisely, insufficiently "legitimated" or underdeveloped in French and foreign institutions. This presupposes a difficult, ongoing theoreticoinstitutional exploration that is turned toward the outside and the inside...

Q.: What will be the relations of the Collège with other institutions?

J.D.: We hope they will be complementary and reciprocally provocative (intense exchanges, circulation, cooperation). But the Collège will remain a paradoxical and singular institution: the absence of chairs, the presence of foreigners in the direction and decision-making as well as in the research groups; careful selection of research projects in a place that nevertheless ought not to become an aristocratic and closed "center for advanced studies," or even a center for higher education; openness to technical and artistic performances; recruitment without consideration for academic rank; constant interest in the problems of primary and secondary teaching that will *also* be addressed by those who are primarily concerned, and so forth. I cannot mention here all the new arrangements and all the projects that have already been elaborated. But in underscoring what distinguishes the CIPh from other fundamental and indispensable institutions, I am not talking about an exteriority and still less a rivalry. We will do everything to assure that the CIPh becomes a supplementary instrument *at the disposal* of other institutions (universities, high schools, colleges, Hautes Etudes, EHESS, the Collège de France, CNRS, and so forth[1]), as well as to those who work outside any institution: in short, a place open to experiment, exploration, encounters, and debates.

Q.: Probably the last books of philosophy are being written today. Does the Collège envision a reflection on this predictable uncoupling of thinking from the book, and an anticipation of its entry into new support networks?

J.D.: I am not so sure that the last books of philosophy are being written today, nor that this is possible or desirable. We would like to pose the question of the future of the book—and especially of those books whose existence is threatened—in all its technical, commercial, and other dimensions. But it is clearer than ever that the book is not the unique medium of thought—whether philosophical or not. Even as we develop a reflection already under way, we will try to experiment with new techniques, new "supports." This does not exclude "basic" meditations on art, technics, the sciences, religion, ethics, on so many apparently classical themes, and even on the received opposition between "basic" research and so-called applied research, on the politics of research or the professionalization of education. These problems are more forbidding and urgent than ever. They are linked to the severe difficulties of philosophical education, in both high schools and at the university. By itself, the existence of the Collège cannot resolve them, of course, but it will not overlook them, it will not distract us from them, on the contrary. We are all determined not to let that happen. Many of the members of the Collège (in the university and in the high schools where they still teach) have fought and are still fighting for the extension of the teaching of philosophy. You know that among the other premises of the Collège, there is also the GREPH and the Estates General of Philosophy in 1979.[2]

Q.: In announcing the creation of the Collège International de Philosophie, several newspapers have reported that you will be its President.

J.D.: In fact, the Collège will not have a President. And in September a provisional Collège will elect its *directeur* or *directrice* (for there are five women, more than a third of the membership, and not two as has been reported: those who put faith in this kind of arithmetic should get the facts straight). Yes, we insist on this electoral procedure. It underscores a collegial rule and a concern for independence that, I hope, will continue to be borne out.

Q.: What do you think of the debate initiated around the "silence of the intellectuals of the left"?[3] Does the creation of the Collège International de Philosophie signify something in this respect?

J.D.: A debate? Was it a debate? For that, there would have to be other conditions, less murkiness, fewer traps. For a long time now—and how can one be unaware of this?—this notion of "intellectual" has undergone a critical re-elaboration. This should inspire caution in whoever improvises a survey on this question. And since it all began with an appeal or a salute to "modernity," let us ask ourselves what an "intellectual" is in an industrial society. How does one set the demographic limits? Who is an intellectual? Who is not? What is the identifying trait? How does it manifest itself? and so forth. Very difficult questions. And this is to say nothing of the "intellectual-of-the-left" sub-species.

Now, if he were to read a certain article in *Le Monde*, a Persian[4] might conclude that the individuals of this sub-species can be counted on one's fingers; and that, another manual operation, it suffices to pick up one's telephone to get to the bottom of the question just as everyone is leaving for vacation. Attentive to what he calls the "external signs" and in order to ground his diagnosis, the investigator made do with "digging," he said, "through back issues of *Le Monde*" and with counting up the voices of those who are "altogether in favor." As if a partisan position or a political activity of an "intellectual-of-the-left" could only take this form: the "altogether in favor" in the op-ed pages of *Le Monde*! And as if whoever does not declare him- or herself "altogether in favor" or "altogether against" in the newspaper were not an "intellectual" or were to be counted among the "silent ones"! This is ludicrous and insulting—especially when it becomes the topic of dinner-table conversation—but it is certainly unrelated to the seriousness and complexity of things. In order to talk about it, one would need to proceed at a different rhythm, according to different requirements, with more respect for the problems and for persons.

The real work is going on elsewhere, without breaking through, alas (this is a shared responsibility), the barriers of a certain kind of information. Now, precisely, what is so hastily called "the silence of the intellectuals" stems perhaps, in part, from a growing reservation not with regard to *the* political or a *particular* politics, but with regard to the "bully" style of public speech-making, with regard to a type of manifestation that has sometimes set the tone in the media: overblown, dogmatic, noisy, second-rate theatrics. "Intellectuals" and the media deserve better. The current reservation—which is not silence and which was already shaping up, I believe, before May 10th[5]—is perhaps the transition into another mode of manifestation, including in the media.

Oh, I am not suggesting that everything is rosy between the current powers-that-be and a "people-of-intellectuals-of-the-left" collected together like a single individual. But solidarity and participation doubtless go deeper and are more active than some are trying to make us believe for their own reasons. If it exists, this set ("intellectual-of-the-left") is differentiated (as is "Power"!), it is even heterogeneous, which does not necessarily weaken it. It is undertaking evaluations articulated according to which aspect or which phase of a political strategy is in question. To support a political program, in a given situation, is not only to vote or to pass judgments, and still less to rule off-limits any reflection on the very principles of this politics. On the contrary, this reflection must be continuous and radical: that is an elementary responsibility. Governments, moreover, have every interest in seeing this vigilance and this critical liberty maintained. I believe that they realize this.

So yes, as you suggested, the creation of a Collège International acquires a certain meaning in this conjunction even if it is not limited to that. And all the problems we are touching on here ("intellectuals," civil society and the State, the new role of the State and of media in culture, in teaching, and in research, and so forth) will be, among many others, taken up by the Collège, I hope, in an analytical, free, open, and diverse fashion.

Unsealing
("the old new language")

Q.: "An interview with Derrida? At last maybe we're going to understand something about him!" That's what some people said when I announced I was preparing this work with you. It is said your texts are difficult, on the limit of readability. Some potential readers are discouraged in advance by this reputation. How do you live with that? Is it an effect you are seeking to produce or, on the contrary, do you suffer from it?

J.D.: I suffer from it, yes, don't laugh, and I do everything I think possible or acceptable to escape from this trap. But someone in me must get some benefit from it: a certain *relation*. In order to explain this, it would be necessary to draw out some very ancient things from my history, and make them speak with others, very present, from a social or historical scene that I try to take into account. It is out of the question to analyze this "relation" while improvising in front of this tape recorder, at this speed. But don't you think that those who accuse me in the way you described understand the essential of what they claim not to understand, namely, that it is a matter first of all of putting into question a certain scene of reading and evaluation, with its familiar comforts, its interests, its programs of every kind? No one gets angry at a mathematician or a physicist whom he or she doesn't understand at all, or at someone who speaks a foreign language, but rather at someone who tampers with your own language, with this "relation," precisely, which is yours...

I assure you that I never give in to the temptation to be difficult just for the sake of being difficult. That would be too ridiculous. It's just that I believe in the necessity of taking time or, if you prefer, of letting time, of not erasing the folds. For philosophical or political reasons, this problem of communication and receivability, in its new techno-economic givens, is more serious than ever for everyone; one can live it only with malaise, contradiction, and compromise.

Q.: In short, you demand for the philosopher what is accorded at the outset to the scientist: the necessity of a translation, of an explanation that will be performed by others.

J.D.: We are all mediators, translators. In philosophy, as in all domains, you have to reckon with, while not ever being sure of it, the implicit level of an accumulated reserve, and thus with a very great number of relays (teaching, newspapers, journals, books, media), with the shared responsibility of these relays. Why is it apparently the philosopher who is expected to be "easier" and not some scientist or other who is even more inaccessible to the same readers? And why not the writer, who can invent, break new paths only in "difficulty," by taking the risks of a reception that is slow to come, discreet, mistaken, or impossible? In truth—here is another complication—I believe that it is always a "writer" who is accused of being "unreadable," as you put it, that is, someone who is engaged in an explanation with language, the economy of language, the codes and the channels of what is the most receivable.

The accused is thus someone who re-establishes contact between the corpora and the ceremonies of several dialects. If he or she is a philosopher, then it's because he or she speaks neither in a purely academic milieu, with the language, rhetoric, and customs that are in force there, nor in that "language of everyone" which we all know does not exist.

Things became virulent (since it's the case, isn't it, and fortunately so, that people do not always complain about those they cannot read) when, after some books on Husserl, I accelerated or aggravated a certain contamination of the genres.[1] "Mixing the genres," people thought, but that's not the right word. So certain readers resented me perhaps when they could no longer recognize their territory, their "being-at-home" or "among-themselves," their institution, or—still worse—when these were being perceived from this angle or this distance...

Q.: In short, in order to read you, one must have an idea not only of philosophy but also of psychoanalysis, literature, history, linguistics, or the history of painting...

J.D.: There is especially the potential that opens up necessarily, whether one wishes it or not, from one text to another, a kind of chemistry...

Q.: To read you, one has to have read Derrida...

J.D.: But that's true for everyone! Is it so wrong to take account of a past trajectory, of a writing that has in part sealed itself, little by little? But it is also interesting to undo, to unseal. I also try to begin over again in proximity to the simplest thing, which is sometimes difficult and dangerous.

You know, the "thinking" that has it out with [*s'explique avec*] philosophy, science, or literature as such does not totally belong to them. It calls for a writing that sometimes can be read with an *apparent* facility...

Q.: Like the "Envois" in *The Post Card*, for example...

J.D.: ... but a writing whose status, in a certain way, is impossible to assign: Is it or is it not a theoretical utterance? Are the signatories and addressees identifiable in advance or produced and divided by the text? Do the sentences describe something or are they doing something? For example, when I say, in an undecided tone: "You come." Do we have sure criteria for deciding it? Where is science, where is philosophy in this regard? You can treat or rather follow language to the point where these decisions are no longer possible. Not in order to put one off the trail or cause anxiety but because, once this limit is reached, the question of the decision or of the interpretation is laid bare (and thus the question of responsibility, of the response). You reach a border from which what seemed to be certain appears in its precariousness or in its history, without necessarily disappearing or collapsing.

Q.: You say that it is not in order to cause anxiety, but this precariousness must worry you a little.

J.D.: When one writes, one is always trying to outsmart the worst. Perhaps so as to prevent it from taking everything away, but the last word, you know, always belongs to non-mastery, for both the reader and oneself. And it's good that this is the way it is. The living desire to write keeps you in relation to a terror that you try to maneuver with even as you leave it intact, audible in that place where you may find yourself, understand yourself, you and whoever reads you, beyond any partition, thus at once saved and lost.

Q.: To escape partition, is that the same thing as escaping destiny? Your destiny as a philosopher, for example?

J.D.: Do you seriously want to get me to speak about my "destiny" under these conditions? No. But if by destiny one means a singular manner of not being free, then what interests me is especially that, precisely and everywhere: this intersection of change and necessity, the *line of life*, the proper language of a life, even if it is never pure. For example, so as not to leave your question unanswered: Why do I have this relation and not another to philosophy? Why, as a "professional" philosopher, have I always occupied this position, on a margin that is not indeterminate, and so forth? (I know that I am going to annoy certain people, as you said, if I speak of "margin" and "solitude"—but all the same...)

My "first" desire no doubt did not lead me toward philosophy, but rather toward literature, no, toward something that literature makes room for better than philosophy. I feel myself to be engaged, for the last twenty years, in a long detour that will lead me back to this thing, this idiomatic writing whose purity, I realize, is inaccessible, but about which I continue to dream.

Q.: What do you mean by "idiomatic"?

J.D.: A property that one cannot appropriate; it signs you without belonging to you; it only appears to the other and it never comes back to you except in flashes of madness that bring together life and death, that bring you together dead and alive at the same time. You dream, it's unavoidable, about the invention of a language or of a song that would be yours, not the attributes of a "self," rather the accentuated paraph, that is, the musical signature, of your most unreadable history. I'm not talking about a *style* but an intersection of singularities, habitat, voices, graphism, what moves with you and what your body never leaves. In my memory, what I write resembles a dotted-line drawing that would be circling around a book to be written in what I call for myself the "old new language," the most archaic and the most novel, therefore unheard-of, unreadable at present. (In Prague, you know, the oldest synagogue is called the Old-New Synagogue.) This book would be something completely different from the path that it nevertheless still resembles. In any case, an interminable anamnesis whose form is being sought: not only *my* history, but culture, languages, families, Algeria first of all...

Q.: Are you going to write it?

J.D.: You must be joking... But the accumulation of dreams, projects, or notes no doubt weighs on what is written in the present. One day, some piece of the book may fall out like a stone that keeps the memory of a hallucinatory architecture to which it might have belonged. The stone still resonates and vibrates, it emits a kind of painful and indecipherable bliss, one no longer knows whose or for whom...

Q.: Was *The Post Card* one of these stones?

J.D.: I don't know any longer.

Q.: You mentioned a moment ago Algeria. That is where it all began for you.

J.D.: Ah, you want me to say things like "I-was-born-in-El Biar-on-the-outskirts-of-Algiers-in-a-petit-bourgeois-family-of-assimilated-Jews-but…" Is that really necessary? I can't do it. You will have to help me…

Q.: What was your father's name?

J.D.: Ok, here we go. He had five names, all the names of the family are encrypted, along with a few others, in *The Post Card*, sometimes unreadable even for those who bear these names; often they are not capitalized, as one might do for "aimé" or "rené."

Q.: How old were you when you left Algeria?

J.D.: You really are persistent. I came to France at the age of nineteen. I had never left El Biar. The war of 1940 in Algeria, thus the first underground rumblings of the Algerian war. As a child, I heard them coming in an animal fashion, with a feeling of the end of the world which was at the same time the most natural habitat, in any case the only one I had ever known. Even for a child who was unable to analyze things, it was clear that it would all end in fire and blood. No one could escape that violence and that fear, even if all around it…

Q.: Do you have specific memories of that fear?

J.D.: Are you thinking I must have retained something of all that? Yes, and I knew from experience that the daggers could be bared at any moment, as one left school, in the football stadium, in the midst of the racist taunts that spared no one: the Arab, the Jew, the Spaniard, the Maltese, the Italian, the Corsican… Then, in 1940, the singular experience of the Algerian Jews. The persecutions, which were unlike those of Europe, were all the same unleashed in the absence of any German occupier.

Q.: Did you suffer personally from that?

J.D.: It is an experience that leaves nothing intact, an atmosphere that one goes on breathing forever. Jewish children expulsed from school. The principal's office: You are going to go home, your parents will explain. Then the Allies landed, it was the period of the so-called two-headed government (de Gaulle–Giraud): racial laws

maintained for almost six months, under a "free" French government. Friends who no longer knew you, insults, the Jewish high
school with its expulsed teachers and never a whisper of protest from
their colleagues. I was enrolled there but I cut school for a year...

Q.: Why?

J.D.: From that moment, I felt—how to put it?—just as out-of-
place in a closed Jewish community as I did on the other side (we
called them "the Catholics"). In France, the suffering subsided. At
nineteen, I naively thought that anti-Semitism had disappeared, at
least there where I was living at the time. But during adolescence, it
was *the* tragedy, it was present in everything else (for there was
everything else, and it was perhaps just as determinant: you see, we
give in to facileness or a certain kind of curiosity when we select out
this sequence; why are you leading me first of all in this direction?).
Paradoxical effect, perhaps, of this brutalization: a desire for inte-
gration in the non-Jewish community, a fascinated but painful and
suspicious desire, nervously vigilant, an exhausting aptitude to
detect signs of racism, in its most discreet configurations or its
noisiest disavowals. Symmetrically, sometimes, an impatient distance with regard to the Jewish communities, whenever I have the
impression that they are closing themselves off by posing themselves as such. Whence a feeling of non-belonging that I have no
doubt transposed...

Q.: Into philosophy?

J.D.: Everywhere. You spoke of chance and destiny; well, look at
the "profession" of philosopher. Right after the *baccalauréat*, I
knew that I wanted, as one says, "to write," but I barely knew what
a university was. On the radio, I happen upon a program on
scholastic preparation: a professor of *hypokhâgne*[2] was describing
his class and mentioned one of his former students, Albert Camus.
Two days later, I was enrolled in this class without knowing then
what the Ecole Normale was...

Q.: It is then that you began to read Sartre, right?

J.D.: A little earlier. He played a major role for me then. A model that I have since judged to be nefarious and catastrophic, but that I love; no doubt as what I had to love, and I always love what I have loved, it's very simple...

Q.: Nefarious and catastrophic! That's a bit strong; you'll have to explain...

J.D.: Do you think we should keep that or cut it? Okay. First of all, I repeat, Sartre no doubt, well, guided me, as he did so many others at the time. Reading him, I discovered Blanchot, Bataille, Ponge—whom I now think one could have read otherwise. But finally, Sartre was himself the "unsurpassable horizon"![3] Things changed when, thanks to him but especially against him, I read Husserl, Heidegger, Blanchot, and others. One would have to devote several dozen books to this question: What must a society such as ours be if a man, who, in his own way, rejected or misunderstood so many theoretical and literary events of his time— let's say, to go quickly, psychoanalysis, Marxism, structuralism, Joyce, Artaud, Bataille, Blanchot—who accumulated and disseminated incredible misreadings of Heidegger, sometimes of Husserl, could come to dominate the cultural scene to the point of becoming a great popular figure? It is true that works can traverse their time like tornadoes, overturn the historical landscape, interpret it without seeming to understand anything about it, without being sensitive or acquiescing to every "novelty." I don't think this is the case with Sartre but, while asking myself a lot of questions, even about his likeable and legendary generosity, I sometimes share the almost familial affection that many feel for this man whom I have never seen. And who does not belong to the age of those works that matter for me...

Q.: And that were being written at the same time...

J.D.: Or even much earlier, look at Mallarmé! What must a French intellectual be if such a phenomenon can happen or happen again? What grants authority to his evaluations? What interests me still today is especially the France of Sartre, the relation of our culture to this man (rather than to his work). And also Sartre's relation to the University. It is said that he escaped it or resisted it. It seems to me that university norms determined his work in the most internal fashion, as they did for so many writers who don't realize or who deny this fact. An analysis of his philosophical rhetoric, of his literary criticism, and even of his plays or novels would be greatly helped if it took into account, for better or worse, the models and the history of education, the *lycée*, the *khâgne*, the Ecole Normale, and the *agrégation*.[4] I began this exercise, one day, with some students, taking the example of Sartre's *Saint Genet*. Thus an enormous screen of French culture. But reading it, I no doubt learned a lot and, even if it goes against him, I am indebted to him. But tell me, is this an interview about Sartre!

Q.: So, in short, you see in Sartre the perfect example of what an intellectual should not be...

J.D.: I didn't say that...

Q.: But, then, what should be the attitude of an intellectual in relation to political affairs?

J.D.: No one stands to gain by there being a model, especially just one model. Also the category of "intellectual" no longer has very strict limits, and probably never did. It is true that Sartre's example, which is why one has to insist upon it, incites one to prudence. His academic legitimacy (graduate of the Ecole Normale, *agrégé*) and his legitimacy as a writer for a major publishing house[5] (don't ever separate these two things, but I am going too quickly) lent to his most impulsive remarks, whether or not you take them seriously, a formidable authority, the authority that was not granted to stricter and more interesting analysts. In political affairs especially, as everyone knows. One could take other examples today, because the thing is being amplified here and there as new powers and new structures appear (media, publishing, and so forth). Not that one has therefore to go into retreat or avoid taking public positions: quite to the contrary, the moment has perhaps come to do more and better, that is, otherwise...

Q.: How so?

J.D.: Paradoxically: by campaigning for the extension and increase in the number of media, of places of publication and broadcast, for their transformation especially, against monopolies, homogeneity, and appropriation. Wherever this power is concentrated today, it tends to put technical modernity to work in the service of worn-out things that keep droning on and sometimes in the service of the most glaring silliness. It actively encourages platitude and pomposity. Yes, I know, but the two are not incompatible. The most dismaying things go over better and better, and they are *designed to go over*, they are *over* in advance. I'm speaking particularly about philosophy, literature, and "ideological" discourse. One can see by a certain number of signs, fortunately, that a sort of resistance is organizing itself, in a number of places that, by definition, one never hears about. The future will tell (perhaps!) what we do not want to hear about or cannot hear about. I think it is necessary—and I hope that this will not be altogether impossible—to redefine the relation between "culture" and the State, the double responsibility that this relation implies. State culture has always represented the most serious danger, and one can never be too vigilant in this regard. But a certain kind of massive antistatism can, on the one hand, be incapable of situating the State in modern society (it is often represented there where one thought and pretended to think it was absent), and, on the other hand, it can misapprehend or combat the role that, in certain conditions (which are difficult to bring together), the State could, should play today, a role which is also paradoxical: to give "counter-culture" its chance, to limit the mechanisms of standardization, appropriation, and monopolization, and so forth. Walter Benjamin said something like this: the responsibility of the writer is not first of all to put forward revolutionary theses. These are defused as soon as they present themselves in language and according to the existent devices of culture. It is the latter that must *also* be transformed. And that is very difficult, the very definition of "difficult." One could try, for example, to understand why *Le Nouvel Observateur*, why me, and now rather than yesterday or tomorrow, why you, who are leading me in this direction among so many other possible directions, why the fact of occupying this platform counts perhaps more than what one says there or reads there in a cursive fashion, and so forth.

Q.: One could pose the question differently. If you accepted to give an interview to *Le Nouvel Observateur*, it is with the idea of transmitting something. For a professor of philosophy, the natural site of transmission is the lecture hall. Can one, in your opinion, talk about philosophy in a newspaper? Or is the message necessarily distorted?

J.D.: A message, if there is any, never remains intact. Why should philosophy be the preserve of professional philosophers? It is, moreover, a profession in which competence is doubtless indispensable, but one whose unity and history are so problematic! A vast work is being undertaken on this subject; it should be pursued both within and without the University, in particular in the press...

Q.: Philosophy for everybody: that's an idea you've held dear for a long time, for which you campaigned with the Research Group on the Teaching of Philosophy (GREPH) and at the Estates General of Philosophy.[6] Can one really, as you have maintained, teach philosophy to a junior high school pupil?

J.D.: Of all the so-called basic disciplines, why is philosophy absent from almost the whole secondary cycle? Other disciplines are taught very early—mathematics, languages, literature, history, economics—precisely because they are difficult and one needs more time. If children had access to philosophy, the problems of reading that we are talking about would be posed differently. Obviously, no one is suggesting that one teach an eighth-grader the same things, and in the same way, one teaches a high school senior, but new pedagogical situations have to be invented, and texts, themes, programs, and relations among the disciplines have to be redefined.

The experiments that we tried out (and published) with GREPH testify to the fact that children between the ages of ten and twelve can, in certain conditions, accede to a kind of reflection and texts that are considered difficult. In certain classes, I heard children complain and accuse: Why had this been *forbidden* to them, thus also depriving them of a certain pleasure? There is here a mass of solidified prejudices, interests, and phantasms. The history of that mass is inseparable from the history of philosophy itself and from a stricter analysis of our society. GREPH is attempting to carry out this work of analysis even as it campaigns for the extension and transformation of philosophical teaching.

Q.: What gains have you made?

J.D.: First of all (at its time and along with others) that the "Haby proposal" not be instituted (it threatened even the final year of philosophy, the "terminale").[7] At the Estates General in 1979, a majority voted for the extension...

Q.: You seem to be saying that for the State, philosophy is a dangerous discourse that one must be wary of. What are the reasons for this wariness?

J.D.: That depends on the state of the State. Political wariness (sometimes shared by a segment of the teaching faculty) toward this or that discourse is not always the essential obstruction. Whatever kind of regime they may have, industrial societies tend, out of concern for profitability, to reduce the share of discourses and formations that have a low productivity (a very difficult evaluation, often erroneous; this is the whole problem today with the "application" of research and the professionalization of university education—a very, very difficult problem, too difficult for the amount of space we have here, so I'll drop it). As I said at the Estates General, a political change was necessary for this but not sufficient; it would not automatically take care of the problem. On the eve of his election, François Mitterrand wrote to the GREPH that the extension of philosophy ought to occur. We have not stopped reminding those in charge at the Ministry of Education of this commitment.

Q.: Does the mission you were charged with by the government to create a Collège International de Philosophie have a relation to these problems?

J.D.: Only partly. It is difficult to say something in a few words about this project. It cannot be reduced to the novelty of certain of its institutional aspects: effective internationality, absence of any permanent chairs or positions, opening onto the problems of research and pedagogical institutions, crossing of philosophical, artistic, scientific activities, and so forth. But this very singularity, which ought to make this new place more "useful" and better situated in the overall domain of research facilities, is also a "high risk" for it. And a good risk to take. An institution without adventure would be without future [*avenir*]. Everything is only beginning for this one; let's give it time.

Q.: You are one of the very rare philosophers to be interested in psychoanalysis and to give it a place in your work, not only as a simple reference but in a movement of continual coming and going. Are there philosophical reasons for this interest of yours?

J.D.: Without speaking of the content, how can one know that a writing—that of psychoanalysts as well as that of philosophers— sometimes keeps not a single trace of psychoanalysis? Now, if there is some affinity between something of psychoanalytic "subversion" and the "deconstructive" affirmation, let's say, of philosophy, the latter can also take aim at a certain "philosophy" of psychoanalysis.

Q.: What do you mean by psychoanalytic "subversion"?

J.D.: That's not the right word, I used it for the sake of convenience. Psychoanalysis should oblige one to rethink a lot of certainties, for example to reconstruct the whole axiomatics of law, of morality, of "human rights," the whole discourse constructed on the agency of the self and of conscious responsibility, the politician's rhetoric, the concept of torture, legal psychiatry and its whole system, and so forth. Not in order to rule out ethical and political statements, on the contrary, for their very future. In this regard, we all live in a state of daily dissociation, one that is terrifying and comical at the same time, the most singular thing about our historical fate.

Q.: Last year, you went to Prague to meet some Czech intellectuals. At the airport, as you were leaving, the customs agents "found" drugs in your suitcase. You spent twenty-four hours in prison and were freed thanks to the intervention of the French government. What was, during those twenty-four hours, your experience of this dissociation?

J.D.: Perhaps a somewhat more ruthless insight, but also a sort of compassion. Despite everything, before my imprisonment, there was that eight-hour interrogation with some terrifying State officials whom one could also have pity for. The prosecutor, the police chief, the translator, and the lawyer assigned to me knew very well why this trap had been set, they knew that the others knew, were watching each other, and conducted the whole comedy with an unshakable complicity. They put on another play when the same ones came to liberate me, while addressing me respectfully as "Monsieur le Professeur." Since I had often spoken of Kafka (at that time I was working on a little text on "Before the Law" which I had with me, and no doubt it was when I went to visit Kafka's grave that they took care of my valise in the hotel), the lawyer said to me in an aside: "You must have the impression of living in a Kafka story." And then later: "Don't take things too tragically; consider it a literary experience." I responded that I did take it tragically, but first of all for him—or for them, I don't remember exactly. And then, as for me, the dissociations were different but just as indescribable in a few words. I knew the scenario and I did, I think, everything that *had* to be done. But how to describe all the archaic movements that are unleashed below that surface, at the moment when the trap was sprung at customs, during the interrogation, during the first incarceration—the guards' yells and insults through the reinforced door and even in the solitary cell where one of them made a gesture to hit me because I asked for a French lawyer, and then the nudity, the photographs (I have never been more photographed in my life, from the airport to the prison, clothed or naked before putting on the prisoner's "uniform")? All of this is part of such a common experience, alas, that it would be indecent to tell it unless I could recapture some absolute singularity, which I cannot do while improvising in front of a microphone. The very first time I spoke before a television camera, I had to be silent about what *my* experience was, which at that moment didn't hold any great interest. It was at night, in Germany, on the train that brought me back from Prague. It seemed to me that, at that moment, I ought to speak of what had just happened, to which I was the only one capable of testifying and which had some general interest. Still I had to be satisfied with broad stereotypes of the sort: "I-went-there-out-of-solidarity-with-those-who-are-struggling-for-the-respect-of-human-rights, etc." This was all true, and I wanted especially to salute those whom I had met there, both in and out of prison. But how can you expect me, in that situation, to say to someone from Channel 2 who puts a microphone in front of me: "You know, I am asking myself certain questions about the State, the foundations, and the function of the discourse on human rights today"? Or else: "The essential thing is what was said there in the outlawed seminar about the political question of the 'subject' and other related things"? Or else: "What I really lived through there would demand a completely different form of narration, another poetics than that of the evening news"? Or else: "There was someone in me who seemed, in spite of everything, to take pleasure in something about that prison, who seemed to be reliving some hallucination, who seemed to want it to last longer, and to regret bitterly the betrayal he felt at the moment of leaving the five kids who were with me in the second prison cell"?

Just imagine the look on the faces of the reporters and the TV viewers. But the difficulty I felt in the most acute way at that moment is permanent, and it is what paralyzes me every time I have to take the floor and speak in public. Even here, still now.

Q.: Listening to you talk about this Prague experience, one understands how you could, on the basis of those twenty-four hours, write a book that would involve at once literature, history, politics, and philosophy.

J.D.: I have written books with several columns or several voices ("Tympan" in *Margins—of Philosophy*, "The Double Session" in *Dissemination, Glas, The Truth in Painting*, "Pas" in *Parages, The Post Card*). But for this multiplicity of levels or tones, one would have to invent still other forms, other kinds of music. How is one to get them accepted when the "dominant" demand always requires, or so people want to make us believe, more linearity, cursivity, flattening? A single voice on the line, a continuous speech, that is what they want to impose. This authoritarian norm would be like an unconscious plot, an intrigue of the hierarchies (ontological, theologico-political, technico-metaphysic), the very ones that call for deconstructive analyses. Deployed with a certain consistency, these analyses destabilize the concepts as well as the institutions and the modes of writing. But since one may presume that the *whole* of tradition is at stake there, I don't know where such upheavals are situated. They situate us. These events do not take place, rather they are seeking their place, within and without; their space is already foreign, in any case, to what is called the history of philosophy, but they also affect it in another way.

For my part, I feel that I am also an heir: faithful as far as possible, loving, avid to reread and to experience the philosophical joys that are not just the games of the esthete. I love repetition, as if the future were entrusted to us, as if it were waiting for us in the cipher of a very ancient speech—one which has not yet been allowed to speak. All this, I realize, makes for a bizarre mixture of responsibility and disrespect. My attention to the present scene is at once intense, desperate, and a little distracted, as if anachronistic. But without this bizarreness, nothing seems to me desirable today. We have gotten more than we think we know from "tradition," but the scene of the gift also obligates us to a kind of filial lack of piety, at once serious and not so serious, as regards the thinking to which we have the greatest debt. I would have liked to speak here about Kant, Schelling or Hegel, Marx, Kierkegaard or Nietzsche, and then about Levinas or Blanchot, or still other thinkers today who are my friends. But take the example of Heidegger: well, it is at the moment in which what he calls "ontological difference" or the "truth of Being" seems to assure the most "gathering" [*rassemblante*] reading of philosophy that I believe it is urgent to question this very gathering, this presumption of unity, what it still excludes or reduces to silence. Why? In view of what? Does one have the right to speak of one—of *the*—Western metaphysics, of *its* language, of a sole destiny or "sending of Being," and so forth? Therefore everything remains open, still to be thought. This in order to respond to your question about the multiplicity of levels. It does not always require a stage device or a labyrinthine typography; it can cause to tremble a very simple sentence, a word, a timbre of the voice...

Q.: Like the "Come" that resonates at the end of "Of an Apocalyptic Tone"?[8]

J.D.: Exactly. This "Come" is a call anterior to any other discourse and any other event, to any order and any desire, an apocalypse that ends and unveils nothing... But it was agreed that we would not talk today about the texts themselves, not directly...

« Dialanguages »

Q.: I have just read the interview you gave to *Le Nouvel Observateur.*[1] I found that your voice came through there, and that, in a certain way, everything is resonance there. And so our original project (to ask you about the question of taste with reference to "Economimesis") has gotten displaced from the mouth to the ear. I think it was a tone or different tones that struck me, a particular manner of enunciating that would try to make itself heard beneath the words. We had not decided whether we would talk about you or your texts, or about you and your texts at the same time. That is precisely my first question. I don't know if I am addressing the man or the "writer-thinker," I don't know what their relation is. This question was suggested to me by the chronological reading of your texts, up to the latest interview; you seem to be putting yourself on stage more and more, or to be revealing yourself—revealing what "constitutes" you, the questions that constitute you, such as the questions of address and destination, which are all the more disturbing when the address is not certain.

J.D.: You say that you heard a voice in this interview. It is true that I spoke of voice and timbre or tone. I insisted several times on the idiom and a certain number of things of that kind, but it was also the effect of an effort to cause a voice to be heard through an extremely complicated apparatus. I realize that for the reader that interview, and I very rarely give them, might seem to have been in fact spontaneous or improvised; but one should know that, however perfunctory the content of what I say there, however limited it is in its scope, it is totally artificial. These things have to be said, one must not pretend to believe that interviews published in the newspapers are real interviews; it is an extremely artificial device, one that I tried to get through, while adhering to the rules of the genre, so as to put across what you said you heard, that is, the voice, a certain "spontaneity," which, I think, is most audible in the little remarks I made about the malaise I felt in that situation.

There are some things that were dropped, and not by my choice, which concerned the media—and what was at stake with *Le Nouvel Observateur*. So a certain number of things, after various compromises that I thought I had to make, were dropped in order that other things could remain. In short, this interview is a totally fabricated effect, but through which a certain number of symptoms or spontaneous, uncontrollable things come across, as in a photo for which one composes one's face: through the composition, there is a certain "truth," as one says, that comes across.

Since I began to write, I have almost always refused interviews; I accepted to go through the rite in that case for very precise, very clear reasons: it was a matter of the necessity of speaking or causing to speak of a certain number of political things that I care about and to which I am committed, namely, the GREPH, the Collège International de Philosophie, but also solidarity with the Czech intellectuals or still more recently with those who are struggling for the abolition of apartheid.[2] That said, as for this staging of myself, of "things" that look to be more unveiled or indiscreet than elsewhere, I have the impression that in texts published elsewhere, which are more written or more elaborated, in *Glas* or *The Post Card*, it is at once more violent and more revealing; it's just that, since this is done according to the code of the book, for a certain kind of public, and not in a newspaper that prints 150,000 or 200,000 copies, it does not have the same effect.

Q.: In any case, I didn't mean "voice" in the sense of spontaneity. I was including your interview in a kind of path marked out by *Glas* and *The Post Card*, where it seems to me that, in a certain way and to a greater and greater extent, a place of emission or, as you put it, a type of far more violent unveiling is indicated, while at the same time it escapes one's grasp. It is true that any assignment to an exact place of emission would be a lure, as you yourself often say; but doesn't this revealing of the place of emission, at the same time as, perhaps, something escapes the grasp, still indicate a desire that would be double or divided, a desire at once to say and not to say, or as you put it in your latest text, a certain "cryptophilia"?[3] Or perhaps, according to you, "it" is spoken or given still better through a certain reserve?

J.D.: What is reserved or held back in the unveiling is not something that is hidden, that one decides not to show: from the moment something escapes me myself, from the moment it is held back from me, as long as (and this "as long as" can last a long time) this reserve remains one for me, I would find it at once laughable, brutal, perfunctory, and false to pretend to reveal it. To keep in reserve the unveiling of the reserve, I maintain a kind of discretion, even when I expose myself. There is a secret of "me" for "me." To protect and preserve the possibility for me to accede to it or to show it, I deem for the moment any exhibition hurried or anecdotal. It would be giving in to conventional channels or to the anecdote; it would be a mystification, mystifying and exhibitionist—exhibitionist in the derisory sense of the term. But at the same time, obviously, there is an affirmation of a theoretical or philosophical or impersonal sort at the bottom of this: this reserved origin is in fact always divisible and consequently without identity, thus indefinitely inaccessible in its identifiable presence; this affirmation is at the center of all these recent texts, such as *The Post Card*.

Q.: Does not the place of emission, in that case, depend on the field in which it is inscribed? The problematic of the veil and unveiling is an eminently "philosophical" one in your formulation;

at the same time, how far can unveiling go in the philosophical field?

J.D.: The philosophical field, if it has an identity, if it has strict limits (and that are such as can be located on the basis of its traditions), has nothing to do with the unveiling of the identity of the thinker or the philosopher; this field was constituted, precisely, by cutting itself off from the autobiography or the signature of the philosopher. The field of the philosopheme in the traditional sense had to become essentially independent from its place of emission, from the subject or from the signatory of the text called philosophical. From the moment one speaks of signature or of autobiographeme, one is no longer in the philosophical field, in the traditional sense of the term.

Q.: So where is one then?

J.D.: I don't know. It's the same question; I don't know where I am when I give myself over to operations of this kind. I am there merely as someone who, like others, is seeking his place, and is not speaking from an already identifiable place. When the voice trembles, when one hears that voice, one hears a non-localizable voice; it makes itself heard *because* its place of emission is not fixed. In an elliptical manner, I would say that, when a voice has its localizable place in a social field, it is no longer heard; when one does hear it, it is the voice of a ghost, a voice that is seeking its place like a will-o'-the-wisp; when you hear a voice over the telephone, on the radio, you don't see where it comes from; as for the one who seems to be the bearer of the voice, you don't know with a certain knowledge either where or who he or she is; the bearer him- or herself does not know either.

Q.: Concerning this voice, you speak of phantomization from the moment it has no assignable place, from the moment it leaves any constituted field; this is something that comes back all the time in everything you say. One hears a tone that, as you say in "Of an Apocalyptic Tone," attracts one toward the source of its emission. At one point you say that, for lack of an assignable emitter or receiver, or for lack of an assignable subject or body, or at least for lack of knowing whether one must assign it and to what one must assign it, the tone is resolved in "a pure differential vibration." The apocalyptic tone "wants to attract, to cause to come to it, to cause to happen to it . . . to the place where the first vibration of tone is heard, whether one calls it, as one wishes, subject, person, sex, or desire (I think rather of a pure differential vibration), without support, insupportable."[4] I have a double question about this "pure differential vibration": Is it still the dream of a primary purity, almost inaccessible or inaudible, which you speak about elsewhere? And likewise, is not this fate of the voice in your text the result, in spite of everything, of a certain type of relation to objects, a certain type of symbolization that, if only at its borders, is provoked by the work of philosophy?

J.D.: As for the dream of a unity, or finally of a place: In *Le Nouvel Observateur*, at several points, I speak of the dream of an idiomatic writing, and I call it Necessity; this dream is forever destined to disappointment; this unity remains inaccessible; that does not mean that the dream is but a fantasy, imaginary, a secondary moment; this "dream" institutes speech, writing, the voice, its timbre. There cannot not be this dream, this dreamed-of desire of a purely idiomatic voice that would be what it is and would be in some way indivisible. Even if this dream is destined to remain a dream, the promise—it is better to speak of promise instead of dream—the promise, as promise, is an event, it exists; there is the promise of unity and that is what sets desire in motion; there is desire. To say that desire is destined to remain desire does not prevent desire, and desire is the essential motion of this speech or this writing. Thus, to speak of dream is not to speak of an accidental surplus; it is the essence of the thing, this "dream." The words "dream," "desire," or "ghost" must be redetermined on the basis of this necessity, the thinking of this necessity.

Q.: You say that you prefer to think that this voice attracts one toward its source, but at the same time, where is the source since this is resolved in a kind of "pure differential vibration"?

J.D.: In saying "pure differential vibration," one has the impression of seeing any identity, presence, fullness, or content disappear; from then on, one is dealing with only a vibrating or resonating system of relations. One would thus have only disappointment or lack. But I don't imagine that any bliss (let's not speak any more here of desire but of bliss [*jouissance*]) is thinkable that does not have the form of this pure difference; a bliss that would be that of a plenitude without vibration, without difference, seems to me to be both the myth of metaphysics—and death. If there is something that can be called living bliss or life, it can be given only in this form of painful bliss which is that of differential vibration. No self-identity can close on itself. When I reread the interview in *Le Nouvel Observateur*, I noticed that many things were said in a symptomatic manner without my having calculated them; for example, at several points the word "pain" or "suffering" was associated with joy or bliss; and the word "terrifying" or "terror" appeared I don't know how many times, without my having done it on purpose. Effectively, then, I let come across the image of someone who is terrified, fundamentally in pain in his bliss. This "differential vibration" is for me the only possible form of response to desire, the only form of bliss, and which can therefore be only a remote bliss, that is, bliss for two or more, bliss in which the other is called; I cannot imagine a living bliss which is not plural, differential. This is marked in a minimal fashion by the fact that a timbre, a breath, a syllable is already a differential vibration; in a certain way, there is no atom.

Q.: In your interview, you say that you are "avid to reread and to experience the philosophical joys [*jouissances*] that are not just the games of the esthete." I wanted to ask you what kind of philosophical "joys" you mean. I was thinking of "Economimesis," where you make philosophy swallow even that which cannot be swallowed, the disgusting, the unavowable; in this case it was, in the context of the work you were doing on "judgments of taste," "the vomited" which you described as "the elixir of bad taste," but still the elixir of philosophy. The question of bliss or joy is linked to that of taste, and I would like to ask the reverse question of the one you treat in "Economimesis": Does philosophy, finally, have any taste for you? What kind of taste? Is it that of an elixir? The quintessence of the drink? Is it a poison-remedy? What kind of taste do you have for philosophy?

J.D.: In a summary and contradictory fashion, I would say that first of all I have no taste for philosophy. There is someone in me (that's a convenient formula for indicating that desire is divided among several instances), there is one in me who has no taste for philosophy and who could get along very well without reading any philosophy or without doing any philosophical exercises. Something I could very well do without is writing or reading philosophy as such. But the contrary is also true: at the same time, I have a great taste for philosophy, I love "to do philosophy," that is, to read the texts, to understand them, explicate them, write philosophy, and have it out with philosophical texts, philosophical systems. What is happening in this double relation? The two things coexist; in what I write, it must be readable that the two things coexist. If, in the sentence you cited, I hasten to add that these are not the games of an esthete, it is because the deconstructive attitude toward philosophy risks looking like an esthete's game. Here and there I say, quoting Nietzsche or Valéry, that philosophy is literature, an art among others, and that one can be interested in Spinoza's systematics as a construction, a work of art that can be put up and taken down, with a certain ludic pleasure. Moreover, when one has reached that phase of history where it seems the combination of possibilities has been exhausted and any rereading can consist only in explaining this combination of concepts, when it seems there is a sort of finite space of philosophical possibilities and every system is a manner of explaining oneself over against this finite field of concepts, at that moment, the risk is estheticism or else archeology: one is interested in philosophy the way an archeologist is interested in things of the past. This is the estheticizing risk of a certain conception of deconstruction against which I am defending my-self, because I think the relation to philosophy today must also be a serious one. Even if I am strongly tempted by the esthete's game, there is also something else. Whence the insistence on the aspect of a loving and faithful bliss. This is not always the language I use; it's part of the scene of the question.

Nevertheless, where does the serious taste for philosophy come from? What resists the esthete's game, or inversely, what resists simple disgust? It's that I have the impression—and here, we come upon the question of the voice again—that across all the philosophical texts, and through all the very complicated mediations and relays that allow us or forbid us access to them, there is a hidden voice, a speech, a writing or a signature, which is there, dissimulated, in a scene of an unheard-of violence, and which in general the academic institution comes along to cover up. I would not say that, when I read Plato, I have a one-on-one conversation with him, or with Descartes, or with Kant, but that this spoken scene interests me very much, the scene in which, first of all, the philosophers in question had to explain themselves over against their interlocutors, tradition, but also with us. One could say that there is the paternal image, the maternal image... a true family scene. While reading in a certain way, one can, I won't say try to hear—because I don't think one can really hear Plato—but one can pose the question of Plato's signature, even if it is inaccessible, one can pose the question of this dramaturgy of signatures and voices; and when I manage to expose, to begin to expose that dramaturgy, I get a taste for it, I find there a much greater pleasure than in so many other exercises of an apparently political or literary sort. The philosopher is someone whose desire and ambition are absolutely mad; the desire for power of the greatest politicians is absolutely minuscule and juvenile compared to the desire of the philosopher who, in a philosophical work, manifests both a design on mastery and a renunciation of mastery on a scale and to a degree that I find infinitely more powerful than can be found elsewhere, for example, with the great politicians or military men, or those who have economic power at their disposal. There is an adventure of power and unpower, a play of potency and impotence, a *size* of desire that seems to me, with the philosophers, much more impressive than elsewhere. It is out of all proportion with other types of discourse and sometimes even with all the rules of art.

Q.: That seems to me to be an interesting, but very peculiar position. This desire interests you, and it is all the more formidable in that it is repressed. At the beginning, you were speaking of a violent dissimulation, and all the more violent in that it is dissimulated; one might imagine there are other spaces, such as the literary or artistic space (since we began with the question of taste, since you were speaking of the signature, the unconscious stakes, the figure of the father or the mother), where something is given, where something is more openly revealed. Thus, in a certain way, what would lend to philosophy its colossal dimension would be the apparent retreat of this kind of scene?

J.D.: But it's a retreat of the will to mastery. What is colossal here is that the philosopher is more in retreat to the extent to which his fundamental project is to render an account of all possible discourses and all possible arts. He wants to situate himself in a place where everything done and said can be thought, theorized, and finally mastered by him. It is the place of absolute mastery, the project of absolute knowledge. Even if this takes this express form only in Hegel, absolute knowledge is indeed the truth of the philosophical project. To situate oneself in this place is simultaneously to project the greatest mastery over all the possible discourses of mastery, and to renounce it. The two things go together: it is the place at the same time of the greatest discretion, of the greatest effacement, of retreat, of modesty—a modesty haunted by the devil. That's what interests me.

Since we are talking about *taste* in the strict sense, perhaps all of this comes together in the question of the voice, the mouth, orality. You mentioned a moment ago the destiny of the voice in what I write; people who are in a bit too much of a hurry have thought that I wasn't interested in the voice, just writing. Obviously, this is not true. What interests me is writing in the voice, the voice as differential vibration, that is, as trace. Philosophical discourse, the mastery of every other possible discourse, tends to gather itself up in the philosophical utterance, in something that, all at once, the philosopher's voice can say, bring together, utter; it is the position of the speaker's mastery that interests me. I don't mean to say that I am seeking it (I seek it just like everyone else); it interests me insofar as it both assures *and* destroys mastery. For example, my preferred pleasure is not at all to publish or to write texts; I don't really like writing in order to publish, I would rather speak from the position of the writer; what I like to do, for example, is to give courses in my own manner: to let be heard in what I write a certain position of the voice, when the voice and the body can no longer be distinguished—and obviously this passes by way of the mouth. I have a taste only for that taste, for what is written by tongues/languages, from mouth to ear, from mouth to mouth, or from mouth to lips...

Q.: A moment ago you were saying that you could get along very well without reading philosophy or philosophical texts. I had a quite simple question about what you like to read, what you like to read in literature. What one hears about are the literary or philosophical texts on which you work, but is there reading you do outside of work, a reading that would be on the side of a simple pleasure?

J.D.: For some time now, I have experienced as a real misfortune the fact that I am less and less able to read without that reading getting involved in a writing project, thus a selective, filtering, preoccupied, and preoccupying reading. When I read, it is in short spurts and most often when I am in the middle of writing, of grafting the writing onto what I read. But as for reading in large, welcoming waves, I feel myself more and more deprived of it. It is a real deprivation.

Q.: Do you not have certain "fetish" books, even old ones? Or genres: poetry, novels, fiction, theater?

J.D.: There are the texts on which I have worked. I don't have any secret corners, authors or texts that I haven't talked about, which would remain in a kind of attic. No, that's not altogether true, but there are such limits...

Q.: I will ask the question again in terms of writing. You spoke in *Le Nouvel Observateur* about "the book to be written, but that I will not write."

J.D.: That was simply a kind of exorcism [*conjuration*]. I wanted to cut things off. She said to me: "Are you going to write it one day?" I was not going to respond: yes, I hope so. So I said no.

It's probable that I will not write it, but I have not given up. The desire to write it is not yet altogether dead. Everything I read—to link up with your two questions—whether it be philosophy, literature (but I also read sacred texts, ethnology, social science, psychoanalysis), everything I read is directly or indirectly oriented, worked over, attracted by the idea of this book. I have only one idea for a book, I have only one project. What has been published in the form of collections of texts, or *Glas* or *The Post Card*, even these two books, was not conceived at the outset as a book. As for a book project, I have only one, the one I will not write, but that guides, attracts, seduces everything I read. Everything I read is either forgotten or else stored up in view of this book.

Q.: That gives me the urge to speculate. Joyce was supposed to want to write the "book of the day," and after his death everyone wondered what he would have written, what the "book of the day" would have been.

J.D.: One of the many differences is that he wrote a lot. I don't; I take notes; there are periods when I have writing compulsions around this book, and then for long periods, nothing.

Q.: Would it take the form of a poem, of fiction?

J.D.: It would be at least a crossing of multiple genres. I am looking for a form that would not be a genre and that would permit me to accumulate and to mobilize a very large number of styles, genres, languages, levels... That's why it is not getting written.

Q.: A moment ago you were speaking of the way in which pain came across, even in your interview. I was wondering if what came across and undid philosophical closure, or what caused the mastery and the neutrality of the utterance to tremble, was not a certain relation to loss, which philosophy usually avoids? I was thinking that the palpitation of the subjective in your texts and in your interview was linked, perhaps, to some loss which you do not simply avoid, but which you turn into a very complex economy, at once a work of mourning and of non-mourning. There were an enormous number of stones and steles, unsealed or not, in your interview. Does not the dream of the book to be written, but that you would not write or have not yet written, have some relation to this? It would be as if, in a certain way, you knew the place that would allow you to write it, as if you had found it, and at the same time it were lost to you.

J.D.: What you say is very true. You put very well everything I try to say, so I will not try to respond. In what you say, which is true, which is pertinent and apt, I will pick up on the word *loss*: as if, you said, all of this were moving ahead in mourning, in the feeling or the experience of loss. I rarely speak of loss, just as I rarely speak of lack, because these are words that belong to the code of negativity, which is not mine, which I would prefer not to be mine. I don't believe desire has an essential relation to lack. I believe desire is affirmation, and consequently that mourning itself is affirmation as well; I would accept more readily to say that my writing is bereaved [*endeuillée*], or a writing of semi-mourning, without intending that to mean loss.

Nevertheless, if there were an experience of loss at the heart of all this, the only loss for which I could never be consoled and that brings together all the others, I would call it loss of memory. The suffering at the origin of writing for me is the suffering from the loss of memory, not only forgetting or amnesia, but the effacement of traces. I would not need to write otherwise; my writing is not in the first place a philosophical writing or that of an artist, even if, in certain cases, it might look like that or take over from these other kinds of writing. My first desire is not to produce a philosophical work or a work of art: it is to preserve memory. Let's imagine a kind of machine, which by definition is an impossible one, that would be like a machine for ingrammatizing [*engrammer*] everything that happens and such that the smallest thoughts, the smallest move- ments of the body, the least traces of desire, the ray of sunlight, the encounter with someone, a phrase heard in passing, are inscribed somewhere; imagine that a general electroencephalocardiosomato- psychogram were possible: at that moment my desire would be absolutely fulfilled—and finitude accepted (and by the same token denied). Thus, what pains me, over and above all the other possible kinds of suffering, is the fact that things get lost. That's not all. As for interior discourse, interior monologue, interior thinking, my misfortune is that between what goes on in my head at every mo- ment, which can take all possible forms and sometimes discursive forms that are quite elaborated, and what remains when I write, there is no relation or a relation that is so indirect and distorted that the suffering comes out there. What we do, think, speak, say is incommensurably richer and finer, more pertinent and inventive than anything we can inscribe with our typewriters, tape recorders, papers, in books, interviews, and elsewhere. It is there that I have the feeling of loss; I struggle against this loss, this loss of memory; in that case, I would accept to speak of loss, of a loss without return.

Q.: One might think that the tape recorder restores, repeats things, but obviously all of the person is not there.

J.D.: It's a little speck of repetition. When I say: "I love repeti- tion," I am lamenting the impossibility of repeating. I would like to repeat all the time, to repeat everything, which is affirmation. It is even the Nietzschean sense of affirmation: to be able to repeat what one loves, to be able to live in such a way that at every moment one may say, "I would like to relive this eternally." As for me, and in this I am fortunate, I do not have any negative experience in this sense; everything that I live, or perhaps almost everything, a good portion of what I live, is such that I would be capable of wishing it to start over again eternally. This is an affirmative desire in the sense in which Nietzsche defined the eternal return in its relation to desire: let everything return eternally. I have the feeling there is loss when I know that things don't repeat and that the repetition I love is not possible; this is what I call loss of memory, the loss of repetition, not repetition in the mechanical sense of the term, but of resurrection, resuscitation, regeneration. So I write in order to keep. But keeping is not a dull and dead archiving. It is at bottom a question of infinite memories, of limitless memories which would not necessarily be a philosophical or literary work, simply a great repetition. What I admire in the philosophers, what interests me most in others, finally, is that they try to construct the most *economical* machines for repeating. They place themselves at that point of the discourse where one has the greatest mastery over it, over discourse as an act of memory, of all memory in advance, which permits the formalization in an economical manner of the maximum of things to be said and thought. In this sense, for me, the philosopher is above all a guardian of memory: someone who asks himself questions about truth, Being, language, *in order to keep*, between truth and keeping. You must have read the texts in which Heidegger speaks of truth as keeping; truth is what allows for keeping, self-keeping. In this sense, the philosopher is a guardian, in the noblest sense of the term: not just a guardian of the institution, or a watchdog, but the guardian of truth, the guardian of what keeps or guards itself, the desire to keep.

Q.: Perhaps in keeping, the philosopher keeps keeping, but what does he keep?

J.D.: He keeps keeping, which is to say he keeps nothing at all. Truth as non-truth, Heidegger also says. But the philosopher is someone who, having thought about keeping, says: one must first of all keep keeping if one wants to keep something. Afterwards he ends up with "nothing," but he has said keeping, he has thought keeping, he has thought memory. I prefer "keeping" [*garde*] to "memory" because the latter is a somewhat psychologizing, subjective definition of this dimension of keeping which is much more than memory.

Q.: One could imagine that this very desire causes one to run endlessly the greatest risk of loss, for wishing to keep...

J.D.: Of course, the keeping of keeping doesn't keep anything.

Q.: That's it.

J.D.: It is at once an extremely protected, protective, protectionist attitude and the most threatened, exposed attitude: forgetting itself. In the register of the interview, of confiding or confessing personal things, let us say that I have a huge desire to keep, and yet I am seriously amnesic. I am at the same time astonished by my capacity for forgetting, the facility with which I forget. It frightens even me. These are not incompatible.

Q.: I had a question that goes in this direction. It concerned the mortal risk that must be conjured away (you spoke of it in *Le Nouvel Observateur* and elsewhere), the risk of partition—within oneself, or between self and the other in the self, or between self and the other outside the self. Is not partition or division, in a certain fashion, fundamental for you, and doesn't it entail in part that relation of voluntary indecision that you seem to maintain with the objects of your thought, and perhaps with "reality" in general? I was also thinking of the musical score [*partition*] which you likewise spoke about, but precisely under the stamp of division. My question about the destiny of the voice came from there; it was like a music without support or, perhaps, I said to myself, a music that hesitated between the support of the page and that of the body, if one can divide them thus; this is what you were talking about with your dream of keeping.

My question bears on the decision, if that's what it is, of indecision, the position of scrupulous indecision.

J.D.: There is no such thing as voluntary indecision, calculated indecision; there is no deciding strategy of indecision. Indecision happens. One grapples with indecision. If it were nothing but a calculation, it would be a sinister tactic. As for division, it has two meanings for me. The meaning of division itself divides. On the one hand, it is fate, seen in its painful aspect: the inability to bring together in the one. It is necessity, inevitable. In this sense, it is what exposes to dissociation, to dehiscence; and at the same time, on the other hand, in another meaning, division can also be a line of strategy, a profound movement of keeping itself. From the moment one divides oneself, one keeps something always in reserve, one doesn't expose oneself all at once to the threat. There is always another place, there is not just one side, just one place; there are always several places, and this differentiation is a protection, a strategy of the living. This is not a little calculation, it's a strategy of desire which divides itself in order to keep something in reserve: I remain free, I am not just there, you will see that I am also elsewhere, and thus that I have resources, I still have a reserve, some life, and that you will not kill me off so quickly. From this point of view, division, inasmuch as it is a structural phenomenon of the living, which can live only by dividing itself *up to a certain point* (death is also a division, a dissociation), a certain type of division of the living is at once exposure to suffering, but also a measure taken to save and to keep, a kind of reserve or holding back. The theme of divisibility and indecision, of undecidability, happens to have the greatest theoretical and philosophical effectiveness right now in every domain. Questions always come back to this one, to the question of the divisibility of the letter, the divisibility of the signifier, to the theorem of the undecidable. This is not a manipulation, at least not by me, in view of producing a paralysis or of guaranteeing oneself a mastery. It is from the moment one surrenders to the necessity of divisibility and the undecidable that the question of decision can be posed; and the question of knowing what deciding, affirming—which is to say, also deciding—mean. A decision that would be taken otherwise than on the border of this undecidable would not be a decision. Thus the gravest decision—the Wager, the Sacrifice of Isaac—the great decisions that must be taken and must be affirmed are taken and affirmed in this relation to the undecidable itself; at the very moment in which they are no longer possible, they become possible. These are the only decisions possible: impossible ones. Think here of Kierkegaard. The only decision possible is the impossible decision. It is when it is not possible to *know* what must be done, when knowledge is not and cannot be determining that a decision is possible as such. Otherwise the decision is an application: one knows what has to be done, it's clear, there is no more decision possible; what one has here is an effect, an application, a programming.

Q.: Does something somewhere limit indecision in the real or in the reading of the real? When you say: there is something that would be a great decision, an impossible decision, and that at that moment one must take...

J.D.: It is taken. I would not say it is a free subject who takes it, I would not say it is the greatest freedom in that case which decides: it is decided at that moment, at that moment the great symptom appears. Imagine the following scene: Someone says, "I don't know if I am going to do this or that, I will never manage to decide if it is better to do this or that." This scene betrays decision. Or else, for example, I can't decide whether or not I am going to do this interview, or while I'm doing it, at each moment, I don't know if I want to answer, if I should go in this direction or that. After an hour's hesitation, a certain truth appears: Here is someone who is constituted in such a way that he can't manage to decide, and who finally decides. He lets himself decide to do this while he is in indecision. Where did all this get decided? I don't know, but it was decided in the tensest possible relation with the impossibility of deciding. It's like the photograph of someone who says: don't take my picture; and then one has the picture of someone who puts his hand in front of his face and says: don't take my picture. It is the truest photograph.

Q.: Your style, your way of writing, and concepts such as that of the undecidable, which are a manner of describing this performance, all manifest a particular relation to truth or to the absence of truth: if one doesn't decide, one also decides. I was thinking of what you say about the "come"; this is not just any utterance but one that appeals to another or to some other, that is struck with indecision, even "total" indecision; not only the tone is undecided, but the coming itself is likewise, the question of to whom it is addressed is undecided.

J.D.: To remain undecided means to turn oneself over to the decision of the other. There has to be decision, as I was saying a moment ago: don't take my picture. This means that in front of me there is another, with his or her camera and look, and who is going to see or to say the truth, or fix it as one says in photography. *To make* the truth. Indecision, from this point of view, is in fact being unable to decide as a free subject, "me," free consciousness, and thus to be paralyzed, but first of all because one turns the decision over to the other: what has to be decided comes back, belongs to the other. In the case of Abraham, it is effectively God who decides. That doesn't mean that Abraham does nothing; he does everything that has to be done, but he knows in a certain sense that he is obeying the Other; it is the Other who will decide what "come" means; that is where the response is.

Q.: This "come" that comes back incessantly is somewhat like the image of what you were describing a moment ago as at the same time a desire to keep and an impossible keeping. What about this "coming back" of the "come"?

J.D.: The keeping is always confided to the other; one cannot keep oneself. When one writes, one accumulates as much as possible a certain reserve, a treasury of traces, whatever they may be, whatever they're worth; but for them to be more safely protected or guarded, one confides them to the other. If one writes them, if one puts them on tape or on paper, or simply in the memory of others, it's because one cannot keep oneself. The keeping can only be confided to the other. And if one wants to keep everything in oneself, at that moment it is death, poisoning, intoxication, turgidity. To keep means to give, to confide: to the other.

Q.: Concerning this "come," you say in your interview and in "Of an Apocalyptic Tone" that, in a certain way, it is an utterance anterior to any order and any desire, as if the moment of utterance were altogether lost or so ancient that it would date from elsewhere or before life; in a certain way, it was almost pointing toward nothingness or death.

J.D.: When I said anterior to any desire, I meant less "anterior" to any order or any desire in itself—since it is at once an order and a desire, a demand, etc.—than "anterior" to all logical and grammatical *categories* of order, of desire as these have come to be determined in Western grammar or logic and which permit us to say: "come" is an imperative, thus "come" is an order. It is anterior to these categories that have been fixed since the origin of the Greco-Latin thought and grammar in which we think. "Come" resists this categorization. This does not mean it is foreign to desire or to order; it is desire, order, injunction, demand, need, but these are categories, derived conceptual oppositions without pertinence as regards the "come."

Q.: You say that it is the word of the end [*la fin*] or of the end of the end, but it is also, in "Of an Apocalyptic Tone," the word of *hunger* [*la* faim].

J.D.: From the moment one is no longer satisfied with the now classic distinction between desire and need, one can say that it is also the expression of hunger.

Q.: That is what set the tone, however undecided it may be, in your interview; ... I saw a tragic dimension appear in certain of your texts.

J.D.: It is there... said he with a laugh.

Q.: In the question of decision and indecision, there is obviously also that of the break [*la coupure*]. Beyond a certain conceptual work you are doing on the break, a certain double but divided position that you affirm with regard to a form of non-break seems to me to be a fundamental one, not only a conceptual but an ethical position, not only ethical... I am thinking of all you have said about fidelity, fidelity to what you have loved, and that you love having loved, the whole relation you point to with tradition, even if it gets divided, that kind of fidelity or faith [*fiance*] you affirm at many different moments as regards something with which you would not break, even if you have a divided relation to it, or as you say, a relation of "filial lack of piety." This fidelity to the other, or to yourself, isn't it at the same time a position of fidelity in a certain mourning where memory and forgetfulness are combined? This is no doubt the source of a very great strength that I would not know how to qualify: should one call it moral strength? Doubtless another term would be necessary. Paradoxically, this perhaps makes possible your very controlled and decided relation to division and to indecision, even if, as you said, indecision is not some vulgar strategy.

J.D.: What is the most decided, the most firmly decided is the decision to maintain the greatest possible tension between the two poles of the contradiction. This is an affirmation of fidelity that runs throughout the interview along with the contrary: the archaic and the brand-new, faithfulness and filial lack of piety, responsibility and carefreeness; I imagine one could do a caricature of these double affirmations that come back all the time.

Q.: For example, when you say that you find yourself "on a margin that is not indeterminate"...

J.D.: What is the most decided is the will not to give up one or the other, either fidelity or a certain infidelity, either a certain responsibility or a certain carefreeness.

Q.: In this latter sense, indecision would be the most precise trait of a kind of economy. Most of the time you work on possible economies, with their losses and gains; indecision would allow a balance of loss and gain.

J.D.: There is no balance, there are two stances each one just as mad as the other; each one separately is a kind of madness, a death, and thus the frenetic desire I affirm is to renounce neither one nor the other, because each of them by itself is mortal. Pure and simple fidelity is death, and so is infidelity. So it is a matter of affirming the most tense, most intense difference possible between the two extremes. Is it then a matter of mourning? Is fidelity mourning? It is also the contrary: the faithful one is someone who is in mourning.

Mourning is an interiorization of the dead other, but it is also the contrary. Hence the impossibility of completing one's mourning and even the will not to mourn are also forms of fidelity. If to mourn and not to mourn are two forms of fidelity and two forms of infidelity, the only thing remaining—and this is where I speak of semi-mourning—is an experience between the two. I cannot complete my mourning for everything I lose, because I want to keep it, and at the same time, what I do best is to mourn, is to lose it, because by mourning, I keep it inside me. And it is this terrible logic of mourning that I talk about all the time, that I am concerned with all the time, whether in "Fors" or in *Glas*, this terrible fatality of mourning: semi-mourning or double mourning. The psychoanalytic discourse, despite its subtlety and necessity, does not go into this fatality, this necessity: the double constraint of mourning.

Q.: At the same time, all of this can only be uttered in the music of love, because it is obvious that the questions of fidelity, of mourning, of non-mourning are thought only in a relation of love. One could imagine that someone is in a hate relation, a relation of affirmed rejection, and so forth.

J.D.: I let drop this sentence, which really was not calculated: "I always love what I have loved." This is a childishly simple sentence and yet it is one of the things I have the least trouble subscribing to. I have this fortunate nature that dictates that at no moment in my life—including the worst things I have lived through—have I wanted to say: I would prefer not to have lived this; in this sense, I am always reaffirming, always repeating. So when I say, "I love what I have loved," it is not only this or that thing or person, but rather: I love love, if one can say that, I love every experience I have had, and it's true, I want to keep everything. That is my good fortune. And yet I very rarely have the feeling in the present of being happy, of loving simply what I am living, but in the past everything seems to have been loved, and to have to be reaffirmed.

Q.: What a great chance that is, both a great misfortune and great good fortune.

J.D.: I don't know if we are going to leave all of this in.

Q.: Because you retract it?

J.D.: No, I don't retract it, but it is said in a particularly exposed and naive manner. We'll see...

Q.: I had other circumstantial questions concerning your present commitment, your engagement—willingly or not so willingly—with reality, with the Collège International de Philosophie. Since Prague, you have become a public person, the interviews have accumulated, there is a chain reaction. Does this engagement with "reality" or this "real" engagement coincide with the phenomenon of your appearance on the social scene? Is there a form of engagement you have truly wanted? What is your relation to this?

J.D.: I don't know what you mean by "wanted" here. If you mean calculated, decided at some moment, I would say no. You mentioned first "Prague": yes, the first time my name was seen on the front page of the newspapers was when I was imprisoned, that is, when I was as passive as it is possible to be. If anything is uncalculated apparently, it is that, although I may have calculated a certain carelessness. When I returned from Prague, in the early morning, a journalist said to me on the train platform: "But really, after what happened in Poland ten days ago, weren't you throwing yourself into the lion's den by going to Prague?" I replied: perhaps. It was particularly foolhardy on my part at that time, and perhaps in a completely unconscious fashion I did seek out what happened, it's not impossible. In any case, it was the result of a preceding history, which dictated that at that moment, and for reasons that would take a long time to analyze (an academic, political trajectory, a general political situation, and so forth), I found myself pushed into that place without ever having taken much initiative. To save the time of the analysis that we cannot take up again here, let's say that I am not at all at ease in this character, on this stage, with these interviews. Having done what I thought had to be done for "ethico-political reasons," on this stage, as quickly as possible, my desire is to retire in order to continue to do what I have done up till now: to write in obscurity, from a certain retreat.

Q.: You said that what you liked was to talk...

J.D.: As I have been doing for a long time in my teaching, or otherwise. Even if I continue to speak of the institution, I prefer to do it in my own way, from a certain place of thinking; but as for institutional "practice," I feel very ill at ease there, even if I consider it indispensable in order to be consistent with what I write.

Q.: You are recognizable, but one may wonder who one recognizes in you.

J.D.: I have never been more dissimulated, more eclipsed, more marginalized than I am now despite appearances. In any case that is my feeling.

Q.: Your interviews are read passively because they pass by way of the journalistic media. But what about the reading of your books? Who reads philosophy today?

J.D.: In certain cases, the interviews may orient someone toward a reading of the books. For the greatest majority, however, they "take the place of"; an image is constructed that gets along very well without texts, without books. And I find that worrisome.

Q.: A question appended to the question on the reading of philosophy and that comes back to a more personal terrain: Does a book like *The Post Card* modify the type of addressee? I don't know if you're the one who can answer that. There is explicitly some present-absent woman—and for what reason?—in this text and in others. This is once again the question of the address. I am thinking of Beaumarchais, who says in his prefaces that he writes his plays for women; you, on the contrary, state your hesitation about the address. Is there not a privilege given or an attention paid in a general manner to the feminine interlocutor, or to the feminine-in-the-masculine interlocutor? And would this be a question and an effect of history or of story?

J.D.: I cannot give an elaborated or certain response. The only response passes by way of the texts. In *The Post Card*, in *Spurs*, the so-called women question is no doubt posed, you are right. *Women* is even the title given to *Spurs* on the back cover...

Q.: On the level of the public, would the reception modify what is traditionally called the philosophical field?

J.D.: I'm not aware of it. That the receptivity to my text is probably greater from the "feminine" side, what does that mean? How is that to be interpreted? What does that say about my texts?

Q.: One more question about "filiation": On the one hand, you describe yourself in a relation of filiation, of respect with regard to "symbolic fathers," even if that is a strategic matter, but on the other hand you have other types of address. I had the feeling that you address questions or appeals more than you transmit messages, the latter being more consistent with the symbolic notion of the Father (I am thinking of figures like Lacan); I was thinking that you create around yourself a network that is more one of affinity or attraction (in response perhaps to the "come"), than of affiliation.

J.D.: Perhaps...

Voice II

Cassis, October 31, 1982

Dear Jacques Derrida—

In a recent interview, in a discussion on sexual difference, you let yourself be carried off by a dream of a different relationship to the other, to others, and you write:

> This double dissymmetry perhaps goes beyond known or coded marks, beyond the grammar and spelling, shall we say (metaphorically), of sexuality. This indeed revives the following question: what if we were to reach, what if we were to approach here (for one does not arrive at this as one would at a determined location) the area of a relationship to the other where the code of sexual marks would no longer be discriminating? The relationship would not be a-sexual, far from it, but would be sexual otherwise: beyond the binary difference that governs the decorum of all codes, beyond the opposition feminine/masculine, beyond bisexuality as well, beyond homosexuality and heterosexuality which come to the same thing. As I dream of saving the chance that this question offers I would like to believe in the multiplicity of sexually marked voices. I would like to believe in the masses, this indeterminable number of blended voices, this mobile of non-identified sexual marks whose choreography can carry, divide, multiply the body of each "individual," whether he be classified as "man" or as "woman" according to the criteria of usage. Of course, it is not impossible that desire for a sexuality without number can still

protect us, like a dream, from an implacable destiny which immures everything for life in the number 2. And should this merciless closure arrest desire at the wall of opposition, we would struggle in vain: there will never be but two sexes, neither one more nor one less. Tragedy would leave this strange sense, a contingent one finally, that we must affirm and learn to love instead of dreaming of the innumerable. Yes, perhaps; why not? But where would the dream of the innumerable come from, if it is indeed a dream? Does the dream itself not prove that what is dreamt of must be there in order for it to provide the dream?[1]

Where do these voices traverse? In what region which cannot be reduced to a precise locus? Of what kind of voices is it a question? Do they have "attachments" to some specific point? Are they voices of identifiable people or are they unidentifiable? of a multiplicity of "men" or "women" one carries within oneself, one's father, mother, son, daughter, all of whom have to be thought outside of a social role, of course, and other *he's* and *she's*, known or unknown with whom one is in dialogue and who dialogue in each of us. Does this dialogue take place with the other, with the other of the other or of others toward a displacement of what you call the number 2, or is it the result of it?—Are these voices linked to pulsions? Would it limit their multiplicity if one advanced the hypothesis of a difference, of differences in libidinal economies which would be, for lack of better things, qualified by traditional adjectives, "masculine," "feminine"—adjectives which, at the limit, one should be able to replace with other qualifiers, color adjectives for example. These two economies would be defined in the following way: the masculine would be marked by traits of reserve, of retention, of reappropriation, of organization, of centralization and the feminine by overflowing, overabundance, spending, a relation to loss which would be more often positive than negative. These qualifiers do not refer in an exclusive way to one or the other of the sexes but today, for cultural and political reasons, one would tend to find a libidinal economy said to be feminine more easily in a woman because a man, if he does not accept the phallic contract for his entry into society, runs the risk of effacement, death, and castration.

How does this multiplicity of voices which traverse a singular being inscribe itself on the level of artistic practices? How can one write so that there will not be an I that triumphs and that it be the one which signs with its proper name? The organization of the artistic "book," would it be modified by these voices? It would no longer be possible to enclose them in a "book" and the text, as a weave of voices, would be sustained by different rhythms, tones, breaths which ebb and flow. These voices would not be enclosed in a system or logic, nor in a theory, yet they would modify the discourse you chose, the discourse of philosophy, the most strongly marked as masculine.

But we still flounder in the old, in phallocentric binaries or in their different inversions. Almost the totality of writing is based on the phantasm of castration, a problem you yourself addressed and displaced in many of your texts. How would these multiple voices of which you dream displace these phantasms? What would be the relation between those multiple voices, the law (of castration) and artistic inscription?—

You speak of an implacable destiny of the number 2 and you desire a dissymmetry in every relation to the other, against "democratic equality." The figure 2, in our culture, that is 1 + 1, or rather 1 against 1. Would it be possible to approach that number otherwise, from the "feminine" border, by thinking the feminine as double (metaphorically), as habitable, as being able to contain and to be contained at once, in an endless process of birth, hence as being able to think the other, to feel and not just to see the other and to have a relation to other(s) different from "man." To "woman," this time sexually marked, things happen from the inside, a child for example, whereas to "man" they always happen from the outside. "Woman" therefore would have a relation to inside and outside (and to others) different from "man." This double feminine, of feminine voices, could introduce a dissymmetry in any relation which would not come back to a closed binary opposition but which would let the other(s) enter and leave in infinite play. This is not to fall into the trap of biology, because the body is in any case a ciphered body and we attempt here to raise the question of the traces of these libidinal economies in artistic practices.

Without waking you from your dream of a multiplicity of voices—to which one should add of course that of timbre, rhythm, tone, etc.—one could say that those qualifiers about which I spoke to you, "masculine" and "feminine," should at the limit disappear. Then, "man" would no longer repress his libidinal economy said to be "feminine." But we are far from it and in these times of transformation which engage each being in her or his singularity in a daily endeavor of questioning, negotiating, etc., rather than simply bypassing, or discarding "femininity" as a masculine construct, should one not at least give woman a chance to speak herself, to write herself from *her* border before acceding to a beyond?

There are myriads of colors in your texts and many tonal variations. You glide from a more "masculine" position to 2 + n and beyond... ? Is it the feminine voices in you, outside of you that provoke the shifts in strategy from the cavalier in spurs to the dreamer of multiplicities not coded by two, a shift away from a masculine position? All this, of course, without your ever occupying a feminine position which, in any event, you are unable to assume. Is it possible to avoid speaking from one's border? Especially in an organized society?—In spite of this multiplicity of voices, is it not always the signature of a sexually marked body that triumphs? Yet the displacement toward the other, toward different sexual relations, should not, at the level of thought, enclose itself, in the system, the ready-made answer, the recipe; it should be pursued in multiple voices, in ever-changing dialogues even if, today, for political reasons a certain binarism to be displaced (and which displaces itself) between masculine and feminine cannot yet be totally absent...

V.

December 25, 1982

Dear Verena,

How difficult your questions are, and how they are necessary but impossible! I shall try to answer your letter, but would it not have been better to *speak* about all this? And to speak of our voice, of our voices, since in sum that is the topic you have chosen for us?

I am going to begin by taking up your words. Forgive me if, too often, I not only seem to take up your words but take you at your word (and how are you going to translate this? and why, in this exchange, are you yourself the translator? I leave the question aside). If I take you at your word, it is not in order to harry you or to inculpate you but, on the contrary, in order to hear you better, to answer you, to avoid losing myself (the risk and temptation are great) and to follow you to the letter. So I'll take up your word: yes, where do these voices "traverse"? Right here, in this exchange, it would be hard to tell. But I do not know whether the question must be asked. I do not know whether these voices must *pass through*, *across*, or *in* some space that pre-exists them, commands them, borders or supports them. And even if it lets them pass, such a space would still threaten to submit them to its law.

No doubt this is inevitable. In order to think this fatality, in order to think it otherwise, we should perhaps not rely too much on names commonly attributed to that "space." It may not be a space, a locus, even a "region," but a strange force of dislocation. Even if, as you say, these "regions" may not be reduced to a precise locus, there remains the risk of surrendering to this topological injunction which you reject at the same time. Not that it be formidable or avoidable as such. But it is often translated into a language overloaded with confused presuppositions fraught with slogans. Are we dealing with "regions" of the body? But what do we think in the name of the "body" when we wish to remove the word from the whole system of oppositions that determines it? When we try to think or listen to voice without any presuppositions, whether it be of philosophy, of "objective" science, or of everyday language, when we try to speak or to hear voice without reference to a fixed place in an objective topology and without "attachments" (once again, I take up your word). A voice detaches itself, that is its way of "attaching itself." In any case, if there is any "locus" where the figure of connection (attachment/detachment, binding/unbinding) no longer offers the least security, then surely it is atopical voice, this madness of the voice.

Instead of exchanging arguments through the mail, we should listen-demonstrate this by way of song. The vocal operation of which I speak is also opera.

Nowadays, some technical devices offer us the occasion to witness this demonstration: the telephone, the radio, the record, and so forth. In general, telephony is the scene of "detachment" of which I just spoke with you. A voice may detach itself from the body, from the very first instant it may cease to belong to it. By which it traces, it is a trace, a spacing, a writing, but neither a simple presence nor a dispersion of meaning. It is part of the body but because it traverses the body, because it disposes of it, it retains almost nothing of it, it comes from elsewhere and goes elsewhere, and in passing it may give to this body a locus but does not depend upon it, that is, for example, it does not depend on it insofar as "its own place" is sexually determined. "Sexually determined" is to be understood here according to dominant criteria. Voice can betray the body to which it is lent, it can make it ventriloquize as if the body were no longer anything more than the actor or the double of another voice, of the voice of the other, even of an innumerable, incalculable polyphony. A voice may give birth—there you are, voilà—to another body.

But why are we talking about voices at such great length when our subject is sexual difference?

Perhaps because where there is voice, sex becomes undecided. From this "there" where there is voice, we will be able to speak of the unheard—the very old and the very new—only if we come back, revenons as we say in French (but how are you going to translate this into your language? You see, for me translation between languages or between sexes is just about the same thing: both very simple and impossible in any rigorous way, once given over to chance. It is, in fact, the only occasion, the occasion of the oeuvre) if we come back from all that knowledge and philosophy have to take for granted in voice. Neither physics, phonetics, linguistics, psychoanalysis, nor philosophy teach us anything whatsoever of this essence of voice. They just imply it, they construct "grammar" (not only the one distinguishing the active, passive, or median voices in order to fix local identities, bodies or souls, subjects, "selves")—or sexes going two by two. These grammars of nautical surveillance [*arraisonnement*] could be uncovered everywhere—in the social, political, economic, judicial, sexual, logical, or linguistic registers. To oversee or watch over a vessel, at least according to maritime lexicons, is to request a declaration of identity or of appurtenance, in sum, to stop in order to ask: under what flag are you sailing? Everywhere from then on a voice, voices, or vocal differences would be subjected to a system of oppositions destined to machinery; the polyphony which vibrates in each timbre is assigned to one of the marks of the same and very limited binary code.

In order to be exposed to the braided polyphony which is coiled up in every voice, perhaps we must come back to a vocal *difference* rebellious to any *opposition* and which is not derived from anything else: it belongs to no one, it carries spacing and does not let any space be assigned to it. As organ or signifying power, it cannot remain at the disposal of either a person or a self, either a consciousness or an unconscious, either one of the two sexes. Even bisexuality is insufficient for it. Nor does it "express" a community, if we mean by that a totality of subjects, a "we," a collection of *egos*, men or women ("we men," "we women"). This writing of voice represents nothing, it is not the representative of a "drive," a "word," or a "thing." This voice lets itself be heard, and it speaks otherwise, watching out for all these violent assignations, of which there are always more to come.

Assignations: this word rings in its tongue, in its idiom, very close to *assignation à résidence* [house arrest], to a judicial assignation, or more coyly, according to an artifice probably still more difficult to translate, to the regime of signification as if "to assign" meant to assign to a subject, to the *law of the sign*, of the signifier or the signified.

Despite a certain appearance, this should not lead to a kind of hypostasis of VOICE: anonymous and asexual, having come from nowhere. Provided that one hears this well. To the contrary, it is the brutality of assignation which multiplies hypostases in order to oppose vocal difference, to turn difference into opposition, into an opposition without multiplicity, lacking internal spacing, or bearing the very homogeneity of a dialectic.

I do not know what this vocal difference is made of (timbre, tone, accent?), nor even if it must be "liberated." In its widely accepted usage, the lexicon of liberation still belongs to the so-called political register dominated by values of "person," "self," even of the "body" as referential identity: what we must have nearest to us, we assume, as our most personal property, that which we must be able to keep for ourselves, intact and free (for, as one says, "my body belongs to me," like "my desire," and so forth). Today, one often says "body" with the same degree of credulousness or dogmatism, at best with the same faith as, previously, one used to speak of "soul"—and that turns out to be or amounts to nearly the same thing.

Why don't we liberate ourselves from that very "liberation"? Why don't we turn our ears toward a call which addresses and provokes *above all else*, above and beyond whatever says "me," my "body," as a "man" or a "woman," or my sex? To turn one's ears to the other when it speaks to "whom," to "what," to this "who" which has not yet been assigned an identity or, for example, since we have to speak of it, to either one sex or the other?

Surely, and you are already telling it to me again, that what I have just suggested may seduce in order to immobilize. This "above all else" runs the risk of neutralizing. We should therefore be aware of it, be careful not to hear it as an indeterminate, empty, negative vigil, or as a kind of abstract *a priori*. I rather think of a rebellious force of affirmation. Despite all appearances, demobilization comes from systems of binary assignations. In the end, it is their order which neutralizes more convincingly: not sexual Difference with a capital D which is always determined as duality and which they—those systems—drag into a dialectic, but sexual differences in the plural. It could be demonstrated, as I had attempted, for example, in *Glas*. It would need time, attention to minute details, a thousand protocols, and certainly much more than a letter.

In order to speak, in a letter, about this innumerable sexuality in open series, I prefer to speak, as you do, of the "colors" of the voice. And there would still be more sexes than colors.

But somebody all ready to take us at our word might mutter an objection to *colors*. My God, you're talking through your hat, my *eye*, a lure, sure, like a snake swallower, you'll try to make us gobble up anything (how are you going to translate *couleuvre à avaler*, Verena?). With these spectrums, with these variations which would no longer even be variations on a theme (this is the objection speaking), would you not rather try to loosen the terrible constraint of the 1/2, the fatality of which would still watch over your revelry or over your unbridled denegation?

No doubt, I would answer. I do not doubt for one instant that this surveillance is relentless and ends up by overdetermining everything.

Yes, yes, but—is it not enough to *think* this law which is the very Law, in order to have, not its proof, but the precarious announcement of its limit and of its sterility with regard to what desires in me and which keeps this *thought* awake? An announcement is essentially threatened, and risked, an announcement of the improbable and with regard to that which, desiring in me, may no longer even be *my* desire. We can no longer be sure here of the very word *desire*. Suffice it to evoke that which, beyond the fatality of the 1/2, would give me pleasure, the idea of a bliss of colors; at the very limit of this distribution, of this destiny to be *divided* according to the law (*nomos, moira*), at the moment of its victory, its defeat. The very experience of this limit is a bliss greater than my bliss, it exceeds both myself and my sex, it is sublime, but without sublimation. If there is a sublime, it would be there where there might be no more sublimation, *n'est-ce pas*. And in order to be sublime, sexual difference must no longer be subject to dialectics.

There is what is announced when I write *this* for example, even if it is false. Very simply, when I *write it* and what is produced is that ecstasy that consists in thinking, in order to love it, the impossible. Even if what I am writing is false, well, the fact that I write it, I sing it according to such and such a voice, that I think I am desiring what I cannot know, the impossible, this is what comes to bear *witness*, right here, if you like, that through falsehood there must be announced what is inscribed as "false" against the "true"...

For me, that's really now the truth of sexual differance. I do not know how you are going to translate *c'est ça pour moi, maintenant, la vérité de la différance sexuelle*. And what passes from language through sexual differance, is that to be translated? Question.

When I say "for me," this does not come back to me (cf. above), certainly. At stake is nonetheless a singular writing, the idiom of an inimitable difference that is not true to a type.

Writing of the singular voice. Type, since there is inscription, *typtein*, timbre and tympanum, but without a type, that is to say, without a model, without a prescriptive form, type without "type" and without a stereotype. Why does one say a "type" for a "guy" in common French? Is there a relation?

I write here without erasure, without correcting myself, the dreamed form of my desire. So you touch on something of my truth, of mine, today, it is a style as they used to say not long ago. The style does not belong to me, it does not come back to me, it makes me come to myself from the other. Let us say that this is the sexual differance of me. I am asking you: what can be done with all that in another language?

December 30. On this day a year ago I was in prison in Prague. Naturally, during the twelve hours of examination at the customs bureau and at the police station, and then in the prison itself, there were only men. Prison will always be the last place for the sexes to mingle. But among other things, I meditated on the following: of the two sole women I met during that experience, one was a translator (the official translator during the examination) and the other was the prison nurse. As for the female customs official whom I faced at the airport, a male customs agent took her place when it was my turn and when they had to put into place—in order to "trap" me—the terrifying scenario of "drug traffic." The man, an enormous type of a guy, came out from behind a curtain, like a *deus ex machina* at the very moment I was arriving.

I am still following you, aren't I, and from colors I go on to what you say, with the very finest motives in the world, about the "cultural and political" reasons which would lead us to mark the two economies. This logic seems in fact irrefutable. But I fear that, more subtly than ever, one is putting together again an atrocious trap: the *same* system, and one is not sure if it is being inverted. The opposition would no longer be from one mark to another but that of a *determining*, masculine mark, which would be a mark insofar as it would remain on board, within its own border; and that of a non-mark, of a mark that is not marked in a certain way, the feminine: overflowing, spendthrift, generous, overabundant, and affirming over and beyond all borders. From this dissymmetry they risk (how are you going to translate this *ils* without neutralizing the masculine contraband?) drawing an argument from it once again so as to reiterate the great phallogocentered phratry: once again the elevation of woman, of a woman so originary that she is not even marked yet, that she is at the source of every "formation," she is generous and overflowing like Mother Nature, Mother Earth, the indeterminate ground that gives, loses and affirms relentlessly, without exchange, without contract...

This would still be too much and yet not enough. Terrible, really, that we still have to calculate in our discourse, still accept the rules of an endless strategy, at the very moment when we would like to lay down our arms, *when we love only (by) laying down our arms.*

So you talk about "cultural and political reasons," and so forth. By that I believe I know what you mean, that you are only making a concession, the time of this indispensable transaction with a historical conjuncture and the real state of forces present. But then, one no longer has to be only prudent. I would say rather that the greatest prudence at times dictates an unarmed, incalculable, uncalculating audacity failing to calculate its very freedom with infinitesimal differences according to the idioms of the "soul and the body," the margins, the rings, and the marks, the indiscernible variations from one instant to the next, the inflections among cultures and languages, public and private, day and night, and then the passage of seasons, the invention of myths, arts, and religions, the infinite powers of fiction, of poetry, and of irony, without ever

being able to stop, not even at the point of an accusation: relativism, empiricism, anything! These offer perhaps (perhaps) the
chance—which must remain incalculable—to divert the "contract"
of the phallogocentric terror which you just recalled. *It must leave
something to be desired.* I prefer to stop today at this sentence which
I am not sure is very intelligible but which, I am convinced,
remains untranslatable. But what can't be translated leaves something to be desired when it appears as such, and it makes us think,
which is what I like to write. And before the questions you ask of
me, that must be my only rule...

January 1, 1983... Why would you still want to call "feminine"
that which escapes that contract, and "masculine" what succumbs
to it? Masculine and feminine are not the subjects but the effects of
such a contract, the subjects produced by the law of this contract
which, besides, is not one, in any strict sense. Hence probably its
power, for it has never been signed in due form—thus it must
always be presupposed—but hence, too, its inconsistency. Masculine and feminine are not even the adverse and possibly contract-
ing parts, but rather the parts of a pseudo-whole determined by the
symbolon of this fictitious contract.

In truth, even in the logic of your tautology (I am quoting you:
"These two economies would be defined in the following way: the
masculine would be marked by traits of reserve, of retention, of
reappropriation, of organization, of centralization and the feminine by overflowing, overabundance, spending, a relation to loss
which would be more often positive than negative. These qualifiers
do not refer in an exclusive way to one or the other of the sexes but
today, for cultural and political reasons, one would tend to find a
libidinal economy said to be feminine more easily in a woman
because a man, if he does not accept the phallic contract for his
entry into society, runs the risk of effacement, death, and castration"), in this strange tautology, I follow you with difficulty.
Of what "woman" are you speaking? If you appeal to some statistical evaluations, the protocol and criteria would be very uncertain:
what does "more often positive" mean? What group of women is

in question? Where? When? To what extent? For reasons of certain structural possibilities (identification, interiorization, reversal, subjugation, metonymical appropriation, specularization, and so forth), we are as little assured of this economy that you call "feminine" in what is called "woman" as that which you call a "masculine" economy in what is meant to be called "man." The names of "woman" and of "man" which, in everyday language, retain authority between quotation marks, continue to designate all that "anatomical destiny" governs in its name. This recourse to anatomy still dominates "modern discourse," I mean the discourse riddled to death by psychoanalysis. I have attempted to show that elsewhere and cannot do it here. Phallocentrism remains an androcentrism, and the phallus adheres to the penis. Despite so many apparently subtle and sophisticated disavowals the so-called anatomical difference of the sexes makes the law, and its tyranny still passes through so many dogmas and so much ignorance! The "anatomical" thing in question is reduced to its most summary phenomenality.

More and less anatomy! That is what we need today. *Less*: we know why and you did well to recall the "traps" of biology or of the alleged objectivity of anatomy—yes, the body is a "ciphered body." *More*: the disciplines of knowledge, which nevertheless remain stammering as to this ciphered body, are no longer what they were at the moment when these axiomatics of psychoanalysis were established. They go very, very quickly. Even if it is not a question of "building" on them a discourse about sexual difference, without displacement and reinterpretation, what obscurantism there would be in ignoring current or future mutations!

In brief, you see, like the unconscious—the unconscious that I am, that I follow—I do not want to give up anything.

1. Neither what has just been said *about* sexual differences (2 + n, beyond phallogocentrism, beyond oppositional dialectics, beyond psychoanalytic philosophy when it repeats that phallogocentrism).

2. Neither a re-elaboration of what is "psychoanalytic"—in other words, no looking back in this respect.

3. Nor an attentive opening (by contrast with what is happening in the "world" of psychoanalysis) onto all new forms of knowledge

about the body," about "biology," without considering as "closed"
the so-called anatomical question...

January 3, 1983. I have already been too long, this letter is
dragging on, so I am going to speed up a little, this being another
way of saying that I will be even more aphoristic and even less
demonstrative.

· · ·

I am not sure, or as sure as you seem to be, that I have "chosen a
philosophical discourse, the most strongly marked as masculine."
On each of these words, I would try to bandy words with you, texts
in hand, but in the instance of my first essays, on the whole the
appearance proves you to be correct. And what if I invoked (a long-
term) strategy? You do the same for me right afterwards...

· · ·

I do not know whether these "multiple voices" displace "phantasms." I have always had difficulty in thinking something that is
rigorous or stable—if it needs to be done—in the name of *phantasm*. But yes—I think that I would say at least this about it: even if
the word, from the roots in ancient Greek, signals in the direction
of light, visibility, image, phenomenon, the thing cannot go without voice. No phantasm, I would say, without the possibility of
voice. So: how could these voices not "displace" phantasms? An
open question. But maybe you want to suggest that women's voices
which pass through a signed writing, or through the body of a man
or vice versa, are *nothing but* phantasms in displacement, even
phantoms (but that would be yet something else). . . . In all the
texts where voices of women are heard as such, did I ever *make*
women speak? Which ones? Those who are in me, who are outside
of me? What does *me* mean here? Or did I *let* them speak? Unless
beyond "making" and "letting" (already very different things), they
did not even ask me for my opinion, and they let me or made me
speak myself, keeping for themselves the whole initiative. . . . But
who are these *she*'s?

· · ·

Your question on "artistic inscription": too difficult. And then, I
would also have to ask as many questions in return. Why would I

be the one to answer questions asked of him "on woman"? What do you mean by "artistic inscription" in this context? There has been so much recent talk about "feminine writing": should we not have insisted on the fact that inscription, the gesture imprinting for example a form (*eidos, typos*) in a matter (typography), was often associated with a masculine power? To claim that power cannot be done without a thousand cunning, cautious protocols, foiling the maneuvers of reappropriation. How are we going to cope with all this? With a thinking of the trace which would be unscathed by this interpretation of the "type" and of the signature? How to negotiate with phallogocentric axiomatics that have dominated so long, and in such an interior manner, the concept of art and the classification of the arts?

. . .

"Habitable," the woman, you say. Without further precautions, that would still remain easy to *domesticate* for this very same dominating logic. Has he not always desired, "he," that the woman be in fact habitable, attached to values of habitation, to the hearth, to the private life, to the inside, and so forth? Old symbolics of the woman as "house". . . . And "being able to contain," is that the same as "being able to think the other"? Some would like to claim just the opposite.

. . .

"...a feminine position which, in any event, you are unable to assume..."
So you say

. . .

amitié
Jacques Derrida

TRANSLATED BY VERENA ANDERMATT CONLEY

Language (*Le Monde* on the Telephone)

Q.: Hello? Could you write an article on language for *Le Monde Dimanche*...

J.D.: Are you asking me whether *I am capable of it*, which is doubtful, or whether *I would accept* to do it? In the latter case, the question would be a request or an invitation. My interpretation will depend on intonation, on our relation at the two ends of the line, on a thousand other givens—in short, on a context which is not immediately linguistic. It is a larger and always open text that is not limited to discourse.

In the first hypothesis (are you capable of...?), the question calls for an answer that some, ever since Austin, would call *constative*. My *yes* would mean: I am indeed able to do it. I would be claiming to say in this way *what the case is*, to define, describe, state. But if the question had the value or the effect of an invitation, my *yes* would not state anything, it *would do* something, it would obligate me. My promise would produce an event that had no chance of appearing, and in fact had no meaning, before my response. The latter essentially has no longer any constative value, it is a *performative*.

Q.: Yes, okay. You remind me of Brecht, his two operas for school: *The One Who Says Yes* and *The One Who Says No*... If I play

171

your game, you could still answer *yes, but no* (yes, I am capable of it, but no I do not accept to write…), *yes, yes* or *no, no,* or *no but yes* (I am not capable of doing it, but I accept, too bad for *Le Monde*). This indispensable distinction (constative-performative) remains nevertheless rather crude, it has required some refinement that continues to make its difficulty more acute.

J.D.: Yes, performatives were first studied as strange curiosities. Now one sees them everywhere in this language that some nevertheless believed was destined to say what is or to communicate information. At stake, therefore, is the essence of language, authority, and the limits of the linguistic as such, notably in the determination of context which, as you saw, is decisive. Now, there are no certain limits on a context and no symmetry between the two *yeses*. The constative *yes* is ventriloquized by a performative *yes* (I affirm, I say that, I believe that, I think that I am…). What is more, by itself a *yes* never states anything more than a *hello*; it answers, obligates, appeals. If I now affirm, and this is no fiction, that I did not clearly understand your question and that I could not answer it unless you said more about it…

Q.: I was expecting as much: This summer *Le Monde Dimanche* is devoting a page per week to philosophy. A brave thing to do, especially during vacation. To start off this series, you would speak about language, as that is the best place to begin: nine pages of twenty-five lines each. But the majority of your readers will not be trained philosophers…

J.D.: I'm familiar with that warning. But you have to admit that it remains obscure, even cryptic. In whose name and of what readers are you speaking? What are you holding, what secret? To whom *do you want* me to address myself? For centuries now, I have been waiting for statistical arguments on this subject. Does this addressee exist? Does he or she exist *before* a reading which can also be active and determinant (in the sense that it is only then that the reader *would determine himself or herself*)? How do you construct the image and the program of these readers, selecting what they can decipher, receive, or reject? And then you assume that these "trained philosophers" have *one* particular *language*; so you wish to "talk philosophy" without having recourse to it...

Q.: Perhaps one has to accept this contradiction. The stakes of philosophy, for example language, *also* concern all those who are in no way prepared to understand the secret language in which certain philosophers indulge themselves.

J.D.: Not at all, and the sad thing is that there is more than one of them. They are not really dialects, more like relatively coded and formalized discourses (like so many others) on the basis of what are called natural languages or "ordinary language," if such a thing exists. Within the so-called philosophic community, the essential adventure has always been a (hi)story of deciphering, translation, interpretive pedagogy, the enigma of a destination. On the other hand, on the side of that which you assume to be estranged from "the" training of philosophy, there are a thousand ways to receive and to respond to a discourse that has a certain philosophic air. The variables are new and more numerous than ever. The access to philosophic writings was more or less reserved, in the past, to a limited milieu. Today, the permeability of socio-linguistic codes increases still faster than social mobility.

Education is not the only condition for these displacements, but they cannot be analyzed if one neglects the devices and the norms of the "educational system." In such a centralized country, a decision concerning the orientation of the different sections in the *lycées*, the *terminale*,[1] the school governing board, the publishing market (not just for textbooks) can in a few years completely overturn the landscape of "non-philosopher-readers-curious-about-articles-on-philosophy-in-*Le-Monde-Dimanche*." Outside of school, interfering with it, the techno-economy of information (publishing, media, information systems, telecommunication...) causes the profile of this supposedly typical reader to change faster and faster. And journalists are not in some observatory; their normative ("performative") interventions bring into play their social situation, their training, their history, and their desire.

In short, a whole machinery of filters and types for the rhetoric of discourses, its effects and affects. An enormous authority today, a terrible responsibility concerning that which dispenses with philosophy. In cases where ignorance or foolishness would be guaranteed a kind of long-term theatrical and inevitably commercial monopoly, the disaster could take on national dimensions...

Q.: One would think, listening to you, that an emergency relief plan ought to be put into effect. One could thus never know to what extent the media produce or reproduce their addressee, always needing, toward that end, to maintain the simulacrum of an addressee. But if language cannot be separated from a certain *techne* and a coded repetition, how is one to avoid these risks? That is why I was proposing that you do a preliminary article on language.

J.D.: Yes, but your decision is philosophical, it already situates language. Well, let's drop it. In any case, if I wrote this article, I would strongly underline the conditions of the thing: why such an article in *Le Monde* at this particular moment? Why me? By whose intermediary, in view of whom and of what? How does this or that framing (for example 225 lines) come to constrain each of my sentences from within?

Q.: Of course, go ahead and do it, why not? Up to now, you have indeed been speaking to me about language and it's clearer than what you usually write. I'll give you some advice: dictate your books over the telephone. Your article should stay in this register, don't go back into the isolation booth.

J.D.: You think I have been all that clear? For whom? What I have just outlined would remain quite inaccessible for a mass of readers. They would perceive its stakes only through a silhouette of meaning. I am thinking of some of those who never open *Le Monde*, and of certain readers of this newspaper who play an important and singular role in the (prescriptive) formation of a rather cultivated public, one that is open to a language with a philosophic air (but not too specialized) and, in certain conditions, to a discourse on discourse. At least in the micro-milieu that we inhabit within francophone society.

For another fraction, for whom you have assumed the role of ambassador by asking me to aim my remarks precisely in their direction, what I have just attempted would no doubt be easy, clear, but would have no interest except on the condition of being unwrapped in one fashion or another, everyone having his or her own idea on that subject and thus his or her own impatience. But it is this fraction that is already annoyed by this manner of backing up and slowing down: I should get on with it, say things instead of asking myself how to say them without saying them, in view of what, on what conditions. Doing the latter is already *too* philosophical, redundant, uneconomical, insufficiently "informative."

Q.: That's not true. And I do not confuse "high performance" (the quantity of information and knowledge contained in a given space) with the "performative," as you put it...

J.D.: Well, a minority of readers will accuse me of simplifying excessively things that are now considered trivial, such as that theory called the "pragmatics" of utterances which is evolving very quickly. I am not thinking only of philosophers or linguists, but of all those who, convinced that they would make better use of this forum, rage and speculate. But all of this remains to be carefully modulated. Never all or nothing, that is one simple thing that must be said about access to the text.

Meaning and effect are never produced or refused absolutely; they always keep a reserve at the disposition of a potential reader, a reserve that has less to do with a substantial wealth and more with an aleatory margin in the trajectories, an impossibility of saturating a context. The "same" utterance (*Could you write...?*) can refer to a large number of other "texts" (phrases, gestures, tones, situations, marks of all sorts) and to other "others" in general; it can open onto other effects, intersections, grafts, iterations, citations... These possibilities and these differential forces are not strictly linguistic, which is why I prefer to speak of traces or text rather than language, because...

Q.: Now you are starting to become hermetic. Permit me to recall...

J.D.: Me to order? Go ahead, say it. I heard the words "isolation booth" a moment ago. This is a quarrel people have been picking with philosophy for centuries. Of course, you said you were speaking in the name of the supposed reader, but it is almost always, for some unknown reason, the same vaguely aggressive demand, the dictate of a threatening desire: "So talk like everybody else, what you are saying concerns us all, you confiscate our bets and our stakes, you possess us and dispossess us, your language games are power games." These summonses are programmed, even if the catalog of arguments is adapted to each situation and to the new hands being dealt by society, technical systems, or school systems. The same accusation, moreover, rages among philosophers who are separated by language, style, tradition, implicit contracts.

Q.: Yes, but precisely, must not philosophy liberate itself from them in order to become immediately available and open to everybody?

J.D.: No text opens itself immediately to everyone. The "everybody" our censors talk about is an interlocutor determined by social situation, often that of a minority, by academic training, by the state of culture, of the media, and of publishing. The abuse of power is always on the side of the censors and "decision makers." Pedagogical talent or good intentions do not suffice: no one can reach an anonymous public, even if it were a single individual, without schools, books, and the press, and thus without the relays of a politics which is not simply governmental. And particularly without the work or the coming of the other.

Q.: Of course, that's all very obvious...

J.D.: So the question must be somewhere else: why, in fact, not ask it of the geneticist or the linguist? Why is the philosopher alone suspect and why is the subpoena served only on him? Why not allow him what is allowed to everybody, beginning with the professional journalist: the right and the duty to superimpose on his sentence the encoded memory of a problem, the formalized allusion to systems of concepts? Without this economy, he would have to redeploy at each moment an infinite pedagogy. This is impossible and paralyzing: how many lines would he need? Not that the history of philosophical language is that of the *progress* of a continuous capitalization. Thought must also interrupt it. A decisive return to the meditation on what one could term the simplest statements ("Being is," "Being is not"), on words as apparently clear as "word," "appearance," "clarity," "science," "research," "technique," "language"—such a return comes along to disturb this progressivism there where it proceeds, at times, like a self-assured sleepwalker.

Q.: Yes, but perhaps this latter movement goes precisely in the direction of a repopularization of philosophy.

J.D.: Yes and no. Sometimes the simplest is the most difficult. Popularization must not renounce rigor and analysis. I know some "professional" philosophers who are made more anxious than any lesson-givers by this double imperative: to "democratize" the exchange without compromising philosophical demands, to take into account the transformation of the social field, of the techniques of transmission and archiving, of education and the press, without giving in to easy seduction and demagogic abuse. When the norms imposed by the media demand too high a price, then silent retreat remains sometimes the most philosophical response, the well-understood strategy. But for the reasons already given, this calculation will always be a shot in the dark. Some singular utterance, whispered like a secret, can still, incalculably, over the centuries... Hello?

Q.: I was playing the devil's advocate: isn't esoterism the shelter sought by weak, commonplace thinking? People also say: usurpation of authority, instrument of terror, password for a sect or a closed club that, along with the power of interpreting—that of evaluating or legitimating—keeps for itself power in general.

J.D.: Yes, but this would not be the case only for philosophers, and competency in the usage of signs can just as easily *serve* as *thwart* these mystifications. These *two* possibilities have been inciting philosophy since the beginning. Without going back to the Sophists and to Plato, look at Descartes. He went after the sophistication of those who, having stumbled onto "something certain and obvious . . . never let it appear except wrapped in various enigmatic turns of phrase, whether because they fear the simplicity of the argument would diminish the importance of their discovery, or because they malevolently refuse to give us the truth in all its frankness (*nobis invident apertam veritatem*). . ."

Q.: So now you're speaking Latin over the telephone?

J.D.: I'm being militant: let us extend the teaching of philosophy well before the *terminale* (that is *one* of the answers to all these questions), but also the teaching of Greek and Latin. . . As to the relations between "turns of phrase" and "truth," one may have certain reservations about what Descartes, who is himself, let us remember, an obscure and difficult author, understood by that. Also, when he decided to write his *Discourse* in French, supposedly in order to address himself to everybody, he did it during a particular socio-political phase, at a moment of violent extension of state control over language. He was not speaking to everybody, but let's let that drop.

As for jealousy or envy (*invident*), he's right on target. There is a war raging for and by means of the property of language, among philosophers and between them and others. On both sides, there is also a desire for innocence. Some describe the laws of war, others appeal to laws and to the rules of the game. Some demand a general and immediate disarmament; others, weighing the risks, want it to be progressive and controlled. Kant, who spoke of an "imminent conclusion of a treaty of perpetual peace in philosophy," wanted also to democratize discourse, denounce crypto-politics and mystagogy. Nietzsche analyzes the politics of philosophical language, its relation to the State, to the process of democratization, to the power of priests and interpreters in the teaching institution and in the press. Already Marx in *The German Ideology*, and still closer to us, despite a very different situation...

Q.: Yes, but that would take too long. In a few words, if you had to write this article, what would you emphasize, today, now? If, instead of calling you on the phone, I placed a microphone in front of you: What direction is being taken by research on language?

J.D.: Thought does not always have the form of what is called "research," with its institutions and its programmed productivity. In any case, I would hazard this answer, in three words and six points: across the dividing walls (national languages, institutions, theoretical traditions and codes, philosophy, linguistics, psycho-analysis, literature, communications and translation technology), most questions, it seems to me, crowd around that "pragmatics" we were speaking about a moment ago. Not necessarily by this name or in the well-known forms that these problems were first ap-proached by Austin and his disciples. Besides its internal diffi-culties, which is a sign of richness, this first theorization was both served and held back by the limits of its axiomatics; it was little concerned with the history of these concepts, beginning with the distinction between production and non-production, production as creation of event and production as a bringing to light, *praxis* and *theoria*, act and speech, and so forth.

Briefly: (1) to think (speak, write) the *logos* "before" these opposi-tions, "before" voice and meaning (*phōnē, sēmainein*)—another "history of philosophy," let's read Heidegger, for example; (2) to recognize that what is called trace, text or context (and among other things, all the so-called conventional conditions of a "perfor-mative") is not limited to something linguistic or phonic, and, moreover, it is not limited to anything; (3) to put psychoanalysis to the test of "pragmatics," but first of all to remove the latter from an axiomatics of intentional consciousness and of the "self" present to itself; (4) to take account of the technology of what is called "information," before and after our technology of the telephone; (5) to keep from confusing the "performative"—its fictions and its simulacra—with the "high performance" profitability of technoscience; (6) not to run away too much from the paradoxes of alterity, the trace, destination, destinerrance or clandestination—in sum, the paradoxes of writing and of signature—I would have suggested all of that and... Hello?

Q.: Hello, I can't make you out very well...

J.D.: ... insisted on this provisional name—"pragmatics"—on what it presupposes about the text in general and that has been, let's say, "disavowed." The effects of this "disavowal" have left a powerful mark on philosophy, the philosophy of philosophical or scientific language, the institutions of research and teaching that depend on it, their interpretation of interpretation, meaning, reference, truth. The theoretical (constative) value of discourse was thus linked to efficiency, to the technical and productive performance of research.

What I rather hastily call the "disavowal" of the "performative" was not a judgment, but a tremendous event—itself performative and normative. What would happen if something happened to these norms? Upheavals difficult to calculate, I believe, in the aforementioned institutions and elsewhere. And what if that were the chance or the risk of what happens, while we are speaking about it, at this very moment...

Q.: Hello? So finally, you could write this article couldn't you?

J.D.: I don't think so. Nine pages, that's just about the time of an overseas phone call on Sunday. Listen, I'll never make it...

Q.: But look, it's almost done, yes it is, yes it is...[2]

Heidegger, the Philosophers' Hell

Q.: Your two books are appearing a few days after the book by Victor Farías[1] that vigorously recalls Heidegger's political positions and activities. What do you think of Farías's conclusions?

J.D.: Concerning the majority of the "facts," I have yet to find anything in this investigation that was not already known, and for a long time, by those who take a serious interest in Heidegger. As for the research into a certain archive, it is a good thing that its results are being made available in France. The most solid of these results were already available in Germany ever since the work of Bernd Martin and Hugo Ott, which Farías draws on extensively. Beyond certain aspects of the documentation and some factual questions, which call for caution, discussion will focus especially—and it is important that the discussion remain open—on the interpretation, let us say, that relates these "facts" to Heidegger's "text," to his "thinking." The reading proposed, if there is one, remains insufficient or questionable, at times so shoddy that one wonders if the investigator began to read Heidegger more than an hour ago. It is said that he was Heidegger's student. These things happen. When he calmly declares that Heidegger, I quote, "translates" "a certain fund of notions proper to National Socialism" into "forms and a style that, of course, are his alone,"[2] he points toward a chasm, more than one chasm, a chasm beneath each word. But he doesn't for an instant approach them and doesn't even seem to suspect they are there.

Is there anything here to cause a scandal? No, except in those places where too little interest is taken in other, more rigorous and more difficult work. I am thinking of the work of those who, especially in France, know the majority of these "facts" and these "texts," who condemn unequivocally both Heidegger's Nazism and his silence after the war, but who are also seeking to *think* beyond conventional and comfortable schemas, and precisely to *understand*. Understand what? Well, that which ensures or does not ensure an immediate passage, according to some mode or other of the aforementioned "translation," between the Nazi engagement, in whatever form, and what is most essential, acute, and sometimes most difficult in a work that continues and will continue to give cause for thinking. And for thinking about politics, I have in mind first of all the works of Lacoue-Labarthe, but also certain texts, each very different, by Levinas, Blanchot, and Nancy.

Why does this hideous archive seem so unbearable and fascinating? Precisely because no one has ever been able to reduce the whole work of Heidegger's thought to that of some Nazi ideologue. This "record" would be of little interest otherwise. For more than a half century, no rigorous philosopher has been able to avoid an "explanation" with [*explication avec*] Heidegger. How can one deny that? Why deny that so many "revolutionary," audacious, and troubling works of the twentieth century have ventured into or even committed themselves to regions that, according to a philosophy which is confident of its liberal and leftist-democratic humanism, are haunted by the diabolical? Instead of erasing or trying to forget it, must one not try to account for this experience, which is to say, for our age? And without believing that all of this is already clear for us? Is not the task, the duty, and in truth the only new or interesting thing to try to recognize the analogies and the possibilities of rupture between, on the one hand, what is called Nazism— that enormous, plural, differentiated continent whose roots are still obscure—and, on the other hand, a Heideggerian thinking that is also multiple and that, for a long time to come, will remain provocative, enigmatic, still to be read? Not because it would hold in reserve, still encrypted, a good and reassuring politics, a "Heideggerianism of the left," but because it opposed to actual Nazism, to its dominant strain, only a more "revolutionary" and purer Nazism!

Q.: Your last book, *Of Spirit*, also deals with Heidegger's Nazism. You inscribe the political problematic at the very heart of his thinking.

J.D.: *Of Spirit* was first of all a lecture given at the closing session of a colloquium organized by the Collège International de Philosophie under the title "Heidegger, questions ouvertes." The proceedings of this colloquium will soon be published.[3] The so-called political question was broached in an analytic manner during a number of the presentations, and without indulgence either for Heidegger or for the sententious judgments that, no less on the side of the "defense" than on that of the "prosecution," have so often managed to prevent reading or thinking, whether one is talking about Heidegger, his Nazism, or Nazism in general. At the beginning of the book, and in certain essays in *Psyché*, I explain the trajectories that led me, and once again this goes back a long way, to attempt this reading. While it is still preliminary, it seeks to knit a multiplicity of motifs around Nazism, motifs concerning which I have always had trouble following Heidegger: questions of the proper, the near [*proche*], and the fatherland (*Heimat*) [*patrie*], of the point of departure of *Being and Time*, of technics and science, of animality or sexual difference, of the voice, the hand, language, the "epoch," and especially, this is the subtitle of my book, the question of the question, which is almost constantly privileged by Heidegger as "the piety of thinking." As regards these themes, my reading has always been, let's say, actively perplexed. I have indicated my reservations in *all* my references to Heidegger, as far back as they go. Each one of these motifs of worry, it's obvious, has an import that one can, to go quickly, call "political." But from the moment one is having it out with [*s'explique avec*] Heidegger in a critical or deconstructive fashion, must one not continue to recognize a certain necessity of his thinking, its character, which is inaugural in so many respects, and especially what remains to come for us in its deciphering? This is a task of thinking, a historical task and a political task. A discourse on Nazism that dispenses with this task remains the conformist opinion of "good conscience."

For a long time I have been trying to displace the old alternative between an "external" history or sociology, which in general is powerless to take the measure of the philosophemes that it claims to explain, and on the other hand, the "competence" of an "internal" reading, which for its part is blind to historico-political inscription and first of all to the pragmatics of discourse. In the case of Heidegger, the difficulty of articulating the two is particularly serious. There is the seriousness of what is at stake: Nazism from the day before yesterday to tomorrow. The difficulty is serious as well to the extent that Heidegger's "thinking" destabilizes the deep foundations of philosophy and the human sciences. I am trying to shed some light on certain of these missing articulations between an external approach and an internal approach. But this is pertinent and effective only if one takes into account the destabilization I just mentioned. I therefore followed the practical, "pragmatic" treatment of the concept and the lexicon of spirit, in the "major" texts as well as in, for example, the Rectorship Address. I have the same concern when I study various connected motifs in "Heidegger's Hand" and other essays collected in *Psyché*.

Q.: People will not fail to ask you: from the moment you situate Nazism at the very heart of Heidegger's thinking, how is it possible to continue to read this work?

J.D.: The condemnation of Nazism, whatever must be the consensus on this subject, is not yet a thinking of Nazism. We still do not know what it is and what made possible this vile, yet overdetermined thing, shot through with internal contradictions (whence the fractions and factions among which Heidegger situated himself—and his cunning strategy in the use of the word "spirit" takes on a certain sense when one thinks of the general rhetoric of the Nazi idiom and the biologizing tendencies, à la Rosenberg, that won out in the end). After all, Nazism did not grow up in Germany or in Europe like a mushroom...

Q.: *Of Spirit*, then, is a book as much about Nazism as about Heidegger?

J.D.: In order to think Nazism, one must not be interested only in Heidegger, but one must *also* be interested in him. To think that the European discourse can keep Nazism at bay like an object is, in the best hypothesis, naive, and in the worst it is an obscurantism and a political mistake. It is to act as if Nazism had no contact with the rest of Europe, with other philosophers, with other political or religious languages...

Q.: What is striking in your book is the rapprochement you effect between Heidegger's texts and those of other thinkers, such as Husserl, Valéry...

J.D.: At the moment when his discourse situates itself in a spectacular fashion in the camp of Nazism (and what demanding reader ever believed that the rectorship was an isolated and easily delimitable episode?), Heidegger takes up again the word "spirit," whose avoidance he had prescribed; he raises the quotation marks with which he surrounded it. He limits the deconstructive movement that he had begun earlier. He maintains a voluntarist and metaphysical discourse upon which he will later cast suspicion. To this extent at least, the elevation of spirit, through the celebration of its freedom, resembles other European discourses (spiritualist, religious, humanist) which are generally opposed to Nazism. This is a complex and unstable knot which I try to untangle by recognizing the threads common to Nazism and to anti-Nazism, the law of resemblance, the inevitability of perversion. The mirroring effects are sometimes dizzying. This speculation is staged at the end of the book...

It is not a question of mixing everything together, but of analyzing the traits that prohibit a simple break between the Heideggerian discourse and other European discourses, whether old ones or contemporary ones. Between 1919 and 1940, everyone was wondering (but are we not still wondering the same thing today?): "What is Europe to become?" and this was always translated as

"How to save the spirit?" Frequently analogous diagnoses are proposed of the crisis, the decadence, or the "destitution" of spirit. But we should not limit ourselves to discourses and to their common horizon. Nazism was able to develop only with the differentiated but decisive complicity of other countries, other "democratic" States, academic and religious institutions. Across this European network, this hymn to the freedom of spirit surged up and still arises, a hymn which is at least consonant with Heidegger's, precisely at the moment of the Rectorship Address and other analogous texts. I try to grasp the common and terribly contagious law of these exchanges, partitions, reciprocal translations.

Q.: To recall that Heidegger launches his Nazi profession of faith in the name of "the freedom of spirit" is a rather stinging reply to all those who have recently attacked you in the name of "conscience," "human rights," and who reproach you for your work on the deconstruction of "humanism," taxing you with...

J.D.: With nihilism, with anti-humanism... You know all the slogans. I am trying, on the contrary, to define deconstruction as a thinking of affirmation. Because I believe in the necessity of exposing, limitlessly if possible, the profound adherence of the Heideggerian text (writings and acts) to the possibility and the reality of all Nazisms, because I believe this abysmal monstrosity should not be classified according to well-known and finally reassuring schemas, I find certain maneuvers to be at the same time ludicrous and alarming. They are very old but we are seeing them reappear. There are those who seize upon the pretext of their recent discovery in order to exclaim: (1) "It is shameful to read Heidegger." (2) "Let's draw the following conclusion—and then pull up the ladder: everything that, especially in France, refers to Heidegger in one way or another, even what is called 'deconstruction,' is part of Heideggerianism!" The second conclusion is silly and dishonest. In the first, one reads the political irresponsibility and renunciation of thinking. On the contrary, by setting out from a certain deconstruction, at least the one that interests me, one can pose, it seems to me, new questions to Heidegger, decipher his discourse, situate in it the political risks, and recognize at times the limits of his own deconstruction. Permit me, if you will, to cite an example of the sort of bustling confusion I would like to warn against. It is from the preface of the investigation by Farías that we were just evoking. At the end of a harangue clearly meant for domestic consumption (it is once again *la France* that is speaking!), one reads this: "For numerous scholars, [Heidegger's] thinking has *an effect of the obvious* [un effet d'évidence] that no other philosophy has been able to achieve in France, with the exception of Marxism. Ontology culminates in a methodical deconstruction of metaphysics as such."[4] The devil! If there is some *effect of the obvious*, it must be for the author of this hodgepodge. There has never been an *effect of the obvious* in Heidegger's text, neither for me nor for those I mentioned a moment ago. If there were, we would have stopped reading. And one can no more speak of an "ontology" with regard to the deconstruction that I try to put to work than one can speak, if one has read a little, of "Heidegger's ontology" or even "Heidegger's philosophy." And "deconstruction"—which does not "culminate"—is certainly not a "method." It even develops a rather complicated discourse on the concept of method that Mr. Jambet would be well advised to meditate on a little. Given the tragic seriousness of these problems, doesn't this Franco-French, not to say provincial, operation seem alternately comic and sinister?

Q.: Perhaps this confusion has to do with the fact that your books are difficult to read. It is often said that in order to read Derrida one has to have read all Derrida. In this case, one has to have read also Heidegger, Husserl, Nietzsche...

J.D.: But this is true of so many others! It is a question of economy, of saving time. Although they don't get asked about it, all scientific researchers have to confront this question. So why is the question asked only of philosophers?

Q.: But it is particularly true for you.

J.D.: In order to unfold what is implicit in so many discourses, one would have each time to make a pedagogical outlay that it is just not reasonable to expect from every book. Here the responsibility has to be shared out, mediated; the reading has to do its work and the work has to make its reader.

Q.: *Of Spirit* is taken from a lecture, and its style is fairly demonstrative. But your earlier works, such as *Parages* or "Ulysses Gramophone," were more like literary attempts on literary texts.

J.D.: I always try to be as demonstrative as possible. But it is true that the demonstrations are taken up in forms of writing that have their own, sometimes novel rules, which are most often produced and displayed. They cannot correspond, at every point, to the traditional norms that precisely these texts are questioning or displacing.

Q.: Your book on Joyce was, all the same, rather disconcerting.

J.D.: I was writing about Joyce. It would be a shame therefore to write in a form that in no way lets itself be affected by Joyce's languages, by his inventions, his irony, the turbulence he introduced into the space of thinking or of literature. If one wants to take the event named "Joyce" into account, one must write, recount, demonstrate in another fashion, one must take the risk of a formal adventure

Q.: Do you adapt your style to each object you fasten on?

J.D.: Without mimeticism, but while incorporating in some way the other's signature. With some luck, another text can begin to take shape, another event, irreducible to either the author or the work about which nonetheless one should speak as faithfully as possible.

Q.: So with each book you have to invent a new "tone," as Robert Pinget would put it?

J.D.: Yes, the most difficult thing is the invention of the tone, and with the tone, of the scene that can be staged, that you can let be staged, the pose that adopts you as much as you adopt it.

Q.: Do you consider yourself to be a writer?

J.D.: The attention paid to language or writing does not necessarily belong to "literature." If one is to interrogate the limits of these spaces, "literature" or "philosophy," I wonder if one can still be altogether a "writer" or a "philosopher." No doubt I am neither one nor the other.

Q.: One gets the impression that you have, in the course of the last few years, deserted France for the sake of an American career. Is this a choice you are making?

J.D.: No, I am not emigrating! I have no American "career"! Like others, I teach every year, for no more than a few weeks, in the United States. It is true that my work is generously translated, received, or discussed in other countries. But I did not choose this situation. I live, teach, and publish in France. If there is some imbalance, I am not responsible for it.

Q.: And do you regret it?

J.D.: On the French side, yes. The debates and the work that interest or concern me are more developed in other countries. This is true not only for me or for the field in which I work. As regards so-called difficult things, even and especially when they are closely related to the French idiom, the debates are richer and more open abroad.

Q.: How do you explain that?

J.D.: It has to do with the state of the French university, notably in philosophy. It also has to do with what is called the cultural field, with its media filters, it should be noted, with the Parisian space, its cliques and its pressure groups. And then, as we were saying, it has to do as well with the way in which these texts are written. They suppose a formalization, a potentialization of previously acquired knowledge that cannot be immediately deciphered. If certain texts are overcoded, if the cultural translation of them remains difficult, this situation has nothing to do with anybody's deliberate will...

Q.: In *Psyché*, there is a text on Mandela and apartheid.[5] This is one of your rare political texts...

J.D.: And what if someone were to have fun showing you that these two books on soul and spirit are also the books of a political activist? That the essays on Heidegger and Nazism, on Mandela and apartheid, on the nuclear problem, on the psychoanalytic institution and torture, on architecture and urbanism, etc., are "political writings"? But you are right, I have never been, as you were saying, a "militant or an engaged philosopher in the sense of the Sartrean figure, or even the Foucauldian figure, of the intellectual." Why? But it's already too late, isn't it?

Comment donner raison?
« How to Concede, with Reasons? »

Who would prohibit us, henceforward, from reading Heidegger? Who, therefore, claims to have already read him? To respond with an act to these questions, but also out of concerns for economy, I shall confine myself to a text I discovered this very day. It is in 1942. Heidegger seems *to concede* [donner raison]. But he asks that his thought, and he understands then all *thought*, be spared the "disaster" of an "*immediate presentation*":

"You are right [*avez raison*]. This writing is a disaster (*Unglück*). *Sein und Zeit* was also a disastrous accident. And every *immediate presentation* [my emphasis, J.D.] of my thought would be today the greatest of disasters. Perhaps that is a first testimony to the fact that my attempts sometimes arrive in the nearness of a true thought."[1] The letter previously denounced an "error" for which "the interruption of *Sein und Zeit* before the decisive step" would have been "responsible," the error of believing thus that Heidegger would have attained "safety" in some kind of "certainty."

An elliptical response to Max Kommerell's gripping, admiring, but also anguished appeal on the subject of Hölderlin. (In 1942! Is such a correspondence on the subject of Hölderlin then ill-timed, abstracted, and academic, or on the contrary terribly fit to that very year? I have no "yes or no" response to this question; it is doubtless badly posed.) Kommerell asked: wouldn't it be necessary to "begin by first agreeing on what is properly speaking a hymn of Hölderlin, before being able to interpret it with that sublime and monstrously insistent care for the letter, which constitutes the privilege, but also by its violence the terrifying character of your reading . . . your essay could, I am not saying that it is, could even be a disaster." In 1941, he also said to Gadamer that Heidegger's discourse on Hölderlin "is a productive rail accident, before which the crossing guards of the history of literature must raise their arms to the sky (to the extent of their decency)."

Let us transpose, just barely. Beyond what would concern only or "properly"(?) Hölderlin, should one remain indifferent to these two voices, to something they ask or prescribe, differently to be sure, but both of them at the edge of the greatest misfortune, when absolute aberration always remains possible and the errant way perhaps irreversible? These letters foretell the always announced disproportion of the worst; they prepare for it, foresee the fatal test in wariness, respect, a dark night of vigilance and of suicidal sacrality, holding their breath.

Each one wonders: what happens *meanwhile*, at this very moment? What can I know? What must I do? (The interest of reason since Kant.)

Doubtless one must not, in certain situations, suspend the imperative of moral or political judgment, that is, that of an "immediate"—or nearly so—"presentation." This no longer directly concerns Hölderlin or *Sein und Zeit*. This concerns, let us never be distracted from this, the *fact* named Nazism and what Heidegger had taken on of this himself from before 1933, approving it at least by his silence in 1942 and again after the war. Doubtless also the letter of the thinker remains cunning, trying to take advantage of what could pass for a confession of humility. No matter, the letter asks us not to "present" thought "immediately," not to condemn a thought too quickly as if its presentation, and also its appearance *before the law*, was immediately possible without disaster, as if one *knew what thought is*, what it is *presently, all things considered*. (But what can I know of this, and how many still today pretend to know in order to free themselves, without waiting, from a task of thinking or from an unbearable nearness?)

What is called "thinking"? Without even knowing, even less than Heidegger, what content to give this word beyond science and philosophy, I propose to call "thought" here *what keeps the right to ask* [*for*], *I am saying only to ask* [*for*] *just that*: not the immediate acquittal for whatever may present itself, immediately or nearly, but the right to the experience of the disaster, to that risk at least *for thought*. Not the right to something calculable (there are tribunals for that; for whatever they're worth, they have already pronounced themselves on the subject of Heidegger and we think here, *at least by analogy*, of the questions raised by the *résistant* Paulhan after the war, even if one does not necessarily approve—such is my case—of all the conclusions), but the right only asked for to that risk incalculable *for thought* and for whoever *surrenders* to thought, *inasmuch as* s/he surrenders to it. Can one imagine a thought without this risk? The most violent mistake [*méprise*], and scorn [*mépris*], isn't that to require from thought its *immediate presentation*, to refuse it the endurance of another duration? and even that of the non-presentable [*imprésentable*]?

Doubtless there is a suffering today common to those who do not want to foreclose a thought, Heidegger's, for example. Suffering because they do not have a sure rule with which to discern between the imperative of immediate—or nearly so—judgment (the denunciation without equivocation and without delay of every known complicity with Nazism) and the demand of thought, such as it perhaps has just made itself heard, even if it exposes itself to madness, to disaster, and to the inhuman.

A suffering without measure, for we must indeed suspect that the rule does not exist, never in any case as a given rule, and which it would suffice to apply. The rule will always be to come, an impossible and contradictory definition for a rule. Now if this or that historic "rail accident" could take place, if something "productive," as Kommerell says, was monstrously allied to the nameless crime and to the bottomless misfortune, if this double memory has allowed us no respite for more than half a century (for, finally, why isn't the case closed? why is Heidegger's trial never over and done with?), it is perhaps because we have to, we've *already* had to, respect the possibility *and* impossibility of this rule: *that it remains to come.* That in the name of which we immediately—or nearly so— condemn Nazism can no longer, must no longer, I believe, be formulated so simply in the language of a philosophy that, for essential reasons, *has never been sufficient for this* and that Heidegger has *also* taught us to question: a certain state of eloquence on the proper of man, the self, consciousness, subject, object, right, truth, a certain determination of freedom or of the spirit, and then of some other things I can say nothing more about here, constrained as I am in the system of a nearly immediate presentation. At the risk of clashing with the card-carrying anti-Heideggerians and the new prosecutors, I shall recall this, very quickly: more than ever, the vigilant but open reading of Heidegger remains in my view one of the indispensable conditions, one of them but not the least, for trying to comprehend better and to tell better why, with so many others, I have always condemned Nazism, in the horror of what, in Heidegger precisely, and so many others, in Germany or elsewhere, has ever been able to give in to it.

No *immediate presentation* for thought could also mean: less facileness in armed declarations and morality lessons, less haste toward platforms [*tribunes*] and tribunals [*tribunaux*], even if one does so to respond to acts of violence, rhetorical or other. There have been some these past weeks, and I reproach myself now and then for having, right here, in an almost immediate fashion, replied to them.

The question of "immediate presentation" is also that of the press. The press lacks the room for the patient analysis of this problem. Referring to other places for other consequences, I con- clude then with a word: even if certain newspapers have been content to stage, and spectacularly, what those among us have been taking into account for a long time in their work (publication and teaching), these "images" themselves will change something, per- haps beyond "opinion," in the very approach to Heidegger's texts. These images have at least contributed to dissipating, and justly so, what in a social authority or a professorial legitimacy depended too much, for some, on an artificial landscape, on a fictive immediacy destined to mask other theaters. Some will henceforward let themselves be less easily taken in by the innocent imagery of the seminar, of the hut, of withdrawal [*retrait*], of the clearing, and of the country path. They now have at their disposal, another symbolic, another film, other photographs which they see now in turn exhibited in the foreground.

What may be hoped for? That this does not exempt us from, but on the contrary prompts us to read: the symbol, the image, the photograph, the film, which are no more, as one at times would like to have us believe, "immediate presentations"—and what is written [*l'écrit*].

TRANSLATED BY JOHN P. LEAVEY, JR.

« There is No *One* Narcissism »
(Autobiophotographies)

Q.: Jacques Derrida, what strikes me, what strikes your readers is your great vigilance with regard to public manifestations, as well as a certain retreat. One could cite many examples of this: very few photographs of you, very few interviews in the press. Is this a deliberate choice, a necessity, or probably both at the same time?

J.D.: I would like to pick up on the word vigilance... I take it to be an evaluation on your part. If you say vigilance, it is because you suppose I have a desire to be lucid on this subject. I don't know how far lucidity can go in this domain. In any case, I will begin with a precaution. If there is, in fact, as you said, retreat, a rarity of photographic or journalistic manifestations, this is not the result of a will not to appear. Like many, I must have a certain desire to appear; but also a misgiving as regards the way in which the modalities of appearing are generally programmed in what is called the cultural field. Let's take the example of the photograph since you alluded to it. I have nothing against photography, on the contrary, photography interests me a lot and I will even say: photographs of myself interest me. During the fifteen or twenty years in which I tried—it was not always easy to do with publishers, newspapers, etc.—to forbid photographs, it was not at all in order to mark a sort of blank, absence, or disappearance of the image; it was because the code that dominates at once the production of these images, the framing they are made to undergo, the social implications (showing the writer's head framed in front of his bookshelves, the whole scenario) seemed to me to be, first of all, terribly boring, but also contrary to what I am trying to write and to work on. So it seemed to me consistent not to give in to all of this without some defense. This vigilance is probably not the whole story. It is likely that I have a rather complicated relation to my own image, complicated enough that the force of desire is at the same time checked, contradicted, thwarted. What I have just told you about photography is valid for other manifestations. You mentioned interviews, live broadcasts, the organized appearance of what is called an author: there too I have the same worry. I have never found a kind of rule or coherent protocol in this regard. No doubt there is a lot of improvisation and inconsistency.

Q.: In your text, one always feels a lot of pleasure, a pleasure in writing, even a certain playfulness. For you, is the pleasure of philosophizing or the pleasure of philosophy essentially a pleasure of writing?

J.D.: That's a very difficult question. To stick with what I know for sure, I will say that it must be the case that I take a certain pleasure in philosophy, in a certain way of doing philosophy. There is much philosophy and many books of philosophy that I find terribly boring, that I do not like to read, and before which I have great resistance. I try to find a certain economy of pleasure in what is called philosophy. Your question asked about the pleasure of writing: Yes, if one uses this word "writing" very carefully. I don't believe, for example—and perhaps contrary to what certain people might tend to believe—that I get a lot of pleasure out of writing, that is, in finding myself before a sheet of paper and in devising sentences. I probably even have a certain immediate aversion for the thing. On the other hand, and also contrary to what certain people might think, I love to *talk* philosophy. Of course, it is also a writing, it is a certain form of writing. I don't particularly like improvising, except in very favorable conditions (which is not the case here!), but I do like a certain manner of talking philosophy which, for me, is a way of writing. And I believe that in what I write in the graphic sense or the sense of publication, the experience of the voice, of rhythm, of what is called speech is always marked. I insist on this point because, in general, at least for those who are interested in what I do, I am presented as someone who is for writing, a man of writing rather than speech. Well, that's wrong! Yes, it's wrong. It's just that I think that the concept of writing has now been sufficiently transformed that we should no longer let ourselves be taken in by the somewhat trivial opposition between speech and writing.

So pleasure, yes, but, you know, pleasure is a very complicated thing. Pleasure can accumulate, intensify through a certain experience of pain, ascesis, difficulty, an experience of the impasse or of impossibility; so, pleasure, yes, no doubt, but in order to respond seriously and philosophically to your question, we would have to open up a whole discourse on the pleasure principle, on beyond the pleasure principle, etc.

Q.: What is more, your taste for philosophy also always takes a path through risk, adventure, high stakes...

J.D.: To get the very complicated pleasure we were just talking about, to get this pleasure, I suppose one must, at a given moment, stand at the edge of catastrophe or of the risk of loss. Otherwise, one is only applying a surefire program. So, one must take risks. That's what experience is. I use this word in a very grave sense. There would be no experience otherwise, without risk. But for the risk to be worth the trouble, so to speak, and for it to be really something risky or risking, one must take this risk with all possible insurance. That is, one must multiply the assurances, have the most lucid possible consciousness of all the systems of insurance, all the norms, all that can limit the risks, one must explore the terrain of these assurances: their history, their code, their norms in order to bring them to the edge of the risk in the surest way possible. One has to be sure that the risk is taken. And to be sure that the risk is taken, one has to negotiate with the assurances. And thus speak... in the mode of philosophy, of demonstration, of logic, of critique

so as to arrive at the point where that is no longer possible, so as to
see where that is no longer possible. What I am calling here
assurance or insurance are all the codes, the values, the norms we
were just talking about and that regulate philosophical discourse:
the philosophical institution, the values of coherence, truth, demonstration, and so forth.

Q.: What also sometimes attracts you is the will to provoke: first
of all to provoke philosophical events, but also to provoke, in the
common sense of provocation. An example among others is this
sentence drawn from "Right of Inspection": "the right to narcissism has to be rehabilitated..."[1]

J.D.: Narcissism! There is not narcissism and non-narcissism;
there are narcissisms that are more or less comprehensive, generous, open, extended. What is called non-narcissism is in general
but the economy of a much more welcoming, hospitable narcissism, one that is much more open to the experience of the other as
other. I believe that without a movement of narcissistic reappropriation, the relation to the other would be absolutely destroyed, it would be destroyed in advance. The relation to the
other—even if it remains asymmetrical, open, without possible
reappropriation—must trace a movement of reappropriation in the
image of oneself for love to be possible, for example. Love is
narcissistic. Beyond that, there are little narcissisms, there are big
narcissisms, and there is death in the end, which is the limit. Even
in the experience—if there is one—of death, narcissism does not
abdicate absolutely.

Q.: Closest to, farthest from narcissism or narcissisms, or rather
I should say, closest to the idiom and to singularity, you have often
repeated that deconstruction is not a method, that there is no
"Derridean method." How, then, is one to take account of your
work? How do you evaluate its effects? To whom is your work
addressed and, finally, who reads you?

J.D.: By definition, I do not know to whom it is addressed. Or
rather yes I do! I have a certain knowledge on this subject, some

anticipations, some images, but there is a point at which, no more than anyone who publishes or speaks, I am not assured of the destination. Even if one tried to regulate what one says by one or more possible addressees, using typical profiles, even if one wanted to do that it would not be possible. And I hold that one ought not to try to master this destination. That is moreover why one writes. Now, you mentioned idiom. Yes, but I also do not believe in pure idioms. I think there is naturally a desire, for whoever speaks or writes, to sign in an idiomatic, that is, irreplaceable manner. But as soon as there is a mark, that is, the possibility of a repetition, as soon as there is language, generality has entered the scene and the idiom compromises with something that is not idiomatic: with a common language, concepts, laws, general norms. And consequently, even if one attempts to preserve the idiom of the method— since you spoke of method—of a system of rules which others are going to be able to use, so even if one wants to preserve, then, the idiom of the method... well, by the fact that the idiom is not pure, there is already method. Every discourse, even a poetic or oracular sentence, carries with it a system of rules for producing analogous things and thus an outline of methodology. That said, at the same time I have tried to mark the ways in which, for example, deconstructive questions cannot give rise to methods, that is, to technical procedures that could be repeated from one context to another. In what I write, I think there are also some general rules, some procedures that can be transposed by analogy—this is what is called a teaching, a knowledge, applications—but these rules are taken up in a text which is each time a unique element and which does not let itself be turned totally into a method. In fact, this singularity is not pure, but it exists. It exists moreover independently of the deliberate will of whoever writes. There is finally a signature, which is not the signature one has calculated, which is naturally not the patronymic, which is not the set of stratagems elaborated in order to propose something original or inimitable. But, whether one likes it or not, there is an *effect of the idiom for the other*. It is like photography: whatever pose you adopt, whatever precautions you take so that the photograph will look like this or like that, there comes a moment when the photograph surprises you and it is the other's gaze that, finally, wins out and decides. So, I think that in what I write in particular—but this is valid for others—the same thing happens: there is idiom and there is method, generality; reading is a mixed experience of the other in his or her singularity as well as philosophical content, information that can be torn out of this singular context. Both at the same time.

Q.: In one of your recent books, *Feu la cendre* [*Cinders*], you note that you write "in the position of non-knowing rather than of the secret"; is it this non-knowing that marks the idiom, that magnetizes desire?

J.D.: It is not a non-knowing installed in the form of "I don't want to know." I am all for knowledge [laughter], for science, for analysis, and... well, okay! So, this non-knowing... it is not the limit... of a knowledge, the limit in the progression of a knowledge. It is, in some way, a structural non-knowing, which is heterogeneous, foreign to knowledge. It's not just the unknown that could be known and that I give up trying to know. It is something in relation to which knowledge is out of the question. And when I specify that it is a non-knowing and not a secret, I mean that when a text appears to be crypted, it is not at all in order to calculate or to intrigue or to bar access to something that I know and that others must not know; it is a more ancient, more originary experience, if you will, of the secret. It is not a thing, some information that I am hiding or that one has to hide or dissimulate; it is rather an experience that does not make itself available to information, that resists information and knowledge, and that immediately encrypts itself. That is what I try to underscore about Celan, who is supposed to be a difficult and cryptic poet, for example, in the way in which he arranges dates, allusions to experiences he has had, and so forth, with all the problems of decipherment that this supposes... What I suggested is that he didn't do it out of calculation, in order to put generations of academics to work looking for the keys to a text. It is the experience of writing and language that is involved in this crypt, in this cryptics.

Q.: If we continue what we've been doing for the last while, that is, trying not to identify but, perhaps, to mark how one can understand and receive your work, there is a word that comes to mind, the word "thought" or "thinking" [*pensée*], in its Heideggerian overtones. At the same time, you seem to be almost more on guard in relation to this word than in relation to the word "philosophy."

J.D.: Yes and no. There are situations in which the word "pensée" takes on in fact very marked connotations, which I would tend to want to guard against. But, generally, I prefer it to the words "philosophy" and "knowledge," with reference, in effect, to Heidegger's gesture. But here, one would have to speak of different languages, because *pensée*, the French word, is not at all the Heideggerian *Denken*. But with reference to what Heidegger did when he distinguished precisely thinking from *philosophy* and from *science*, I care about... a "thinking," let's say, that is not confined within the particular way of thinking that is philosophy or science. There are forms—I don't dare say forms of questions because it is not at all certain that thinking means questioning, that it is essentially questioning; I am not sure that the question is the ultimate form or the worthiest form of thinking—there are perhaps "pensées" that are more thinking than this kind of thinking called philosophy. So, I have used this word "pensée" from this point of view, with these intentions, since this is the way Heidegger's distinction between *philosophy* and *thinking* gets translated. But perhaps in Latin, in a Latinate language like French, *pensée* should be replaced by something else. Here, one would have to go into that which, in Heidegger's text, makes the link between thinking and other meanings that are not linked to the word *pensée* in French: *Andenken*, memory, gratitude, thanking. None of this is present in the Latin or the French *penser*. So, to a certain extent, it's a conventional word for me, it's a translation; it's not necessarily the best word.

Q.: You just mentioned memory, which is a word to which I would like to return and first of all by asking an "indiscreet" question. It is part of those autobiographical elements which are, a priori, more or less certain: you were born in Algeria.

J.D.: That's true.

Q.: You confirm it! So, what memory do you have of Algeria, of that time? What is the legacy of that link and that period? But first of all is there a possible narration [*récit*] of this?

J.D.: I wish that a narration were possible. For the moment, it is not possible. I dream of managing one day, not to recount this legacy, this past experience, this history, but at least to give a narration of it among other possible narrations. But, in order to get there, I would have to undertake a kind of work, I would have to set out on an adventure that up until now I have not been capable of. To invent, to invent a language, to invent modes of anamnesis... For me, it is this adventure that interests me the most in a certain way, but which still today seems to me practically inaccessible. So, having said that, am I going to take the risk here, while improvising, of telling you things that would resemble a narration? No! Unless you ask me precise factual questions that I will not dodge, but I don't feel capable of giving myself over to... variations on my memory, my inheritance. All the more so in that this inheritance— if it is one—is multiple, not very homogenous, full of all kinds of grafts; and to talk about it seriously, we would need a different apparatus than the one at our disposal for this program. I was born in Algeria, but already my family, which had been in Algeria for a long time, before the French colonization, was not simply Algerian. The French language was not the language of its ancestors. I lived in the pre-independent Algeria, but not all that long before Independence. All of this makes for a landscape that is very, very... full of contrasts, mixtures, crossings. The least statement on this subject seems to me to be a mutilation in advance.

Q.: During a colloquium in Canada, you said to the only Frenchman present in the room: "You are French, I'm not; I come from Algeria. I have therefore a different relation to the French language." Can one speak of an exile in language?

J.D.: I don't know if one ought to speak simply of language, in the strict sense of the term. I have only one language. I don't know any other. Thus, I was raised in a monolingual milieu—absolutely monolingual. Around me, although not in my family, I naturally heard Arabic spoken, but, except for a few words, I do not speak Arabic. I tried to learn it later but I didn't get very far. Moreover, one could say in a general way, without exaggerating, that learning Arabic was something that was virtually forbidden at school. Not prohibited by law, but practically impossible. So, French is my only language. Nevertheless, in the culture of the French in Algeria and in the Jewish community of the French in Algeria, there was a way in which, despite everything, France was not Algeria; the source, the norm, the authority of the French language was elsewhere. And, in a certain manner, confusedly, we learned it, I learned it as the language of the other—even though I could only refer to one language as being mine, you see! And this is why I say that it is not a question of language, but of culture, literature, history, history of French literature, what I was learning at school. I was totally immersed, I had no other reference, I had no other culture, but at the same time I sensed clearly that all of this came from a history and a milieu that were not in a simple and primitive way mine. Not counting what I was saying a moment ago about the gap between the figure of the French of France and the French of Algeria, a very marked social gap—about which there would be a lot to say. It's that the Frenchman of France was an other. And an other who was, to be sure, higher on the ladder: he was the model of distinction, what one should say and how one should say it. So, it was the master's language in a certain way—I mean this also in the pedagogical sense of the term, it was what we were taught by the schoolmasters. And yet, there was and there still is—I think this is still true for the *pieds-noirs*[2] who returned to France—in relation to the French of France a condescendence on the part of the *pieds-noirs*, a suspicion, and, at the same time, the feeling that these people, when you get right down to it, are still naive or innocent [*niais*]. Innocent with the sexual connotation that this word can have. They are credulous, in a certain way. People from the South often have this feeling about Northerners; it's also true within France. The Southerner tends to think—I'm talking about a very

primitive but strong feeling—that the Northerner is more credulous, less cunning, and there was some of this among the *pieds-
noirs*. So, the Frenchman was the master, the norm, the authority,
the source of legitimation, and at the same time, he was the one
who had not yet really opened his eyes, who was credulous, who is
not going to put one over on me, and so forth.

Q.: You just evoked your Judaism. Were you raised in a family
context that was strongly marked by Judaism?

J.D.: My family was observant in a very banal way, but I must
say, unfortunately, that this observance was not guided by a true
Jewish culture. There were rituals to be observed in a rather
external way, but I was not really raised in what is called Jewish
culture. I regret this, moreover. I don't regret it simply out of
nostalgia for a sense of Judaic belonging, but because I think it is a
lacuna in anyone's culture, mine in particular. The paths of this
inheritance have to be extremely complicated for it to be passed
along neither by genes, nor by a thematics, nor by language, nor by
religious instruction. It can follow other trajectories. So what are
they? It is very difficult to improvise an answer, but one can
imagine that a community cut off from its roots can, by way of
non-conscious paths, communicate with... a certain manner of
managing its unconscious, of reading, deciphering, living its anxiety. All of this can give rise to a certain relation to the world, a
certain attitude that compels one to write in this way or that. I
know I am giving a very inadequate answer concerning these
trajectories, but it is in the direction of these very singular trajectories that one must look in order to pose the question. That is,
neither in the direction of religion, nor themes, nor language, nor
content, but of another mode of transmission.

Q.: Reading you, one has at first the feeling that your intellectual
and cultural heritage is Greek and German, which is not surprising
for a philosopher: Plato, Aristotle, Kant, Heidegger, the list of
names could be extended. Might there not also be with you a sort
of Judaic intrusion, difficult to define, which would come along to

undo again, deconstruct this line of division that is so traditional between the Greek and the German? An inscription of Judaism within the Greco-German?

J.D.: Perhaps. I hesitate for all the reasons given up until now, I hesitate to call it Judaic. There is certainly (and here I am describing naively a naive experience) a feeling of exteriority with regard to European, French, German, Greek culture. But when, as you know I do, I close myself up with it because I teach and write all the time about things that are German, Greek, French, even then it is true that I have the feeling I am doing it from another place that I do not know: an exteriority based on a place that I do not inhabit in a certain way, or that I do not identify. That is why I hesitate to call it Judaic. There is an exteriority! Some might say to me: But it's always like that, even when a German philosopher writes about the German tradition, the fact that he is questioning, writing, interrogating inscribes him in a certain outside. One always has to have a certain exteriority in order to interrogate, question, write. But perhaps beyond this exteriority, which is common to all those who philosophize and write, ask questions… beyond this exteriority there is perhaps something else, the feeling of *another* exteriority. Finally, if I wanted to rush toward a more coherently formulated response, also perhaps a more elegant one, I don't know—and which perhaps would not be true to the extent it was elegant—this place, which for the moment I cannot identify and which I refuse to call the place of Judaism, is perhaps what I am looking for, very simply. If I were optimistic enough on this subject, I would say that I see the journey of my brief existence as a journey in view of determining and naming the place from which I will have had the experience of exteriority. And the anamnesis we were talking about at the outset, this anamnesis would be in view of identifying, of naming it—not effacing the exteriority, I don't think it can be effaced—but of naming it, identifying it, and thinking it a little better than I have done so far. And that's it, finally, the narration I refused to give a moment ago, because a *récit*, as you know, is not simply a memory reconstituting a past; a *récit* is also a promise, it is also something that makes a commitment toward the future. What I dream of is not only the narration of a past that is inaccessible to me, but a narration that would also be a future, that would determine a future.

Q.: Does this signal toward that experience that also traverses your work and that one can read as, in its own way, an experience of loss?

J.D.: Yes, it's a very common experience. I would say that what I suffer from inconsolably always has the form, not only of loss, which is often!—but of the loss of memory: that what I am living not be kept, thus repeated, and—how to put it?—decipherable, as if an appeal for a witness had no witness, in some way, not even the witness that I could be for what I have lived. This for me is the very experience of death, of catastrophe. I would be reconciled with everything I live, even the worst things, if I were assured that the memory of it would stay with me, or stay as well as the testimony that gives meaning or that brings to light, that permits the thing to reappear. The experience of cinders is the experience not only of forgetting, but of the forgetting of forgetting, of the forgetting of which nothing remains. This, then, is the worst and, at the same time, it is a benediction. Both at once.

Q.: If one were to try to measure your... well, I don't know!—there are a lot of words one could propose: route, path, adventure, experience, trajectory... Which one do you prefer from among all these words? Perhaps it is in fact a different one?

J.D.: Adventure, trajectory, experience...?

Q.: ... trajectory, route, path... to designate, then, your...

J.D.: I don't know. I rather like the word experience whose origin evokes traversal, but a traversal with the body, it evokes a space that is not given in advance but that opens as one advances. The word experience, once dusted off and reactivated a little, so to speak, is perhaps the one I would choose.

Q.: So, in order to try to take the measure of your experience, one could, for example, start out from "cinder." It seems to me that a displacement has occurred from the question of writing, of trace toward, precisely, the question of cinders. First of all, is this a thread that permits one to describe the experience and what would be the principal stages?

J.D.: That's not the right word! But perhaps it is the least bad word for gathering all this together. If I say that at a given moment, I collected in *Cinders* everything that had received the name "cinders" in a number of earlier texts, it was not with the systematic aim of bringing out a continuity. Moreover, I also wrote that text, as I frequently do, in response to a demand. At that moment, I remembered that I had written a very crypted, deliberately crypted little sentence, which is: "Il y a là cendre." It's on the last page of *Dissemination*, in a paragraph of acknowledgments. So I began by wishing to read this sentence, which is, in its brevity, very overcharged. And then, along the way, I became more vividly, clearly aware of the fact that cinders formed a very, let's say, insistent motif in a number of earlier texts. Whence this sort of "polylogue," an indeterminate number of voices on the subject of this text of ashes or cinders, or on cinders, in the course of which I tried to show... or someone tried to show that the words I had somewhat privileged up till now, such as trace, writing, gramme, turned out to be better named by "cinder" for the following reason: Ashes or cinders are obviously traces—in general, the first figure of the trace one thinks of is that of the step, along a path, the step that leaves a footprint, a trace, or a vestige; but "cinder" renders better what I meant to say with the name of trace, namely, something that remains without remaining, which is neither present nor absent, which destroys itself, which is totally consumed, which is a remainder without remainder. That is, something which is not. To explain it in a consistent manner, one would have to undertake a meditation on Being, on "is," on what "is" means, what "rest" means in the texts in which I distinguish "to remain" from "to be."[3] The cinder is not! The cinder is not: This means that it testifies without testifying. It testifies to the disappearance of the witness, if one can say that. It testifies to the disappearance of memory. When I keep a text for memory, what remains there is apparently not cinders. Cinders is

the destruction of memory itself; it is an absolutely radical forgetting, not only forgetting in the sense of the philosophy of consciousness, or a psychology of consciousness; it is even forgetting in
the economy of the unconscious by repression. Repression is not
forgetting. Repression keeps the memory. Cinders, however, is an
absolute non-memory, so to speak. Thus, it communicates with
that which in the gift, for example, does not even seek to get
recognized or kept, does not even seek to be saved. Well, to say that
there are cinders there [*il y a là cendre*], that there is some cinder
there, is to say that in every trace, in every writing, and consequently in every experience (for me every experience is, in a certain
way, an experience of trace and writing), in every experience there
is this incineration, this experience of incineration which is experience itself. Of course, then, there are great, spectacular experiences
of incineration—and I allude to them in the text—I'm thinking of
the crematoria, of all the destructions by fire, but before even these
great memorable experiences of incineration, there is incineration
as experience, as the elementary form of experience.

In the text on Celan (*Shibboleth*), I evoke certain poems by
Celan on ashes or cinders, on the disappearance not only of the
cherished one, but of his or her name—when *mourning* is not even
possible. This is the absolute destruction of testimony and, in this
regard, the word "cinder" says very well—provided, of course, that
one also makes it say this in a text that writes the cinder, that writes
on cinders, that writes in cinders—cinder says very well that which
in the trace in general, in writing in general, effaces what it
inscribes. Effacement is not only the contrary of inscription. One
writes with cinders on cinders. And not only is this not nihilistic,
but I would say that the experience of cinders, which communicates with the experience of the gift, of the non-keeping, of the
relation to the other as interruption of economy, this experience of
cinders is also the possibility of the relation to the other, of the gift,
of affirmation, of benediction, of prayer...

Q.: With "cinder," for example, one may note in your work a
certain inflection: the desire to rework on a philosophical plane

words that are less "technical" or at least less philosophically charged than those on which you previously insisted, such as margin, writing, or differance...

J.D.: Certainly. In the text *Cinders*, I do what I cannot do again here while improvising in front of a microphone, which would be both impossible and indecent: I take an interest in the word "cinder," effectively. Everything that can happen to it and everything that it can cause to happen in the French language, for example, and in other languages, since *Cinders* is also concerned with the translation of the word "cinder" into other languages. Yes, so beyond an analysis—which is not only an analysis, which is also a manner of writing the word "cendre" in French in other languages—beyond this analysis which I undertook in *Cinders*, one might get the impression that I am trying to bestow a philosophical legitimacy on this or that word, such as "cinder" for example, to transform it into a philosophical concept. This is true and false. No doubt, that interests me and I am tempted to take a word from everyday language and then make it do some work as a philosophical concept, provoking thereby restructurations of philosophical discourse. That interests me. For example, in *Glas*, I tried to talk about cinders in Hegel, to see what the meaning of fire was in Hegel: sun, fire, holocaust, the total destruction by fire. There are passages that could be read as a kind of philosophy of cinders. And, at the same time, I restrain this movement because to write a philosophy of cinders, to give to the word "cinder" a philosophical dignity, is also to lose it. It is to make of it precisely something other than what I think it "is" or remains, since "cinder" cannot be an essence, a substance, a philosophical meaning. It is on the contrary what ruins philosophy or philosophical legitimacy in advance, in a certain way. Whence this double gesture that proposes a philosophical thinking of cinders and shows how "cinder" is that which prevents philosophy from closing on itself.

Q.: "Toward deconstruction": an affirmation (which I am responsible for) on the cover of an issue of *Digraphe* and perhaps as well, the occasion to recall what deconstruction is or is not?

J.D.: I have constantly insisted on the fact that the movement of deconstruction was first of all affirmative—not positive, but affirmative. Deconstruction, let's say it one more time, is not demolition or destruction. Deconstruction—I don't know if it is something, but if it is something, it is also a thinking of Being, of metaphysics, thus a discussion that has it out with [*s'explique avec*] the authority of Being or of essence, of the thinking of what is, and such a discussion or explanation cannot be simply a negative destruction. All the more so in that, among all the things in the history of metaphysics that deconstruction argues against [*s'explique avec*], there is the dialectic, there is the *opposition* of the negative to the positive. To say that deconstruction is negative is simply to reinscribe it in an intra-metaphysical process. The point is not to remove oneself from this process but to give it the possibility of being thought.

Q.: Here, I am going to interrupt to say that the word "deconstruction" is one you have used a lot, although less now. I am doing what many others have done, no doubt somewhat pointlessly, when they throw the word back to you, despite everything, very often.

J.D.: I don't use it, let's say, spontaneously; I use it only in a context that requires it. I didn't think, moreover, when I used it for the first time that it would become, even for me, a particularly indispensable word. I am saying very simply, very naively that I didn't think, when I first used it, that it would be accentuated to such a degree by readers. I don't say this in order to erase it, and I am not saying that it never should have gotten repeated; I used it and I underlined it in a certain way but, for me, it was not a master word. I have tried to explain several times how this word imposed itself on me: it is a part of the French language, rather infrequently used it is true, but it can be found in the Littré; it plays on several registers, for example linguistic or grammatical, but also mechanical or technical. What people retained of it at the outset was the allusion to structure, because at the time I used this word, there was the dominance of structuralism: deconstruction was considered then at the same time to be a structuralist and anti-structuralist gesture. Which it was, in a certain manner. Deconstruction is not simply the decomposition of an architectural structure; it is also a question about the foundation, about the relation between foundation and what is founded; it is also a question about the closure of the structure, about a whole architecture of philosophy. Not only as concerns this or that construction, but on the architectonic motif of the system. Architectonic: here I refer to Kant's definition, which does not exhaust all the senses of "architectonic," but Kant's definition interests me particularly. The architectonic is the art of the system. Deconstruction concerns, first of all, systems. This does not mean that it brings down the system, but that it opens onto possibilities of arrangement or assembling, of being together if you like, that are not necessarily systematic, in the strict sense that philosophy gives to this word. It is thus a reflection on the system, on the closure and opening of the system. Of course, it was also a kind of active translation that displaces somewhat the word Heidegger uses: "Destruktion," the destruction of ontology, which also does not mean the annulment, the annihilation of ontology, but an analysis of the structure of traditional ontology.

An analysis which is not merely a theoretical analysis, but at the same time another writing of the question of Being or meaning: deconstruction is also a manner of writing and putting forward another text. It is not a *tabula rasa*, which is why deconstruction is also distinct from doubt or from critique. Critique always operates in view of the decision after or by means of a judgment. The authority of judgment or of the critical evaluation is not the final authority for deconstruction. Deconstruction is also a deconstruction of critique. Which does not mean that all critique or all criticism is devalued, but that one is trying to think what the authority of the critical instance signifies in history—for example in the Kantian sense, but not only the Kantian sense. Deconstruction is not a critique. Another German word of which deconstruction is a kind of transposition is "Abbau," which is found in Heidegger, and also found in Freud. With this latter word, I wanted to place what I was writing in a network with the kinds of thinking that are important to me, obviously.

Q.: One notices, for example in your most recent publications (I'm thinking of *Psyché, Inventions de l'autre*), an increasingly lively interest in architecture. To deconstruct/architecture: some will hasten to see there a paradox! And yet you are involved in a project with architects who describe themselves as "deconstructivists"...

J.D.: In fact, there are two aspects of this project: on the one hand, at the initiative of Bernard Tschumi, there is a project in which I am associated with another American architect, named Peter Eisenman, who also talks a lot about deconstruction in his texts. A project that concerns the development of a certain space at the Villette.[4] You know that Tschumi is responsible for the park overall with his project of the "Follies." And then, on the other hand, there are exchanges with Tschumi. I have just written a text, in fact, for a boxed book in which will be assembled all the designs, the whole graphic but also architectural work on the subject of the "Follies" at the Villette.[5]

Q.: Your interest for architecture in general?

J.D.: My interest in architecture is not that of an expert, nor is it very cultivated. And I even have to say that, when I read certain texts written by those in the milieu of Tschumi and Eisenman about their architecture and their projects, when I saw the concepts, the words, the schemas of deconstruction appear, I at first thought naively of a sort of analogic transposition or application. And then I realized, by working, precisely, by seeing these projects, by preparing this text, that that was not at all what was going on, and that, in fact, what they are doing under the name of deconstructive architecture was the most literal and most intense affirmation of deconstruction. Deconstruction is not, should not be only an analysis of discourses, of philosophical statements or concepts, of a semantics; it has to challenge institutions, social and political structures, the most hardened traditions. And, from this point of view, since no architectural decision is possible that does not implicate a politics, that does not put into play economic, technical, cultural, and other investments... an effective, let's say radical deconstruction must pass by way of architecture, by way of the very difficult transaction that architects must undertake with political powers, cultural powers, with the teaching of architecture. All of philosophy in general, all of Western metaphysics, if one can speak in this global way of a Western metaphysics, is inscribed in architecture, which is not just the monument in stone, which gathers up in its body all the political, religious, cultural interpretations of a society. Consequently, deconstruction can also be an architectural deconstruction, which once again does not mean a demolition of architectural values. On the one hand, one has to consider that this architecture called deconstructive, to go quickly, begins precisely by putting into question everything to which architecture has been subjugated, namely, the values of habitation, utility, technical ends, religious investments, sacralization, all of those values which are not in themselves architectural... If, therefore, they have tried to extract architecture from these partly extrinsic ends, one may say that, not only do they not demolish architecture, but they are reconstituting architecture itself in what it has that is properly architectural. That would be a first moment. But in fact, to say this would be to let oneself once again be taken in by the desires, the phantasms, the illusion of something *properly* architectural that would have to be rescued from its subjugation or its contamination. In fact, when one sees what people like Eisenman or Tschumi are doing, it is something else altogether. First of all, they do not only destroy, they construct, effectively, and they construct by putting this architecture into a relation with other spaces of writing: cinematographic, narrative (the most sophisticated forms of literary narration), finally experimentations with formal combinations... all of this is something other than a restoration of architectural purity, even though it is also a thinking of architecture as such, that is, architecture not simply in the service of an extrinsic end. So, I am now increasingly tempted to consider this architectural experience to be the most impressive "deconstructive" audacity and effectivity. Also the most difficult because it is not enough to talk about this architecture; one has to negotiate the writing in stone or metal with the hardest and most resistant political, cultural, or economic powers... It is these architects who come up against the resistances, which are the most solid ones in some way, of the culture, the philosophy, the politics in which we live.

Is There a Philosophical Language?

Q.: You have suggested several times that the philosophical text should be taken as is, before moving beyond it toward the thinking that directs it. You have in this way been led to read philosophical texts with the same eye as you read texts generally considered to be "literary," and to take up again these latter texts from within a philosophical problematic. Is there a specifically philosophical writing, and in what way is it distinct from other forms of writing? Does not the concern with literality distract us from the demonstrative function of philosophic discourse? Do we not risk in this way effacing the specificity of the genres, and measuring all texts on the same scale?

J.D.: All texts are different. One must try never to measure them "on the same scale." And never to read them "with the same eye." Each text calls for, so to speak, another "eye." Doubtless, to a certain extent, it also responds to a coded, determined expectation, to an eye and to an ear that precede it and dictate it, in some way, or that orient it. But for certain rare texts, the writing also tends, one might say, to trace the structure and the physiology of an eye that does not yet exist and to which the event of the text destines itself, for which it sometimes invents its destination no less than it regulates itself by that destination. To whom is a text addressed? Just how far can this be determined, on the side of the "author" or on the side of the "readers"? Why is it that a certain "play" remains irreducible and even indispensable in this very determination? These questions are also historical, social, institutional, political.

To restrict myself to the *types* you evoke, I have never assimilated a so-called philosophical text to a so-called literary text. The two types seem to me irreducibly different. And yet one must realize that the limits between the two are more complex (for example, I don't believe they are *genres*, as you suggest) and especially that these limits are less natural, ahistorical, or given than people say or think. The two types can be interwoven in a same corpus according to laws and forms that it is not only interesting and novel to study but indispensable if one wants to continue to refer to the identity of something like a "philosophic discourse" while having some idea what one is talking about. Must one not be interested in the conventions, the institutions, the interpretations that produce or maintain this apparatus of limitations, with all the norms and thus all the exclusions they imply? One cannot approach this set of questions without asking oneself at some moment or other: "What is philosophy?" and "What is literature?" More difficult and more wide open than ever, these questions in themselves, by definition and if at least one pursues them in an effective fashion, are neither simply philosophical nor simply literary. I would say the same thing, ultimately, about the texts I write, at least to the extent that they are worked over or dictated by the turbulence of these questions. Which does not mean, at least I hope, that they give up on the necessity of *demonstrating*, as rigorously as possible, even if the rules of the demonstration are no longer altogether, and above all constantly, the same as in what you call a "philosophic discourse." Even within the latter, you know, the regimes of demonstrativity are problematic, multiple, mobile. They themselves form the constant object of the whole history of philosophy. The debate that has arisen as regards them is indistinguishable from philosophy itself. Do you think that for Plato, Aristotle, Descartes, Hegel, Marx, Nietzsche, Bergson, Heidegger, or Merleau-Ponty, the rules of demonstrativity had to be the same? And the language, the logic, the rhetoric?

To analyze "philosophic discourse" in its form, its modes of composition, its rhetoric, its metaphors, its language, its fictions, everything that resists translation, and so forth, is not to reduce it to literature. It is even a largely philosophical task (even if it does not remain philosophical throughout) to study these "forms" that are no longer just forms, as well as the modalities according to which, by interpreting poetry and literature, assigning the latter a social and political status, and seeking to exclude them from its own body, the academic institution of philosophy has claimed its own autonomy, and practiced a disavowal with relation to its own language, what you call "literality" and writing in general; it thereby misrecognized the norms of its own discourse, the relations between speech and writing, the procedures of canonization of major or exemplary texts, and so forth. Those who protest against all these questions mean to protect a certain institutional authority of philosophy, in the form in which it was frozen at a given moment. By protecting themselves against these questions and against the transformations that the questions call for or suppose, they are also protecting the institution against philosophy. From this point of view, it seemed interesting to me to study certain discourses, those of Nietzsche or Valéry for example, that tend to consider philosophy as a species of literature. But I never subscribed to that notion and I have explained myself on this point. Those who accuse me of reducing philosophy to literature or logic to rhetoric (see, for example, the latest book by Habermas, *The Philosophical Discourse of Modernity*[1]) have visibly and carefully avoided reading me.

Conversely, I do not think that the "demonstrative" mode or even philosophy in general is foreign to literature. Just as there are "literary" and "fictional" dimensions in any philosophical discourse (and a whole "politics" of language, a politics period is generally contained there), likewise there are philosophemes at work in any text defined as "literary," and already in the finally altogether modern concept of "literature."

This explanation between "philosophy" and "literature" is not only a difficult problem that I try to elaborate as such, it is also that which takes the form of writing in my texts, a writing that, by being neither purely literary nor purely philosophical, attempts to sacrifice neither the attention to demonstration or to theses nor the fictionality or poetics of languages.

In a word, and to respond to the very letter of your question, I don't believe that there is "a specifically philosophical writing," a sole philosophical writing whose purity is always the same and out of reach of all sorts of contaminations. And first of all for this overwhelming reason: philosophy is spoken and written in a natural language, not in an absolutely formalizable and universal language. That said, within this natural language and its uses, certain modes have been forcibly imposed (and there is here a relation of force) as philosophical. These modes are multiple, conflictual, inseparable from the philosophical content itself and from its "theses." A philosophical debate is also a combat in view of imposing discursive modes, demonstrative procedures, rhetorical and pedagogical techniques. Each time a philosophy has been opposed, it was also, although not only, by contesting the properly, authentically philosophical character of the other's discourse.

Q.: Your recent work seems to be marked by a growing concern for the question of the signature, the proper name. In what way does this question have weight in the field of philosophy where for a long time the problematics were considered to be impersonal and the proper names of philosophy were considered the emblems of these problematics?

J.D.: From the outset, a new problematic of writing or of the trace was bound to communicate, in a strict and strictly necessary fashion, with a problematic of the proper name (it is already a central theme in *Of Grammatology*) and of the signature (especially since *Margins—of Philosophy*). This is all the more indispensable in that this new problematic of the trace passes by way of the deconstruction of certain metaphysical discourses on the constituting subject, with all the traits that traditionally characterize it: identity to itself, consciousness, intention, presence or proximity to itself, autonomy, relation to the object. The point was, then, to resituate or to reinscribe the function said to be that of the subject or, if you prefer, to re-elaborate a thinking of the subject which was neither dogmatic or empiricist, nor critical (in the Kantian sense) or phenomenological (Cartesian-Husserlian). But simultaneously, while taking into account the questions that Heidegger addresses to the metaphysics of the *subjectum* as the support of representations, and so forth, I thought that this gesture of Heidegger's called for new questions.

All the more so since, despite many complications that I have tried to take into account, Heidegger in fact most often reproduces (for example in his "Nietzsche") the classical and academic gesture that consists of dissociating, *on the one hand,* an "internal" reading of the text or of "thinking," or even an immanent reading of the system from, *on the other hand,* a "biography" that remains finally secondary and external. This is how in general, in the university, a sort of classical, "novelized" narrative of the "life of the great philosophers" is opposed to a systematic, or even structural, philosophical reading, which is organized either around a unique and ingenious intuition (this motif is finally common to Bergson and to Heidegger) or else around an "evolution"—in two or three stages.

I have tried to analyze the presuppositions of this gesture and to undertake analyses around the borders, limits, frames, and marginalizations of all sorts that in general have authorized these dissociations. The questions of the signature and of the proper name seem to me in fact to offer advantages for this re-elaboration. The signature in general is neither *simply* internal to the immanence of the signed text (here, for example, the philosophical corpus), nor *simply* detachable and external. If either of these hypotheses were the case, then it would disappear as signature. If your signature did not belong in a certain manner to the very space that you sign and that is defined by a symbolic system of conventions (the letter, the post card, the check, or any other attestation), it would not have any value as commitment. If, on the other hand, your signature were simply immanent to the signed text, inscribed in it as one of its parts, it again would not have the performative force of a signature. In the two cases (inside and outside), you would be doing no more than indicating or mentioning your name, which is not the same thing as signing. The signature is neither inside nor outside. It is situated on a limit defined by a system and a history of conventions; I am still using these three words, system, history, and convention, in order to save time, but in the problematic I am talking about they cannot be accepted unquestioned.

It was necessary, then, to take a look at these problems: the "convention" and "history" of a topology, the borders, the framings, but also performative responsibility and force. It was also necessary to remove them from the oppositions or alternatives that I have just mentioned. How does a signature operate? The thing is complicated, always different, precisely, from one signature and from one idiom to another, but this was the indispensable condition for preparing a rigorous access to the relations between a text and its "author," a text and its conditions of production, whether they be, as one used to say, psychobiographical or socio-historico-political. This is valid in general for any text and any "author," but then requires many specifications according to the types of texts considered. The distinctions do not fall only between philosophical and literary texts, but also within these types and, at the limit— the limit of the idiom—between all texts, which may also be juridical, political, scientific (and differently according to the different "regions," and so forth). While tracing this analysis in, for example, Hegel or Nietzsche, Genet, Blanchot, Artaud, or Ponge, I proposed a certain number of general axioms even as I tried to take account of the idiom or of the desire for idiom in each case. I cite here these examples because the work concerning the signature also passes by way of the proper name in the ordinary sense, I mean the patronym in the form I have just cited. But without being able to reconstitute this work here, I would like to specify a few points and recall several precautions.

a. Even when the signifier of the proper name, in its public and legal form, exposes itself to this analysis of the signature, the latter cannot be reduced to the name. It has never consisted in writing, simply, one's proper name. That is why, in my texts, the references to the signifier of the proper name, even if they seem to occupy center stage, remain preliminary and have a finally limited importance. As often as possible, I signal my distrust of the facile, abusive, or self-satisfied games to which this can give rise.

b. The "proper name" is not necessarily to be confused with what we commonly designate as such, that is, the official patronym, the one inscribed by a civil status. If one calls "proper name" the singular set of marks, traits, appellations by means of which someone can identify him- or herself, call him- or herself, or still yet be called, without having totally chosen or determined them him- or herself, you begin to see the difficulty. It is never certain that this set gathers itself together, that there is only one of them, that it does not remain secret for some, or even for the "consciousness" of the bearer of the name, and so forth. This opens up a formidable field for analysis.

c. A possibility thus remains open: the proper name may not exist in all purity and the signature may finally remain impossible in all strictness, if at least one still supposes that a proper name must be absolutely proper, a signature absolutely autonomous (free) and purely idiomatic. If, for reasons that I try to analyze, there is never a pure idiom, in any case an idiom that I can give *to myself* or invent in its purity, then it follows that the concepts of signature and of proper name, without being necessarily ruined, have to be re-elaborated. This re-elaboration, it seems to me, can give rise to new rules, to new procedures of reading, notably as concerns the relations of the philosophical "author" with his or her text, society, the institutions of teaching and publication, traditions, inheritances, but I am not sure it can give rise to a general theory of the signature and the proper name, on the classical model of theory or of philosophy (formalizable, constative, and objective metalanguage). For the very reasons I have just mentioned, this new discourse on the signature and the proper name must once again be signed and carry with it *in itself* a mark of the performative operation that one cannot simply and totally remove from the set under consideration. This does not lead to relativism but imprints another curvature on theoretical discourse.

Q.: You have inscribed your works under the title of "deconstruction," while explicitly opposing this thematic to the Heideggerian thematic of destruction. From "*retrait*" to "*pas*," from "the post card" to "the envoi," from "margins," to "*parages*," deconstruction weaves a tighter and tighter network of names that are neither concepts, nor metaphors, but rather seem to be landmarks or roadsigns.[2] Does deconstructive activity resemble that of the surveyor or geometer? Does not this "spatialization" of the relation to tradition reinforce the idea of a "closure" of this tradition to the detriment of a more differentiated perception of the plurality of filiations?

J.D.: Yes, the relation of "deconstruction" to Heideggerian "destruction" has always, for more than twenty years now, been marked by questions, displacements, or even, as is sometimes said, by criticisms. I pointed this out once again at the beginning of *Of Spirit* (1987), but this has been the case since *Of Grammatology* (1967). Heidegger's thought remains nonetheless for me one of the most rigorous, provocative, and necessary of our time. Permit me to recall these two things in order to say how shocking and ridiculous I find all the simplistic classifications, the hasty homogenizations that certain people have indulged in over the last few months (I am not speaking only of the newspapers). These abuses and this crudeness are as threatening as obscurantism itself, and this threat is equally moral and political, to say nothing of philosophy itself.

To pick up on your words, while the "network" you evoke is reducible neither to a weave of concepts nor to a weave of metaphors, I am not sure that it consists only in "landmarks" or "roadsigns." I would have been tempted to ask you what you mean by that. The next sentence, in your question, seems to indicate that with these words you are privileging the relation to space and, within space, to the experience of the "geometer" or the "surveyor." But you realize of course that the geometer is no longer a "surveyor" (see my translation and introduction to Husserl's *Origin of Geometry*) and that there are many other experiences of space besides those two.

But first of all I would like to return to this question of the concept and the metaphor to which you just alluded. Two clarifications: I have never reduced the concept to metaphor or, as I was accused again recently of doing by Habermas, logic to rhetoric (no more than I reduced philosophy to literature, as we were just saying). This is clearly said in numerous places, in particular in "The White Mythology,"[3] which proposes an altogether different "logic" of the relations between concept and metaphor. I can only refer to this here. Whatever may be in fact the attention I give to questions and to the experience of space—whether we're talking about *The Origin of Geometry*, or about writing, painting, drawing (in *The Truth in Painting*)—I don't think that the "spacing [*espacement*]" I talk about is simply "spatial" or "spatializing." It doubtless permits the rehabilitation, so to speak, of the spatiality that certain philosophical traditions had subordinated, marginalized, or even ignored. But, on the one hand, "spac*ing*" also says the becoming space of time itself; it intervenes, with differance, in the movement of temporalization itself; spacing is also time, one might say. On the other hand, irreducible by virtue of being a differential interval, it disrupts presence, the self-identity of any presence, with all the consequences that this can have. One may trace these consequences in the most diverse fields.

I confess now I am not sure I see how this gesture, which is certainly not a "spatialization," could mark the "closure" of "tradition." Differential spacing indicates on the contrary the impossibility of *any* closure. As for the "plurality of filiations" and the necessity of a "more differentiated perception," this will always have been my "theme" in some way, in particular as signaled by the name "dissemination." If one takes the expression "plurality of filiations" in its familial literality, then this is virtually the very "subject" of "Dissemination," "Plato's Pharmacy," and especially of *Glas* and *The Post Card*. If one steps back a bit farther (I am trying to understand the thinking behind your question), I have always distinguished "closure" from end (*Of Grammatology*) and have often recalled that the tradition was not homogeneous (which explains my interest in non-canonical texts that destabilize the representation a certain dominant tradition gave of itself). I have often said how problematic I find the idea of Metaphysics, capital M, and the Heideggerian schema of the epochality of Being or of the reassembled unity of a history of Being, even if the claim, the desire, the limit, or the failure of this "auto"-interpretation has to be taken into account. I put "auto" in quotation marks because it is always this identity and especially this self-identity, this power of transparent, exhaustive, or totalizing reflexivity that is found to be in question here.

Q.: Your recent research concerns "philosophical nationality." In what way does language seem to you to be constitutive of an identity? Is there a French philosophy?

J.D.: Everything depends obviously on what one means by language. And also, if you will pardon my saying so, by "identity" and "constitution." If, as I seem to understand, by identity you mean identity of a "philosophical nationality" or in a larger sense of a philosophical tradition, I would say that language, of course, plays a very important role there. Philosophy finds its element in so-called natural language. It has never been able to formalize itself integrally in an artificial language despite several fascinating attempts to do so in the history of philosophy. It is also true that this formalization (according to artificial codes constituted in the course of a history) is always, up to a certain point, at work. This means that philosophical language or languages are more or less well defined and coherent subsets within natural languages or rather the uses of natural languages. And one may find equivalents and regulated translations between these subsets from one natural language to another. Thus German and French philosophers can refer to more or less ancient and stable conventions in order to translate their respective uses of certain words that have a high degree of philosophical content. But you know all the problems this provokes, problems which are not distinguishable from the philosophical debate itself.

If, on the other hand, there is no thinking outside of some language (a proposition that would nevertheless have to be accompanied by many precautions that I cannot enumerate here), then, of course, an identity and especially a national identity in philosophy is not constituted outside of the element of language.

That said, I don't believe one can establish a simple correspondence between a national philosophical tradition and a language, in the ordinary sense of this term. The so-called Continental and Anglo-Saxon (or analytic) traditions, to use these very crude and imprecise labels, are divided, and in a very uneven fashion, among English, German, Italian, Spanish, and so forth. The philosophical "language" (by which I mean the subcode) of analytic philosophy or of some tradition or other (Anglo-American, e.g., Austin; Austro-Anglo-American, e.g., Wittgenstein) is caught up in a number of overdeterminations in relation to the so-called national language, which is itself spoken by citizens of different countries (the English of Americans, the French spoken outside of France). This explains why there sometimes develops outside of the so-called language of origin (of the original text) a tradition of reading that is reassimilated only with difficulty by the very people who speak or think they speak this language of origin. This is true in very different ways for both Wittgenstein and Heidegger. The French "readings" or "reception" of Heidegger encounter a strong resistance in Germany (as does Heidegger himself, and for reasons that are not only political). As for French specialists of Wittgenstein, neither Germanophones nor Anglophones are very interested in it, to the point that one cannot even say they resist it.

Is there, then, a French philosophy? No, less than ever if one considers the heterogeneity, as well as the conflictuality, that marks all manifestations called philosophical: publications, teaching, discursive forms and norms, the relations to institutions, to the sociopolitical field, to the power of the media. One would even have trouble establishing a typology, since every attempt at typology would presuppose precisely an interpretation that takes sides in the conflict. It would encounter right away a predictable hostility from almost all sides. Therefore, although I do have my own little idea about this, I will not risk it, here, now. On the other hand, despite all the debates and battles over philosophical "positions" or "practices," who can deny that there is a configuration of French philosophy, and that over its history, despite the succession of hegemonies, despite the mobility of dominant strains, this configuration constitutes a tradition, which is to say a relatively identifiable element of transmission, memory, heritage? In order to analyze it, one would have to take into account a very large number of always overdeterminable givens—historical, linguistic, social—across very specific institutions (which are not only the institutions of teaching and research), but without ever forgetting that rather capital over-determination which we call philosophy, if there is any! This is too difficult and too touchy for me to risk getting into it here in a few sentences. I think that the identity of French philosophy has never been more severely tested than it is today. The signs of this are a growing rigidity of the power of the University as exercised in its official capacities as well as, and often going in the same direction, a certain journalistic aggressivity. To take only one current example, I will cite the decision handed down just recently (by the CNU) that prevents [Philippe] Lacoue-Labarthe and [Jean-Luc] Nancy, which is to say two philosophers whose work has been recognized and respected in France and abroad for many years, from becoming full professors in the university.[4] Through these sometimes laughable signs of war, which finally paralyze nothing but what is already inert and paralyzed, the severe test I mentioned a moment ago confers its singularity on this thing we call "French philosophy." It belongs to an idiom which is, as always, more difficult to perceive at home than abroad. The idiom, if there is one, is never pure, chosen, or manifest on its own side, precisely. The idiom is always and only for the other, in advance expropriated (exappropriated).

The Rhetoric of Drugs

Q.: You are not a specialist in the study of drug addiction, yet we suppose that as a philosopher you may have something of particular interest to say on this subject, if only because of the concepts common both to philosophy and addictive studies, for example dependency, freedom, pleasure, *jouissance*.

J.D.: Okay. Let us speak then from the point of view of the non-specialist which indeed I am. But certainly you will agree that in this case we are dealing with something other than a delimitable domain. The criteria for competence, and especially for professional competence, are very problematic here. In the end, it is just these criteria that, whether directly or not, we will be led to discuss. Having identified me as a philosopher, a non-specialist in this thing called "drug addiction," you have just named a number of highly philosophical concepts, concepts that philosophy is obliged to consider as priorities: "freedom," "dependency," "pleasure" or "jouissance," and so forth. So be it. But I propose to begin quite simply with "concept," with the concept of concept. "Drugs" is both a word and a concept, even before one adds quotation marks to indicate that one is only mentioning them and not using them, that one is not buying, selling, or ingesting the "stuff itself" [*la chose même*].

Such a remark is not neutral, innocently philosophical, logical,

228

or speculative. Nor is it for the same reasons, nor in the same manner that one might note, just as correctly, that such and such a plant, root, or substance is also for us a concept, a "thing" apprehended through the name of a concept and the device of an interpretation. No, in the case of "drugs" the regime of the concept is different: there are no drugs "in nature." There may be "natural" poisons and indeed naturally lethal poisons, but they are not poisonous insofar as they are drugs. As with drug addiction, the concept of drugs supposes an instituted and an institutional definition: a history is required, and a culture, conventions, evaluations, norms, an entire network of intertwined discourses, a rhetoric, whether explicit or elliptical. We will surely come back to this rhetorical dimension. There is not, in the case of drugs, any objective, scientific, physical (physicalistic), or "naturalistic" definition (or rather there is: this definition may be "naturalistic," if by this we understand that it attempts to naturalize that which defies any natural definition or any definition of natural reality). One can claim to define the *nature* of a toxin; however, not all toxins are drugs, nor are they considered as such. Already one must conclude that the concept of drugs is a non-scientific concept, that it is instituted on the basis of moral or political evaluations: it carries in itself norm or prohibition, and allows no possibility of description or certification—it is a decree, a buzzword [*mot d'ordre*]. Usually the decree is of a prohibitive nature; occasionally, on the other hand, it is glorified and revered: malediction and benediction always call to and imply one another. As soon as one utters the word "drugs," even before any "addiction," a prescriptive or normative "diction" is already at work, performatively, whether one likes it or not. This "concept" will never be a purely theoretical or theorizable concept. And if there is never a theorem for drugs, there can never be a scientific competence for it either, one attestable as such and which would not be essentially overdetermined by ethico-political norms. For this reason I have seen fit to begin with some reservations about the division "specialist/non-specialist." No doubt the division may prove difficult for other reasons.

From these premises one may draw different, indeed contradictory ethico-political conclusions. On the one hand, there would be a *naturalist* conclusion: "Since 'drugs' and 'drug addiction,' " one might say, "are nothing but normative concepts, institutional evaluations or prescriptions, this artifice must be reduced. Let us return to true natural freedom. Natural law dictates that each of us be left the freedom to do as we will with our desire, our soul, and our body, as well as with that stuff known as 'drugs.' Let us finally do away with this law which the history of conventions and of ethical norms has so deeply inscribed in the concept of 'drugs'; let's get rid of this suppression or repression; let's return to nature."

To this naturalistic, liberal, and indeed laxist decree [*mot d'ordre*] one may, on the basis of the same premises, oppose an artificialist policy and a deliberately repressive position. Occasionally, this may, just like its liberal counterpart, take on a therapeutic guise, preventativist, if I can put it like that, inclined to be persuasionist and pedagogical: "we recognize," one might say, "that this concept of drugs is an instituted norm. Its origin and its history are obscure. Such a norm does not follow analytically from any scientific concept of natural toxicity, nor, despite all our best efforts to establish it in this sense, will it ever do so. Nonetheless, by entirely assuming the logic of this prescriptive and repressive convention, we believe that *our* society, *our* culture, *our* conventions require this interdiction. Let us deploy it consistently. At stake here are the health, security, productivity, and the orderly functioning of these very institutions. By means of this law, at once supplementary and fundamental, these institutions protect the very possibility of the law in general, for by prohibiting drugs we assure the integrity and responsibility of the legal subject, of the citizens, and so forth. There can be no law without the conscious, vigilant, and normal subject, master of his or her intentions and desires. This interdiction and this law are thus not just artifacts like any other: they are the very condition of possibility of a respect for the law in general in our society. An interdiction is not necessarily bad, nor must it necessarily assume brutal forms; the paths it follows may be twisted and symbolically overdetermined, but no one can deny that the survival of our culture originarily comprises this interdiction. It belongs to the very concept of our culture, and so forth."

From the moment we recognize the institutional character of a certain concept of drugs, drug addiction, narcotics, and poisons, two ethico-political axiomatics seem to oppose each other. Briefly put, I am not sure that this contradiction is more than superficial; nor am I convinced that either of these logics can follow through to their conclusions; and finally I am not sure that the two so radically exclude each other. Let us not forget that both start from the same premises—that is, the opposition of nature and institution. And not simply of nature and the law, but indeed already of two laws, of two decrees. Naturalism is no more natural than conventionalism.

Q.: The word *toxicomanie* first came into use just before the end of the last century; the kinds of behavior which we now call addictive were previously not considered a medical, nosological phenomenon. In England one used the old term *addiction*, which emphasized the subject's dependency on a given product, but there was as yet no question of a drug pathology, of a toxicomania. Toxicomania, the notion of drug addiction as a disease, is contemporaneous with modernity and with modern science. "Flash," a term introduced by photography, was, oddly enough, picked up by addicts.[1] And at some point, someone, abusively consuming certain products, was for the first time called a toxicomaniac.

J.D.: Actually, in the eyes of the law, dependency on a toxic product or even on harmful medications does not, as such, belong to toxicomania. But let's take a moment to consider this modernity. As always, drugs are here the effect of an interpretation. Drugs are "bad" but the evil in them is not simply a "harmfulness." Alcohol and tobacco are, as objects of consumption, just as artificial as any drug, and no one will now dispute their harmfulness. One may prescribe—as does the medical community and a certain segment of society—abstinence from drinking (especially while driving—a decisive question for the public/private distinction) and abstinence from smoking (especially in *public* places). Still, even if they are considered somehow "bad," as driving or health hazards, alcohol and tobacco are never denounced as narcotics, they are never branded with such a moral stigma. The relation to "public safety" is thus different.

One can, of course, refer to alcohol or tobacco as "drugs," but this will necessarily imply a sort of irony, as if in so doing one only marked a sort of rhetorical displacement. Tobacco and alcohol, we tranquilly assume, are not really drugs. Of course, their harmfulness can become the object of dissuasive campaigns and of a whole quasi-moral pedagogy, but the simple consumption of these products, in and of itself, does not form the object of moral reprobation or, more important, of criminal prosecution. One can prosecute a drunkard because he is *also* a dangerous driver, but not because alcohol might have been "classified" as a narcotic (to use the legal terminology of the articles defining the "Struggle Against Toxicomania"[2]). The (secular) prohibition of alcohol, if I'm not mistaken, will be seen as a brief and unique interlude in the history of mankind; and, for well-known reasons, more unthinkable in France than anywhere else. This should remind us that, in France, the drug market, unlike the wine market, is supplied mainly by *foreign* productions. And this is also the case in many Western nations. But of course this fact hardly suffices to explain our modern legislation, that of the [French] laws of 1970 in particular.

What, then, is the modernity, if indeed there is one, of the phenomenon of drug addiction, of its definition, which, as we were just saying, is always a normative or prescriptive interpretation? This is a very difficult question—in fact a swarm of obscure questions. One of these leads back to the entire, massively intertwined history of the division between public and private. I wouldn't presume to take on the issue here. Let us simply note that the legislation of 1970 also condemns the *use*, whether public or *private*, and not just the dealing of drugs—what article 626 calls "production, conveyance, importation, exportation, holding, tender, transfer, acquisition." One might have thought this would be enough to prosecute anyone who used drugs, for one cannot very well use drugs without having in one way or another "acquired" them. Were such the case, the principle dictating respect for private life and a right to freely dispose of one's person would have been at least formally and hypocritically respected. But no, the law explicitly specifies that the "use" of classified substances will be punished by fine and imprisonment. The word "use" completes the list of acts that I cite above.[3]

And the opening of title VI of the law establishing the "Struggle Against Toxicomania" also speaks of simple *use*: "Any person who illicitly uses plants or substances classified as narcotics is to be placed under the surveillance of the health authorities." The non-illicit use of substances thus "classified" is the supervised, medical use, the other version of the same *pharmakon* (an enormous problem, and now more timely than ever before).

Another question is tied up with the technical one and with any given technological mutation. The definition of toxicomania, as you were saying, suggests not just a casual use, but rather a frequent and repeated drug use: thus, not simply an ample supply (numerous techno-economical transformations of the marketplace, transportation, international communication, etc.), but the technical possibility for an individual to reproduce the act, even when alone (the question of the syringe, for example, to which we shall have to return).

It is this crossing of a quantitative threshold that allows us to speak of a modern phenomenon of toxicomania: namely, the number of individuals that have easy access to the possibility of repeating the act, alone or otherwise, in private or in public, and throughout the zone where this distinction loses all pertinence or rigor.

I think that now, at this moment, it is no longer possible to dissociate this narcotic "modernity" from what is happening to humanity as one of the major events, that is, one of the most revealing and, what amounts to the same thing, one of the most "apocalyptic" in its most essential and "interior" history: what is called AIDS. But we will no doubt have to come back to this...

Q.: Do you link this modernity to mass production? to repetition? Do we rediscover here a questioning of writing, of the *pharmakon*?

J.D.: I have indeed attempted to link up the problematic of the *pharmakon* with the very disconcerting "logic" of what we casually call "repetition." In the *Phaedrus*, writing is presented to the king, before the law, before the political authority of power, as a beneficial *pharmakon* because, as Theuth claims, it enables us to repeat, and thus to remember. This then would be a good repetition, in the service of anamnesis. But the king disqualifies this repetition. This is not *good* repetition. "You have found a *pharmakon* not for memory (*mnēmē*), but rather for recollection (*hypomnesis*)."[4] The *pharmakon* "writing" does not serve the good, authentic memory. It is rather the mnemotechnical auxiliary of a bad memory. It has more affinity with forgetting, the simulacrum, and *bad* repetition than it does with anamnesis and truth. This *pharmakon* dulls the spirit and rather than aiding memory, it loses it. It is thus in the name of authentic, living memory, and in the name of truth, that power accuses this bad drug, writing, of being a drug that leads not only to forgetting, but also to irresponsibility. Writing is irresponsibility itself, the orphanage of a wandering and playful sign. Writing is not only a drug, it is a game, *paideia*, and a bad game if it is no longer ruled by a concern for philosophical truth. Thus, in the rhetoric of a familial scene, there is no father to answer for it any longer, and no living, purely living speech can help it. The bad *pharmakon* can always parasitize the good *pharmakon*, bad repetition can always parasitize good repetition. This parasitism is at once accidental and essential. Like any good parasite, it is at once inside and outside—the outside *feeding* on the inside. And with this schema of food we are very close to what, in the usual sense of the word, we call drugs, which are usually to be "consumed." "Deconstruction" is always attentive to this indestructible logic of parasitism. As a discourse, deconstruction is always a discourse about the parasite, itself a device parasitic on the subject of the parasite, a discourse "on parasite" and in the logic of the "superparasite."

That said, however tempting and instructive it might be, the transposition of this problematic (which for lack of time I have very much simplified) toward what you call "modern toxicomania," together with its theoretical and practical interpretations, requires, as you may well imagine, the greatest caution.

Q.: Certain drug-users unwittingly tell us that by writing they seek to end their addiction. When they carry out this project, we often witness an intensification of their anxiety and of their addiction. And yet, some psychoanalysts insist on the function of writing in providing a release from symptoms. By writing itself, does drug addiction end?

J.D.: We cannot trust in the simple opposition of symptom and cause, of repression and the release from repression, any more than we can count on a simple opposition of memory and forgetting, especially considering the paradoxes of repetition and of the relation to the other. "Good" repetition is always haunted or contaminated by "bad" repetition, so much the better and so much the worse for it. The *pharmakon* will always be apprehended as both antidote *and* poison. As you were just saying, the drug addict may seek to forget even as he takes on the work of an anamnesic analysis, may at once seek repression and a release from repression (which indeed suggests that this is not the pertinent boundary, and that it has other, more twisted forms...). To this end the addict uses a "technique," a technical supplement which he also interprets as being "natural".... Another thread would bring us to that very common distrust as regards the artificial, the instrumentalization of memory, thus as regards the *pharmakon, both* as poison *and* as antidote, along with that supplementary discomfort stemming from the indecidability between the two...

Q.: In this regard, we might also compare the results of Platonic *mimesis*, itself the product of a technique which at once recalls and opposes itself to an original model.

J.D.: The question of *mimesis*, or, if I might risk a shortcut, the question of drugs as the question—the great question—of truth. No more no less. What do we hold against the drug addict? Something we never, at least never to the same degree, hold against the alcoholic or the smoker: that he cuts himself off from the world, in exile from reality, far from objective reality and the real life of the city and the community; that he escapes into a world of simulacrum and fiction. He is reproached for his taste for something like hallucinations. No doubt, we should have to make some distinction between so-called hallucinogens and other drugs, but this distinction is wiped out in the rhetoric of fantasy that is at the root of the interdiction: drugs, it is said, make one lose any sense of true reality. In the end, it is always, I think, under this charge that the interdiction is declared. We do not object to the drug user's pleasure per se, but to a pleasure taken in an experience without truth. Pleasure and play (now still as with Plato) are not in themselves condemned unless they are inauthentic and void of truth. This, then, is the system which ought to be analyzed carefully and articulated with the political question of fiction or literature. If he does not at least subordinate his poetics to philosophy and to the politics of the philosopher, the man of the simulacrum will find himself driven from the community by Plato (etc.). If, in "modernity," we still suppose there to be some affinity between, on the one hand, the experience of fiction (literary or otherwise, whether from the perspective of the "producer," the distributor, or the consumer) and, on the other hand, the world of drug use; and if we imagine this affinity even when the poet does not search for any "artificial paradise," in that case the writer is accepted only to the degree that he allows himself to be reintegrated by the institutions. He restores the normal order of intelligible production; he produces and his production generates value. This legitimation has to do with the evaluation of a productivity which is at least interpreted as a source of truth, albeit one that comes through the medium of fiction. The drug addict, in our common conception, the drug addict as such produces nothing, nothing true or real. He is legitimated, in certain cases, secretly and inadmissibly, by certain portions of society, only in as much as he participates, at least indirectly, in the production and consumption of goods...

Q.: With certain writers—those of the "Grand Jeu,"[5] Burroughs currently, Artaud when he was with the surrealists, in his "Letter to the Legislator"—drugs are advanced as the object of a political battle, indeed the definitive political battle. With Burroughs, drugs are a "weapon" used in a terminal war, as the final form of "world trade." Such a consideration seems rather timely.

J.D.: Certainly, for Artaud, in any case, there was the project of lifting a system of norms and prohibitions which constitute European culture and especially European religion. From Mexican drugs, he sought the power to emancipate the subject, to end that subjection which from birth had somehow expropriated the subject, and most of all to end its subjection to the very concept of the subject. Already at birth, God had stolen his body and his name. Indeed, at stake in this experience was a desire to be done with the judgment of God. But speaking thus extemporaneously we oversimplify the matter, and I would rather go back to Artaud's texts, to those written not simply "on drugs" and under the influence, but which moreover call into question, in language itself, and wrestle with systems of interpreting drugs. And then we would have to distinguish carefully between discourses, practices, and experiences of writing, literary or not, which imply or justify what we call drugs. Abysses often lie between them. There is not a *single* world of drugs. Artaud's text is not Michaux's or Benjamin's (I am thinking in particular of his "Hashish in Marseilles"[6]), neither of which should be confused with Baudelaire's text which in turn is not that of Coleridge nor of De Quincey. To conflate such differences in a homogeneous series would be delirious, indeed narcoticizing. But then, can one ever condemn or prohibit without also somehow confusing?

Q.: In literature at least, we can date the concept of toxicomania, in the modern sense of the word, from the publication of De Quincey's *Confessions of an English Opium-Eater*. By the same token, alcoholism first appeared in French literature with Zola.

J.D.: This path deserves to be followed. Pending a more thorough investigation, we might perhaps risk a hypothesis. Let us consider literature, in a fairly strict sense, distinguishing it, at least in Europe, from poetry and belles lettres, as a modern phenomenon (dating from the sixteenth or seventeenth century). Well then, is it not thus contemporaneous with a certain European drug addiction? In fact, one that was tolerated? You've mentioned De Quincey, but we also have Coleridge. We might, just this once, add a word on coffee and tobacco: whole theses, even whole departments of literature (general or comparative) should perhaps be devoted to the study of coffee and tobacco in our literatures. Consider Balzac or Valéry: two otherwise and obviously very different cases. Would we not be rather hard-pressed to find anything analogous, from Homer to Dante, *before* this literary modernity? We will soon enough come back to Homer. But first consider the figures of dictation, in the asymmetrical experience of the other (of the being-given-over-to-the-other, of the being prey to the other, of quasi-possession) that commands a certain writing, perhaps all writing, even the most masterful (gods, the daemon, the muses, inspiration, and so forth). These forms of originary alienation, in the most positive, productive and irreducible sense of the word, these figures of *dictation*—are they not drawn into a history in which drugs, following "the flight of the gods," one day came to take a place left vacant, or to play the role of an enfeebled phantom? Rather it would be a matter of a methodical provocation, of a technique for calling up the phantom: the spirit, the ghost (*Geist*), inspiration, dictation. More precisely, and what makes the matter even more convoluted, we would be dealing here with a methodology of the counter-phantom. What is a counter-phantom? It is the phantom that one plays against another phantom, yet it is also the phantom of the phantom, the alibi phantom, the other phantom. Have we then a choice only between phantoms, or between the simulacra of phantoms?

But let's not act as if we knew what a phantom or a phantasm was, and as if it were enough simply to set out the consequences of such a knowledge. As long as we have not recognized the full magnitude of this enigma ("What is a phantom?" "What is a phantasm?" "What is the flight of the gods?"), beyond the opposition of presence and absence, of the real and the imaginary, even beyond a properly ontological question, the philosophical, political, and ideological "answers" to what we call "the drug problem" will remain expedients incapable of any radical auto-justification. We're back where we began, back to the problem of the criteria of competence and the impossibility of any theorem. The responsibilities that anyone (and first and foremost the "decision maker"—the legislator, educator, citizen in general, and so forth) must take in such an emergency are only all the more serious, difficult, and ineluctable. Depending on the circumstances (tirelessly analyzed, whether macroscopically or microscopically) the discourse of "interdiction" can be justified *just as well or just as badly* as the liberal discourse. Repressive practice (in all its brutal or sophisticated, punitive or re-educational forms) can be justified just as well or just as badly as permissive practice (with all its ruses). Since it is impossible to justify absolutely either the one or the other of these practices, one can never absolutely condemn them. In an emergency, this can only lead to equivocations, negotiations, and unstable compromises. And in any given, progressively evolving situation, these will need to be guided by a concern for the singularity of each individual experience and by a socio-political analysis that is at once as broadly and as finely tuned as possible. I say this not to avoid the question, any more than I do to argue for relativism or opportunism; rather, I would simply describe the state of affairs in which such decisions have to be made when the ultimate extent and boundaries of the problem remain unanalyzed and unthought.

This "state of affairs," this equivocation of discourses incapable of any radical justification, this is just what we observe both in the customs and in the discourses that now dominate our society. The only attitude (the only politics—judicial, medical, pedagogical, and so forth) I would *absolutely* condemn is one which, directly or indirectly, cuts off the possibility of an essentially interminable questioning, that is, an effective and thus transforming questioning.

By effective and transforming questioning I mean, of course, the work of analysis (in every sense, from psychoanalysis to the socio-economico-political study of the conditions of drug addiction: unemployment, the geopolitics of the marketplace, the "real" condition of what we call democracy, the police, the state of criminal law and of medical institutions, and so forth), but also a thoughtful reflection on the axioms of this problematic and on all those discourses that inform it. We have just spoken of the phantom and of ontology, before that we were talking about the simulacrum, truth, and repetition. Thus at stake here is the very genealogy of a vast number of conceptual oppositions: nature/culture or nature/convention, nature/technique, emancipation/alienation, public/private, and so forth.

To continue on the subject of the inspired trance in what we habitually call writing, ought we not attempt some sort of a history of dictation, and more precisely, of what we call *inspiration*: if possible, literally, that is to say "physically" (for example, inhalation), or figuratively? What is still "inspired," what "inspires," and who "inspires," in the proper or the figural sense, in the experience of drugs? Where is the boundary here between poetry and prose, between poetry and the novel, and between various types of novels and various structures of fictionality, and so on?

There are those who would say, and not without "common sense": when the sky of transcendence comes to be emptied, and not just of Gods, but of any Other, a sort of fated rhetoric fills the void, and this is the fetishism of drug addiction. Not religion as the opiate of the people, but drugs as the religion of the atheist poets—and of some others, more or less atheists, more or less poets.

We have neither enough time nor enough space to do it, but were we to follow this thread further, we might come back to those questions we touched upon earlier, questions of nature and of production. These two concepts also belong to a series of oppositions and refer back to their "history." But let us for the moment put this aside for it is not something that lends itself to improvisation (a brief treatise, in parentheses, on the question of drugs and improvisation, in the arts and elsewhere). We imagine that the drug addict–writer seeks to discover a sort of gracious and graceful inspiration, a passivity that welcomes what repression or suppression would otherwise inhibit: "By the grace of the technical or artificial, and ever-*interiorizing* violence of an injection, inhalation, or ingestion, by taking into my self, inside myself a foreign body, or indeed a nutriment, I will provoke a state of productive receptivity:

the word being at once received and sent forth, in a sort of creative spontaneity or transcendental imagination, I will let it go, and the violence will have put an end to violence. Reappropriation will be induced by the foreign body and production will take place without effort, and so forth." This transcendental-imaginary discourse (imaginary for anyone who would profess it as well as for anyone who might hope to unmask it), this is what is condemned by a society based on work and on the subject answerable as subject. A poem ought to be the product of *real* work, even if the traces of that work have been washed away. It is always non-work that is disqualified. The authentic work [*oeuvre*], as its name seems to suggest, ought to be the result of an effort (with merit and rewards) and of a responsible effort, even up to the point where the effort effaces itself, erasing its traces or erasing itself before that which is given to it. And even if the work [*oeuvre*] comes from an effortless labor, a work without work, submitted to the dictation of the other, still we require that this alterity be authentic and not factitious, neither simulated nor stimulated by artificial projections. It is in the name of this authenticity that drug addiction is condemned or deplored. This authenticity can be *appropriated*—either simultaneously (in confusion) or successively (in denial) to the values of natural or symbolic normality, of truth, of a real relation to true reality, of free and responsible subjectivity, of productivity, and so forth. And it *appropriates* such different values, makes them *proper* to itself the more so in that it is itself founded on the value of *properness or property*, and of the appropriation or reappropriation of self. It is the making proper of the proper itself [*propriation du propre même*], in as much as the proper is opposed to the heterogeneity of the im-proper, and to every mode of foreignness or alienation that might be recognized in someone's resorting to drugs. And this value might just as easily be the mainstay of a right-wing as of a left-wing discourse, and just as easily in the East as in the West.

This specularity should not surprise you. It is inexhaustible. A certain form of drug addiction can, moreover, also reflect this same phantasm of reappropriation. It can do so naively or with a great "cultivation," dreaming also of emancipation and of the restoration of an "ego," of a self, or of the self's own body, or even of a subject once and for all reclaimed from the forces of alienation, from oppression and repression, and from the law that speaks in religion, metaphysics, politics, the family, and so forth.

As convoluted and paradoxical as this "logic" of reappropriation may be, especially when it gets mixed up with the simulacrum, still one can never quite escape from it. Certainly, for example, it is not missing from certain of Artaud's texts. This logic goes together with a thinking or an experience of the proper that no doubt carries it beyond itself, that gets carried away and otherwise expropriates itself. The boundaries here are not between two opposed camps or between two metaphysics in which one might clearly recognize certain commonalities. They are not the boundaries between "repression" and "lifting of repression," between suppression and non-suppression. Rather, even if up to a point they could or should yield to certain more or less refined typologies, these boundaries run between a non-finite number of *experiences*.

And I find no better word than *experience*, that is to say, the voyage that crosses the boundary. An experience *between* two experiences: on the one hand, the passage, the odyssey, with or without *nostalgia*—you are perhaps familiar with Adorno and Horkheimer's text on the lotus-eaters and on this Homeric *nostos*[7]—the wandering from which one cannot return, so many possibilities wrapped up in a certain etymology of the word "experience," occasionally associated, like the "trip," with the experience of "drugs," with the relation to the other and with an opening up to the world in general; and, on the other hand, we have the organized experiment, the *experimental* as an "organized voyage." What does this *between* signify? Perhaps it means that the experience to which I am referring, the thought of this experience or this experience as thought does not as yet yield to a determination within the usual series of oppositions, for example nature/technics, nature/artifice, non-work/work, natural experience/artificial experimentation, and so forth. Thus I am not speaking merely of experiences with drugs or experiences with non-drugs (which, after all, are no more natural than drugs), but rather of experiences which are qualitatively highly differentiated, occasionally even for the same "individual," and which we cannot mention without multiplying qualifications and points of view. Every name and every concept which one might use to define these criteria, these qualifications and points of view, is already caught up in very restrictive discursive sequences. All of them answer to a highly stabilized program, one that is particularly difficult to undo. We are dealing here with a metaphysical burden and a history which we must never stop questioning. At stake here is nothing less than the self, consciousness, reason, freedom, the responsible subject, alienation, one's own body or the foreign body, sexual difference, the unconscious, repression or suppression, the different "parts" of the body, injection, introjection, incorporation (oral or not), the relationship to death (mourning and interiorization), idealization, sublimation, the real and the law, and I could go on.

Q.: Do all drug addicts then tell of a lost body or a body they seek to discover, an ideal body, a perfect body?

J.D.: Here again the opposition between *dominant* or *canonical* discourses is not a radical one. It seems rather secondary to an axiomatic that remains common to the majority of those who speak or act *against* drug addiction as well as to the majority of those who act or argue *for* it—or who would at least redirect the interdiction toward more liberal, softer forms (for example, the legalization of "soft" drugs) or toward more intelligent forms, compromises, mediations, negotiations (after all, in our society one rarely finds anyone who publicly advocates drug use). From the prohibitionist, then, we hear of a need to protect society from everything we associate with drug use: irresponsibility, non-work, irrationality, unproductivity, delinquency—either sexual or not—illness and the social costs it entails, and more generally, the very destruction of the *social bond*. But this protection of the social bond, and thus of a certain symbolicity, indeed of rationality in general—this is almost always presented as the protection of a "natural" normality of the body, of the social body and the body of the individual member.

In the name of this organic and originary naturalness of the body we declare and wage the war on drugs, the war against these artificial, pathogenic, and foreign aggressions. Again we find a desire to reconstitute what you just called the "ideal body," the "perfect body." But as you also just pointed out, from the other side of the problem, so to speak (for you see how this opposition remains problematic), "products" otherwise considered as dangerous and unnatural are often considered apt for the liberation of this same "ideal" or "perfect body" from social oppression, suppression, and repression, or from the reactive violence that reduces originary forces or desire, indeed the "primary processes." And this is the same naturalistic metaphysics that, in order to restore a "prior" body—we could almost say prior to the fall—is translated through codes that can occasionally turn out to be quite diverse (of a sort that is vaguely "Nietzschean," "Freudian," "Artaudian," "Marcusian," and so forth).

In outlining this false opposition and exaggerating its characteristics, I have spoken of *canonical or dominant* discourses. Now, in analyzing, as I intend to do, the common grounds of these two discourses, we must ask ourselves how and why they have become, precisely, "canonical or dominant." Where does their force or their authority come from? What contract binds them together? What do the two together exclude, and so forth? What contradictions or tensions are at work even inside the canonical? As I see it these are the fundamental questions, or rather, and by the same token, the most indispensable "philosophico-political" moves. Their necessity cannot, moreover, fail to be felt throughout every "crisis" or "symptom" of "crisis" that our societies are currently undergoing.

Neither of the two opposed "canons" takes into account what we might call the *technological condition.* There is no natural, originary body: technology has not simply added itself, from the outside or after the fact, as a foreign body. Or at least this foreign or dangerous supplement is "originarily" at work and in place in the supposedly ideal interiority of the "body and soul." It is indeed at the heart of the heart.

Rushing things a bit, I would say that what now takes on particular and macroscopic forms, without being absolutely new, is this paradox of a "crisis," as we superficially call it, of naturalness. This alleged "crisis" also manifests itself, for example, throughout the problems of biotechnology and throughout the new and so-called artificial possibilities for dealing with life, from birth to death, as if there had once been some standard of naturalness and as if the boundary between nature and its other were susceptible to objectification. Let me just quickly add that in certain always singular circumstances, the recourse to dangerous experimentation with what we call "drugs" may be guided by a desire to think this alleged boundary from both sides at once, and thus to think this boundary as such, in any case to approach its formation, its simulation, or its simulacrum as it takes form (for this boundary does not exist, is never *present*, and has no essence). This experience (one to which artists and thinkers occasionally devote themselves, but which is by no means the unique privilege of those who claim or to whom we grant such a status), this experience may be sought with or without "drugs," at least without any "narcotic" "classified" as such by the law. We will always have unclassified or unclassifiable supplements of drugs or narcotics. Basically everybody has his own, and I don't just mean stuff that is patently comestible, smokable, or shootable. As you know, the introjection or incorporation of the other has so many other resources, stratagems, and detours... It can always invent new orifices, in addition to and beyond those, for example the mouth, which we think we naturally possess. Besides, orality does not open up only to receive, but also, as they say, to emit, and we should ask ourselves whether drug addiction consists simply and essentially in receiving and taking in, rather than in "expressing" and pushing outside, for example in a certain form of speaking or of singing, whether or not we drink what we "spit out." There is no doubt, at least for orality, for hearing, and for hearing-oneself-speak, a zone of experience where giving and receiving, inspiration and expiration, impression and expression, passivity and activity can only with great difficulty be opposed to one another, or even distinguished. And then, even supposing that we could delimit it, oral consumption is no more limited to any particular classified narcotic than it is to all sorts of non-classified objects of compulsive ingestion, things like chocolate or marzipan, liquor, coffee, or tobacco.

And since I've just mentioned coffee and tobacco you might think of that really very "French," very "Cartesian" writer, one who was also a philosopher of vigilance and freedom, of the will, self-consciousness and self-mastery both in thinking and in writing—I have in mind Valéry, who every day at dawn organized his trances of writing and lucidity in a secular temple dedicated to the cult of coffee and cigarettes. Another very "French," very "Cartesian" writer, himself also a philosopher of vigilance and freedom, of the will, self-consciousness, and so forth—here I have in mind Sartre, who was at one time, so they say, a serious user of pharmaceutical drugs and "abused" these non-"classified" substances for his writing... Fine, enough of that, but as you see this *coincidentia oppositorum* always takes us back to the question of consciousness, reason and work, truth, the good memory, and the anamnesis of allegedly primary or natural processes. In the end, or in the very long run (for by definition there will never be any absolutely final term), a thinking and a politics of this thing called "drugs" would involve the simultaneous displacement of these two opposed ideologies in their common metaphysics.

Do not ask me whether I am for or against one of these ideologies at this precise moment. Today, here and now, in my private-public life, and in the determined situation of "our" society, I feel rather more inclined toward an *ethos*, shall we say, that, according to the dominant codes, would be interpreted as somewhat repressive and interdictive, at least in the case of the "classified" drugs. (As I suggested above, one can also extend the concept and the experience of drugs far beyond its legal, medical definition, and in a space at once idiosyncratic and public, arrange all sorts of practices, pleasures, and pains that no one could rigorously show to be unrelated and without analogy to drug addiction. The possibilities are innumerable and quasi-idiomatic. Every phantasmatic organization, whether collective or individual, is the invention of a drug, or of a rhetoric of drugs, be it aphrodisiac or not, including production, consumption, semi-secrecy, and a semi-private market...) But to attempt to justify the *ethos* which draws me toward an apparently "repressive" attitude (in the case of "classified" drugs), I should not, in the final analysis, rely on any of those discourses or axiomatics which I have just sketched out. This much would be strictly necessary, and yet so hard! Thus, in an unprepared interview, in the space of a few pages I cannot, so to speak, do right by this justification. However, what most matters to me, as you might guess, is precisely the necessity—or the difficulty—of such a justification, and it is this that guides me in all that I say or do, whether in "public" or in "private," and even when there is apparently no question of drugs as such. And if you consider that I believe neither in the infallible pertinence of the distinction between public and private (a distinction threatened by the very structure of language, and even before language, by the iterability of any mark) nor in the simple essence of the aphrodisiac (the economy of pleasure is so very convoluted...), you will understand even better my reserve...

As we were saying, the logic of *technological supplementarity* is not much tolerated by either of these two sides, by either of these two "canons." The "new" (new thinking, new practice, new politics) here supposes a formalization powerful enough to allow us to comprehend *both canons at once*, by displacing their shared axiomatics. On the subject of this newness one may have two contradictory feelings. *On the one hand*, as they say, "that day is a long way off." Such a formalization will never be fully accessible. Granted, but then "fully accessible," plenitude, and absolute access, is this not still the language of these two "canons," the shared desire of the drug user and of the one who would "just say no"? *On the other hand*, and no less obviously, this formalization and displacement are *practically* under way and following a laborious, turbulent, apparently chaotic course; indeed, this is the very experience of our current "crisis." If today so many socio-ethico-political problems intersect and condense in the problem of drugs, it is not simply because of the modern technology we were just talking about. The indissociability of all these emergencies, the impossibility of isolating a "drug problem" only becomes all the more clear; and, by the same token, so does the necessity of treating a "general logic" as such of discourses on the subject of drugs, and *simultaneously* discourses on the subject of artificial insemination, sperm banks, the market for surrogate mothers, organ transplants, euthanasia, sex changes, the use of drugs in sports, *and especially, especially* on the subject of AIDS, which we will finally have to discuss. For isn't it true that henceforth AIDS will offer us a privileged and inevitable access into all these questions?

Q.: It is ironic that athletes, offered up as role models to our children, should find themselves, because of steroids, in the front lines of the war on drugs. A bike racer says that he does drugs in order to be the first one at the top of the hill. And yet, doesn't the drug addict also say that he wants to come in, if not in first place, in any case at the top of the hill that is life?

J.D.: Yes, basically, the farther we go, the more the question of drugs seems inseparable not only from such tremendous questions as "the concept," "reason," "truth," "memory," "work," and so forth, but also from the centers of urgency where all these things appear to gather symptomatically: for example, what does a society do with literature? What of birth, death, and AIDS? And, yes, you are quite correct, what of sports? and so forth. Everything about the politics of sports today (discourses, markets, entertainment) opens up a new main line for the analysis of the social bond. And in this case we can never get around the problem of drug use by athletes: where does it begin? How can we classify and track its products? And by what authority do we condemn this drug use or such and such a chemical prosthesis? And what about women athletes who get pregnant for the stimulating, hormonal effects and then have an abortion after their event? In any case, as the basis of this condemnation, one still supposes that the athletic hero should treat his body *naturally*. As such he works out, he makes his body work in a production that is not simply individual. Through the social-

ization of sports, whether it be professional or not, this so-called
disinterested work brings into play everything that relates to education: and first and foremost to the education of the will as the
overcoming of self in the self. In this sense not only should sports
avoid drugs, but as the anti-drug itself, the antidote for drugs, *the
pharmakon of the pharmakon*, it is the very thing which should be
kept safe from drugs, far from any possible contamination. Thus,
and nothing could have been easier to foresee, we have here the
zone closest, most analogous, and most exposed to the evil it
excludes. And not merely because, whether as exercise or as entertainment, sports can become literally intoxicating and depoliticizing (if you prefer, the arena for a certain drunkenness)—and as
such, moreover, sports can be manipulated by the political powers
that be—but also because competition seeks to stretch, and precisely by the use of such things as steroids, the body's "natural"
powers (and also the soul's: there are no sports without soul! I
would bet that someone will recognize in sports the essence of man.
Man, the rational, political animal, alone privileged with the possession of language and laughter, with the experience of death and
with other experiences "proper to man"—among them drugs!—let
us not forget that he is also an athletic animal). When one seeks to
extend these "natural powers," it is altogether natural, I mean
inevitable, that one should think of using such artificially natural
methods to go beyond man, toward the hero, the superman, and
other figures of a man who would be more man, more man than
man. . . The use of drugs in sports is condemned because it cheats
nature, but also because it cheats a certain idea of justice (the
equality of all participants in the contest). One wants to uphold the
integrity not only of the natural body but also of good will, of
consciousness, and of the spirit which maneuvers the body in the
athletic effort, in this free work or in this politically healthy game
which is, and from Plato on has been, athletic competition.

And yet those who, under certain prescribed conditions, would
defend the use of steroids claim that, after all, such drug use does
not corrupt an independent will, and thus cannot constitute drug
addiction. And furthermore, steroids do not provide any pleasure

as such, none that is individual and desocializing. Anyway, as I
think we've made clear, drugs in general are not condemned for the
pleasure they bring, but rather because this aphrodisiac is not the
right one: it leads to suffering and to the disintegration of the self,
in short, it desocializes. It belongs to that diabolical couple, pleasure and suffering, denounced in every indictment of drugs. The
hierarchy of pleasures goes together with that metaphysics of work
and activity (practical and theoretical, thus occasionally contem-
plative) which is mixed up in the history of Western reason. Here
again, Adorno and Horkheimer correctly point out that drug
culture has always been associated with the West's other, with
Oriental ethics and religion.[8]

So it cannot be said that the pleasure of drug use [*la jouissance
toxicomanique*] is in itself forbidden. Rather we forbid a pleasure
that is at once solitary, desocializing, and yet contagious for the
socius. We pretend to believe that if it were purely private, if the
drug user only availed himself of the sacred right to do as one will
with one's own body and soul, then even the most insidious
delights would be permissible. But such a hypothesis is ruled out in
advance: the consumer is a buyer and so takes part in dealing which
means that he participates in the open market, and thereby par-
takes in public discourse. Besides, you might even say that the act
of drug use is structured like a language and so could not be purely
private. Straightaway, drug use threatens the social bond. Again,
and just when it had been rather obscurely and dogmatically
crossed over, we come back to the problematic instability of the
boundary between public and private. The Enlightenment (*Aufklärung*), identified essentially by the motif of publicity and with
the public character of every act of reason, is in itself a declaration
of war on drugs.

Apparently, in the case of what is called sexual perversion, the
boundary between public and private would lie elsewhere. In fact,
here again things are very twisted, but since you have asked me
about a certain modernity of the problem, let us limit ourselves in
any case to this fact of our time that I believe to be absolutely
original and indelible: the appearance of AIDS. This is not just an

event with immeasurable effect on humanity, both on the world's surface and within the experience of the social bond. The various forms of this deadly contagion, its spatial and temporal dimensions deprive us henceforth of everything that a relation to the other, and first of all desire, could invent to protect the integrity and thus the inalienable identity of anything like a subject: in its "body," of course, but also in its entire symbolic organization, the ego and the unconscious, the *subject* in its separation and in its absolute secret. The virus (which belongs neither to life nor to death) may *always already* have broken into any "intersubjective" trajectory. And given its spatial and temporal dimensions, its structure of relays and delays, no human being is ever safe from AIDS. This possibility is thus installed at the heart of the social bond as intersubjectivity. And at the heart of that which would preserve itself as a dual intersubjectivity it inscribes the mortal and indestructible trace of the third party—not the third term as condition of the symbolic and the law, but the third as destructuring structuration of the social bond, as social disconnection [*déliaison*] and even as the disconnection of the interruption, of the "without relation" that can constitute a relation to the other in its alleged normality. The third itself is no longer a third, and the history of this normality more clearly displays its simulacra, almost as if AIDS painted a picture of its exposed anatomy. You may say this is how it's always been, and I believe it. But now, exactly as if it were a painting or a giant movie screen, AIDS provides an available, daily, massive *readability* to that which the canonical discourses we mentioned above had to deny, which in truth they are destined to deny, founded as they are by this very denial. If I spoke a moment ago of an event and of indestructibility, it is because already, at the dawn of this very new and ever so ancient thing, we know that, even should humanity some day come to control the virus (it will take at least a generation), still, even in the most unconscious symbolic zones, the traumatism has irreversibly affected our experience of desire and of what we blithely call intersubjectivity, the relation to the alter ego, and so forth.

Enough said; I'll stop this digression. You may tell me that this is not our subject. Quite right, for if there is no theorem for drugs, it is because there is no longer any purely identifiable and delimitable *subject* here. But let's at least remember this: the modern problem of drugs was already judged to be indissociable, in its genesis and thus in its treatment, from the problem of delinquency in general (and not just of delinquency *as* drug addiction). From now on it is indissociably tied up with—and subordinated to—the problem of AIDS. If we consider the fact that the phenomenon AIDS could not be confined, as some had thought or hoped, to the margins of society (delinquency, homosexuality, drug addiction), we have here, within the social bond, something that people might still want to consider as a destructuring and depoliticizing poly-perversion: a historic (historial!) knot or denouement which is no doubt original. In these circumstances, the (restructuring and supposedly repoliticizing) reactions are largely unforeseeable and may reproduce the worst political violence.

In any case, were we to attempt the impossible and limit our discussion to drugs, you know that henceforth, in order to treat all these problems as we should, simultaneously and systematically, we can organize a hierarchy, play the bad against the worse, liberalize the sale of syringes in order to fight the spread of AIDS, liberalize sex education like never before, ever *econdomizing* the full range of social visibility, starting with the schools and the media. AIDS is in the process of redrawing the political front lines and the face of politics, the structures of civil society and of the State, at the very moment when governments thought they could organize against an identifiable enemy, the international counter-state of the drug lord. And this is a result in particular, though not solely, of the fact that, as I recently read in *Libération*, "AIDS Hooks Junkies."

Q.: We see, for example in Latin America, how the drug lords have organized themselves as a state within the State. We hear the mayors of major American cities talk about a need for "tolerance" in order to confront delinquency. As we've said, and all this is evoked in terms of war, the major dealers are notoriously allied with the extreme right-wing. A strange paradox with the drug addict seen as a marginal figure. The legalization of crack? The State as dealer?

J.D.: One very brief remark. People hardly talk about it, but in this case the opposition between different regimes and types of society becomes more paradoxical than ever. In so-called socialist societies, those based on a philosophy of work and the ideal of its reappropriation by the worker, certain forms of unemployment and unproductivity need to be disguised, but also the phenomena of drugs need to be dissembled. A book written in Czechoslovakia has recently revealed a considerable drug problem in the Eastern bloc nations, despite the severity of their laws and criminal prosecution. (In Prague on my way back from an outlawed seminar, the authorities planted and pretended to discover a quantity of drugs in my luggage. Once I was charged and in jail, I learned that no one ever gets off without at least two years of prison without parole, *for the slightest contact* with the drug-world.) Since AIDS does not respect international borders, how are these regimes going to react when, as in the West, they have to adopt a more liberal attitude toward one problem in order to better cope with the other, for example by relaxing restrictions on the sale of syringes? And when they will have to work together with the international police to control this double network? If now the AIDS virus were spliced onto a computer virus, you can imagine what might happen tomorrow to Interpol's computers and the geopolitical unconscious.[9] What then would become of the diplomatic corps? What would become of spies? And let's not even talk about soldiers—we can now no more distinguish between military and civilian than we can between public and private.

A small and henceforth secondary contradiction: the production and distribution of drugs are, of course, primarily organized by right-wing forces or regimes, by a certain form of capitalism. But in Western Europe drug consumption and a certain drug culture are often associated with a vaguely anti-establishment, left-leaning ideology, whereas the brutality of repressive politics generally has the characteristics of the right, and indeed of the extreme right-wing. We can in principle account for all these phenomena: they are not so strange as they first appear. In its particulars and within its boundaries, the code of these paradoxes is destined for an upheaval, and, to tell the truth, it is already undergoing one. But by recording, transcribing, or translating such an upheaval, we can only try to mitigate its threat. To economize it. This is always possible and it always works: up to a point. As sudden and over-whelming as it may be, this event had heralded itself even before we could talk about history or memory. The virus has no age.

TRANSLATED BY MICHAEL ISRAEL

«Eating Well,» or the
Calculation of the Subject

J.D.: From your question one might pick out two phrases: first, "Who comes after the subject?" the "who" perhaps already pointing toward a grammar that would no longer be subjected to the subject; and, second, "a prevalent discourse of recent date concludes with its [the subject's] simple liquidation."

Now should we not take an initial precaution with regard to the *doxa*, which in a certain way dictates the very formulation of the question? This precaution would not be a critique. It is no doubt necessary to refer to such a *doxa*, if only to analyze it and possibly disqualify it. The question "Who comes *after* the subject?" (this time I emphasize the "after") implies that for a certain philosophical opinion today, in its most visible configuration, something named "subject" can be identified, as its alleged passing might also be identified in certain identifiable thoughts or discourses. This "opinion" is confused. The confusion consists at least in a clumsy mixing up of a number of discursive strategies. If over the last twenty-five years in France the most notorious of these strategies have in fact led to a kind of discussion around "the question of the subject," none of them has sought to "liquidate" anything (I don't know moreover to what philosophical concept this word might correspond, a word that I understand more readily in other codes: finance, crime, terrorism, civil or political criminality; one only speaks of "liquidation" therefore from the position of the law, indeed, the police). The diagnostic of "liquidation" exposes in general an illusion and an offense. It accuses: they tried to "liquidate," they thought they could do it, we will not let them do it. The diagnostic implies therefore a promise: we will do justice, we will save or rehabilitate the subject. A slogan therefore: a return to the subject, the return of the subject. Furthermore, one would have to ask, to put it very briefly, if the structure of every subject is not constituted in the possibility of this kind of repetition one calls a return, and more important, if this structure is not essentially *before the law*, the relation to law and the experience, if there *is* any, of the law, but let's leave this. Let's take some examples of this confusion, and also some proper names that might serve as indexes to help us along. Did Lacan "liquidate" the subject? No. The decentered "subject" of which he speaks certainly doesn't have the traits of the classical subject (and even here, we'd have to take a closer look...), though it remains indispensable to the economy of the Lacanian theory. It is also a correlate of the law.

Q.: Lacan is perhaps the only one to insist on keeping the name...

J.D.: Perhaps not the only one in fact. We will speak later on about Philippe Lacoue-Labarthe, but we might note already that Althusser's theory, for example, seeks to discredit a certain authority of the subject only by acknowledging for the instance of the "subject" an irreducible place in a theory of ideology, an ideology that, *mutatis mutandis*, is just as irreducible as the transcendental illusion in the Kantian dialectic. This place is that of a subject constituted by interpellation, by its being-interpellated (again being-before-the-law, the subject as a subject subjected to the law and held responsible before it). As for Foucault's discourse, there would be different things to say according to the stages of its development. In his case, we would appear to have a history of subjectivity that, in spite of certain massive declarations about the effacement of the figure of man, certainly never consisted in "liquidating" the Subject. And in his last phase, there again, a return of morality and a certain ethical subject. For these three discourses (Lacan, Althusser, Foucault) and for some of the thinkers they privilege (Freud, Marx, Nietzsche), the subject can be re-interpreted, restored, re-inscribed, it certainly isn't "liquidated." The question "who," notably in Nietzsche, strongly reinforces this point. This is also true of Heidegger, the principal reference or target of the *doxa* we are talking about. The ontological questioning that deals with the *subjectum*, in its Cartesian and post-Cartesian forms, is anything but a liquidation.

Q.: For Heidegger, nevertheless, the epoch that comes to a close as the epoch of metaphysics, and that perhaps closes epochality as such, is the epoch of the metaphysics of subjectivity, and the end of philosophy is then the exiting of the metaphysics of subjectivity...

J.D.: But this "exiting" is not an exit, it cannot be assimilated to a passage beyond or a lapsing, even less to a "liquidation."

Q.: No, but I can't see in Heidegger what thread in the thematic or the problematic of the subject still remains to be drawn out, positively or affirmatively, whereas I can see it if it's a question of truth, if it's a question of manifestation, a question of the phenomenon...

J.D.: Yes. But two things: The very summary exposition that I have just ventured was a quick response, precisely, to whatever summariness there might be in this *doxa* that doesn't go to the trouble of analyzing, up close, in a differentiated manner, the differential strategies of all these treatments of the "subject." We could have chosen examples closer to us, but let's move on. The effect of the *doxa* consists in saying: all these philosophers think they have put the subject behind them...

Q.: So it would now be a matter of going back to it, and that's the slogan.

J.D.: It's the effect of the slogan I was getting at. Second thing: what you called the "thread to be drawn" in Heidegger, perhaps follows, among other paths, that of an *analogy* (to be treated very cautiously) between the function of the *Dasein* in *Being and Time* and the function of the subject in an ontological-transcendental, indeed, ethico-juridical setting. *Dasein* cannot be reduced to a subjectivity, certainly, but the existential analytic still retains the formal traits of every transcendental analytic. *Dasein*, and what there is in it that answers to the question "Who?" comes to occupy, no doubt displacing lots of other things, the place of the "subject," the cogito or the classical "*Ich denke*." From these, it retains certain essential traits (freedom, resolute-decision, to take up this old translation again, a relation or presence to self, the "call" [*Ruf*] toward a moral conscience, responsibility, primordial imputability or guilt [*Schuldigsein*], etc.). And whatever the movements of Heideggerian thought "after" *Being and Time* and "after" the existential analytic, they left nothing "behind," "liquidated."

Q.: What you are aiming at in my question then is the "coming after" as leading to something false, dangerous...

J.D.: Your question echoes, for legitimate strategic reasons, a discourse of "opinion" that, it seems to me, one must begin by critiquing or deconstructing. I wouldn't agree to enter into a discussion where it was imagined that one knew what the subject is, where it would go without saying that this "character" is the same for Marx, Nietzsche, Freud, Heidegger, Lacan, Foucault, Althusser, and others, who would somehow all be in agreement to "liquidate" it. For me, the discussion would begin to get interesting when, beyond the vested confusion of this *doxa*, one gets to a more serious, more essential question. For example, if throughout all these different strategies the "subject," without having been "liquidated," has been reinterpreted, displaced, decentered, re-inscribed, then, first: what becomes of those problematics that seemed to presuppose a classical determination of the subject (objectivity, be it scientific or other—ethical, legal, political, etc.), and second: who or what "answers" to the question "who"?

Q.: For me, "who" designated a *place*, that place "of the subject" that appears precisely through deconstruction itself. What is the place that *Dasein*, for example, comes to occupy?

J.D.: To elaborate this question along topological lines ("What is the place of the subject?"), it would perhaps be necessary to give up trying to do the impossible, that is to say, trying to reconstitute or reconstruct that which has already been deconstructed (and which, moreover, has deconstructed "itself," offered itself since forever to the deconstruction "of itself," an expression that encapsulates the whole difficulty) and ask ourselves, rather: What is designated, in a tradition that one would have to identity in a rigorous way (let's say for the moment the one that runs from Descartes to Kant and to Husserl) under the concept of subject, in such a way that once certain predicates have been deconstructed, the unity of the concept and the name are radically affected? These predicates would be, for example, the sub-jective structure as the being-thrown—or under-lying—of the substance or of the *substratum*, of the *hypokeimenon*, with its qualities of stance or stability, of permanent presence, of sustained relation to self, everything that links the "subject" to conscience, to humanity, to history... and above all to the law, as subject subjected to the law, subject to the law in its very autonomy, to ethical or juridical law, to political law or power, to order (symbolic or not)...

Q.: Are you proposing that the question be reformulated, keeping the name "subject," but now used in a positive sense?

J.D.: Not necessarily. I would keep the name provisionally as an index for the discussion, but I don't see the necessity of keeping the word "subject" at any price, especially if the context and conventions of discourse risk re-introducing precisely what is in question...

Q.: I don't see how you can keep the name without enormous misunderstandings. But in lieu of the "subject," there is something like a place, a singular point of passage. It's like the writer for Blanchot: place of passage, of the emission of a voice that captures the "murmur" and detaches itself from it, but that is never an "author" in the classical sense. How might one name this place? The question "who" seems to keep something of the subject, perhaps...

J.D.: Yes.

Q.: But the "what" is no better; what about "process," "functioning," "text"...

J.D.: In the case of the text, I wouldn't say a "what"...

Q.: Can you be more precise?

J.D.: Yes, a little later, that can wait. I assumed, rather naively, that in our discussion here we would try to bypass the work that we have both done concerning the "subject." That of course is impossible; in fact, it's idiotic. We will refer to this later. Yes, it's idiotic. Moreover, one could put the subject in its subjectivity on stage, *submit* it to the stage as the *idiot* itself (the innocent, the proper, the virgin, the originary, the native, the naive, the great beginning: just as great, as erect, and as autonomous as *submissive*, etc.).

In the text or in writing, such as I have tried to analyze them at least, there is, I wouldn't say a place (and this is a whole question, this topology of a certain locatable non-place, at once necessary and undiscoverable) but an instance (without stance, a "without" without negativity) for some "who," a "who" besieged by the problematic of the trace and of differance, of affirmation, of the signature and of the so-called proper name, of the *je[c]t* (above all subject, object, project), as *destinerring* of missive. I have tried to elaborate this problematic around numerous examples.

Let's go back a little and start out again from the question "who?" (I note first of all in passing that to substitute a very indeterminate "who" for a "subject" overburdened with metaphysical determinations is perhaps not enough to bring about any decisive displacement. In the expression the *"question 'Who'?"* the emphasis might well later fall on the word "question." Not only in order to ask *who* asks the question or *on the subject of whom* the question is asked [so much does syntax decide the answer in advance], but to ask if there is a subject, no, a "who," before being able to ask questions about it. I don't yet know who can ask himself this nor how. But one can already see several possibilities opening up: the "who" might be there before, as the power to ask questions [this, in the end, is how

Heidegger identifies the *Dasein* and comes to choose it as the exemplary guiding thread in the question of Being] or else it might be, and this comes down to the same thing, what is made possible by its power, by its being able to ask questions about itself [Who is who? Who is it?]. But there is another possibility that interests me more at this point: it overwhelms the question itself, re-inscribes it in the experience of an "affirmation," of a "yes" or of an "en-gage" [this is the word I use in *De l'esprit* to describe *Zusage*, that acquiescing to language, to the mark, that the most primordial question implies], that "yes, yes"[1] that answers before even being able to formulate a question, that is responsible without autonomy, before and in view of all possible autonomy of the who-subject, etc. The relation to self, in this situation, can only be differance, that is to say alterity, or trace. Not only is the obligation not lessened in this situation, but, on the contrary, it finds in it its only possibility, which is neither subjective nor human. Which doesn't mean that it is inhuman or without subject, but that it is out of this dislocated *affirmation* [thus without "firmness" or "closedness"] that something like the subject, man, or whoever it might be can take shape. I now close this long parenthesis.)

Let's go back. What are we aiming at in the deconstructions of the "subject" when we ask ourselves what, in the structure of the classical subject, continues to be required by the question "Who?"

In addition to what we have just named (the proper name in exappropriation, signature, or affirmation without closure, trace, differance from self, destinerrance, and so forth), I would add something that remains required by both the definition of the classical subject and by these latter nonclassical motifs, namely, a certain *responsibility.* The singularity of the "who" is not the individuality of a thing that would be identical to itself, it is not an atom. It is a singularity that dislocates or divides itself in gathering itself together to answer to the other, whose call somehow precedes its own identification with itself, for to this call I can *only* answer, have already answered, even if I think I am answering "no" (I try to explain this elsewhere, notably in "Ulysses Gramophone"). Here, no doubt, begins the link with the larger questions of ethical, juridical, and political responsibility around which the metaphysics of subjectivity was constituted. But if one is to avoid too hastily reconstituting the program of this metaphysic and suffering from its surreptitious constraints, it's best to proceed more slowly and not rush into these words...

Q.: For me, the subject is above all, as in Hegel, "that which can retain in itself its own contradiction." In the deconstruction of this "property," it seems to me that the "that which," the "what" of the "itself" brings forth the place, and the question, of a "who" that would no longer be "in itself" in this way. A *who* that would no longer have *this* property, but that would nevertheless be a *who*. It is "him/her" I want to question here.

J.D.: Still on a preliminary level, let's not forget Nietzsche's precautions regarding what might link metaphysics and grammar. These precautions need to be duly adjusted and problematized, but they remain necessary. What we are seeking with the question "Who?" perhaps no longer stems from grammar, from a relative or interrogative pronoun that always refers back to the grammatical function of subject. How can we get away from this contract between the grammar of the subject or substantive and the ontology of substance or subject? The differant singularity that I named perhaps does not even correspond to the grammatical form "who" in a sentence wherein "who" is the subject of a verb coming after the subject, and so forth. On the other hand, if Freudian thought has been consequential in the decentering of the subject we have been talking about so much these last years, is the "ego," in the elements of the topic or in the distribution of the positions of the unconscious, the only answer to the question "Who?" And if so, what would be the consequences of this?

Thus, if we retain the motif of "singularity" for the moment, it is neither certain nor a priori necessary that "singularity" be translated by "who," or remain the privilege of the "who." At the very moment in which they marked, let us say, their mistrust for substantialist or subjectivist metaphysics, Heidegger and Nietzsche, whatever serious differences there may be between the two, continued to endorse the question "Who?" and subtracted the "who" from the deconstruction of the subject. But we might still ask ourselves just how legitimate this is. *Conversely*, and to multiply the preliminary precautions so as not to neglect the essential entanglement of this strange history, how can one forget that even in the most marked transcendental idealism, that of Husserl, even where the origin of the world is described, after the phenomenological reduction, as originary consciousness in the form of the ego, even in a phenomenology that determines the Being of beings as an object in general for a subject in general, even in this great philosophy of the transcendental subject, the interminable genetic (so-called passive) analyses of the ego, of time and of the alter ego lead back to a pre-egological and pre-subjectivist zone. There is, therefore, at the heart of what passes for and presents itself as a transcendental idealism, a horizon of questioning that is no longer dictated by the egological form of subjectivity or intersubjectivity.

On the French philosophical scene, the moment when a certain central hegemony of the subject was being put into question again in the 1960s was also the moment when, phenomenology still being very present, people began to become interested in those places in Husserl's discourse where the egological and more generally the subjective form of the transcendental experience appeared to be more *constituted* than *constitutive*—in sum, as much grounded as precarious. The question of time and of the other became linked to this transcendental passive genesis...

Q.: Still, it was by penetrating *into* this Husserlian constitution, by "forcing" it, that you began your own work...

J.D.: It is within, one might say (but it is precisely a question of the effraction of the within) the living present, that *Urform* of the transcendental experience, that the subject conjoins with nonsubject or that the *ego* is marked, without being able to have the originary and presentative experience of it, by the non-*ego* and especially by the *alter ego*. The *alter ego* cannot present itself, cannot become an originary presence for the *ego*. There is only an analogical a-presentation [*apprésentation*] of the *alter ego*. The *alter ego* can never be given "in person," it resists the principle of principles of phenomenology—namely, the intuitive given of originary presence. This dislocation of the absolute subject from the other and from time neither comes about, nor leads *beyond* phenomenology, but, rather, if not in it, then at least on its border, on the very line of its possibility. It was in the 1950s and 1960s, at the moment when an interest in these difficulties developed in a very different way (Levinas, Tran-Duc-Thao, myself)[2] and following moreover other trajectories (Marx, Nietzsche, Freud, Heidegger), that the centrality of the subject began to be displaced and this discourse of "suspicion," as some were saying then, began to be elaborated in its place. But if certain premises are to be found "in" Husserl, I'm sure that one could make a similar demonstration in Descartes, Kant, and Hegel. Concerning Descartes, one could discover, following the directions of your own work,[3] similar aporia, fictions, and fabrications. Not identical ones, but similar ones. This would have at least the virtue of de-simplifying, of "de-homogenizing" the reference to something like The Subject. There has never been The Subject for anyone, that's what I wanted to begin by saying. The subject is a fable, as you have shown, but to concentrate on the elements of speech and *conventional* fiction that such a fable presupposes is not to stop taking it seriously (it is the serious itself)...

Q.: Everything you have recalled here comes down to emphasizing that there is not, nor has there ever been any presence-to-self that would not call into question the *distance* from self that this presence demands. "To deconstruct," here, comes down to showing this distance at the very heart of presence, and, in so doing, prevents us from simply separating an outdated "metaphysics of the subject" from another thinking that would be, suddenly, elsewhere. However, *something has happened*, there is a *history* both of the thinking of the subject and of its deconstruction. What Heidegger determined as the "epoch" of subjectivity, has this taken place, or has the "subject" always been only a surface effect, a fallout that one cannot impute to the thinkers? But in that case, what is Heidegger talking about when he talks about subjectivity?

J.D.: An enormous question. I'm not sure that I can approach it head-on. To whatever degree I can subscribe to the Heideggerian discourse on the subject, I have always been a little troubled by the Heideggerian delimitation of the epoch of subjectivity. His questions about the ontological inadequacy of the Cartesian view of subjectivity seem to me no doubt necessary but inadequate, notably in regard to what would link subjectivity to *representation*, and the subject-object couple to the presuppositions of the principle of reason in its Leibnizian formulation. I have tried to explain this elsewhere. The foreclosure of Spinoza seems to me to be significant. Here is a great rationalism that does not rest on the principle of reason (inasmuch as in Leibniz this principle privileges both the final cause and representation). Spinoza's substantialist rationalism is a radical critique of both finalism and the (Cartesian) representative determination of the idea; it is not a metaphysics of the cogito or of absolute subjectivity. The import of this foreclosure is all the greater and more significant in that the epoch of subjectivity determined by Heidegger is also the epoch of the rationality or the techno-scientific rationalism of modern metaphysics...

Q.: But if the foreclosure of Spinoza stems precisely from his having distanced himself from what was dominant elsewhere, does that not confirm this domination?

J.D.: It's not Spinoza's case that is most important to me. Heidegger defines a modern hegemony of the subject of representation or of the principle of reason. Now if his delimitation is effected through an unjustified foreclosure, it is the interpretation of the epoch that risks becoming problematic. And so everything becomes problematic in this discourse.

And I would graft on another remark at this point. We were speaking of dehiscence, of intrinsic dislocation, of differance, of destinerrance, and so forth. Some might say: but what we call "subject" is not the absolute origin, pure will, identity to self, or presence to self of consciousness but precisely this noncoincidence with self. This is a riposte to which we'll have to return. By what right do we call this "subject"? By what right, conversely, can we be forbidden to call this "subject"? I am thinking of those today who would try to reconstruct a discourse around a subject that would not be pre-deconstructive, around a subject that would no longer include the figure of mastery of self, of adequation to self, center and origin of the world, etc. . . . but which would define the subject rather as the finite experience of non-identity to self, as the underivable interpellation inasmuch as it comes from the other, from the trace of the other, with all the paradoxes or the aporia of being-before-the-law, and so on. Perhaps we'll pick this up again later on. For the moment, since we're speaking of Heidegger, let me add this. I believe in the force and the necessity (and therefore in a certain irreversibility) of the act by which Heidegger *substitutes* a certain concept of *Dasein* for a concept of subject still too marked by the traits of the being as *vorhanden, and hence by an interpretation of time*, and insufficiently questioned in its ontological structure. The consequences of this displacement are immense, no doubt we have not yet measured their extent. There's no question of laying these out here in an improvised manner, but I simply wanted to note this: the time and space of this displacement opened up a gap, marked a gap, they left fragile, or recalled the essential ontological fragility of the ethical, juridical, and political foundations of democracy and of every discourse that one can oppose to National Socialism in all its forms (the "worst" ones, or those that Heidegger and others might have thought of opposing to them). These foundations were and remain essentially sealed within a philosophy of the subject. One can quickly perceive the question, which might also be the task: can one take into account the necessity of the existential analytic and what it shatters in the subject and turn toward an ethics, a politics (are these words still appropriate?), indeed an "other" democracy (would it still be a democracy?), in any case toward another type of responsibility that safeguards against what a moment ago I very quickly called the "worst"? Don't expect from me an answer in the way of a formula. I think there are a certain number of us who are working for just this, who let themselves be worked over by this, and it can only take place by a way of a long and slow trajectory. It cannot depend on a speculative decree, even less on an opinion. Perhaps not even on philosophical discursivity.

Having said this, whatever may be the force, the necessity, or the irreversibility of the Heideggerian gesture, I see the point of departure for the existential analytic remaining tributary of precisely what it puts into question. Tributary in this respect—I am picking this out of the network of difficulties that I have associated with it at the beginning of *Of Spirit* (on the question of the question, technology, animality, and epochality)—which is intimately linked to the axiom of the subject: the chosen point of departure, the exemplary entity for a reading of the meaning of Being, is the entity that *we* are, we the *questioning* entities, we who, in that we are open to the question of Being and of the being of the entity we are, have this relation of presence and proximity, this relation to self, in any case, that is lacking in everything that is not *Dasein*. Even if *Dasein* is not the subject, this point of departure (which is moreover assumed by Heidegger as ontologico-phenomenological) remains analogous, in its "logic," to what he inherits in undertaking to deconstruct it. This isn't a mistake, it's no doubt an indispensable phase, but now...

Q.: I'd like to point something out to you: a moment ago you were doing everything to dismiss, to disperse the idea of *a* "classic" problematic of the subject. Now you are targeting in Heidegger that which would remain tributary of the classical thinking or position of the subject. That seems a bit contradictory...

J.D.: I didn't say "there is no problematic of the subject," but rather that it cannot be reduced to a homogeneity. This does not preclude, on the contrary, seeking to define certain analogies or common sources, provided that one takes into account the differences. For example, the point of departure in a structure of *relation to self as such and of reappropriation* seems to me to be common just as much to transcendental idealism, to speculative idealism as the thinking of absolute subjectivity, as it is to the existential analytic that proposes its deconstruction. *Being and Time* always concerns those possibilities most proper to *Dasein* in its *Eigentlichkeit*, whatever the singularity may be of this "propriation" that is not, in fact, a subjectivation. Moreover, that the point of departure of the existential analytic is the *Dasein* privileges not only the rapport to self but also the power to ask questions. Now I have tried to show (*Of Spirit*, p. 129, n. 5) what this presupposed and what could come about, even in Heidegger, when this privilege of the question was complicated or displaced. To be brief, I would say that it is in the relation to the "yes" or to the *Zusage* presupposed in every question that one must seek a new (post-deconstructive) determination of the responsibility of the "subject." But it always seems to me to be more worthwhile, once this path has been laid down, to forget the word to some extent. Not to forget it, it is unforgettable, but to rearrange it, to subject it to the laws of a context that it no longer dominates from the center. In other words, no longer to speak about it, but to write it, to write "on" it as on the "subjectile," for example.[4]

In insisting on the *as such*, I am pointing from afar to the inevitable return of a distinction between the *human* relation to self, that is to say, that of an entity capable of consciousness, of language, of a relation to death as such, and so forth, and a *nonhuman* relation to self, incapable of the phenomenological *as such*—and once again we are back to the question of the animal.[5] The distinction between the animal (which has no or is not a *Dasein*) and man has nowhere been more radical nor more rigorous than in Heidegger. The animal will never be either a subject or a *Dasein*. It doesn't have an unconscious either (Freud), nor a relation to the other as other, any more than there is an animal face (Levinas). It is from the standpoint of *Dasein* that Heidegger defines the humanity of man.

Why have I rarely spoken of the "subject" or of "subjectivity," but rather, here and there, only of "an effect" of "subjectivity"? Because the discourse on the subject, even if it locates difference, inadequation, the dehiscence within auto-affection, and so forth, continues to link subjectivity with man. Even if it acknowledges that the "animal" is capable of auto-affection (etc.), this discourse obviously does not grant it subjectivity—and this concept thus remains marked by all the presuppositions that I have just recalled. Also at stake here of course is responsibility, freedom, truth, ethics, and law.

The "logic" of the trace or of differance determines this re-appropriation as an ex-appropriation. Re-appropriation necessarily produces the opposite of what it apparently aims for. Ex-appropriation is not what is proper to man. One can recognize its differential figures as soon as there is a relation to self in its most elementary form (but for this very reason there is no such thing as elementary).

Q.: When you decide not to limit a potential "subjectivity" to man, why do you then limit yourself simply to the animal?

J.D.: Nothing should be excluded. I said "animal" for the sake of convenience and to use a reference that is as classical as it is dogmatic. The difference between "animal" and "vegetal" also remains problematic. Of course the relation to self in ex-appropriation is radically different (and that's why it requires a thinking of differance and not of opposition) in the case of what one calls the "nonliving," the "vegetal," the "animal," "man," or "God." The question also comes back to the difference between the living and the nonliving. I have tried to indicate the difficulty of this difference in Hegel and Husserl, as well as in Freud and Heidegger.

Q.: For my part, in my work on freedom, I was compelled to ask myself if the Heideggerian partition between *Dasein*, on the one side, and, on the other side, *Vor-* or *Zuhandensein* would not reconstitute a kind of distinction between subject and object.

J.D.: The categories of *Vorhandenheit* and *Zuhandenheit* are also intended to avoid those of object (correlate of the subject) and instrument. *Dasein* is first of all thrown. What would link the analytic of *Dasein* with the heritage of the subject would perhaps be more the determination of *Dasein* as *Geworfenheit*, its primordial being-thrown, rather than the determination of a *subject* that would come to be *thrown*, but a being-thrown that would be more primordial than subjectivity and therefore [more primordial] than objectivity as well. A passivity that would be more primordial than traditional passivity and than *Gegenstand* (*Gegenwurf*, the old German word for object, keeps this reference to throwing, without stabilizing it into the stance of a *stehen*; I refer you to what I have said about the "*dé-sistance*"[6] of the subject in Philippe Lacoue-Labarthe). I am trying to think through this experience of the throwing/being-thrown of the subjectile beyond the Heideggerian protocols about which I was just speaking and to link it to another thinking of destination, of chance and of destinerrance (see again "My Chances,"[7] where I situate a (foreclosed) relationship between Heidegger and a thinking of the Democritean type).

Q.: What happens to the *who* of the question in this being-thrown?

J.D.: Starting at "birth," and possibly even prior to it, being-thrown re-appropriates itself or rather ex-appropriates itself in forms that are not yet those of the *subject* or the *project*. The question "who" then becomes: "Who (is) thrown?" "Who becomes—'who' from out of the destinerrance of the being-thrown?" That it is still a matter here of the trace, but also of iterability (cf. my *Limited Inc*) means that this ex-appropriation cannot be absolutely stabilized in the form of the subject. The subject assumes presence, that is to say sub-stance, stasis, stance. Not to be able to stabilize itself *absolutely* would mean to be able *only* to be stabilizing itself: relative stabilization of what remains *unstable*, or rather *non-stable*. Ex-appropriation no longer closes itself; it never totalizes itself. One should not take these figures for metaphors (metaphoricity supposes ex-appropriation), nor determine them according to the grammatical opposition of active/passive. Between the thrown and the falling (*Verfallen*) there is also a possible point of passage. Why is *Geworfenheit*, while never put into question, subsequently given to marginalization in Heidegger's thinking? This is what we must continue to ask. And ex-appropriation does not form a boundary, if one understands by this word a closure or a negativity. It implies the irreducibility of the relation to the other. The other resists all subjectivation, even to the point of the interiorization-idealization of what one calls the work of mourning. The non-subjectivable in the experience of mourning is what I tried to describe in *Glas* and in *Mémoires for Paul de Man*. There is, in what you describe in your recent book[8] as an experience of freedom, an opening that also resists subjectivation, that is to say, it resists the modern concept of freedom as subjective freedom. I think we will have to come back to this.

q.: In what you are calling ex-appropriation, inasmuch as it does not close in on itself and *although* it does not close in on itself (let us say in and in spite of its "passivity") is there not also necessarily something on the order of *singularity*? It is in any case something on the order of the singular that I was getting at with my question *who*.

j.d.: Under the heading of *Jemeinigkeit*, beyond or behind the subjective "self" or person, there is for Heidegger a singularity, an irreplaceability of that which remains nonsubstitutable in the structure of *Dasein*. This amounts to an irreducible singularity or solitude in *Mitsein* (which is also a condition of *Mitsein*), but it is not that of the individual. This last concept always risks pointing toward both the ego and an organic or atomic indivisibility. The *Da* of *Dasein* singularizes itself without being reducible to any of the categories of human subjectivity (self, reasonable being, consciousness, person), precisely because it is presupposed by all of these.

q.: You are getting around to the question "Who comes after the subject?" reversing its form: "Who comes before the subject...?"

j.d.: Yes, but "before" no longer retains any chronological, logical, nor even ontologico-transcendental meaning, if one takes into account, as I have tried to do, that which resists here the traditional schema of ontologico-transcendental questions.

q.: But I still do not understand whether or not you leave a place for the question "Who?" Do you grant it pertinence or, on the contrary, do you not even want to pose it, do you want to bypass every question...?

J.D.: What troubles me is what also commands my thinking here: it involves the necessity of locating, wherever one responds to the question "Who?"—not only in terms of the subject, but also in terms of *Dasein*—conceptual oppositions that have not yet been sufficiently questioned, not even by Heidegger. I referred to this a moment ago, and this is what I have been aiming at in all my analyses of Heidegger.[9] In order to recast, if not rigorously re-found a discourse on the "subject," on that which will hold the place (or replace the place) of the subject (of law, of morality, of politics—so many categories caught up in the same turbulence), one has to go through the experience of a deconstruction. This deconstruction (we should once again remind those who do not want to read) is neither negative nor nihilistic; it is not even a pious nihilism, as I have heard said. A concept (that is to say also an experience) of responsibility comes at this price. We have not finished paying for it. I am talking about a responsibility that is not deaf to the injunction of thought. As you said one day, there is a duty in deconstruction. There has to be, if there is such a thing as duty. The subject, if subject there must be, is to come *after* this.

After: not that it takes the rather improbable end of a deconstruction before we can assume responsibilities! But in order to describe the origin, the meaning, or the status of these responsibilities, the concept of subject still remains problematic. What I find disturbing is not that it is *inadequate*: it is no doubt the case that there neither can be nor should be any concept adequate to what we call responsibility. Responsibility carries within it, and must do so, an essential excessiveness. It regulates itself neither on the principle of reason nor on any sort of accountancy. To put it rather abruptly, I would say that, among other things, the subject is also a principle of calculability—for the political (and even, indeed, for the current concept of democracy, which is less clear, less homogenous, and less of a given than we believe or claim to believe, and which no doubt needs to be rethought, radicalized, and considered as a thing of the future), in the question of legal rights (including human rights, about which I would repeat what I have just said about democracy) and in morality. There has to be some calculation, and this is why I have never held against calculation that condescending reticence of "Heideggerian" haughtiness. Still, calculation is calculation. And if I speak so often of the incalculable and the undecidable it's not out of a simple predilection for play nor in order to neutralize decision: on the contrary, I believe there is no responsibility, no ethico-political decision, that must not pass through the proofs of the incalculable or the undecidable. Otherwise everything would be reducible to calculation, program, causality, and, at best, "hypothetical imperative."

It is therefore a certain closing off—the saturating or suturing—of identity to self, and a structure still too narrowly fit to self-identification, that today gives the concept of subject its dogmatic effect. Something analogous perhaps occurs, it seems to me, with the concept of *Dasein*, but at a distance that must never be neglected. In spite of everything it opens up and encourages us to think, to question, and to redistribute, *Dasein* still occupies a place analogous to that of the transcendental subject. And its concept, in *Being and Time*, is determined, it seems to me, on the basis of oppositions that remain insufficiently interrogated. Here once again we find the question of man. The possibility for the indeterminate "who" to become subject, or, more originarily, to become *Dasein* and *Dasein* thrown (*geworfene*) into the world, is reserved for man alone. This possibility, which in sum defines man for Heidegger, stands in opposition to every other form of self-relation, for example, what one calls the living in general, a very obscure notion, for the very reasons we have indicated. As long as these oppositions have not been deconstructed—and they are strong, subtle, at times mainly implicit—we will reconstitute under the name of subject, indeed under the name of *Dasein*, an *illegitimately* delimited identity, illegitimately, but often precisely under the authority of rights!—in the name of a particular kind of rights. For it is in order to put a stop to a certain kind of rights, to a certain juridico-political calculation, that this questioning has been interrupted. Deconstruction therefore calls for a different kind of rights, or, rather, lets itself be called by a more exacting articulation of rights, prescribing, in a different way, more responsibility.

It is thus not a matter of opposing another discourse on the same "things" to the enormous multiplicity of traditional discourses on man, animal, plant, or stone, but of ceaselessly analyzing the whole conceptual machinery, and its interestedness, which has allowed us to speak of the "subject" up to now. And the analysis is always more and something other than an analysis. It transforms; it translates a transformation already in progress. Translation is transformative. This explains the nervous distrust of those who want to keep all these themes, all these "words" ("man," "subject," and so forth), sheltered from all questioning, and who manipulate an ethico-political suspicion with regard to deconstruction.

If we still wish to speak of the subject—the juridical, ethical, political, psychological subject, and so forth—and of what makes its semantics communicate with that of the subject of a proposition (distinct from qualities, attributes viewed as substance, phenomena, and so on) or with the theme or the thesis (the subject of a discourse or of a book), it is first of all necessary to submit to the test of questioning the essential predicates of which all subjects are the subject. While these predicates are as numerous and diverse as the type or order of subjects dictates, they are all in fact ordered around being-present [*étant-present*]: presence to self—which implies therefore a certain interpretation of temporality; identity to self, positionality, property, personality, ego, consciousness, will, intentionality, freedom, humanity, etc. It is necessary to question this authority of the being-present, but the question itself offers neither the first nor the last word, as I have tried to show for example in *De l'esprit,* but also everywhere I have spoken of the "yes, yes," of the "come" or of the affirmation that is not addressed first of all to a subject.[10] This vigil or beyond of the question is anything but precritical. Beyond even the force of critique, it situates a responsibility as irreducible to and rebellious toward the traditional category of "subject." Such a vigil leads us to recognize the processes of differance, trace, iterability, ex-appropriation, and so on. These are at work everywhere, which is to say, well beyond humanity. A discourse thus restructured can try to situate in another way the question of what a human subject, a morality, a politics, the rights of the human subject are, can be, and should be. Still to come, this task is indeed far ahead of us. It requires passing through in particular the great phenomeno-ontological question of the *as such*, appearing as such, to the extent that it is held to distinguish, in the last analysis, the human subject or *Dasein* from every other form of relation to the self or to the other *as such*. The experience or the opening of the *as such* in the onto-phenomenological sense does not merely consist in that which is lacking in the stone or animal; it equally involves that to which one *cannot and should not* submit the other in general, in other words the "who" of the other that could only appear absolutely *as such* by disappearing as other. The enormity involved in questions of the subject, as in the questions of right, ethics, and politics, always leads back to this place.

If we go back to the semantics of throwing or of the "subjectile" that has instituted the concept of subject, we should note that the *Geworfenheit* (thrownness) of *Dasein*, even before being a subjectivity, does not simply characterize a state, a fact, as in being-thrown into the world at birth. It can also describe a manner of being thrown, delivered, exposed to the call (*Ruf*). Consider the analysis of *Gewissen* and originary *Schuldigsein*. Heidegger shows in particular what is insufficient, from the anthropologico-ontological point of view, about both the "picture" (*Bild*) of the Kantian "court of justice" and any recourse to psychical faculties or personal actions (*Being and Time*, p. 271) in order to describe the call and "moral conscience." But the translation remains equivocal. *Gewissen* is not yet the "moral conscience" it renders possible, no more than *Schuldigsein* is a culpability: it is rather the possibility of being guilty, a liability or an imputability. I would be tempted to relate this call to what Heidegger says enigmatically and elliptically about the "voice of the friend," and particularly in terms of "hearing" this voice that every *Dasein* "carries within it" (*Being and Time*, p. 163). I treat this elsewhere.[11] But for the moment I would already say this much: the "who" of friendship, the voice of the friend so described, belongs to the existential structure of *Dasein*. This voice does not implicate just one passion or affect among others. The "who" of friendship, as the call (*Ruf*) that provokes or convokes "conscience" and therefore opens up responsibility, precedes every subjectal determination. On the indefinite openness of this question I would be tempted to read to you from your *The Inoperative Community* or from Blanchot's *The Unavowable Community*, or else these few lines from his *L'amitié*: "And when we ask the question: 'Who has been the subject of this experience?' this question is perhaps already an answer, if, for the one who introduced it, it was affirmed through him in this interrogative form, substituting for the closed and unique 'I' the openness of a 'Who?' without answer. Not that this means that he simply had to ask himself: 'What is this me that I am?' but much more radically he had to seize hold of himself and not let go, no longer as an 'I?' but as a 'Who?,' the unknown and sliding being of an indefinite 'Who?' "[12]

The origin of the call that comes from nowhere, an origin in any case that is not yet a divine or human "subject," institutes a responsibility that is to be found at the root of all ulterior responsibilities (moral, juridical, political), and of every categorical imperative. To say of this responsibility, and even of this friendship, that it is not "human," no more than it is "divine," does not come down to saying that it is simply inhuman. This said, in this regard it is perhaps more "worthy" of humanity to maintain a certain inhumanity, which is to say the rigor of a certain inhumanity. In any case, such a law does not leave us any choice. Something of this call of the other must remain nonreappropriable, nonsubjectivable, and in a certain way nonidentifiable, a sheer supposition, so as to remain *other*, a *singular* call to response or to responsibility. This is why the determination of the singular "Who?"—or at least its determination as subject—remains forever problematic. And it *should* remain so. This obligation to protect the other's otherness is not merely a theoretical imperative.

Q.: In that respect, indeed, the determination of "who" is problematic. But in another respect, is not the interrogative "Who?"— the one I used in my question—determinant? By which I mean that it predetermines—as every question predetermines the order of response—a response from some*one*, from some *one*. What is predetermined—which is also to say, what is called—is a *respondant*. It seems to me that this would link up with the guiding thread of your response. But I would note that with a single gesture, or at least in this same interview, you are keeping at a distance, under suspicion, the question "Who?" while you also increasingly validate the "Who?" You validate it by suppressing that which, a priori, would limit the question to humanity.

J.D.: Yes, I would not want to see the "who" restricted to the grammar of what we call Western language, nor even limited by what we believe to be the very humanity of language.

Q.: An incidental remark. In Heidegger's seminar, to which you alluded in reference to the animal, there is all the same something strange, if I remember correctly: toward the end of the analysis of the animal, Heidegger attributes to it a *sadness*, a sadness linked to its "lack of world." With this single remark, does not Heidegger contradict part of what he said before? How could sadness be simply nonhuman? Or rather, how would such a sadness fail to testify to a relation to a world?

J.D.: The Heideggerian discourse on the animal is violent and awkward, at times contradictory. Heidegger does not simply say "The animal is poor in world (*weltarm*)," for, as distinct from the stone, it has a world. He says: the animal *has* a world in the mode of a *not-having*. But this not-having does not constitute in his view an indigence, the *lack* of a world that would be human. So why this negative determination? Where does it come from? There is no category of original existence for the animal: it is evidently not *Dasein*, either as *vorhandene* or *zuhandene* (Being cannot appear, be, or be questioned as such [*als*] for the animal). Its simple existence introduces a principle of disorder or of limitation into the conceptuality of *Being and Time*. To come back to your remark, perhaps the animal is sad, perhaps it appears sad, because it indeed has a world, in the sense in which Heidegger speaks of a world as world of spirit, and because there is an openness of this world for it, but an openness without openness, a having (world) without having it. Whence the impression of sadness—for man or in relation to man, in the society of man. And of a sadness determined in its *phenomenology*, as if the animal remained a man enshrouded, suffering, deprived on account of having access neither to the world of man that he nonetheless senses, nor to truth, speech, death, or the Being of the being as such. Heidegger defends himself in vain against this anthropo-teleological interpretation, which seems to me to derive from the most acute aspect in his description of having-in-the-mode-of-not-having-a-world. Let us venture, in this logic, a few questions. For example, does the animal hear the call that originates responsibility? Does it question? Moreover, can the call heard by *Dasein* come originally to or from the animal? Is there an advent of the animal? Can the voice of the friend be that of an animal? Is friendship possible for the animal or between animals? Like Aristotle, Heidegger would say: no. Do we have a responsibility toward the living in general? The answer is still "no," and this may be because the question is formed, asked in such a way that the answer must necessarily be "no" according to the whole canonized or hegemonic discourse of Western metaphysics or religions, including the most original forms that this discourse might assume today, for example, in Heidegger or Levinas.

I am not recalling this in order to start a support group for vegetarianism, ecologism, or for the societies for the protection of animals—which is something I might also want to do, and something which would lead us to the center of the subject. By following this necessity, I am trying especially to underscore the *sacrificial* structure of the discourses to which I am referring. I don't know if "sacrificial structure" is the most accurate expression. In any case, it is a matter of discerning a place left open, in the very structure of these discourses (which are also "cultures") for a noncriminal putting to death. Such are the executions of ingestion, incorporation, or introjection of the corpse. An operation as real as it is symbolic when the corpse is "animal" (and who can be made to believe that our cultures are carnivorous because animal proteins are irreplaceable?), a symbolic operation when the corpse is "human." But the "symbolic" is very difficult, truly impossible to delimit in this case, hence the enormity of the task, its essential excessiveness, a certain unclassifiability or the monstrosity of that *for which* we have to answer here, or *before* which (whom? what?) we have to answer.

Keeping to original, typical possibilities, let's take things from another angle: not that of Heidegger but of Levinas, for whom subjectivity, of which he speaks a great deal in a new, forceful, and unusual way, is constituted first of all as the subjectivity of the *hostage*. Rethought in this way, the hostage is the one who is delivered to the other in the sacred openness of ethics, at the origin of sacredness itself. The subject is responsible for the other before being responsible for himself as "me." This responsibility to the other, for the other, comes to him, for example (but this is not just one example among others) in the "Thou shalt not kill." Thou shalt not kill thy neighbor. Consequences follow upon one another, and must do so continuously: thou shalt not make him suffer, which is sometimes worse than death, thou shalt not do him harm, thou shalt not eat him, not even a little bit, and so forth. The other, the neighbor, the friend (Nietzsche tries to keep these two values separate in *Zarathustra*, but let's leave that, I'll try to come back to it elsewhere), is no doubt in the infinite distance of transcendence. But the "Thou shalt not kill" is addressed to the other and presupposes him. It is destined to the very thing that it institutes, the other as man. It is by him that the subject is first of all held hostage. The "Thou shalt not kill"—with all its consequences, which are limitless—has never been understood within the Judeo-Christian tradition, nor apparently by Levinas, as a "Thou shalt not put to death the living in general." It has become meaningful in religious cultures for which carnivorous sacrifice is essential, as being-flesh. The other, such as this can be thought according to the imperative of ethical transcendence, is indeed the other man: man as other, the other as man. Humanism of the other man is a title in which Levinas suspends the hierarchy of the attribute and the subject. But the other-man is the subject.

Discourses as original as those of Heidegger and Levinas disrupt, of course, a certain traditional humanism. In spite of the differences separating them, they nonetheless remain profound humanisms *to the extent that they do not sacrifice sacrifice.* The subject (in Levinas's sense) and the *Dasein* are "men" in a world where sacrifice is possible and where it is not forbidden to make an attempt on life in general, but only on human life, on the neighbor's life, on the other's life as *Dasein*. Heidegger does not say it this way. But what he places at the origin of moral conscience (or rather *Gewissen*) is obviously denied to the animal. *Mitsein* is not conferred, if we can say so, on the living in general, any more than is *Dasein*, but only on that being-toward-death that also makes the *Dasein* into something else, something more and better than a living [thing]. As justified as it may be from a certain point of view, Heidegger's obstinate critique of vitalism and of the philosophies of life, but also of any consideration of life in the structure of *Dasein*, is not unrelated to what I am calling here a "sacrificial structure." This "sacrificial structure," it seems to me (at least for the moment, this is a hypothesis that I am trying to relate to what I call elsewhere the "phallogocentric" structure) defines the invisible contour of all these reflections, whatever the distance taken with regard to ontology in Levinas's thinking (in the name of what he calls metaphysics) or in Heidegger's with regard to onto-theological metaphysics. Going much too quickly here, I would still try to link the question of the "who" to the question of "sacrifice."

It would be a matter not only of recalling the concept of the subject as phallogocentric structure, at least according to its dominant *schema*: one day I hope to demonstrate that this *schema* implies carnivorous virility. I would want to explain *carno-phallogocentrism*, even if this comes down to a sort of tautology or rather heterotautology as a priori synthesis, which you could translate as "speculative idealism," "becoming-subject of substance," "absolute knowledge" passing through the "speculative Good Friday": it suffices to take seriously the idealizing interiorization of the phallus and the necessity of its passage through the mouth, whether it's a matter of words or of things, of sentences, of daily bread or wine, of the tongue, the lips, or the breast of the other. People are going to object: there are ethical, juridical, and political subjects (recognized only quite recently, as you well know), full (or almost full) citizens who are also women and/or vegetarians! But this has been admitted in principle, and in rights, only recently and precisely at the moment when the concept of subject enters into deconstruction. Is this fortuitous? And that which I am calling here *schema* or image, that which links the concept to intuition, installs the virile figure at the determinative center of the subject. Authority and autonomy (for even if autonomy is subject to the law, this subjugation is freedom) are, through this schema, attributed to the man (*homo*

and *vir*) rather than to the woman, and to the woman rather than
to the animal. And of course to the adult rather than to the child.
The virile strength of the adult male, the father, husband, or
brother (the canon of friendship, as I have shown elsewhere,[13]
privileges the fraternal schema), belongs to the schema that dominates the concept of subject. The subject does not want just to
master and possess nature actively. In our cultures, he accepts
sacrifice and eats flesh. Since we haven't much time or space here,
and at the risk of provoking some loud protests (we pretty much
know from which quarter), I would ask you: in our countries, who
would stand any chance of becoming a *chef d'Etat* (a head of State),
and of thereby acceding "to the head," by publicly, and therefore
exemplarily, declaring him- or herself to be a vegetarian?[14] The *chef*
must be an eater of flesh (with a view, moreover, to being "symbolically" eaten himself—see above). To say nothing of celibacy, of
homosexuality, and even of femininity (which for the moment, and
so rarely, is only admitted to the head of whatever it might be,
especially the State, if it lets itself be translated into a virile and
heroic schema. Contrary to what is often thought, the "feminine
condition," notably from the point of view of rights, deteriorated
from the fourteenth to the nineteenth century in Europe, reaching
its worst moment when the Napoleonic Code inscribed the positive right of the concept of subject we are talking about).

In answering these questions, you will have not only a scheme of
the *dominant*, of the common denominator of the dominant,
which is still today of the order of the political, the State, right, or
morality, you will have the dominant schema of subjectivity itself.
It's the same. If the limit between the living and the nonliving now
seems to be as unsure, at least as an oppositional limit, as that
between "man" and "animal," and if, in the (symbolic or real)
experience of the "eat-speak-interiorize," the ethical frontier no
longer rigorously passes between the "Thou shalt not kill" (man,
thy neighbor) and the "Thou shalt not put to death the living in
general," but rather between several infinitely different modes of
the conception-appropriation-assimilation of the other, then, as
concerns the "Good" [*Bien*] of every morality, the question will
come back to determining the best, most respectful, most grateful,

and also most giving way of relating to the other and of relating the other to the self. For everything that happens at the edge of the orifices (of orality, but also of the ear, the eye—and all the "senses" in general) the metonymy of "eating well" [*bien manger*] would always be the rule. The question is no longer one of knowing if it is "good" to eat the other or if the other is "good" to eat, nor of knowing which other. One eats him regardless and lets oneself be eaten by him. The so-called non-anthropophagic cultures practice symbolic anthropology and even construct their most elevated socius, indeed the sublimity of their morality, their politics, and their right, on this anthropophagy. Vegetarians, too, partake of animals, even of men. They practice a different mode of denegation. The moral question is thus not, nor has it ever been: should one eat or not eat, eat this and not that, the living or the nonliving, man or animal, but since *one must* eat in any case and since it is and tastes good to eat, and since there's no other definition of the good [*du bien*], *how* for goodness' sake should one *eat well* [*bien manger*]? And what does this imply? What is eating? How is this metonymy of introjection to be regulated? And in what respect does the formulation of these questions in language give us still more food for thought? In what respect is the question, if you will, still carnivorous? The infinitely metonymical question on the subject of "one must eat well" must be nourishing not only for me, for a "self," which would thus eat badly; it must be *shared*, as you might put it, and not only in language. "One must eat well"[15] does not mean above all taking in and grasping in itself, but *learning* and *giving* to eat, learning-to-give-the-other-to-eat. One never eats entirely on one's own: this constitutes the rule underlying the statement, "One must eat well." It is a rule offering infinite hospitality. And in all differences, ruptures, and wars (one might even say wars of religion), "eating well" is at stake. Today more than ever. One must eat well—here is a maxim whose modalities and contents need only be varied, *ad infinitum*. This evokes a law of need *or* desire (I have never believed in the radicality of this occasionally useful distinction), *orexis*, hunger, and thirst ("one must," "one has to"), respect for the other at the very moment when, in experience

(I am speaking here of metonymical "eating" as well as the very concept of experience), one must begin to identify with the other, who is to be assimilated, interiorized, understood ideally (something one can never do absolutely without *addressing oneself to the other* and without absolutely limiting understanding itself, the identifying appropriation), speak to him or her in words that also pass through the mouth, the ear, and sight, and respect the law that is at once a voice and a court (it hears itself, it is *in us* who are *before it*). The sublime refinement involved in this respect for the other is also a way of "Eating well," in the sense of "good eating" but also "eating the Good" [*le Bien manger*]. The Good can also be eaten. And it, the good, must be eaten and eaten well.

I don't know, at this point, who is "who," any more than I know what "sacrifice" means; to determine what this last word means, I would retain this clue: need, desire, authorization, the justification of putting to death, putting to death as denegation of murder. The putting to death of the animal, says this denegation, is not a murder. I would link this denegation to the violent institution of the "who" as subject. There is no need to emphasize that this question of the subject and of the living "who" is at the heart of the most pressing concerns of modern societies, whether they are deciding birth or death, including what is presupposed in the treatment of sperm or the ovum, surrogate mothers, genetic engineering, so-called bioethics or biopolitics (what should be the role of the State in determining or protecting a living subject?), the accredited criteriology for determining, indeed for "euthanastically" provoking death (how can the dominant reference to consciousness, to the will and the cortex still be justified?), organ removal and transplant (I might recall in passing that the question of the graft in general has always been—and thematically so from the beginning—essential to the deconstruction of phallogocentrism).

Let's go back a little: In relation to whom, to what other, is the subject first thrown (*geworfen*) or exposed as hostage? Who is the "neighbor" dwelling in the very proximity of transcendence, in Heidegger's transcendence, or Levinas's? These two ways of thinking transcendence are as different as you wish. They are as different or as similar as being and the other, but seem to me to follow the same schema. What is still to come or what remains buried in an almost inaccessible memory is the thinking of a responsibility that does not stop at *this* determination of the neighbor, at the dominant schema of this determination. One could, if one so wished, show that the problems or the questions that I am raising here concern not only metaphysics, onto-theologies, and certain claims to go beyond them, but also the ethnology of the religious domains in which these thinkings "presented" themselves. I have tried to suggest, notably in *Of Spirit*, that in spite of many denegations, Heidegger was a Judeo-Christian thinker. (However, an ethnology or a sociology of religions would only be up to these questions if it were no longer itself dominated, as regional science, by a conceptuality inherited from these metaphysics or onto-theologies. Such an ethnology would in particular have to spend quite some time in the complex history of Hinduist culture, which perhaps represents the most subtle and decisive confirmation of this schema. Does it not, precisely, set in opposition the political hierarchy—or the exercise of power—and the religious hierarchy, the latter prohibiting, the former allowing itself, indeed imposing upon itself the eating of meat? Very summarily, one might think of the hierarchy of the *varna*, if not of the castes, and of the distinction between the Brahman priests, who became vegetarians, and the Kshatriya warriors, who are not...)

Q.: I must interrupt you, for in the time remaining I want to ask you some more questions. Beginning with this one: in the shift, which you judge to be necessary, from man to animal—I am expressing myself very quickly and crudely—what happens to language?

J.D.: The idea according to which man is the only speaking being, in its traditional form or in its Heideggerian form, seems to me at once undisplaceable and highly problematic. Of course, if one defines language in such a way that it is reserved for what we call man, what is there to say? But if one re-inscribes language in a network of possibilities that do not merely encompass it but mark it irreducibly from the inside, everything changes. I am thinking in particular of the mark in general, of the trace, of iterability, of differance. These possibilities or necessities, without which there would be no language, *are themselves not only human.* It is not a question of covering up ruptures and heterogeneities. I would simply contest that they give rise to a single linear, indivisible, oppositional limit, to a binary opposition between the human and the infra-human. And what I am proposing here should allow us to take into account scientific knowledge about the complexity of "animal languages," genetic coding, all forms of marking within which so-called human language, as original as it might be, does not allow us to "cut" once and for all where we would in general like to cut. As you can see, in spite of appearances, I am speaking here of very "concrete" and very "current" problems: the ethics and the politics of the living. We know less than ever where to cut—either at birth or at death. And this also means that we never know, and never have known, how to *cut up* a subject. Today less than ever. If we had been given more space, I would like to have spoken here about AIDS, an event that one could call *historial* in the *epoch* of *subjectivity,* if we still gave credence to *historiality,* to *epochality,* and to *subjectivity.*

Q.: Second question: since, in the logic you have deployed, you foresee for a long time hence the possibility of coming back to or coming at last to interrogate the subject of ethical, juridical, political responsibility, what can one say of this or these responsibilities now? Could one speak of them only under the heading of a "provisional morality"? What would this mean? And I would add to this the question of what is today recognized as perhaps "the" question, or as "the" figure of responsibility, namely, Auschwitz. There, where an almost general consensus recognizes an absolute responsibility and calls for a responsibility so that it might not be repeated, would you say the same thing—provisionally or not—or would you say that one must defer the answer to this question?

J.D.: I would not subscribe to the expression "provisional morality." At the very least, an exacting responsibility requires not trusting blindly the axioms of which we have just spoken. These limit still more the concept of responsibility within frontiers that the axioms refuse to answer for, and they constitute, in the form of provisional schemas, the very models of traditional morality and right. But for this surplus of responsibility that summons the deconstructive gesture or that the deconstructive gesture of which I am speaking calls forth, a waiting period is neither possible nor legitimate. The deconstructive explication with provisional prescriptions might require the indefatigable patience of the re-beginning, but the affirmation that motivates deconstruction is unconditional, imperative, and immediate—in a sense that is not necessarily or only Kantian, even if this affirmation, because it is double, as I have tried to show, is ceaselessly threatened. This is why it leaves no respite, no rest. It can always upset, at least, the instituted rhythm of every pause (and the subject is a pause, a stance, the stabilizing arrest, the thesis, or rather the hypothesis we will always need), it can always trouble our Saturdays and Sundays... and our Fridays... I'll let you complete this monotheistic sentence, it's a bit wearying.

Q.: Would you think, then, that Heidegger's silence concerning the camps—this almost total silence, as distinct from his relative silence about his own Nazism—would you think that this silence might have come from such a "deconstructive explication," at once different and comparable, that he might have been trying to carry out in silence, without managing to explain himself on it? (I could ask this question about others, about Bataille, for example, but let's stick to Heidegger for today.)

J.D.: Yes and no. The surplus of responsibility of which I was just speaking will never authorize any silence. I repeat: responsibility is excessive or it is not a responsibility. A limited, measured, calculable, rationally distributed responsibility is already the becoming-right of morality; it is at times also, in the best hypothesis, the dream of every good conscience, in the worst hypothesis, of the petty or grand inquisitors. I suppose, I hope you are not expecting me simply to say "I condemn Auschwitz" or "I condemn every silence on Auschwitz." As regards this last phrase or its equivalents, I find a bit indecent, indeed, obscene, the mechanical nature of improvised trials instigated against all those whom one thinks one can accuse of not having named or thought "Auschwitz." A compulsion toward sententious discourse, strategic exploitation, the eloquence of denunciation: all this would be less grievous if one began by stating, rigorously, what we call "Auschwitz" and what we *think* about it, if we think something. What is the referent here? Are we making a metonymical usage of this proper name? If we are, what governs this usage? Why this name rather than that of another camp, of other mass exterminations, etc. (and who has answered these questions seriously)? If not, why this forgetful and just as grievous restriction? If we admit—and this concession seems to me to be readable everywhere—that the thing remains unthinkable, that we still have no discourse equal to it, if we recognize that we have nothing to say about the real victims of Auschwitz, the same ones we nonetheless authorize ourselves to treat by metonymy or to name *via negativa*, then let's stop diagnosing the alleged silences, forcing avowals of the "resistances" or the "unthought" in everyone indiscriminately. Of course, silence on Auschwitz will never be justifiable; but neither is speaking about it in such an instrumental fashion and in order to say nothing, to say nothing about it that does not go without saying, trivially, serving primarily to give oneself a good conscience, so as not to be the last to accuse, to teach lessons, to take positions, or to grandstand. As for what you call Heidegger's infamous "silence," I think that in order to interpret or to judge it—which is not always the same thing—it would be necessary *at least* to take into account, and this is not easy to circumscribe and would require more space and time, what we have said here about the subject, about man, about the animal, but also about sacrifice, which means also about so many other things. A necessary condition, which would already call for lengthy discourse. As for going beyond this necessary but insufficient condition, I would prefer that we wait for, let us say, *another moment*, the occasion of another discussion: another rhythm and another form.

TRANSLATED BY PETER CONNOR AND AVITAL RONELL

Che cos'è la poesia?

Pour répondre à une telle question—*en deux mots, n'est-ce pas?*—on te demande de savoir renoncer au savoir. Et de bien le savoir, sans jamais l'oublier: démobilise la culture mais ce que tu sacrifies en route, en traversant la route, ne l'oublie jamais dans ta docte ignorance.

Qui ose me demander cela? Même s'il n'en paraît rien, car disparaître est sa loi, la réponse *se voit dictée*. Je suis *une* dictée, prononce la poésie, apprends-moi par coeur, recopie, veille et garde-moi, regarde-moi, dictée, sous les yeux: bande-son, *wake*, sillage de lumière, photographie de la fête en deuil.

Elle se voit dictée, la réponse, d'être poétique. Et pour cela tenue de s'adresser à quelqu'un, singulièrement à toi mais comme à l'être perdu dans l'anonymat, entre ville et nature, un secret partagé, à la fois public et privé, *absolument* l'un et l'autre, absous de dehors et de dedans, ni l'un ni l'autre, l'animal jeté sur la route, absolu, solitaire, roulé en boule *auprès de soi*. Il peut se faire écraser, *justement*, pour cela même, le hérisson, *istrice*.

Et si tu réponds autrement selon les cas, compte tenu de l'espace et du temps qui te sont *donnés* avec cette *demande* (déjà tu parles italien), par elle-même, selon *cette* économie mais aussi dans l'im-

Che cos'è la poesia?

In order to respond to such a question—*in two words, right?*—
you are asked to know how to renounce knowledge. And to know it
well, without ever forgetting it: demobilize culture, but never
forget in your learned ignorance what you sacrifice on the road, in
crossing the road.

Who dares to ask me that? Even though it remains inapparent,
since disappearing is its law, the answer *sees itself (as) dictated
(dictation)*. I am *a* dictation, pronounces poetry, learn me by heart,
copy me down, guard and keep me, look out for me, look at me,
dictated dictation, right before your eyes: soundtrack, *wake*, trail of
light, photograph of the feast in mourning.

It sees itself, the response, dictated to be poetic, by being poetic.
And for that reason, it is obliged to address itself to someone,
singularly to you but as if to the being lost in anonymity, between
city and nature, an imparted secret, at once public and private,
absolutely one and the other, absolved from within and from without, neither one nor the other, the animal thrown onto the road,
absolute, solitary, rolled up in a ball, *next to (it)self*. And for that
very reason, it may get itself run over, *just so*, the *hérisson, istrice* in
Italian, in English, hedgehog.

And if you respond otherwise depending on each case, taking
into account the space and time which you are *given* with this
demand (already you are speaking Italian), by the demand itself,

minence de quelque traversée *hors de chez soi*, risquée vers la langue de l'autre en vue d'une traduction impossible ou refusée, nécessaire mais désirée comme une mort, qu'est-ce que tout cela, cela même où tu viens déjà de te délirer, aurait à voir, dès lors, avec la poésie? Avec le *poétique*, plutôt, car tu entends parler d'une *expérience*, autre mot pour voyage, ici la randonnée aléatoire d'un trajet, la strophe qui tourne mais jamais ne reconduit au discours, ni chez soi, jamais du moins ne se réduit à la poésie—écrite, parlée, même chantée.

Voici donc, tout de suite, *en deux mots*, pour ne pas oublier.

1. *L'économie de la mémoire:* un poème doit être bref, par vocation elliptique, quelle qu'en soit l'étendue objective ou apparente. Docte inconscient de la *Verdichtung* et du retrait.

2. *Le coeur.* Non pas le coeur au milieu des phrases qui circulent sans risque sur les échangeurs et s'y laissent traduire en toutes langues. Non pas simplement le coeur des archives cardiographiques, l'objet des savoirs ou des techniques, des philosophies et des discours bio-éthico-juridiques. Peut-être pas le coeur des Ecritures ou de Pascal, ni même, c'est moins sûr, celui que leur préfère Heidegger. Non, une histoire de "coeur" poétiquement enveloppée dans l'idiome "apprendre par coeur," celui de ma langue ou d'une autre, l'anglaise *(to learn by heart)*, ou d'une autre encore, l'arabe *(hafiza a'n zahri kalb)*—un seul trajet à plusieurs voies.

Deux en un: le second axiome s'enroule dans le premier. Le poétique, disons-le, serait ce que tu désires apprendre, mais de l'autre, grâce à l'autre et sous dictée, par coeur: *imparare a memoria*. N'est-ce pas déjà cela, le poème, lorsqu'un gage est donné, la venue d'un événement, à l'instant où la traversée de la route nommée traduction reste aussi improbable qu'un accident, intensément rêvée pourtant, requise là où ce qu'elle promet toujours laisse à désirer? Une reconnaissance va vers cela même et prévient ici la connaissance: ta bénédiction avant le savoir.

Fable que tu pourrais raconter comme le don du poème, c'est

according to *this* economy but also in the imminence of some traversal *outside* yourself, away from *home*, venturing toward the language of the other in view of an impossible or denied translation, necessary but desired like a death—what would all of this, the very thing in which you have just begun to turn deliriously, have to do, at that point, with poetry? Or rather, with the *poetic*, since you intend to speak about an *experience*, another word for voyage, here the aleatory rambling of a trek, the strophe that turns but never leads back to discourse, or back home, at least is never reduced to poetry—written, spoken, even sung.

Here then, right away, *in two words*, so as not to forget:

1. *The economy of memory.* A poem must be brief, elliptical by vocation, whatever may be its objective or apparent expanse. Learned unconscious of *Verdichtung* and of the retreat.

2. *The heart.* Not the heart in the middle of sentences that circulate risk-free through the interchanges and let themselves be translated into any and all languages. Not simply the heart archived by cardiography, the object of sciences or technologies, of philosophies and bio-ethico-juridical discourses. Perhaps not the heart of the Scriptures or of Pascal, nor even, this is less certain, the one that Heidegger prefers to them. No, a story of "heart" poetically enveloped in the idiom "*apprendre par coeur*," whether in my language or another, the English language (to learn by heart), or still another, the Arab language (*hafiza a'n zahri kalb*)—a single trek with several tracks.

Two in one: the second axiom is rolled up in the first. The poetic, let us say it, would be that which you desire to learn, but from and of the other, thanks to the other and under dictation, by heart; *imparare a memoria.* Isn't that already it, the poem, once a token is given, the advent of an event, at the moment in which the traversing of the road named translation remains as improbable as an accident, one which is all the same intensely dreamed of, required there where what it promises always leaves something to be desired? A grateful recognition goes out toward that very thing and precedes cognition here: your benediction before knowledge.

A fable that you could recount as the gift of the poem, it is an

une histoire emblématique: quelqu'un *t*'écrit, à toi, de toi, sur toi. Non, une marque à toi adressée, laissée, confiée, s'accompagne d'une injonction, en vérité s'institue en cet ordre même qui à son tour te constitue, assignant ton origine ou te donnant lieu: détruis-moi, ou plutôt rends mon support invisible au dehors, dans le monde (voilà déjà le trait de toutes les dissociations, l'histoire des transcendances), fais en sorte en tout cas que la provenance de la marque reste désormais introuvable ou méconnaissable. Promets-le: qu'elle se défigure, transfigure ou indétermine en son *port*, et tu entendras sous ce mot la rive du départ aussi bien que le référent vers lequel une translation se porte. Mange, bois, avale ma lettre, porte-la, transporte-la en toi, comme la loi d'une écriture devenue ton corps: *l'écriture en soi*. La ruse de l'injonction peut d'abord se laisser inspirer par la simple possibilité de la mort, par le danger que fait courir un véhicule à tout être fini. Tu entends venir la catastrophe. Dés lors imprimé à même le trait, venu du coeur, le désir du mortel éveille en toi le mouvement (contradictoire, tu me suis bien, double astreinte, contrainte aporétique) de garder de l'oubli cette chose qui du même coup s'expose à la mort et se protège—en un mot, l'adresse, le retrait du hérisson, comme sur l'autoroute un animal roulé en boule. On voudrait le prendre dans ses mains, l'apprendre et le comprendre, le garder pour soi, auprès de soi.

Tu aimes—garder cela dans sa forme singulière, on dirait dans l'irremplaçable *littéralité du vocable* si on parlait de la poésie et non seulement du poétique en général. Mais notre poème ne tient pas en place dans des noms, ni même dans des mots. Il est d'abord jeté sur les routes et dans les champs, chose au-delà des langues, même s'il lui arrive de s'y rappeler lorsqu'il se rassemble, roulé en boule auprès de soi, plus menacé que jamais dans sa retraite: il croit alors se défendre, il se perd.

Littéralement: tu voudrais retenir par coeur une forme absolument unique, un événement dont l'intangible singularité ne sépare

emblematic story: someone writes *you*, to you, of you, on you. No, rather a mark addressed to you, left and confided with you, is accompanied by an injunction, in truth it is instituted in this very order which, in its turn, constitutes you, assigning your origin or giving rise to you: destroy me, or rather render my support invisible to the outside, in the world (this is already the trait of all dissociations, the history of transcendences), in any case do what must be done so that the provenance of the mark remains from now on unlocatable or unrecognizable. Promise it: let it be disfigured, transfigured or rendered indeterminate in its *port*—and in this word you will hear the shore of the departure as well as the referent toward which a translation is portered. Eat, drink, swallow my letter, carry it, transport it in you, like the law of a writing become your body: *writing in (it)self.* The ruse of the injunction may first of all let itself be inspired by the simple possibility of death, by the risk that a vehicle poses to every finite being. You hear the catastrophe coming. From that moment on imprinted directly on the trait, come from the heart, the mortal's desire awakens in you the movement (which is contradictory, you follow me, a double restraint, an aporetic constraint) to guard from oblivion this thing which in the same stroke exposes itself to death and protects itself— in a word, the address, the retreat of the *hérisson*, like an animal on the autoroute rolled up in a ball. One would like to take it in one's hands, undertake to learn it and understand it, to keep it for oneself, near oneself.

You love—keep that in its singular form, we could say in the irreplaceable *literality of the vocable* if we were talking about poetry and not only about the poetic in general. But our poem does not hold still within names, nor even within words. It is first of all thrown out on the roads and in the fields, thing beyond languages, even if it sometimes happens that it recalls itself in language, when it gathers itself up, rolled up in a ball on itself, it is more threatened than ever in its retreat: it thinks it is defending itself, and it loses itself.

Literally: you would like to retain by heart an absolutely unique form, an event whose intangible singularity no longer separates the

plus l'idéalité, le sens idéal, comme on dit, du corps de la lettre. Le désir de cette inséparation absolue, le non-absolu absolu, tu y respires l'origine du poétique. D'où la résistance infinie au transfert de la lettre que l'animal, en son nom, réclame pourtant. C'est la détresse du hérisson. Que veut la détresse, le *stress* même? *stricto sensu* mettre en garde. D'où la prophétie: traduis-moi, veille, garde-moi encore un peu, sauve-toi, quittons l'autoroute.

Ainsi se lève en toi le rêve d'*apprendre par coeur*. De te laisser traverser le coeur par la dictée. D'un seul trait, et c'est l'impossible et c'est l'expérience poématique. Tu ne savais pas encore le coeur, tu l'apprends ainsi. De cette expérience et de cette expression. J'appelle poème cela même qui apprend le coeur, ce qui invente le coeur, enfin *ce que* le mot de coeur semble vouloir dire et que dans ma langue je discerne mal du mot coeur. *Coeur*, dans le poème "apprendre par coeur" (à apprendre par coeur), ne nomme plus seulement la pure intériorité, la spontanéité indépendante, la liberté de s'affecter activement en reproduisant la trace aimée. La mémoire du "par coeur" se confie comme une prière, c'est plus sûr, à une certaine extériorité de l'automate, aux lois de la mnémotechnique, à cette liturgie qui mime en surface la mécanique, à l'automobile qui surprend ta passion et vient sur toi comme du dehors: *auswendig*, "par coeur" en allemand.

Donc: le coeur te bat, naissance du rythme, au-delà des oppositions, du dedans et du dehors, de la représentation consciente et de l'archive abandonnée. Un coeur là-bas, entre les sentiers ou les autostrades, hors de ta présence, humble, près de la terre, tout bas. Réitère en murmurant: ne répète jamais… Dans un seul chiffre, le poème (l'apprendre par coeur) scelle ensemble le sens et la lettre, comme un rythme espaçant le temps.

Pour répondre en deux mots, *ellipse*, par example, ou *élection*, *coeur* ou *hérisson*, il t'aura fallu désemparer la mémoire, désarmer la culture, savoir oublier le savoir, incendier la bibliothèque des poétiques. L'unicité du poème est à cette condition. Il te faut célébrer, tu

ideality, the ideal meaning as one says, from the body of the letter. In the desire of this absolute inseparation, the absolute non-
absolute, you breathe the origin of the poetic. Whence the infinite
resistance to the transfer of the letter which the animal, in its name,
nevertheless calls out for. That is the distress of the *hérisson.* What
does the distress, *stress* itself, want? *Stricto sensu,* to put on guard.
Whence the prophecy: translate me, watch, keep me yet awhile, get
going, save yourself, let's get off the autoroute.

Thus the dream of *learning by heart* arises in you. Of letting your
heart be traversed by the dictated dictation. In a single trait—and
that's the impossible, that's the poematic experience. You did not
yet know the heart, you learn it thus. From this experience and
from this expression. I call a poem that very thing that teaches the
heart, invents the heart, *that which,* finally, the word *heart* seems to
mean and which, in my language, I cannot easily discern from the
word itself. *Heart,* in the poem "learn by heart" (to be learned by
heart), no longer names only pure interiority, independent spontaneity, the freedom to affect oneself actively by reproducing the
beloved trace. The memory of the "by heart" is confided like a
prayer—that's safer—to a certain exteriority of the automaton, to
the laws of mnemotechnics, to that liturgy that mimes mechanics
on the surface, to the automobile that surprises your passion and
bears down on you as if from an outside: *auswendig,* "by heart" in
German.

So: your heart beats, gives the downbeat, the birth of rhythm,
beyond oppositions, beyond outside and inside, conscious representation and the abandoned archive. A heart down there, between
paths and autostradas, outside of your presence, humble, close to
the earth, low down. Reiterate(s) in a murmur: never repeat... In a
single cipher, the poem (the learning by heart, learn it by heart)
seals together the meaning and the letter, like a rhythm spacing out
time.

In order to respond in two words: *ellipsis,* for example, or *election, heart, hérisson,* or *istrice,* you will have had to disable memory,
disarm culture, know how to forget knowledge, set fire to the
library of poetics. The unicity of the poem depends on this condi-

dois commémorer l'amnésie, la sauvagerie, voire la bêtise du "par
coeur": le hérisson. Il s'aveugle. Roulé en boule, hérissé de pi-
quants, vulnérable et dangereux, calculateur et inadapté (parce
qu'il se met en boule, sentant le danger sur l'autoroute, il s'expose à
l'accident). Pas de poème sans accident, pas de poème qui ne
s'ouvre comme une blessure, mais qui ne soit aussi blessant. Tu
appelleras poème une incantation silencieuse, la blessure aphone
que de toi je désire apprendre par coeur. Il a donc lieu, pour
l'essentiel, sans qu'on ait à le faire: il *se laisse* faire, sans activité, sans
travail, dans le plus sobre *pathos*, étranger à toute production,
surtout à la création. Le poème échoit, bénédiction, venue de
l'autre. Rythme mais dissymétrie. Il n'y a jamais que du poème,
avant toute poïèse. Quand, au lieu de "poésie," nous avons dit
"poétique," nous aurions dû préciser: "poématique." Surtout ne
laisse pas reconduire le hérisson dans le cirque ou dans le manège
de la *poiesis*: rien à faire *(poiein)*, ni "poésie pure," ni rhétorique
pure, ni *reine Sprache*, ni "mise-en-oeuvre-de-la-vérité." Seulement
une contamination, telle, et tel carrefour, cet accident-ci. Ce tour,
le retournement de *cette* catastrophe. Le don du poème ne cite rien,
il n'a aucun titre, il n'histrionne plus, il survient sans que tu t'y
attendes, coupant le souffle, coupant avec la poésie discursive, et
surtout littéraire. Dans les cendres mêmes de cette généalogie. Pas
le phénix, pas l'aigle, le hérisson, très bas, tout bas, près de la terre.
Ni sublime, ni incorporel, angélique peut-être, et pour un temps.

   Tu appelleras désormais poème une certaine passion de la marque singulière, la signature qui répète sa dispersion, chaque fois au-
delà du *logos*, anhumaine, domestique à peine, ni réappropriable
dans la famille du sujet: un animal converti, roulé en boule, tourné
vers l'autre et vers soi, une chose en somme, et modeste, discrète,
près de la terre, l'humilité que tu *surnommes*, te portant ainsi dans
le nom, au-delà du nom, un hérisson catachrétique, toutes flèches
dehors, quand cet aveugle sans âge entend mais ne voit pas venir la
mort.

tion. You must celebrate, you have to commemorate amnesia, savagery, even the stupidity of the "by heart": the *hérisson*. It blinds itself. Rolled up in a ball, prickly with spines, vulnerable and dangerous, calculating and ill-adapted (because it makes itself into a ball, sensing the danger on the autoroute, it exposes itself to an accident). No poem without accident, no poem that does not open itself like a wound, but no poem that is not also just as wounding. You will call poem a silent incantation, the aphonic wound that, of you, from you, I want to learn by heart. It thus takes place, essentially, without one's having to do it or make it: it *lets itself* be done, without activity, without work, in the most sober *pathos*, a stranger to all production, especially to creation. The poem falls to me, benediction, coming of (or from) the other. Rhythm but dissymmetry. There is never anything but some poem, before any *poiesis*. When, instead of "poetry," we said "poetic," we ought to have specified: "poematic." Most of all do not let the *hérisson* be led back into the circus or the menagerie of *poiesis*: nothing to be done (*poiein*), neither "pure poetry," nor pure rhetoric, nor *reine Sprache*, nor "setting-forth-of-truth-in-the-work." Just this contamination, and this crossroads, this accident here. This turn, the turning around of *this* catastrophe. The gift of the poem cites nothing, it has no title, its histrionics are over, it comes along without your expecting it, cutting short the breath, cutting all ties with discursive and especially literary poetry. In the very ashes of this genealogy. Not the phoenix, not the eagle, but the *hérisson*, very lowly, low down, close to the earth. Neither sublime, nor incorporeal, angelic, perhaps, and for a time.

You will call poem from now on a certain passion of the singular mark, the signature that repeats its dispersion, each time beyond the *logos*, a-human, barely domestic, not reappropriable into the family of the subject: a converted animal, rolled up in a ball, turned toward the other and toward itself, in sum, a thing—modest, discreet, close to the earth, the humility that you surname, thus transporting yourself in the name beyond a name, a catachrestic *hérisson*, its arrows held at the ready, when this ageless blind thing hears but does not see death coming.

Le poème peut se rouler en boule mais c'est encore pour tourner ses signes aigus vers le dehors. Il peut certes réfléchir la langue ou dire la poésie mais il ne se rapporte jamais à lui-même, il ne se meut jamais de lui-même comme ces engins porteurs de mort. Son événement interrompt toujours ou dévoie le savoir absolu, l'être auprès de soi dans l'autotélie. Ce "démon du coeur" jamais ne se rassemble, il s'égare plutôt (délire ou manie), il s'expose à la chance, il se laisserait plutôt déchiqueter par ce qui vient sur lui.

Sans sujet: il y a peut-être du poème, et qui *se laisse*, mais je n'en écris jamais. Un poème je ne le signe jamais. L'autre signe. Le *je* n'est qu'à la venue de ce désir: apprendre par coeur. Tendu pour se résumer à son propre support, donc sans support extérieur, sans substance, sans sujet, absolu de l'écriture en soi, le "par coeur" se laisse élire au-delà du corps, du sexe, de la bouche et des yeux, il efface les bords, il échappe aux mains, tu l'entends à peine, mais il nous apprend le coeur. Filiation, gage d'élection confié en héritage, il peut se prendre à n'importe quel mot, à la chose, vivante ou non, au nom de hérisson par exemple, entre vie et mort, à la tombée de la nuit ou au petit jour, apocalypse distraite, propre et commune, publique et secrète.

—Mais le poème dont tu parles, tu t'égares, on ne l'a jamais nommé ainsi, ni aussi arbitrairement.

—Tu viens de le dire. Ce qu'il fallait démontrer. Rappelle-toi la question: "Qu'est-ce que...?" *(tí estí, was ist..., istoria, episteme, philosophia).* "Qu'est-ce que...?" pleure la disparition du poème—une autre catastrophe. En annonçant ce qui est tel qu'il est, une question salue la naissance de la prose.

The poem can roll itself up in a ball, but it is still in order to turn its pointed signs toward the outside. To be sure, it can reflect language or speak poetry, but it never relates back to itself, it never moves by itself like those machines, bringers of death. Its event always interrupts or derails absolute knowledge, autotelic being in proximity to itself. This "demon of the heart" never gathers itself together, rather it loses itself and gets off the track (delirium or mania), it exposes itself to chance, it would rather let itself be torn to pieces by what bears down upon it.

Without a subject: poem, perhaps there is some, and perhaps it *leaves itself,* but I never write any. A poem, I never sign(s) it. The other sign(s). The *I* is only at the coming of this desire: to learn by heart. Stretched, tendered forth to the point of subsuming its own support, thus without external support, without substance, without subject, absolute of writing in (it)self, the "by heart" lets itself be elected beyond the body, sex, mouth, and eyes; it erases the borders, slips through the hands, you can barely hear it, but it teaches us the heart. Filiation, token of election confided as legacy, it can attach itself to any word at all, to the thing, living or not, to the name of *hérisson,* for example, between life and death, at nightfall or at daybreak, distracted apocalypse, proper and common, public and secret.

—But the poem you are talking about, you are getting off the track, it has never been named thus, or so arbitrarily.

—You just said it. Which had to be demonstrated. Recall the question: "What is...?" (*tí estí, was ist..., istoria, episteme, philosophia*). "What is...?" laments the disappearance of the poem—another catastrophe. By announcing that which is just as it is, a question salutes the birth of prose.

Istrice 2: Ick bünn all hier

Q.: "Most of all do not let the *hérisson* be led back into the circus or the menagerie of *poiesis*: nothing to be done (*poiein*), neither 'pure poetry,' nor pure rhetoric, nor *reine Sprache*, nor 'setting-forth-of-truth-in-the-work.' "[1] In *The Origin of the Work of Art*, and by means of the idea of the work as setting-into-work of truth, Heidegger accentuates the serious side of poetry, which would shelter it from the characteristic irresponsibility of literature and imagination. "Poetry, however, is not an aimless imagining of whimsicalities and not a flight of mere notions and fancies into the realm of the unreal. . . . If we fix our vision on the nature of the work and its connection with the happening of the truth of what is, it becomes questionable whether the nature of poetry, and this means at the same time the nature of projection, can be adequately thought of in terms of the power of imagination."[2]

Project, poetics, and politics are brought together in the strictest fashion thanks to this definition of art as setting-into-work of truth and to a degradation of esthetics as play. We are not very far, it seems to me, from a passage in the Rectorship Address that you quote in *Of Spirit*, a passage in which Heidegger writes that " 'spirit' is neither empty acumen nor the noncommittal play of wit (*das unverbindliche Spiel des Witzes*) nor the busy practice of never-ending rational analysis nor even world reason; rather, spirit is the determined resolve to the essence of Being."[3] Like Spirit, poetry promotes a *Versammlung*, a thoughtful gathering that goes beyond dispersion, beyond the letter, and beyond irresponsibility; for the *logos* is what it is only to the extent that it gathers (and Heidegger underscores in *Identity and Difference* that the *logos* is very precisely what reunites everything in the universal; in *What Is Metaphysics?* and elsewhere, he specifies in a specular fashion that science, which does not think and shares precisely a certain irresponsibility of the *unverbindliche Spiel des Witzes*, is now completely dispersed, held together solely in a formal manner by the organization of the teaching disciplines. And it is this dissolution, which has to be understood literally as an absence of link, that is at the origin of the crisis).

J.D.: There was a hedgehog in your very first sentence; it went by very quickly at the beginning of this interview. In memory of this hedgehog, which in the past you were good enough to call up and to translate, allow me first of all to open a parenthesis. It concerns precisely the memory of the hedgehog. In *"Che cos'è la poesia?"* the figure of this animal seems to herald, as if in silence, something about the "by heart" and memory. Well, quite a bit later after publishing this text, I had to give in to a strange certainty: if this hedgehog had appeared to rise up before me, unique, young as on the first day of creation, but also given secretly for the first time, an incomparable present, in truth I must have come across it at least two times before. In two texts that mean a lot to me. But I didn't recall this for a single instant at the moment of writing. I didn't even have the distant feeling of other possible hedgehogs—in my memory or in literature. Before the depth of this forgetting, which effaced even the support of the message, I wonder if I even noticed during my reading, which was perhaps distracted, the two other hedgehogs that now come back like ghosts, or if instead an operation of effective censoring had not already imposed in me the accident that that text talks about. It little matters. And it is true that, although they have the same name, these two hedgehogs don't have much relation to "mine"; they don't belong to the same family, the same species, or the same genre, even though this non-relation

says something about a deep genealogical affinity, but in antago-
nism, in counter-genealogy. Compared to these two hedgehogs,
which turn out to be German hedgehogs, bearing therefore a
German name (*Igel*), the one that occurred to me is a solitary
counter-hedgehog, first of all Italian [*istrice*] or French [*hérisson*].

Who are the two Germans? There is first of all Schlegel, whom I
read or reread in *The Literary Absolute: The Theory of Literature in
German Romanticism*, the very fine book by Philippe Lacoue-
Labarthe and Jean-Luc Nancy.[4] It concerns a fragment (206) on the
fragment: "Like a little work of art, a fragment must be totally
detached from the surrounding world and closed on itself like a
hedgehog."[5] In their "Overture," and precisely in the chapter titled
"The Fragmentary Demand," Lacoue-Labarthe and Nancy underscore the coherent cohesion that commands this concept of the
fragment. Their statements make me better understand why I have
always had reservations with regard to a certain cult of the fragment
and especially of the fragmentary *work* which always calls for an
upping of the ante of authority and monumental totality. Lacoue-
Labarthe and Nancy speak of a "logic of the hedgehog": "The
fragmentary totality, in conformity with what one should venture
to call instead the logic of the hedgehog, cannot be situated at one
point: it is simultaneously in the whole and in each part. Each
fragment is valid for itself and for that from which it is detached.
The totality is the fragment itself in its finished individuality."
Earlier, this romantic hedgehog had Kantian features: "What it
must be [*Son devoir-être*], if not its being (but doesn't one have to
understand that its only being is what it must be, and that this
hedgehog is a Kantian animal?) is indeed formed by the integrity
and the integralness of organic individuality."[6]

In relation to this hedgehog and what it configures (work,
organic individuality, total fragment, poetry), the one that came to
me across this letter ("*Che cos'è la poesia?*") seems very solitary and
deprived of family. It doesn't have the same genealogy. It doesn't
belong to the species or the genre, to the generality of the *gens*
"hedgehog." First of all because, indissolubly linked to the chance
of a language and of signifiers that play the role of temporary

proper name (first *istrice* and then its fragile translation into *hérisson*), come into being via a letter, this "catachrestic" *hérisson* is barely a name, it does not bear its name, it plays with syllables, but in any case it is neither a concept nor a thing. As "poematics" and not "poetics," it remains profoundly estranged from the work and from the setting-to-work of truth. Humble and close to the ground, it can only expose itself to accidents when it tries to save itself, and first of all to save itself from its name and to save its coming. It has no relation to itself—that is, no totalizing individuality—that does not expose it even more to death and to being-torn-apart. Another logic. Or rather: this very young hedgehog is older than "logic." The "logic of the hedgehog" is one of the possible traps in the adventure of this other hedgehog, of its name and of its dispatch.

There is also Heidegger. The silhouette of an *Igel* passes by still more quickly near the end of *Identity and Difference* in "Die onto-theologische Verfassung der Metaphysik."[7] Heidegger there mimes the objection of someone who might reproach him for claiming to contribute something with the difference between Being and being, when in fact Being and being in their difference are already (*immer schon*) there, there where one thinks one has arrived, a "there" which is already a "here" (*Ick bünn all hier*), here where one pretends finally to reach them. The critic is made to say: "It is as in Grimm's fairytale 'The Hedgehog and the Hare': 'I'm here already' [Es ist hier wie im Grimmschen Märchen vom Hasen und Igel: 'Ick bünn all hier']."[8] The Grimms' tale in fact tells of a hedgehog who, to be sure of victory and of winning the race, sends his female hedgehog ahead to the finish line. One or the other of them will always be able to cry out "I am there," already there, whenever some hare will have naively thought he beat them to the finish. The concept, the figure, the sense of the hedgehog, in this case, whatever its language may be and whatever its name may be, mean the "always-already-there," the structure or the logic of the "always already" (and who would dare to claim this "objection" to Heidegger is as naive as it appears when it is the setting-to-work of truth that is in question?), of the "I have always already arrived," here or there, here as there, "*Ick bünn all hier,*" "*Ick bünn all da.*" The *Da* or the *Fort-Da* of the *Dasein* would belong to this logic of destination that permits one to say, everywhere and always, "I have always already arrived at the destination." There would be much to say about the maneuver or the working of the *couple* in this strategy: the delegation of the female to the finish, to the place of arrival, to the end of a race or a competition that is first of all that of the male. But we don't know which voice says "I am here." His or hers? What is the *Geschlecht* of this triumphal voice? The *istrice* that came to me can barely say "*Ich*" and certainly not "*bünn,*" still less "*hier*" and "*da.*" It is still waiting and is not assured of any "always already." Which does not mean that it is deprived of speech, of being-for-death, of being-thrown (for example onto the highway), of *Geworfenheit,* and so forth. Quite to the contrary. It is barely a hedgehog, strictly speaking; it is neither a work, nor poetry, nor truth, only a letter and a few syllables destined to die by accident. There is, in the end, no cogito or work for this hedgehog who cannot gather itself up or gather itself together enough to say "*Ich bin hier*" or "*ergo sum,*" "*immer schon da*"...

The sentence you quoted does in fact allude to, among other things, what Heidegger says of the "setting-to-work of truth." The point would thus be to remove what I am calling the *poem* (or the *poiemata*) from the merry-go-round or circus that brings them back in a circular fashion to *poiein,* to their poetic source, to the act or to the experience of their setting-to-work in poetry or in poetics. By dissociating the poematic from the poetic, one removes it, one makes way for the experience during which it removes itself from the initiative of the setting-to-work, of *poiesis,* the tradition in which, I believe, *The Origin of the Work of Art* is inscribed. But I must not overburden this *letter on the letter in istrice* with too much significance: it must remain elliptical, just barely serious, poematic in some respects, in the manner of the poem about which it *converses with itself,* by means of which it *maintains itself* [*dont elle s'entretient elle-même*], that is to say, blindly (like the hedgehog that Homer recalls), deprived of meaning and responsibility.

If one puts into question again the interpretation of the poem as the "setting-to-work of the truth," if one deems a certain aleatory factor of the letter to be irreducible there, which exposes the hedgehog to catastrophe, then in fact by the same token this puts in question the motif of the *Versammlung*. Whether in Schlegel or Heidegger, it is always a matter of this gathering together, of this being-one with oneself, in all these stories of the hedgehog, of indivisible individuality or of being always already with oneself, from the origin or at the finish line of some *Bestimmung*. I recognize the force and the necessity of this motif of the *Versammlung* in Heidegger, all the more so in that it never excludes difference, on the contrary. But also all the stakes are gathered together here. There where the *Versammlung* doesn't win out, where the force, the *Verwalten* of the *Versammlung* doesn't win out, there is some hedgehog and a solitary hedgehog that no longer belongs to Grimms', Schlegel's, or Heidegger's family. Concerning Trakl, it is true, Heidegger acknowledges the plurivocal (*mehrdeutig*) character of poetic language; but this plurivocity has to be gathered up in a higher univocity, which is the condition of great poetry. Heidegger then shows himself to be rather contemptuous of lightweight poets who play with plurivocity. It is a little surprising to see him praise the security or an assurance (*Sicherheit*) guaranteed by univocity (*Eindeutigkeit*).[9] That is to say, by the force of gathering together. Heidegger would doubtless consider the dissemination of meaning in writing, beyond the controlled polysemia that he basically recommends, to be an effect of *Witz*. I am not making a case for *Witz*. But the writing-hedgehog links the essence of the poematic to the aleatory, not only to the aleatory factor of language or nomination, but to that of the mark, and this is what destines it to a "learning-by-heart" whose letter is not thoroughly nominal, discursive, or linguistic. In all this, a great proximity to Heidegger does not exclude some misgiving on the subject of nothing less than poetry and truth (*Dichtung und Wahrheit*): things are played out between the *Versammlung* (which is to say also, for Heidegger, the *logos*) and dissemination. You are quite right to recall the condemnation of the *unverbindliche Spiel des Witzes* in relation to the seriousness of sacrifice and of the founding act—for example of the State...

Q.: Allow me to quote the complete passage from *The Origin of the Work of Art* to which I was alluding as regards sacrifice and foundation, sacrifice as foundation: "One essential way in which truth establishes itself in the beings it has opened up is truth setting itself into work. Another way in which truth occurs is the act that founds a political state. Still another way in which truth comes to shine forth is the nearness of that which is not simply a being, but the being that is most of all. Still another way in which truth grounds itself is the essential sacrifice. Still another way in which truth becomes is the thinker's questioning, which, as the thinking of Being, names Being in its question-worthiness. By contrast, science is not an original happening of truth, but always the cultivation of a domain of truth already opened."[10]

J.D.: The theme of sacrifice plays a role in Heidegger's thought the stakes of which have yet to be measured. It shows up, in a discreet but determining fashion, in *The Origin of the Work of Art*, in certain seminars on Hölderlin ("Germanien" and "Der Rhein") and in *Identity and Difference*. In the first context, "the essential sacrifice" (*das wesentliche Opfer*) is one of the four modes by which "truth is founded" (*sich gründet*). In the seminar on Hölderlin, and in accord with the aims of *Introduction to Metaphysics*, it is a question of the inevitable sacrifice of the founders. The founders (*Dichter, Denker, Staatsmann*) are those who hear what is unheard-of in the originary *polemos*. So they in their turn cannot be heard or tolerated. They are excluded and sacrificed (the word "sacrifice" is uttered in relation to Hölderlin) by the very ones or the very thing that they found. The founder is excluded from the founded, by the founded itself, which cannot tolerate the abyssal void and thus the violence on which the foundations stand or rather are suspended. Finally, much later, in *Identity and Difference* ("The Onto-Theological Constitution of Metaphysics"), a few pages after the allusion to the Grimms' hedgehog, Heidegger defines the god of the philosophers, the *causa sui* of onto-theology, as a God to whom one does not pray and to whom one does not offer sacrifices.[11] This implies that one ought to address oneself through prayer and sacrifice to the God that is coming or that is heralded beyond metaphysical onto-theology.

Q.: *Ick bünn all hier*: here again it is Heidegger who is the first of the *Zu-künftigen* who knows how to listen to the voice of God, the athlete taking up the flame again. If Oedipus had one eye too many, the sacrificed *Denker*, for his part, has an ear that is a little too sharp. Now, as acts of founding, the action that founds a state, prayer, essential sacrifice, and poetry turn out to be interchangeable. And from this it may follow that, on the biographical level, sacrifice—as well as the emphasis on poetry—represents the speculative consolation or substitute for the political failure of the rectorship. A failure due to Heidegger's practical ineptitude and his isolation, at the center of the party, faced with a Rosenberg or a Bäumler. It is at that moment that he begins to think of himself as a sacrificed hero.

J.D.: Yes, he presents himself, implicitly, as a sacrificial victim. He says in effect to the Germans: "You sacrifice Hölderlin; when are you finally going to hear him?" Which inevitably leads one to understand: "When are you going to hear the one who is saying this to you? When are you going to stop sacrificing the intercessor who reminds you of Hölderlin's historial speech?" This sacrificial scene, whose victim is the historial thinker, if not the historial poet, takes shape around 1933–1935.

Q.: It seems to me that this movement is very clearly confirmed in the *Beiträge* from 1936–38 where a process of identification with Nietzsche, that other sacrificed thinker, is initiated. The very form is Nietzschean, organized in aphorisms subdivided into vast thematic chapters: it mimes the structure that Elisabeth Förster-Nietzsche conferred on her conjectural reconstruction of the *Wille zur Macht*. It is the form that Heidegger had known as a youth (especially in the second revised edition of 1911) and that will continue to impress him throughout his life (one need only think of this massively obvious fact: the Nietzsche that counted in Heidegger's eyes was the Nietzsche of the will to power as the crowning moment of European nihilism). But this identification is not only literary. Gadamer likes to recall that Heidegger used to tell those close to him—who, moreover, may not have understood him, like the Germans with Hölderlin or like the mother and sister with Nietzsche—that Nietzsche had destroyed him, had devastated his experience as thinker. And one may wonder whether Heidegger did not interpret also the psychic depression he went through after 1945 as some kind of identification with the Nietzschean break-down, or else with the gentle madness of Hölderlin in the last years; for finally the vicissitudes of a psyche are never simply individual but always have something to do with *Seinsgeschichte*...

    J.D.: That is to invest every kind of accident with a destinal meaning. The death of the "poematic" hedgehog, if one distin-guishes it from the poetic hedgehog, from the total fragment (Schlegel) or from the setting-to-work of truth (Heidegger), may not even be a sacrifice. Sacrifice always becomes meaningful within the truth of a historial destiny, within an epochal super-teleology. It is never accidental. When there is sacrifice, the ritual victim is not run over by history in an accidental way, as on the highway. Even if he agrees to declare that he was "stupid" [*bête*], that what he did at the moment of the advent of Nazism was a "stupidity" (*Dumm-heit*) [*bêtise*], Heidegger still believes in the sacrificial greatness of his error or erring. This is the sense of his letter to Kommerell on the subject of Hölderlin, at the very moment when, all the same, Heidegger distinguishes himself from Hölderlin. The disaster of the accident is still magnified or sublimated, in a movement of denegation, by thought and as a disaster of thought: "You are right. This writing [that of Heidegger on the subject of Hölderlin] is a disaster (*Unglück*). *Being and Time* was also a disastrous accident. And every immediate presentation of my thought would be today the greatest of disasters. Perhaps that is a first testimony to the fact that my attempts sometimes reach into the vicinity of a true thinking. All straight *thinking* is, unlike that of poets, a disastrous accident in its immediate effect. In this way you see how I *can* not identify with Hölderlin, not at any point. Here the exposition of a thinking to a poet is under way where the ex-position goes so far as to first of all pose what is opposed. Is this arbitrary or a supreme liberty?"[12] This propensity to magnify the disastrous accident is foreign to what I called the humility of the poematic hedgehog: low, very low, close to the earth, humble (*humilis*).

Q.: The notion of *Kehre* in the form in which it is inserted in a text as neuralgic as *The Letter on Humanism* (1946) is indicative of that attitude that tends to impute biographical facts and a man's choice to destiny and to the grandiloquence of the history of Being. The turn, as Heidegger never tires of repeating, does not concern his life; the turn comes about in Being. Again in the "Letter to Richardson" (1962), Heidegger will insist on the fact that the turn takes place at the heart of the question itself, of the *Seinsfrage*, and that therefore he could not have invented it since it does not concern only his own thinking (about life, less than anything).

When does it come about? The chronology does seem to confirm the nexus poetry-and-sacrifice. Again in the "Letter to Richardson," Heidegger maintains that it took place ten years before *The Letter on Humanism*—therefore during the period of the political failure and the writing of the *Beiträge*. This, in a certain sense, is even more impressive because the turn in Heidegger (that is, in Being) does not seem to have been induced by the war, the defeat, and above all by Auschwitz, but rather by the failure of his politico-pedagogical project in the form we find it presented between *What is Metaphysics?* (1929) and *Introduction to Metaphysics* (1935): based in this concept of *paideia* (cf. *Plato's Doctrine of Truth*), thought finds its realization in politics, and the aim of the philosopher is not simply to contemplate the sun of ideas, but to go back down into the cave for the *battle* within it—catabasis or anabasis of the Platonic myth. It is not, moreover, by chance that, coming after the experience of the rectorship, the *Introduction to Metaphysics* is already traversed by a repeated reference to the crisis whose most manifest symptom would have been the *Zusammenbruch* of transcendental idealism. It was when the political pedagogy failed and came to an end that Heidegger began to talk about the turn, about poetry, about the event, and the last God. But even here it is a matter still of a theology and a poetology that are in some way political: a political theology that is both negative and resigned, and a poetology that takes the place of the active aspirations of a thinking that, in *Being and Time*, had shown clear pragmatic traits.

J.D.: Without even coming back to the "biographical," one may say that history, the "current affairs" of our age are always re-inscribed by Heidegger in the history of Being. According to a motif that one begins to find in 1935 at least, *Zur Seinsfrage* (1955) recalls the famous Fragment 53 of Heraclides on the *polemos*, a fragment that Heidegger evokes in a 1933 letter to Carl Schmitt and that he never stopped retranslating even as he de-anthropologized and de-theologized it. The *polemos* arises at the origin of the gods and men, free men and slaves, always already coming before them. Well, he says in 1955, to listen correctly to the fragment on the *polemos* is more decisive than world wars, nuclear confrontation, and so forth.

Q.: I quote once again from *The Origin of the Work of Art*: "Truth establishes itself in the work. Truth is present only as the conflict between lighting and concealing in the opposition of world and earth. Truth wills to be established in the work as this conflict of world and earth. The conflict is not to be resolved in a being brought forth for the purpose, nor is it to be merely housed there; the conflict, on the contrary, is started by it. This being must there-fore contain within itself the essential traits of the conflict. In the strife the unity of world and earth is won. As a world opens itself, it submits to the decision of an historical humanity the question of victory and defeat, blessing and curse, mastery and slavery."[13] This is valid not only for the opening of a historical world, but also for the final act, death, which is not learned in war, for example, but is rather truly comprehended, along with war, through an experience that is more originary than any empirical experimentation: "When confronted with death, therefore, those young Germans who knew about Hölderlin lived and thought something other than what the public held to be the typical German attitude."[14]

II

Q.: *Ick bünn all hier.* Let us come back to Mr. or Mrs. Hedgehog. Perhaps there is a hedgehog even in *The Origin of the Work of Art*, there where Heidegger writes: "A man is not a thing. It is true that we speak of a young girl who is faced with a task too difficult for her as being a young thing, still too young for it, but only because we feel that being human is in a certain way missing here and think that instead we have to do here with the factor that constitutes the thingly character of things. We hesitate even to call the deer in the forest clearing, the beetle in the grass, the blade of grass a thing." The hedgehog's accident is not particularly destinal, and represents a rather abnormal being-for-death.

J.D.: I would rather not re-semanticize this letter. It must remain of little meaning. Without secret but sealed. It is also better not to stuff polysemic vitamins down the throat of a humble little mammal. Let's not entrust it with any message; it's not a carrier pigeon that would carry off into the blue, hidden in its band, a coded order, a law of the heart, or strategic information. But you are right: If there is a being-for-death, it is for the death of an animal, of some "one" that is apprehended, without knowing very well what this means, as an animal, even if it is a catachrestic one, like this hedgehog. In Heidegger, the being-for-death, as strange as this may seem, is not the being of a living creature. Death does not happen to a living creature. Being-for-death is reserved for a *Dasein* whose phenomenon as such does not essentially belong to being-alive. The *Dasein* is not an animal, not even, essentially, an *animal rationale* or a *zoon logon ekhon*. The catachresis of the *hérisson*, in the very aleatoriness of the letter and of its name for me, is the figure of a being-for-death *as living creature*, which is, it seems to me, wholly unacceptable to Heidegger's dominant discourse. Here again one comes upon the difficulties the latter encounters with animality. I have talked about this in *Of Spirit* and elsewhere. I say the "dominant discourse" since we must never exclude the possibility that contrary propositions, which are more discreet or more implicit, are at work within a necessarily heterogeneous discourse. To be sure, Heidegger makes room for accident in the impossible possibility of death. But this accident is, in his view, anticipated, apprehended as such only by the human *Dasein* to which the experience of finitude in the relation to death is reserved. Heidegger would say: the hedgehog does not see death coming, death does not happen to it. I say this as well in another way: the hedgehog "hears but does not see death coming," it is as blind as Homer, but where does one draw the limit? Is it certain that the human *Dasein* sees death coming *as such*? What is the "as such" in the case of death? And how can one maintain that the hedgehog has no apprehension of death when it rolls itself up in a ball? There is therefore in this passage of the catachrestic hedgehog a virtual *Gespräch* with the existential analytic of the *Dasein* as being-for-death. For this hedgehog, there is some poem. For the *Dasein* such as Heidegger delimits it, no poem, only *Dichtung* as setting-to-work of truth. There is perhaps some poetry, some poetic, but no poematic, in the sense that I discerned in the nearest proximity to the *hérisson* in its letter and in its down-to-earthness. One has to choose, or rather one has to be attentive to the limit of a choice that we don't even have to make any longer. Only a *hérisson* of cata-chresis can still give itself over to the poem, the poematic experi-ence, the one of which it is said "a poem, I never sign(s) it," the poem without poetry.

This passes again very close to Heidegger. It crosses the great highway that *The Origin of the Work of Art*, which is an immense repetition of the great Western poetic tradition, travels over again or re-inaugurates. The poematic hedgehog crosses the highway at the risk of being run over by a great discourse that it cannot resist...

Q.: In question is a highway between Greece and Germany, Patmos and Messkirch. Or perhaps it is one of those highways that the Germans had built in Normandy and that—as she recounted it to me—called forth the proud admiration of Elfriede Heidegger in August 1955. What is more, the lecture that Heidegger gave on that occasion at Cerisy, "Was ist das—die Philosophie?," underscores forcefully the link between *Dichten* and *Denken*. Now, it seems to me that to the extent that it is linked to the complete unfolding of the poetic, Heidegger's reflection on poetry is essentially connected to the discourse of German idealism (the excellence of speech over all other arts; the link poetry-thought that is at the basis of both Hegel's decree on art as thing of the past and Heidegger's heralding of art as the setting-to-work of truth, and so forth). But, for example, this poetics is not entirely assimilable to those of the Renaissance and the baroque period that turn resolutely toward a beyond of thinking at the very moment they insist on imitation, and thus on something that is not at all originary or fundamental. I am not saying that is not a highway, but it seems to me that it is a different one.

J.D.: It's another highway but it is still linked to the general network by a great interchange. Heidegger's critique of imitation is necessary and legitimate, but it repeats the most originary foundation of this *mimesis*.

Q.: All the same, can one imagine Heidegger's analyses functioning in the same way and on the same level if they were applied, let's say, to Tasso? Moreover, the German romantic canon with which Heidegger works is much more dispersed than what one is led to think by his readings of Rilke, Trakl, Hebel, or Hölderlin, who finally all look alike, not because of an empirical repetitivity but because of a transcendental coercion toward the gathering of *common thoughts*—and this despite Heidegger's assertion, for example, that Rilke's thinking of the opening is in every way antithetical to Hölderlin's. One might say, finally, that the way in which Heidegger works on his poets is an elevated (spiritual) thematic critique whereby he finds the same thing in different texts and authors— finding there the idea of the spirit that unifies and cancels out the letter, and thus if you like (and Heidegger certainly would not have liked it), art as thing of the past, this *Igel*-Hegel having already arrived at the finish line of the interpretation and saying: *Ick bünn all hier*. I do not want to put the blame on thematic criticism, I just want to observe that this thematicism implies a very powerful *Versammlung* of the poetic text, which in turn, as you have pointed out, finds its own highest form in *Eindeutigkeit*. And thus it is that in *Andenken*, Heidegger underscores emphatically that the variants of *undichtrischen* are: *unendlichen*, *unfriedlichen*, *unbündigen*, *unbändigen*[15]—variants that, paradoxically, lead back to unity, so as to make of harmonious union and extreme gathering together the synonyms or the symbols of poetry.

J.D.: The thematicist tendency in Heidegger is undeniable. But even if one wanted to, one cannot annihilate such a tendency. Heidegger also is tireless in the attention he pays to the German idiom of the poet. This resists semanticization or thematization and makes his texts so difficult and provocative for the translator. What is said about the "by heart" in "*Che cos'è la poesia?*" could be compared with a certain Heideggerian understanding. The irreducibility of song or of consonance in the poem (*Gesang*) is the non-semantic, non-substitutable character of the letter, in a word, of that which has to be learned by heart. This may be consonant with what Heidegger says of that place where the heart, memory, and thought are gathered together. But Heidegger would have more difficulty accepting another dimension of the "by heart" (*auswendig*), the "by heart" of exteriority, of the machine-like, of automaticity, which I do not dissociate from the other. He would see in this the other of thinking. Here everything is being played out between two experiences of the heart and of the by heart. One is very close to thinking—to the gift, to the coming or the event, to memory or gratitude—whereas Heidegger would assimilate the other to automaticity or technicity, in any case to animality, the thing he would like to maintain outside of *Dichtung* and of thinking memory. To go very quickly, we would find once again here the elements of a certain de Manian problematic that I attempted to interpret in *Mémoires*: the opposition between *Erinnerung* and *Gedächtnis*.[16] To the extent to which this opposition is pertinent, the Heideggerian interpretation of memory would be situated in the neighborhood of *Erinnerung*, although this interpretation never places *Gedächtnis* on the side of that involuntary memory which de Man wanted to see in a certain Hegelian tradition.

On the basis of the brief allusion I make in "*Che cos'è la poesia?*"
one must recall the Heideggerian critique of Pascal in *What is
Called Thinking?*. Pascal, according to this critique, interpreted the
heart from within a thinking of science, setting out from the
project of a foundation of scientific reason. And it is true that Pascal
assigns to the heart an immediate knowledge of mathematical first
principles, that is, a founding role in the exercise of this scientific
reason: "And it is in the kinds of knowledge that are the heart and
instinct that reason must find support, and that it founds its whole
discourse. (The heart senses that there are three dimensions in
space, and that numbers are infinite; and reason then demonstrates
that there are no two square numbers of which one is the double of
the other. Principles are felt, propositions are concluded; and the
whole with certainty, although by different paths.)"[17] But then
Pascal was French. He was out of luck in Heidegger's view, as were
Descartes and Bergson.

    q.: They are Frenchmen who belong therefore to the people of
letters, distant from the spirit and dispersed in that technique the
essence of which they do not manage to think. But what is then the
spirit of an interpretation? And what does it mean to "interpret
according to the spirit"? As you point out in *Mémoires*, de Man
himself had written in one of his first essays ("Heidegger's Exegeses
of Hölderlin," 1955), with reference to *Andenken*, that "Hölderlin
says exactly the opposite of what Heidegger makes him say." This is
the theme of "close reading" and of faithfulness to the letter, which
is not literality, and which dictates de Man's method. What de Man
reproaches Heidegger for is a certain hermeneutic *hubris* that, in
my opinion, goes beyond the unquestionable attention to the letter
and carries over in a hyperbolic manner to the spirit conceived as
gathering. And this does not concern only poets: One need only
think of the interpretation of Nietzsche where, moreover, Heidegger explicitly thematizes (cf. "The sentence of Nietzsche 'God
is dead,'" in *Holzwege*) that only the profane invoke a supposed
literality. In principle, Heidegger is certainly right and the notion
of literal meaning is no less improbable and idealist than that, for

example, of originary reader. One must stand in the circle in the correct manner. It would seem, all the same, that this hounding of the profane aims to stigmatize them as weak in spirit, and that it thereby follows a path that is no less idealistic than the originary reader, the author's intention, literal meaning, and so forth.

In this regard, one can cite a very significant example. It concerns the Heideggerian commentary of "Wie wenn am Feiertage," and it is reported by von Herrmann in his afterword to the *Erläuterungen zu Hölderlins Dichtung*.

Responding to a letter from Detlev Lüders, Heidegger concludes: "The question remains of knowing what a 'text' is, how one must read it, and when it is completely appropriated. These questions are so essentially linked to the question of the essence of the language [*Sprache*] and the tradition of the language that I have always limited myself to the strictly necessary when there was something to say as regards interpretation [*Interpretationen*], elucidations [*Erläuterungen*], etc. . . . Is there a text in itself?"

One can understand the importance, but also the depth of the hermeneutic questions that Heidegger evokes in this reply, which is moreover very prompt. But the question remains: not only the question "what is a text," but likewise that of Heidegger's exegetical position, which ends up making the letter dependent on the spirit to the extent that the first exists only to resolve itself—once it is truly understood—in the second. The letter comes first in the order of the de facto truth, but its de jure truth—the teleology functioning transcendentally as archeology—is spirit. Now, it seems to me that this appeal to living spirit and to its power of *Versammlung* that overcomes the dispersion of the letter, runs through all classic German philosophy, from the Fichtean lessons *Über den Unterschied des Geistes und des Buchstabes in der Philosophie* (1794; and one can think of the Fichtean command to interpret Kant according to the spirit and not the letter) up to Heidegger's *Erläuterungen*, and passing by way of Schelling, Hegel, Dilthey, Yorck von Wartenburg, Husserl...

J.D.: One would have to exclude Nietzsche, lover of the Italians and the French. But that is not the only Nietzsche...

Q.: For example, the Nietzsche who writes to Wagner: "It is to you and to Schopenhauer that I owe my fidelity today to the German seriousness of life, to a deepened consideration of this existence that is so enigmatic and so problematic." Is not this German seriousness the one that Heidegger requires from the critique of the *unverbindliche Spiel des Witzes?* The point is not to accuse "the German spirit" or any other abstraction, which would imply a *Versammlung* still more ambiguous than the one accused. It seems to me that Heidegger or the young Nietzsche invokes this German seriousness not so much out of nationalism, but rather because they are classical—with all that classicism implies in terms of vitalism, seriousness, humanism, and suspicion of the letter (Marx never knew how right he was when he said that Feuerbach was the end point of German *classic* philosophy; it's just that classicism didn't end with Feuerbach, nor even with Marx). Why do I say "classicism"? In the *Timaeus,* the priest of Sais, the Egyptian, addresses Solon and says to him that the Greeks are still young because they are not tied to a civilization in which, like the Egyptian civilization, everything is written down. With perfect irony, Plato brings out what we could call the scene of classicism: the classical is the living and still current spirit that operates through dialogue and dialectic, without being weighed down by memories and immemorable antiquities, which would rob dialogue of all currentness by making it into a repetition of letters, citations, and elements not present to spirit. These are all the aspects that you have analyzed so admirably in "Plato's Pharmacy." Now, these traits of classicism outline the physiognomy or the prosopopoeia of philosophy insofar as Plato is functioning as eponymous hero of both classicism and metaphysics. There is thus nothing surprising in the fact that an author as Hellenizing as the first Nietzsche could maintain, in his second *Untimely Meditation,* but finally in all the writings of his earliest period, that the greatness of the Greek world consisted precisely in the fact of having been able to go beyond the stagnation of the Orient, the mass of letters, and enormous cults, in order to arrive at a fundamental amnesia: the Greeks, precisely, are always young, they are not cultivated in the nineteenth-century sense, because they have at their disposal a knowledge that is always current; they presuppose nothing and are not crushed by the weight of letters or the past. It is not by chance that the *Untimely Meditation* of 1874 ends with a speech to the young who are called upon to become Greek and to rid themselves of the heavy legacy of a tradition that historicism has rendered colossal. It is less surprising than ever that Heidegger ends his *Rektoratsrede* by proclaiming in his turn *die junge und jüngste Kraft des Volkes*, which has mobilized and gotten under way with this extraordinary classical revolution. That is why *The Letter on Humanism* blames Roman civilization, taken up again by the peoples of the letter, precisely insofar as the point of departure of Roman humanism is not the absolute youth of the classical Greeks, but rather Alexandrian old age, or else Greece transferred to Egypt, become decrepit and literate, that is, deprived of actuality. Humanism is always Hellenism in the sense of Droysen, which has to do with that declining antiquity from which—according to Nietzsche in 1874—philosophers fashion disciples for themselves. It is this humanism, which—according to the Heidegger of the *Brief*—is still exhausting itself in Lessing or Goethe (those two cosmopolitans in the sense of the antique Romans), that Hölderlin escapes by thinking a still more originary classicness, that is, more authentically Greek, thanks to his proud roots in Swabian soil. Hölderlin, which is to say also Heidegger, if we follow this process of sacrificial identification which you alluded to earlier. The classicism of Plato, but also that of Nietzsche, of Heidegger, and of Husserl (as you have shown in *Speech and Phenomena*), the paradigm of the classical and the metaphysical is consciousness present to itself, monologically self-conscious, which nothing—neither letters, traditions, indexes, nor lists, that is, anything that is of the order of the letter written on paper and not on the soul—can carry away from itself. This is why Hegel confers such an important role to the victory of Oedipus over the Sphinx, symbol of the Orient, of old age, of a consciousness that does not manage to enter into full possession of itself, and remains finally a man's face on an animal's body. (It is also clear that the animal has here a non-peripheral role. Hegel, once again, shows that the birth of the classical as human self-consciousness, as statue of a man who knows himself, brings with it a degradation of the animal in hunting, sacrifices, and metamorphoses—because now, in Greece, the animal is infinitely inferior to self-conscious man, which was not the case in Egypt, where it made no difference whether one buried an ox or a sovereign in a pyramid.) What one sees then is the formation of two series: on the one side, there is spirit, youth, humanity, life, Greece; on the other, there is letter, old age, animality, death, and Egypt as *realm of death* (that logic itself was, for Hegel, a *realm of shadows* is another question that would perhaps deserve a separate development).

Forgive me for this long digression, and I come now to the point. Insofar as there is in Heidegger, as you yourself have pointed out, a constant attention to the letter, and insofar as, moreover, all poetics is inscribed within a classicist circle from which there seems to be no exit—I am nevertheless persuaded that Heidegger would never have been able to give a reading of a poem like Baudelaire's "Spleen" ("J'ai plus de souvenirs que si j'avais mille ans . . . mon triste cerveau. / C'est une pyramide, un immense caveau, / Qui contient plus de morts que le fosse commune. . . . Désormais tu n'es plus, ô matière vivante! / Qu'un granit entouré d'une vague épouvante, / Assoupi dans le fond d'un Saharah brumeux; / Un vieux sphinx ignoré du monde insoucieux, / Oublié sur la carte . . .").[18] At most he would have defined it—like Lukács—as the sign of *a moribund culture ready to collapse on itself* (that is an expression from the Rectorship Address concerning the crisis of the modern world): and he would have done so correctly, moreover, because that is indeed the idea of Baudelaire or Flaubert.

J.D.: But let's be careful. Let's not construct between us a Franco-Italian axis or a southern highway...

III

Q.: "If death comes to the other, and comes to us through the other, then the friend no longer exists except *in us, between us.* In himself, by himself, of himself, he is no more, nothing more. He lives only in us. But *we* are never *ourselves*, and between us, identical to us, a 'self' is never in itself or identical to itself. This specular reflection never closes on itself; it does not appear *before* this *possibility* of mourning, before and outside this structure of allegory and prosopopoeia which constitutes in advance all 'being-in-us,' 'in-me,' between us, or between ourselves. . . . And everything that we inscribe in the living present of our relation to others already carries, always, the signature of *memoirs-from-beyond-the-grave*."[19] This superb passage from one of your most recent books seems to weld the reflection on the letter to themes that in a certain way could be connected to the philosophy of existence. We are in ourselves only as *Andenken*, as a dead letter come from the other; before any living act, and even before any position of the cogito (and already in *Speech and Phenomena* you point out that "I am" means "I am mortal"), we are solicited or interpellated by a dead letter that is addressed to us—whether it be by preceding generations, by the ancientness of language, or the opacity of history. In relation, however, to the analyses of *Being and Time*, it seems to me that this being-for-death presents an important difference: whereas from the perspective of mourning, death presents itself above all as the experience of an expropriation, by which the other lives in us, but we are carried away from the other and, as a consequence, finally half-dead, in Heidegger death has a strictly personal dimension. It is the most inalienable of properties, for no one can die in the place of an other, no one can assume an other's death (*Keiner kann dem Anderen sein Sterben abnehmen*),[20] and this constitutes the most certain character of existence as always-mine.

J.D.: What is said about the death of the other in *Mémoires* does not necessarily contradict the Heideggerian analysis. The other dies his or her own death, substitution is impossible here, no one can die in the place of the other, not even in sacrifice. The difference would stem perhaps from the approach to mourning. Heidegger's texts on mourning are very powerful and very beautiful (not in *Being and Time* but in the seminar on "Germanien," for example, around the "sacred mourning"[21]). But because it supposes a re-elaboration, rather than a simple disqualification of the concept of "subject," the post-Freudian thinking of mourning as importation of the other in me (according to an altogether different topical and "rhetorical" schema) has little chance of interesting Heidegger. This carrying of the mortal other "in me outside me" instructs or institutes my "self" and my relation to "myself" already before the death of the other. This problematic, which I try to articulate, notably in *Glas* and in *Mémoires*, has only a very limited affinity with that of Heidegger, I believe. I speak of mourning as the attempt, always doomed to fail (thus a constitutive failure, precisely), to incorporate, interiorize, introject, subjectivize the other in me. Even before the death of the other, the inscription in me of her or his mortality constitutes me. I mourn therefore I am, I am—dead with the death of the other, my relation to myself is first of all plunged into mourning, a mourning that is moreover impossible. This is also what I call ex-appropriation, appropriation caught in a double bind: I must and I must not take the other into myself; mourning is an unfaithful fidelity if it succeeds in interiorizing the other ideally in me, that is, in not respecting his or her infinite exteriority. I explain this more clearly in "Fors," the foreword to *The Wolf Man's Magic Word* by Nicolas Abraham and Maria Torok. I suggest there that the opposition between incorporation and introjection, however fruitful it may be, remains of a limited pertinence. Faithful mourning of the other must fail *to succeed / by succeeding* (it fails, precisely, if it succeeds! it fails because of success!). There is no successful introjection, there is no pure and simple incorporation. If one wants to reconstruct a concept of the subject "after deconstruction," one has to take this into account, one has to shape a logic and a topic that are rather powerful, supple, articulated, and that therefore can be disarticulated.

Doubtless the death of the other is irreplaceable. I do not die in the place of the other who does not die in my place. But I can have this experience of "my own death" by relating to myself only in the impossible experience, the experience of the impossible mourning at the death of the other. It is because I "know" that the other is mortal that I try to keep him or her in me, in memory. But from that moment on, he or she is no longer radically other. In the experience of fatal, original, and impossible mourning, I anticipate my own death, I relate to myself as mortal. Even if I am the only one to die, I apprehend this solitude on the basis of this impossible mourning. I do not know if this "logic" is very Heideggerian. It should lead one to say that my being-for-death is always mediated (but that word is not very good: one would have to say immediately mediatizable), not only by the spectacle or the perception of the other's death, but in the experience or in the "non-experienceable" structure of impossible mourning. Mourning would be more originary than my being for death.

Q.: Here as well, Nietzsche goes very far, in particular when he says in *Ecce Homo*: "As my father I am already dead, while as my mother I am still living and becoming old." Such is the fatedness of his existence that makes him an expert in decadence and as regards his symptoms, thanks to this father who was "more a gracious memory of life than life itself." But let's come back to Heidegger, not exactly to death and mourning but to memory and vestiges. "*Was bleibet aber stiften die Dichter*": Heidegger remains ambiguous as to this remainder suspended between the eternal and the ephemeral. What relation does this have with the remainder to which you refer in your texts?

J.D.: The way I write it, the word "rest" is closer to the German *Rest*, in the sense of residue, refuse, or trace than to *bleiben* in the sense of permanence.[22] The rest "is" not, because it is not what remains, in the stance, substance, or stability. What I call *restance* no longer comes to modify Being or the presence of Being. It indicates a repetition, an iterability rather, which no longer takes shape only on the basis of Being or beingness. Whence the question of cinders, of the cinder without spirit, without phoenix, without rebirth, and without destiny: perhaps the death of the hedgehog, its exposure to disappearance without remainder [*sans reste*]. But between the remainder and the without-remainder, or between the two senses of the rest there is no more *opposition*. The relation is other. This is the motif of *Glas* and of *Cinders*: The rest "is" always what can radically disappear, without remainder [*reste*] in the sense of what would remain permanently (memory, a memory, vestige, monument). The rest can always not remain [*rester*] in the classic sense of the term, in the sense of substance. This is the condition for there being any remainder. On the condition that it cannot remain, that it can happen to it not to remain. A remainder is finite—or it is not a remainder.

Q.: One might wonder what could motivate someone to prefer the hedgehog to the phoenix, Egypt to Greece, writing to the voice, and so forth, and lead one to expose the formal logic of opposition, what besides a certain ethos, to put it in Benjaminian terms, in favor of the rejected, that is, the rejects of history, society, and so on.

J.D.: Out of a concern to think the couple—and thus to remark it in its retreat, its re-trait. Out of a concern to explore what you call the formal logic of the thing, the functioning of the couple, to rejoin that point at which a formalization remains necessarily incomplete, open to what may come. A hedgehog may always arrive, it may always be given to me. There is something non-formalizable and the concern comes from there, precisely. It is for that very thing that there is concern, interest, desire, non-indifference. One cannot remain in the couple, nor in the dialectic, nor in the third party. Perhaps an "ethical" concern, in fact; in any case, the interested desire comes from a place that no longer belongs either to the couple or to the circle. To the extent at least to which they would be caught in the couple, or even in the circle, none of the names would be apt any longer, writing no more than the voice, Egypt no more than Greece.

Q.: Once again on Heidegger's passage to poetry from the perspective of sacrifice. Basically, before his political experience, Heidegger had concerned himself little with poetry, with the exception, if I am not mistaken, of "Wozu Dichter?" in 1946. In any case, he had not concerned himself with it *as a philosopher*, not to the point of declaring that Rilke, Trakl, and Hölderlin would have been absolutely central to his development. We have seen, more-over, in what circumstances this more or less private interest be-comes public. Pardon me for the triviality of my question, which nevertheless seems to me inevitable in a reflection on Heidegger and poetry: the image of Heidegger, disappointed and defeated by politics, who sets sail for poetry in order to find in Arcadia a safer port, is that not a conventional and finally miserable image?

J.D.: This passage toward the poetic sets sail, as you put it, toward a poetic that is also a mooring, a political mooring or home port, the Hölderlin of "Der Rhein" and "Germanien." And this passage occurs against the background of a mourning, on the theme of sacred mourning, and in a scene of sacrifice. Whether one is talking about that Hölderlin or this Heidegger, there is always some address to the German people, if not a speech to the German nation. It is an address that seeks as much to institute its addressee as to reveal that addressee to itself.

Q.: A lecture, written in 1943—as was the commentary on *An-denken*—and that confers a livid tonality on the nationalist flames of the Hölderlin of 1801 and his river navigation: the German spirit as capacity for meditation, the spirit that loves the colonies, that went as far as Bordeaux, where it encountered the warmth of the Greeks, and that—following in this way the discovery of Indo-European languages—set off for India as the origin of the early Germans. The spirit is fire, tirelessly repeats the Heidegger of *Andenken* following Hölderlin. But in these same pages one also reads that the spirit is shadow, deep shadow that saves poetic speech from the excessive light of the heavenly fire. It seems to me that a duplicity gets registered here that is analogous to the struggle between world and earth in *The Origin of the Work of Art*: art is not only historical institution and opening, but likewise earth, silence, retreat in the face of the historical accomplishments of a people, in such a way that, far from confirming the rhetoric of blood and soil, this appeal to the earth constitutes a powerful contestation. And one would have to ask whether such a counter-positioning would not be valid as well—if one takes into account the sacrificial perspective in which Heidegger situates himself—for those two "neighbors" that are *Dichten* and *Denken*, in which poetry, like earth, would finally be the sign of a retreat before the fire of spirit.

J.D.: The opposition of earth and world is also the opposition between what is hidden and what is exposed, the shelter and the opening. With the catachrestic or poematic hedgehog, the *topos* of earth is marked as what is "low." A low without opposition to height. Is that possible? Is it still a "here-below" [*ici-bas*], but this time a here-below without beyond? No, it must be something else. A low that would rise up—in order to fall, then fall again—against the background of the All-High or the Beyond, such a low would never be very low, an all-low, absolutely low. A hedgehog is low, all-low, "humble," humiliated perhaps, which means close to the earth, down-to-earth, but low also as "signifier," pronounced very low, in a lowered voice, almost without voice, and then the heart that beats, over there, far away. The hedgehog, very low, is something of the earth that does not open, does not open to the "as such," an earth without truth in the sense of the verticality of the sky and the open. This earth can always not open. This earth is not necessarily inscribed in the opposition earth/world. Not that the hedgehog has no world, in the sense in which Heidegger says that the animal is deprived of world or is poor in world. Yes, if one can say that, the hedgehog is poor in world since it is very low, close to the earth, but so is man. And man is also more or less rich, thus more or less poor in world. But it's true, it is truth itself, that one can always bring this hedgehog back into the Heideggerian logic. As we have already seen, this can always happen to it as one of its accidents. As its loss. Its salvation is its loss. There is no longer anything fortuitous about this and the consequences of this strange proposition remain to be drawn.

As for the theme of the proximity of *Dichten* and *Denken*, in the sense of "parallels" that cross, it seems to me to come later. But while it may become explicit in *Unterwegs zur Sprache*, this motif is already heralded in *The Origin of the Work of Art*. To turn toward the poet, to address oneself to him in a *Gespräch* is a gesture motivated, it seems, both by the political history and by the aporia of *Sein und Zeit,* an aporia that nevertheless never gets closed up in an impasse. What remains open is language...

Q.: Even a tongue of fire, burning coals, or match: there is here a history of ashes and flames that perhaps deserves to be mentioned. In 1927, Heidegger leaves *Being and Time* unfinished; the published text consists of the first two parts of the first section, which should have included a third part, *Time and Being.* From a number of elements at our disposal, we are authorized to suppose that Heidegger had planned to take on the themes of the third part in his *Fundamental Problems of Philosophy,* the course given in Marburg in the summer term of 1927, right after the publication of *Being and Time*—and to which Heidegger always attributed a central role, to the point of making it appear as the first volume of the *Gesamtausgabe.* Should we consider this course as the text of *Time and Being*? No, or at least not according to Heidegger. In his philological note to *Being and Time* in the critical edition (1976), von Herrmann writes that, as Heidegger had told him in person, the true *Time and Being* had been written, then immediately burned. That may be, but it is rather improbable that in the space of one year Heidegger would have been able to write *Being and Time, The Fundamental Problems of Philosophy,* and a third work *Time and Being.*

J.D.: I don't see Heidegger burning a manuscript, but perhaps I'm wrong and it's interesting that he talks about it. When it's a matter of burning, the question of the difference between doing and saying is more burning than ever.

Once Again from the Top:
Of the Right to Philosophy

Q.: Jacques Derrida, you are a philosopher whom one imagines totally occupied with writing books and producing a philosophy. It may seem surprising that you have always been interested, and sometimes in a militant way, in problems of the teaching of philosophy at the secondary level, in institutions, in the curricula of the *classes terminales*,[1] in the number of hours of philosophy taught in the technical programs, and so forth.

J.D.: Why would this be "surprising"? Even before one speaks of visible or overriding structures (primary and secondary education, the university, authority, legitimacy), there is the very experience of discourse and language: the interest of philosophy already finds itself involved there in institutions. Everywhere and always, institutions articulate teaching and research, they attempt to dictate our rhetoric, the procedures of demonstration, our manner of speaking, writing and addressing the other. Those who think they stand outside institutions are sometimes those who interiorize its norms and programs in the most docile manner. Whether it is done in a critical or deconstructive way, the questioning of philosophy's relation to itself is a trial of the institution, of its paradoxes as well, for I try to show nonetheless what is unique and finally untenable in the philosophical institution: it is there that this institution must be a counter-institution, one which may go so far as to break, in an asymmetrical fashion, all contracts and cast suspicion on the very concept of institution. And then, however untenable it may be, it is in this institution that I live, for a good part, so to speak, of my life. Not to deny this is, in my view, a duty, first of all a philosophical duty. Also, whether one participates in it or observes it, the *French* philosophical institution is a phenomenon whose singularity seems to me increasingly odd and fascinating. Finally, from all the themes you mentioned, permit me to select the theme of "technical programs." For the last few years (and the Research Group on the Teaching of Philosophy, the GREPH, deserves some credit for this[2]), a philosophical teaching has been offered there. This is the place today of the greatest concentration (historical, social, political) of all the ordeals philosophy is undergoing. That is why we must all be very sensitive to it.

Q.: With Jacques Bouveresse, you chaired the Commission on Philosophy and Epistemology and you submitted your report to the Minister [of Education] in June 1989.[3] Elsewhere, you have published *Du droit à la philosophie*, which collects all the texts you have devoted since 1974 to the teaching of philosophy, to education, to institutions. While putting it together, did you think that it might serve as your... bunker or shield against the attacks of those who "looked askance" at your appointment to write a report on which the future of philosophical teaching in France is going to depend to a large extent?

J.D.: No, really, neither "shield" nor "bunker." Unless it has now become necessary to complain that books are too long (but no one is obliged to read) and then the author has to defend himself by accusing the complainers themselves of being defensive. The Report to which you allude takes up only the last twenty-five pages of the annex in *Du droit à la philosophie*: it is the last and most recent episode in a trajectory that began more than fifteen years ago. I hope that the continuity is not inconsistent, even if a certain coherence is differentially distributed according to the places and times of the interventions and the institutional initiatives. The filmed map of this itinerary (followed by several archives in the "annexes") could also be read as a working document and basis for discussion: not only of what I might have written at one time, of course, but of certain collective movements in which I participated, whether or not I took the initiative for them (the GREPH, the Estates General, the Collège International de Philosophie, the Commission on Philosophy and Epistemology).

As for the "attacks" to which you allude, they are indeed the acts of those who in fact, as you put it so well, "looked askance"—and especially who read askance, that is, badly or little. No one "appointed" me to anything, and especially not, I quote, "to write a report on which the future of philosophical teaching in France is going to depend to a large extent." Pierre Bourdieu and François Gros cordially invited us, Bouveresse and myself, to form a study group and to make proposals: in complete freedom, without being committed to respect the wishes of anyone in power, reciprocity in this regard being also rigorously the case. The government did not choose to follow our advice (alas, I would say, and perhaps one day also our adversaries will say the same). After months of work and consultation (which was very wide-ranging: *all* the unions, *all* the professional organizations, the Inspection Générale,[4] and so many others...), these studies and these proposals were submitted, since this was their address, to the reading and the discussion of *everyone*—and not only the government. To attack such a text, for there were in fact "attacks," is somewhat like hurling insults at a thinking, organizing campaigns against it, calling for it to be shot on sight. To insult, denounce, and get signatures on a petition when it is a matter of discussing proposals or of making counter-proposals, this is not only to take aim at the wrong target, to be incapable of reading and recognizing the status of a text, it is to set a disastrous example, whether we're talking about philosophy or politics. Especially if, as is the case, the outcry is to save the status quo, if no one has anything new, positive, or constructive to say, whereas, in a situation that everyone admits makes philosophical teaching today difficult and painful for many, one has to recognize (as did the most irritable representative of this "attack" in public) that all the "principles" of our Report are, I quote, "excellent."

The Report, then, was *destined* to be discussed and even criticized. This is what we wanted. It is there in order to open and to
widen a debate. I take strong exception only to the falsifications in
the presentation of the text, the obstacles set up to reading it, the
insulting denunciations, and the insinuations about our motives. If
the "attacks" in the form of a signature-gathering campaign (organized even before the publication of the Report and under conditions that more and more witnesses have given us cause to find
disturbing) have made more noise than the thoughtful criticisms,
on the other hand the signs of interest or approval, in the final
analysis, have been more numerous, more serious, more responsible, and in my view more interesting. I am sure that they will have
greater weight in the end. As you point out, the true discussion is in
the process of beginning throughout France. That was our first
concern. If, as I see it, a very large majority of philosophers agrees
on the principles we formulated and if it were then necessary to
complicate, improve, or reconsider the practical consequences we
proposed to draw from these principles, the reflection thus begun
will not have been merely *inaugural* (in particular, for the technical
programs, the extension of philosophy *en première*[5] and in the University, as well as for many other points), but *beneficial*. So no, this
book could not be a "shield" or a "bunker" that I would have been
preparing for my protection over the last fifteen years against a few
colleagues who, in the last few months, have "looked askance": that
would be a little out of proportion, you must admit...

Q.: Faithful to what you said already almost fifteen years ago, at
the time of the founding of the GREPH, you propose that philosophy be taught in three stages: a stage of in-depth study, at the
University, a stage of intense training, in the *classe terminale*, and a
stage of initiation in *première*, the latter being an innovation. What
would be the advantages of such a graduated "ladder" approach to
teaching philosophy? And does it seem "realistic" to you to propose
it when one thinks of the fact that curricula are already very full,
that no discipline is ready to "make room," that thousands of
additional teachers would be required?

J.D.: Yes, more than a thousand additional teachers will be required, teachers who are qualified and who teach philosophy in its most rigorous specificity ("unity" and "specificity" form the leitmotiv of the Report). This is what we demand and will continue to demand. Without that, without the reduction of the number of students per class, of the number of classes per teacher, without the preservation (in *terminale*) or the increase elsewhere of the number of hours of philosophy (all of which are firm and clear demands in our Report), then no improvement is possible and none can even be conceived. Allow me to quote one passage among others from the Report that some people have tried to prevent others from reading: "the concrete and intolerable conditions that are inflicted at present on so many philosophy teachers and professors (excessive number of classes on a reduced schedule, excessive number of students per class, and so forth) ought to be radically transformed. The proposals we are making would have no meaning, no interest, no chance, they would encounter a legitimate opposition on the part of all professors and teachers if they were not put into effect in a new context. Among all the elements of this new context, an absolute priority belongs, then, to these two conditions: reduction of class size . . . or of the maximum number of classes taught by each instructor."[6] The same is valid for the introduction of philosophy in *première*. It is a *realistic compromise* in my view, since I believe one ought to begin even earlier. This idea, which was proposed fifteen years ago by the GREPH and is accepted by many today, seems to make sense for three types of reasons:

(1) Among the disciplines that, by common accord, are called "basic," why should philosophy be subject to a kind of "law of exception"? Why is it the only one to find itself confined, without any possible progression, to the period of several months? Why only one class? For the last fifteen years, we have analyzed the roots of this prejudice and the harmful consequences of this antique artifact which, moreover, has deprived generations of young people of philosophy, all of those who, often for social reasons, never reach the *classe terminale*. (2) Experience shows that it is only after several months, thus right before the *baccalauréat*, that students begin to

understand, in the best of cases, what the demands of philosophy are and what is expected of them. Why not prepare them for this earlier? (3) A large number of students are asking for this and are ready for it. This necessary extension does not consist in "making room" or of taking up room: we are proposing—and this is no doubt what frightens some people—to transform the space and to invent other modalities of teaching which permit the problem to be posed in other terms. Even as we guard the *specificity* of philosophical teaching (our Report insists on it at every step), we believe that the relation to other disciplines must be changed. But do not forget that this question of the specificity of the philosophical ("What is philosophy?") is swarming with tremendous paradoxes. Philosophy is but a "conflict of interpretations" on this subject. Professional philosophers ought to know this better than anyone. We are not going to be able to treat it in a few words here. It's the principal theme of this "big book"!

Q.: Would you endorse today, and in what sense, this remark of Diderot's: "Let us hasten to make philosophy popular"?

J.D.: Yes, on the condition that I be allowed, in a newspaper, to develop all the analyses and all the reservations which this motif of the "popular" seems to me to call for and to which I devoted hundreds of pages in this last book. Since it is not a question *here* (this is the whole problem) of reopening this debate (which is a major one in my view) about the media, democracy to come,[7] and philosophy, I will just recall the following: the Report to which you are confining your questions attempts to respond to the problems of the democratization of education and to come to terms with these enormous stakes. A certain democratization is under way, it is woefully inadequate, but if the conditions and the *givens* of this process are not taken into account (not in order to adapt to them, as we have sometimes stupidly been accused of doing, but in order to take the best advantage of them), then it will be blocked or caused to fail. And I repeat, to take (social, linguistic, etc.) facts into account does not mean simply to record them. To say to someone, "I see, you take account of social differences and the different

backgrounds of your students, or their different 'rhetorical capacities,' so you want to keep them there and to adapt philosophy to
these differences," this is as crude as reproaching someone for
trying to make himself or herself understood or to understand
someone else who, at the outset, does not completely share the
same language. No pedagogy, moreover, has ever been possible that
does not accept the responsibility of these differences: otherwise,
teaching would adopt the rigid and ridiculous stance of someone
who persists in speaking his own language in a foreign country on
the pretext that he does not want to yield to "factual conditions"
and therefore refuses to "adapt" himself to the other's language, so
as not to betray his own language and his noble rhetoric! This is
only an analogy, but I could go very far it with it.

Q.: The presence of philosophy in the technical programs represents, according to you, a "historic opportunity." And yet, taking
into consideration the difficulty represented by the mastery of a
written exercise such as the *dissertation*[8] in these programs, you
propose, for the *baccalauréat*, an oral examination. Is this not
making a virtue out of necessity and isn't there a danger here of
sanctioning an inequality?

J.D.: Our proposal is more complicated. It leaves the choice
open: *either* a "continuous evaluation" (which excludes neither the
written exam nor the *dissertation*, as some have tried to maintain,
and leaves no room for "bootlicking"—I am quoting an objection—provided the instructor has a strict sense of his or her responsibilities), *or else* an obligatory oral examination during which, as
our Report says, "*the candidate would present and defend*" a "dossier" constituted in the course of the year on philosophical topics
and in the conditions that we describe. This dossier, like any
dossier, implies a work of research and *writing* (I am responding to
the grotesque accusation that we are, that I am against "writing").
To be sure, the diversification of the kinds of exercises, without
being directed against the still-valuable *dissertation*, relativizes and
de-fetishizes a certain model of rhetoric and demonstration, and
calls for careful analyses. We think the model of the traditional

dissertation ought to be not destroyed but accompanied by other types of written and oral exercises. This reasonable proposal should not induce panic, unless people see no other salvation for philosophical argumentation (and for themselves) outside the sacrosanct *dissertation*. Moreover, you know that already, in fact, many professors have recourse to other forms of written examination without anyone ever dreaming of reproaching them for it.

Q.: You would like to see in addition to the classical (and impractical?) *dissertation* a series of exercises for the *baccalauréat*, ones that could perhaps be evaluated more "objectively" and that would attest to the acquisition of very precise knowledge. This project has sometimes been caricatured by saying it would lead to "multiple choice questionnaires"—Nietzsche is the author of (1) *The Divine Comedy*, (2) *The Social Contract*, (3) *The Genealogy of Morals*. There is already a manual on the market that proposes "exercises" in which one has to find the missing word in a quotation, or else "attribute the following words ('drive,' 'universal attraction') to those who invented them" (Freud? Marx? Newton?). How will what you envision avoid this kind of "drift"?

J.D.: That is not even caricature; this nonsense has no relation to what we are proposing and which is meant rather to avoid exactly that. For this is what has already been on a certain market for a long time, sometimes supplied, as everyone knows, by one or more of those who are yelling the loudest against a Report that is not very favorable, precisely, to a certain *baccalauréat* industry. I cannot mention all the concrete proposals we make concerning the contracts between instructors and their students, concerning the differentiation of programs (nationally and regionally), concerning the increased freedom of innovation for each instructor and each *lycée*, and so forth. These proposals all contribute to an avoidance of this ridiculous kind of mechanization. But at a certain point, it can no longer be prescribed; the responsibility of each of us finds itself involved. There are those who will always transform philosophy into crossword puzzles, others will never do so. With what we are proposing, I believe there will be less desire for and lower probability of crossword puzzles. That said, let us never forget (it is at present a very serious problem which some deny) that it is always better to know who the author of *The Social Contract* was and who spoke of "universal attraction"! It is better in general, and it is better for philosophy. One must make every effort so that this can be known without seeking to ridicule this demand for knowledge and without deriding those who sustain it. There are other means of dispensing and checking this knowledge than crib sheets.

Who ever learned Latin by learning Latin declensions? Yet, one must know them, particularly if one wants to learn to read Latin and maintain a critical spirit in the reading of texts written in Latin—as are, for example, some great philosophical texts. I don't know what a critical spirit can be if it is alleviated of knowledge, and how it could be exercised without knowledge. I explain myself on this question in a somewhat more complicated way in the preface to the book.

Q.: In this whole present debate concerning philosophy, have you ever suspected that, behind the theoretical positions and even the positions of those in power, there are conservatisms, professionalisms, plans that could be, as one newspaper put it, those of "any other beet-growers' lobby"?

J.D.: No. Doubtless certain conservatisms and professionalisms combined with the impassioned reaction to our Report (once again I distinguish this organized, organic, compulsive reaction from argued criticism, for which I have the greatest respect). But to speak here of a "beet-growers' lobby" is an insulting exaggeration, which not only overlooks the essential differences between several kinds of protectionisms, but recalls the disturbing climate in which certain members of the professional corporation tried to install the reading and reception of this Report.

Q.: If, like... Dion to Plato, one suggested to you that you get your hands dirty by concerning yourself with the institutional implementation of a reform of philosophical education, would you accept to do so even if it meant sacrificing your theoretical work?

J.D.: You're pulling my leg, or else you're generously accumulating the anachronisms. If I would have to stop teaching or writing in order to assume strictly institutional responsibilities, however interesting they may be, my answer would be what it has always been: no, quite simply no. I have neither the taste nor the talent for those kinds of commitments. To the modest extent I have accepted them, for the briefest of periods, it has been only under the tension of "duty" (call it ethico-political, if you like, or philosophical). I still have the hope that, through teaching and publishing, I also play a small role in the transformations under way in philosophical education.

Q.: Some unions have accused the Conseil National des Programmes [National Curricular Board], established in view of the reform of the *lycées*, of envisioning a reduction in the number of hours taught in certain disciplines, including, precisely, philosophy. In your report, you insist to the contrary on the fact that there is no case and no program in which the current number of hours of philosophy could be reduced. Is this to say that the Ministry of Education grants little importance to your proposals, proposals which philosophy professors, on the other hand, saw already as directives, or even "accepted facts"? Are you consulted by the CNP, and do you feel, will you feel responsible for whatever may come out of a future reform?

J.D.: No, the CNP does not consult me. Nothing obliges it to do so. The role of our Commission was finished the day we published our Report. The CNP works in complete freedom, as did we ourselves. It does not have to follow our Report any more than anyone else does. It is true that the CNP can, if it wishes, consult us informally in the course of the considerable work that remains to be done and, without following the letter of our proposals, it can maintain the tradition of the spirit that was ours. I hope this will be the case. But the only colleague who represents philosophy on the CNP is unknown to us; she was named in the absence of any consultation with our Commission, and while certain members of the "technical group" (in philosophy) were named on our suggestion and because we have confidence in them, they constitute a *small majority* in a very diverse group. And there is no reason to suspect any one of them of wishing to harm philosophy! But their power remains advisory. Decisions may be made that contradict their recommendations.

Not only did we underscore several times that the hours "should in no case be decreased from the present number." We asked that these hours be extended, and, in truth, that philosophy be introduced where there has not been any up till now, both before and after the *terminale*. I have repeatedly pointed out, on every occasion, that if there were to be a decrease in hours (and this is in fact, we cannot deny it, the *general* perspective of the reform taking shape which would tend to reduce the number of lecture courses), *this decrease must in no case affect philosophy*, precisely because of the limits that enclose it in a single class year, and then, we hope, even though this is still insufficient, in two years. Any reduction in hours would obviously go *against the clearest and firmest of our proposals*. So we would thus have protested in advance, which will not prevent us from protesting again vigorously. I do not rule out that we will have to do so, which should suffice to show, if this is still necessary, just how ridiculous and indecent is the hypothesis according to which our project, as one misguided colleague was not afraid to shout publicly, was "commissioned" by the government.

The problem of the schedule of hours is not the only one. There is also the problem of teacher training. We made many precise recommendations on this subject (which I cannot repeat here), in particular in view of associating philosophy closely with the training of secondary teachers in all disciplines and at all levels, as is the case in the training of primary teachers. If the new university institutes for the training of secondary teachers do not give philosophy the place it deserves, which unfortunately we have some reasons to fear may happen, then obviously this would go against the spirit and against the letter of our Report. We would once again feel free to issue a warning and to protest strongly. All secondary teachers at the junior as well as at the senior level, we have said, whatever may be the disciplines they are preparing to teach, "should have the

benefit of a philosophical teaching during their years of training."
This extension, which is "horizontal" in some sense, corresponds
moreover to a demand coming from other disciplines, and from
the most scientific among them. It is also in this spirit that we
founded the Collège International de Philosophie: for the last
seven years, a number of secondary teachers (philosophers and
others) have been conducting teaching and research there.

Q.: In what way might this reflection on the teaching of philosophy concern others besides students and professors of philosophy?

J.D.: The question is too broad. Permit me to give it an answer
that is both minimal and maximal. Whether one is talking about
the Report of the Commission or the book I have just published,
the hypothesis is that questions concerning the teaching of philosophy are inseparable from those concerning teaching and research in
all disciplines at all levels. And they are indissociable from the great
question of *democracy to come* (in Europe and elsewhere).

« A 'Madness' Must Watch
Over Thinking »

Q.: Let us imagine your future biographer. One may suppose he will write, in a lazy repetition of the public record: Jacques Derrida was born July 15, 1930, in El Biar, near Algiers. It is up to you perhaps to oppose this biological birth with your true birth, the one that would proceed from that private or public event in which you really became yourself.

J.D.: For starters, that's a bit too much. You go so far as to say: "it is up to you [*il vous revient*]" to say when you are born. No, if there is anything that cannot be "up to me," then this is it, whether we're talking about what you call "biological birth" transferred to the objectivity of the public record, or "true birth." "I was born": this is one of the most singular expressions I know, especially in its French grammatical form.[1] If the interview form lent itself to it, I would prefer, instead of answering you directly, to begin an interminable analysis of the phrase "*je, je suis, je suis né*" in which the tense is not given. Anxiety will never be dispelled on this subject, for the event that is thereby designated can herald itself in me only in the future: "I am (not yet) born," but the future has the form of a past which I will never have witnessed and which for this reason remains always promised—and moreover also multiple. Who ever said that one was born just once? But how can one deny that through all the different promised births, it is a single and same time, the unique time, that insists and that is repeated forever? This is a little what is being recounted in *Circumfession*. "I am not yet born" because the moment that decided my nameable identity was taken away from me. Everything is *arranged* so that it be this way, this is what is called culture. Thus, through so many different relays, one can only try to recapture this theft or this institution which was able to, which *had to* take place more than once. But however iterable and divisible it remains, the "only once" resists.

Q.: Do you mean to say that you do not want to have any identity?

J.D.: On the contrary, I do, like everyone else. But by turning around this impossible thing, and which no doubt I also resist, the "I" constitutes the very form of resistance. Each time this identity announces itself, each time a belonging circumscribes me, if I may put it this way, someone or something cries: Look out for the trap, you're caught. Take off, get free, disengage yourself. Your engagement is elsewhere. Not very original, is it?

Q.: Is the work you do aimed at refinding this identity?

J.D.: No doubt, but the gesture that tries to refind *of itself* distances, it distances itself again. One ought to be able to formalize the law of this insurmountable gap. This is a little what I am always doing. Identification is a difference to itself, a difference with/of itself. Thus *with*, *without*, and *except* itself. The circle of the return to birth can only remain open, but this is at once a chance, a sign of life, and a wound. If it closed in on birth, on a plenitude of the utterance or the knowledge that says "I am born," that would be death.

Q.: In *Circumfession*, you grant a fundamental place to the fact of your circumcision. Is this your secret today?

J.D.: Under the name circumcision, I am often asking myself (and *Circumfession* is also the trajectory of this question or this demand) whether there is a "real" event that I can attempt, not to remember of course, but to re-elaborate, to reactivate in a sort of memory without representation—or whether this is a lure, a simulacrum (but then what gives it its privilege?), a screen destined for the figural projection of so many other events of the same type, which sends me astray as much as it guides me. Circumcision means, among other things, a certain mark that, coming from others and submitted to in absolute passivity, remains on the body, visible and no doubt indissociable from the proper name which is likewise received from the other. It is also the moment of the signature (the other's as well as one's own) by which one lets oneself be inscribed in a community or in an ineffaceable alliance: birth of the subject, as you were suggesting a moment ago, rather than "biological" birth, but there has to be some body and some indestructible mark. Every time there is this mark and this name (and this is not limited to cultures that practice so-called real circumcision), the *figure* at least of a circumcision is imposed on me. What does "figure" mean here? That is what *Circumfession* turns around.

Q.: What relation should one see between the first birth and this other birth that would be your arrival in France, your studies at the *lycée* Louis-le-Grand, the *khâgne*, an inscription in a completely other world?[2]

J.D.: In Algeria, I had begun, let's say, to "get into" literature and philosophy. I dreamed of writing—and already models were instructing the dream, a certain language governed it, and certain figures and names. It's like circumcision, you know, it begins before you do. Very early I read Gide, Nietzsche, Valéry, in ninth or tenth grade. Gide even earlier no doubt: admiration, fascination, cult, fetishism. I no longer know what remains of all this. I remember a young teacher, a redhead, whose name was Lefèvre; he came from the Métropole, which, in the eyes of us young *pieds-noirs* who were a little tough, made him somewhat ridiculous and naive.[3] He sang the praises of the state of love and *Les nourritures terrestres*. I would have learned this book by heart if I could have. No doubt, like every adolescent, I admired its fervor, the lyricism of its declarations of war on religion and families (I probably always translated "I hated the home, families, every place where man thinks he can find rest" into a simple "I am not part of the family"). For me it was a manifesto or a Bible: at once religious and neo-Nietzschean, sensualist, immoralist, and especially very Algerian, as you know. I remember the hymn to the Sahel, to Blida, and to the fruits of the Jardin d'Essai. I read all of Gide, and probably *L'immoraliste* sent me to Nietzsche, which I doubtless understood very badly, and Nietzsche, oddly enough, led me in the direction of Rousseau, the Rousseau of the *Rêveries*. I remember I became the stage for the great argument between Nietzsche and Rousseau and I was the extra ready to take on all the roles. I loved, precisely, what Gide says about Proteus, I identified naively with him who identified, if that's possible, with Proteus. It was the end of the war ("my" Algeria was basically almost constantly at war, because the first uprisings, and thus first portents of the Algerian war, were suppressed at the end of the Second World War). Paris being occupied in 1943–44, the liberated Algiers became a sort of literary capital. Gide was often in North Africa, Camus was talked about a lot, new literary journals and new publishers sprang up everywhere. All of this fascinated me. I wrote some bad poetry that I published in North African journals, I kept a "private diary." But even as I withdrew into this reading or other solitary activities, well, in a dissociated, juxtaposed way, I also led the life of a kind of young hooligan, in a "gang" that was interested more in soccer or track than in studying. In my last two years at the *lycée*, I began to read Bergson and Sartre, who were very important to me for what could be called a philosophical "training," in any case at its beginnings.

Q.: Was it you or your parents who wanted you to go to the Ecole Normale?

J.D.: My parents didn't know what it was. Neither did I, even when I enrolled in *hypokhâgne*.[4] The next year, when I began *khâgne* at Louis-le-Grand, it was quite simply the first trip I made in my life, at nineteen years of age. I had never left El Biar, in the suburbs of Algiers. The boarding-school experience in Paris was very hard, I didn't put up with it very well. I was sick all the time, or in any case frail, on the edge of a nervous breakdown.

Q.: Until you got to the Ecole Normale?

J.D.: Yes. Those were the most difficult, most threatening years. In part, it had to do with a kind of exile, in part with the monstrous torture of the national competitions in the French system.[5] With competitions like those of the Ecole Normale and the *agrégation*, many who found themselves in my situation had the impression of risking everything in this horrible machine or of awaiting a life or death sentence. Failure meant a return to Algiers in a state of absolute precariousness—and I didn't want to go back to Algeria once and for all (both because I felt that I could never "write" while living "at home" and already for political reasons; from the early '50s, colonial politics and first of all colonial society had become unbearable for me). These years of *khâgne* and the Ecole Normale were thus an ordeal (discouragement, despair—failures on the exams themselves: nothing was handed to me on the first try).

Q.: And yet you remained for a long time at the Ecole Normale?

J.D.: This paradox has not escaped you; there would no doubt be a lot to say about that. I have always had "school sickness," as others have seasickness. I cried when it was time to go back to school long after I was old enough to be ashamed of such behavior. Still today, I cannot cross the threshold of a teaching institution (for example the Ecole Normale, where I taught for twenty years, or the Ecole des Hautes Etudes, where I have been teaching for six years) without physical symptoms (I mean in my chest and my stomach) of discomfort or anxiety. And yet, it's true, I have never left school in general, I stayed at the Ecole Normale for almost thirty years altogether. I must suffer also from "school sickness" in the sense this time of homesickness.

Q.: Your name is Jackie. Did you yourself change your first name?

J.D.: You are asking me in fact a very serious question. Yes, I changed my first name when I began to publish, at the moment I entered what is, in sum, the space of literary or philosophical legitimation, whose "good manners" I was practicing in my own way. In finding that Jackie was not possible as the first name of an author, by choosing what was in some way, to be sure, a semi-pseudonym but also very French, Christian, simple, I must have erased more things than I could say in a few words (one would have to analyze the conditions in which a certain community—the Jewish community in Algeria—in the '30s sometimes chose American names, occasionally those of film stars or heroes, William, Jackie, and so forth). But I never would have changed my last name, Derrida, which I have always found to be quite beautiful, don't you think? It has a good resonance in me—but precisely like the resonance of another, in sum, and very rare. That is what allows me to talk this way, and to talk about it so freely. I would have liked to invent it and I probably dream of serving it. With modesty and abnegation, you see what I mean, and out of duty, but I will avoid talking about it here on another level. Time is short.

Q.: In *Circumfession*, you indicate that you have another first name, Elie.

J.D.: Which is not inscribed in the civil record, I don't know why. I have a few theories about that. This is a whole other story, the one that *Circumfession* more or less turns around. I would not be able to talk about it here in this fashion...

Q.: It seems to play a big role for you.

J.D.: Perhaps, I don't know, I don't know if it's true, spontaneous, or if I reinvented it little by little, if I made it up, if I told myself a story in this regard, and in fact rather late, only in the last ten or fifteen years.

Q.: Your earliest work, *The Problem of Genesis in the Philosophy of Husserl* (written in 1954 and published in 1990), and your *Introduction to "The Origin of Geometry"* (1962) dealt with Husserl. Did you already know what your philosophical project was to be?

J.D.: An obsessive thematics already organized a whole space of questions and interpretations: that of writing, between literature, philosophy, and science. This concern was at the heart of the *Introduction to "The Origin of Geometry,"* a text that I chose to translate in particular because Husserl there *runs into* writing. I insisted at the time on the status of the written thing in the history of science. Why does the very constitution of ideal objects, and in an exemplary fashion mathematical objects, require, as Husserl says without drawing all the consequences from it, incorporation in what is called the "spiritual body" of what is written? The passage through Husserl was not just a detour. But it is true that I have also turned away from him, unjustly I more and more believe. The texts that followed the *Introduction to "The Origin of Geometry"* or *Speech and Phenomena* remain nevertheless guided by this problematic of writing, in the way I formalized and systematized it, up to a certain point, in *Of Grammatology.*

Q.: So your question is: what is literature?

J.D.: For instance, but to the extent that this question went beyond the sense that Sartre gave to it. I had learned a lot from Sartre's *What is Literature?* and *Situations,* which introduced me to works that I have continued to admire (Ponge, Blanchot, Bataille), but at the beginning of the '60s, it no longer satisfied me.

Q.: How did you formulate the question for yourself?

J.D.: I find the Sartrean question necessary but insufficient, at once too socio-historical and too metaphysical, external to the specificity of the literary structure that Sartre does not question, or that he pre-interprets on the basis of very determined literary models (also in ignorance of certain literary writings of this century, which either he almost never speaks of—Joyce, Artaud—or else he speaks of them in what I find to be a very minimal way—Mallarmé, Genet, to say nothing of the other three I named above). In order to give full measure to the socio-political or socio-historical questions about literature (what is the function of literature? what does the writer do in society? and so forth), one must read literature otherwise and construct another axiomatics. Do not ask me to specify this axiomatics, because I could not do so in these conditions, but this is everything I try to do elsewhere in almost each one of my texts.

Q.: Why did literature constitute for you such an important object?

J.D.: What counted for me (but why do you make me talk about this in the past tense?), is the act of writing or rather, since it is perhaps not altogether an act, the experience of writing: to leave a trace that dispenses with, that is even destined to dispense with the present of its originary inscription, of its "author" as one might say in an insufficient way. This gives one a way that is better than ever for thinking the present and the origin, death, life, or survival. Given that a trace is never present without dividing itself by referring to another present, then what does being-present, or the presence of the present mean? The possibility of this trace no doubt carries beyond what is called art or literature, beyond in any case the identifiable institutions of that name. No more than philosophy or science, literature is not an institution among others; it is at once institution and counter-institution, placed at a *distance* from the institution, at the angle that the institution makes with itself in order to *take a distance from itself, by itself* [s'écarter d'elle-même]. And if literature maintains here some privilege in my view, it is in part by reason of what it thematizes about the event of writing, and in part because of what, in its political history, links literature to that principal authorization to "say everything" whereby it is related in such a unique fashion to what is called truth, fiction, simulacrum, science, philosophy, law, right, democracy.

Q.: What was at stake in these descriptions?

J.D.: Perhaps, among other things, an economic stake in a strategy of formalization—and of impossible formalization. Perhaps even the stake of economy itself and the limit of any formalization. It was an attempt to think a large dominant structure within a set called philosophy. Why is it that the trace (neither presence nor absence, beyond being, therefore, even beyond Being—which is the whole border of negative theologies that has always interested me, notably in "How to Avoid Speaking?") "is" that which puts philosophy into motion and thereby refuses itself to philosophy, resists *properly ontological, transcendental, or philosophical comprehension* in general? Without being foreign to philosophy, this attempt was neither philosophical nor solely theoretical or critical; it *promised* (it was this very promise itself), it engaged new bodies of writing, pledges of other signatures, new bodies in which neither philosophy, nor literature, nor perhaps knowledge in general would reassemble their image or their history. "Autobiography" is certainly just an old name for designating one of the bodies thereby pledged.

Q.: But why is it so important to write? What does one engage of oneself by writing?

J.D.: I just spoke of a "pledge" [*gage*] or an "engagement" of *oneself* in a strange autobiography; yes, but the self does not exist, it is not present to itself before that which engages it in this way and which is not it. There is not a constituted subject that engages itself at a given moment in writing for some reason or another. It is *given* by writing, by the other: *born* as we were bizarrely saying a moment ago, born by being given, delivered, offered, and betrayed all at once. And this *truth* is an affair of love and the police, of pleasure and the law—all at once. The event is at once grave and microscopic. It is the whole enigma of a truth *to be made*. Saint Augustine speaks often of "making the truth" in a confession. In *Circumfession*, I try, by citing him often, to think how this truth rebels against philosophical truth—a truth of adequation or revelation.

Q.: In 1968, you were teaching at the Ecole Normale, one of the hotbeds of dissent. Were the events of May important for you?

J.D.: I was not what is called a "soixante-huitard" [a "sixty-eighter"]. Even though I participated at that time in demonstrations and organized the first general meeting at the time at the Ecole Normale, I was on my guard, even worried in the face of a certain cult of spontaneity, a fusionist, anti-unionist euphoria, in the face of the enthusiasm of a finally "freed" speech, of restored "transparence," and so forth. I never believed in those things...

Q.: You thought it was a little naive?

J.D.: I was not against it, but I have always had trouble vibrating in unison. I didn't feel I was participating in a great shake-up. But I now believe that in this jubilation, which was not very much to my taste, something else happened.

Q.: What?

J.D.: I won't be able to name it: a seismic jolt that came from far away and that carried very far. In the culture and in the University, these shock waves are not yet stabilized. I was more sensitive to it after the fact when I saw the spectacle of resentment and the reassertion of control by the most conservative, even retrograde forces, notably in the University. It is in this aftermath that I began to give a more visibly, let us say "militant" form to my work as a teacher. The formation of the GREPH dates from those years...

Q.: What was May '68? What was this event that does not end? What had to be sutured? Why were some people so frightened?

J.D.: Through the cult of spontaneity and a certain naturalist utopianism, people doubtless became aware of the artificial, artifactual character of institutions. One didn't need May '68 to realize this, to be sure, but perhaps one was able to realize it more practically, more effectively, because these non-natural, founded, historical things were clearly no longer functioning. As usual, it is the breakdown that lays bare the functioning of the machine as such. And with that, because these non-natural, historical, founded institutions were no longer working, they were found to be altogether unfounded, unfounded in law, illegitimate. Add to this the fact that the media and with them the whole culture were taking on forms and dimensions that marked a veritable mutation, including the very production of the "event" May '68. This freed up all sorts of questions about legitimacy and the source of the powers to sanction, evaluate, publish, communicate, and so forth.

Q.: Does May '68 designate a philosophical event?

J.D.: No doubt, no doubt one of those philosophical events that do not take the form of a work or a treatise but that *carry*, that always carry with them the philosophical events identifiable thanks to titles or the name of an author. To question practically a social or discursive state, which some were interested in naturalizing or dehistoricizing, to question it by shaking it up or participating in its transformation, to ask the question of the historicity of these structures is also a philosophical event or a promise of one. Whether one knows it or wishes it or not, it changes things in philosophy. The trajectories and repercussions are difficult to trace, one would have to invoke other categories and other historiographic instruments. To take just the most ordinary manifestations of philosophical work: books of philosophy, with a few exceptions, are no longer written in the same manner today. One no longer teaches, one no longer talks to students, and especially with students, as before. They no longer speak among themselves in the same way. This didn't change in a day, in a month, but no doubt in the undercurrent that gathered itself together, as it were, on the crest of its manifestation or demonstration, in the advancing tide of May '68, in France and elsewhere.

Q.: *Glas*, which appeared in 1974, was a book that, at least in the way it was put together, was at once very new and very disconcerting. What was the project, the stake of an enterprise like *Glas*?

J.D.: Without renouncing classical norms and requirements of philosophical reading, for which I have always maintained the greatest respect, the point in *Glas* was doubtless to treat seriously certain themes (the family, the proper name, religion, the dialectic, absolute knowledge, mourning—and thus several others), but by juxtaposing, column against column, the interpretation of a great canonical corpus of philosophy, that of Hegel, and the re-writing of a more or less outlaw, barely receivable writer-poet, Genet. Hegel and Genet at the same time, face to face, one in the other, one before or behind the other at the same time, if the geometry or the mobility of that posture is possible. Later, the question of what is decorum [*bienséance*] will be posed, in *The Post Card*, with Socrates, well seated [*bien assis*] and writing *in front of* Plato, who is standing up and pointing his finger. This contamination of a great philosophical discourse by a literary text that passes for scandalous or obscene, and of several norms or kinds of writing by each other other may seem violent—already in the "page layout." But it also rejoined or reawakened a very old tradition: that of a page that set out otherwise its blocks of texts, interpretation, interior margins. And thus of another space, another practice of reading, of writing, of exegesis. It was for me a manner of assuming in practice the consequences of certain propositions in *Of Grammatology* concerning the book and the linearity of writing. And, contrary to what is sometimes said by those who haven't read, of doing something altogether other than mixing literature and philosophy.

Q.: When you write a book like that, do you write in a relation to yourself or do you address a certain public?

J.D.: I no doubt address readers who I presume will be able to help me, to accompany me, recognize, respond. The typical profile of a possible reader is prefigured in the examples of existing readers (sometimes just one is enough). Perhaps, but in an always ambiguous manner, you hope to pull others into it, or rather to discover or invent others who do not yet exist, but who nevertheless know something about it already, know more about it than you do. This is where we get into the most obscure, the most disconcerting, disrupted topology, the disruption of destination: of that which I thought it convenient to nickname *destinerrance* or *clandestination*.

Q.: So the book induces certain modes of reading?

J.D.: Perhaps as well but without forming or closing a reading program, without suturing a system of formalizable rules. It is always an *opening*, at once in the sense of an unclosed system, of the opening *left* to the other's freedom, but also in the sense of overture, advance, or invitation *made* to someone else. The intervention of the other, whom one should perhaps no longer call simply the "reader," is an indispensable but always *improbable* counter-signature. It must remain something one cannot anticipate. The chance of the absolute event always has a bottomless fund of initiative which must always return to it.

Q.: Does this amount to instituting a group?

J.D.: More like an *open* "quasi"-community of people who, because they "like this stuff," signal their reception by going off elsewhere, reading and writing in their turn altogether differently. This is the generous response, always more faithful and at the same time more ungrateful.

Q.: Have you found this community?

J.D.: It is never found, one never knows if it exists, and given the opening I was talking about a moment ago, to think one has found it would be not only mystified, but would right away cause one to lose it, destroy it. Such a community is always to come, it has an essential relation to the singularity of the event, of that which is coming but (therefore) "has not happened."

Q.: Yet it seems that in the United States, there is a certain number of readers around you who have managed to formalize this practice of reading and writing.

J.D.: Some very interesting things have happened in this regard in the United States. It would require long analyses—that I have begun here and there. But I am very suspicious concerning this very frequent and very interested calculation that consists in referring me back to the United States or putting me under American house arrest. What is one trying to do or to defend in this way? I leave you to imagine it. No, I spend only a few days, a few weeks in the United States each year. Whatever may be the intensity of this experience, whatever may be the generosity but also the aggressivity (you have no idea) that I encounter there, the things that count for my work are also going on elsewhere, outside of Europe, in Europe, and for example, yes, in France.

Q.: Your published work is considerable. What is the relation between one book and the other? Is it your aim each time to reinvent, to leave behind the preceding trace in order to produce another? Or is there continuity?

J.D.: I must give you a contradictory but typical and unoriginal reply: "Something" insists, to be sure, and is recognizable from one book to the other. This is undeniable, and moreover I must want it that way. Yet each text belongs to a completely other history: discontinuity of tone, of vocabulary, of the sentence even, and finally of address. It is really as if I had never before written anything, or even known how to write (I mean, very sincerely, in the most elementary and almost grammatical fashion). Each time I begin a new text, however modest it may be, there is dismay in the face of the unknown or the inaccessible, an overwhelming feeling of clumsiness, inexperience, powerlessness. What I have already written is instantly annihilated or rather thrown overboard, as it were.

Q.: How do you get the idea for a book or an article?

J.D.: A sort of animal movement seeks to appropriate what always comes, always, from an *external* provocation. By responding to some request, invitation, or commission, an invention must nevertheless seek itself out, an invention that defies both a given program, a system of expectations, and finally surprises *me* myself—surprises me by suddenly becoming for me imperious, imperative, inflexible even, like a very tough law. The more singular the form, approaching what is called no doubt inappropriately "fiction" or "autobiography," as in *Glas, The Post Card*, or *Circumfession*, the more this compulsion surprises me. But all these books also recount in their own way the staged history of their formation, and each time a new scene is described. Then I forget almost everything from the moment this "internal" constraint has bent me to its will.

Q.: An internal constraint: that means it is not a cultural or political constraint.

J.D.: One is always calculating with what one perceives of the cultural field. But even if this calculation negotiates in a very

cunning fashion, it always consents to serve a more unruly, dis-
armed, naive desire, or in any case another culture that no longer
calculates, and certainly not according to the norms of "present"
culture or politics. One is coming to terms with someone, with
someone *other, dead or alive, with some others* who have no identity
in this cultural scene.

Q.: At the same time as the solicitation that incites you, there is
also a remarkable fact: all the texts you write are indexed to
important references: Husserl, Plato, Heidegger, Hegel, Rousseau,
Jabès, Celan. The list is considerable.

J.D.: There is always someone else, you know. The most private
autobiography comes to terms with great transferential figures,
who are *themselves* and themselves *plus* someone else (for example,
Plato, Socrates, and a few others in *The Post Card*, Genet, Hegel,
Saint Augustine, and many others in *Glas* or *Circumfession*, and so
forth). In order to speak of even the most intimate thing, for
example one's "own" circumcision, one does better to be aware that
an exegesis is in process, that you carry the detour, the contour, and
the memory inscribed in the culture of your body, for example.
Here's an example among thousands of others, and which I've
never talked about: a coming to terms with Meister Eckhart, who
reported what Maimonides said on the subject with as much
knowledge as naïveté, namely, "the foreskin that was cut off served
concupiscence and the pleasure of the flesh more than generation.
That is why," as this author puts it, "one could hardly separate a
woman from an uncircumcised man. Whence one sees that God's
commandment to circumcise the male prevented the superfluous
in woman, that is, the excess of carnal concupiscence." Don't ask
me why, in a detour from all these detours, Heidegger, who read
Eckhart throughout his life as a master, never speaks of either
circumcision or Maimonides; that's another story. I just wanted to
suggest that these reading grids, these folds, zigzags, references, and
transferences are, as it were, in our skin, right on the surface of our
sex organ when we claim to be treating our "own circumcision." In
short, since there is no brute nature and no opposition between

nature and culture that holds up, only the *différance* from one to the other, well, a text in which the name of the other would be absent always looks like it's dissimulating, effacing, or even censoring. Violent, ingenuous—or both at the same time. Even if the name of the other does not appear, even if it remains secret, it is there, it teems and maneuvers, it screams sometimes, it makes itself all the more authoritarian. One does better to know this and to say it. And anyway others are so much more interesting. Whom are we going to be interested in otherwise, tell me? Even within oneself?

Q.: What is the relation of all these texts among themselves? Do they form a work?

J.D.: What is a work?

Q.: A set of texts, books, linked by an identity.

J.D.: From the socio-juridical point of view, this is hardly debatable. There is a legal copyright and a civil identity, texts signed by the same name, a law, a responsibility, a property, guarantees. All this interests me very much. But it is only one stratum of the thing or the singular adventure called a work, which I feel is at every moment in the process of undoing itself, expropriating itself, falling to pieces without ever collecting itself together in a signature. I would be tempted to retain from the old concept of work the value of singularity and not that of identity to itself or of collection. If anything repeats itself in me in an obsessive fashion, it is this paradox: there is singularity but it does not collect itself, it "consists" in not collecting itself. Perhaps you will say that there is a way of not collecting oneself that is consistently recognizable, what used to be called a "style."

Q.: Can you say in what way it is recognizable?

J.D.: This can be perceived only by the other. The idiom, if there is any, that by which one recognizes a signature, does not reappropriate itself, as paradoxical as that may seem. It can only be apprehended by the other, given over to the other. Of course, I may think I recognize myself, identify my signature or my sentence, but only on the basis of experience and of an exercise which I will have undertaken and in which I will have been trained *as other*, the possibility of repetition and thus of imitation, simulacrum, being inscribed at the very origin of this singularity.

Q.: You urge two things: to displace the practices of reading and to create a sort of community of your readers.

J.D.: I don't much like the word community, I am not even sure I like the thing.

Q.: You were the one who used it.

J.D.: If by community one implies, as is often the case, a harmonious group, consensus, and fundamental agreement beneath the phenomena of discord or war, then I don't believe in it very much and I sense in it as much threat as promise.

Q.: I am thinking of the work of Roger Chartier on reading, when he explains that the meaning of a book is linked to the practices of reading that one undertakes with it. I was wondering if one couldn't say that the work of your writing is to induce those practices of reading that will be themselves productive of meaning?

J.D.: There is doubtless this irrepressible desire for a "community" to form but also for it to know its limit—and for its limit to be its *opening*. Once it thinks it has understood, taken in, interpreted, *kept* the text, then something of this latter, something in it that is altogether *other* escapes or resists the community, it appeals for another community, it does not let itself be totally interiorized in the memory of a present community. The experience of mourning and promise that institutes that community but also forbids it from collecting itself, this experience stores in itself the reserve of another community that will sign, otherwise, completely other contracts.

Q.: Something that might seem surprising about our discussion: we have not talked of "deconstruction."

J.D.: That is never indispensable, I don't insist upon it at all.

Q.: Does the term "deconstruction" designate your fundamental project?

J.D.: I have never had a "fundamental project." And "deconstructions," which I prefer to say in the plural, has doubtless never named a project, method, or system. Especially not a philosophical system. In contexts that are always very determined, it is one of the possible names for designating, by metonymy in sum, what happens or doesn't happen to happen, namely, a certain dislocation that in fact is regularly repeated—and wherever there is something rather than nothing: in what are called the texts of classical philosophy, of course and for example, but also in every "text" in the general sense that I try to justify for this word, that is, in experience period, in social, historical, economic, technical, military, etc., "reality." The event of the so-called Gulf War, for example, is a powerful, spectacular, and tragic condensation of these deconstructions. In the same conflagration, in the same seism there trembles the split genealogy of all these structures and all these foundations that I have just mentioned: the West and the history of philosophy, what links it, on the one hand, to several great and (despite what people say) irreconcilable monotheisms, on the other hand, to natural languages and national feelings, to the idea of democracy and to the theologico-political, and finally to the infinite progress of an idea of international law, whose limits are manifesting themselves more than ever. The manifestation of these limits is occurring not only because those who represent international law or refer to it always take it over for the profit of determined hegemonies and moreover can do no more than approach that law inadequately to infinity, but also because it is founded (and thereby limited) on concepts of European philosophical modernity (nation, State, democracy, relations of parliamentary democracy among States, either democratic or not, and so forth)—not to mention what links science, technics, and the military, from within, to these formidable problems. These violent deconstructions are under way, *it is happening*, it doesn't wait for someone to complete the philosophico-theoretical analysis of everything I have just evoked in a word: this analysis is necessary but infinite and the reading that these cracks make possible will never dominate the event; that reading only intervenes there, it is inscribed there.

Q.: What is the relation between deconstruction and critique?

J.D.: The *critical* idea, which I believe must never be renounced, has a history and presuppositions whose deconstructive analysis is also necessary. In the style of the Enlightenment, of Kant, or of Marx, but also in the sense of evaluation (esthetic or literary), *critique* supposes judgment, voluntary judgment between two terms; it attaches to the idea of *krinein* or of *krisis* a certain negativity. To say that all this is deconstructible does not amount to disqualifying, negating, disavowing, or surpassing it, of doing the *critique of critique* (the way people wrote critiques of the Kantian critique as soon as it appeared), but of thinking its possibility from another border, from the genealogy of judgment, will, consciousness or activity, the binary structure, and so forth. This thinking perhaps transforms the space and, through aporias, allows the (non-positive) affirmation to appear, the one that is presupposed by every critique and every negativity. I try to say something about this necessary aporetics in *Of Spirit* and, with regard to Europe, in *The Other Heading*.

Q.: Could one say that deconstruction is the techniques you use for reading and writing?

J.D.: I would say instead that this is one of its forms or manifestations. This form remains necessarily limited, determined by a set of open contextual traits (the language, the history, the European scene in which I am writing or in which I am inscribed with all manner of more or less aleatory givens that have to do with my own little history, and so forth). But as I was saying, there is deconstruction, there are deconstructions everywhere. What takes the form of techniques, rules, procedures, in France or in the West, in philosophical, juridico-political, esthetic, and other kinds of research, is a very delimited configuration; it is carried—and thus exceeded—by much broader, more obscure and powerful processes, between the earth and the world.

Q.: So deconstruction is not just the critical activity of a litera-ture or philosophy professor in a university. It is a historical move-ment. Kant characterized his age as that of the critique. Can one say that we are in the age of deconstruction?

J.D.: Let's say the age of a certain *thematics* of deconstruction, which in fact receives a certain name and can formalize itself up to a certain point in methods and modes of reproduction. But decon-structions do not begin or end there. It is certainly necessary but still very difficult to account for this intensification and this passing into the theme and the name, into this beginning of formalization.

Q.: What would be the appropriate historical marker?

J.D.: I don't know. To be sure, one should never give up on the historical recognition of such signposts, but I wonder whether something can take the form here of a sole "historical marker," whether even the question can be posed in this fashion without implying precisely a historiographical axiomatics that ought per-haps to be suspended, since it is too bound up with deconstructible philosophemes. The things we are talking about ("deconstruc-tions" if you will) do not happen within what would be recogniz-ably called "history," an orientable history with periods, ages, or revolutions, mutations, emerging phenomena, ruptures, breaks, *episteme*, paradigms, *themata* (to answer according to the most diverse and familiar historiographic codes). Every "deconstructive" reading proposes another one of these multiple "markers," but I do not know around which great axis they are to be oriented. If, as is the case with me, one also has reservations about history or the epochality of Being, in Heidegger's sense, then what is left? That said, from a phenomenal and even trivial point of view, the inten-sification and thematization we were talking about are indeed "contemporary" with the double worldwide post-war, with what is happening to Europe, with what is cleaving Europe and violently relating it to an other that is no longer even *its* other. Here again I take the liberty of referring you to what I try to suggest in *Of Spirit* and *The Other Heading...*

Q.: Are you talking about the consequences of anthropology?

J.D.: Anthropology as a scientific project is certainly not a cause, no more than any other form of knowledge in itself. Ethnological knowledge would be rather one of the impacts, a highly significant one in fact, of this general shake-up. It reflects, in all senses of this word, the (European) history of culture as colonization and decolonization, as mission in the broad sense, import-export of national or statist models, ex-appropriations, crisis of identification, and so forth.

Q.: All of this is going toward what? We are in a period in which no one knows any longer what he should want, in a period of highly perfected, nearly consummate nihilism. Everyone is waiting to know where we are going, toward what we are moving, toward what we should be moving, directing ourselves. Toward what does work such as yours lead?

J.D.: I don't know. Or rather: I believe this is not on the order of knowledge, which does not mean that one must give up on knowledge and resign oneself to obscurity. At stake are responsibilities that, if they are to give rise to decisions and events, must not follow knowledge, must not flow from knowledge like consequences or effects. Otherwise, one would unfold a program and conduct oneself, at best, like "smart" missiles. These responsibilities, which will determine "where things are going" as you put it, are heterogeneous to the formalizable order of knowledge and no doubt to all the concepts on which the idea of responsibility or decision (conscious self, will, intentionality, autonomy, and so forth) have been constructed, I would even say *arrested*. Each time a responsibility (ethical or political) has to be taken, one must pass by way of antinomic injunctions, which have an aporetic form, by way of a sort of experience of the impossible; otherwise the application of a rule by a conscious subject identical to itself, objectively subsuming a case to the generality of a given law, manages on the contrary to *irresponsibilize*, or at least to miss the always unheard-of singularity of the decision that has to be made.

Since the event is each time singular, on the measure of the other's alterity, one must each time *invent*, not without a concept but each time exceeding the concept, without assurance or certainty. The obligation can only be double, contradictory or conflictual, from the moment it appeals to a responsibility and not to a moral or political technique. For example, how is one to, *on the one hand*, reaffirm the singularity of the idiom (either national or not), the rights of minorities, linguistic and cultural difference, and so forth? How is one to resist uniformization, homogenization, cultural or linguistico-media leveling, its order of representation and spectacular profitability? But, *on the other hand*, how is one to struggle for all that without sacrificing the most univocal communication possible, translation, information, democratic discussion, and the law of the majority? Each time one must *invent* so as to betray as little as possible both one and the other—*without any prior assurance* of success. Another example: not to renounce the idea of international law, of the indisputable progress it has made by embodying itself in institutions, to reaffirm this immense idea in an effective and consistent way, but to continue to analyze and to criticize (effectively and not just in a theoretical manner) all the premises that have motivated this or that effectuation of the said international law, the mystifications of the references that can be made to it, its hijacking to the advantage of determined interests, indeed, as I was suggesting a moment ago, *to deconstruct* (*also, and then* in another manner but *already* and without delay in another manner) the conceptual and historical limits of *this* institution of international law—I am speaking of the U.N. and of the Security Council, of course.

But naturally, once this double imperative (weighed down with so many contradictions) has been recognized, once engaged the implacable critique of the politics, of *all* the politics that have, in the distant or immediate past, constituted the premises of this war, the decision that remained to be made could only be a terrible strategic wager, betting on the possibility—once the tragedy had been appeased (and nothing will ever compensate for the number of dead it will have cost)—of being able to keep the memory, to draw lessons, and to respond better to this double imperative. And a decision (for example in politics) is always made at a moment when the most critical theoretical analysis can no longer modify irreversible premises. No matter how necessary and rigorous the case one makes against Western, Israeli, and Arab-Islamic politics (and there is more than one politics in each category, moreover), no matter how far back one goes and *must* go in this case (and one must go back very, very far in articulated stages), the decision to be made (embargo or not, war or not, this or that "goal of war") has to be made in a "today," at a unique moment in which no past error or wrong can be effaced or even repaired any longer. This terrifying strategic wager cannot be guaranteed by anything in advance, not even by the computation (always necessarily speculative) that a contrary wager would have led to the worst. I think we can easily translate these abstract schemas today, can we not. (We will have to date this interview: on the eve of the stage of the war curiously named the "land war.") I merely wanted to suggest that any assumption of assurance and of non-contradiction in such a parox-ystic situation (but this is valid for every situation) is an optimistic gesticulation, an act of good conscience and irresponsibility—and thus it is indecision, profound inactivity beneath the appearance of activism or resolution.

Q.: One can put it in other terms: Is there a philosophy of Jacques Derrida?

J.D.: No.

Q.: There is thus no message.

J.D.: No.

Q.: Is there anything normative?

J.D.: Of course there is, there is nothing but that. But if you are asking me implicitly whether what I am saying there is normative in the ordinary sense of the term, I would have more trouble an-swering you. Why don't I particularly like this word "normative" in this context? What I have just suggested about responsibility signals instead in the direction of a law, of an imperative injunction to which one must finally respond *without norm*, without a presently presentable normativity or normality, without anything that would finally be the object of knowledge, belonging to an order of being or value. I am not even sure that the concept of *duty* [devoir] (or in any case of *having-to-be* [devoir-être]) can measure up to it. No doubt one will be tempted to reply: From all these apparently negative or abstract propositions, it is difficult to deduce a politics, a morality, or a right. I think the opposite. If they economize on such doubts, questions, reservations, clauses of non-knowledge, aporias, and so forth, then politics, morality, and right (which I do not confuse here with justice) take assurance from and reassure themselves in illusion and good conscience—and are never far from being or from doing *something other* than morality, politics, and right.

Q.: Do you draw this from your philosophy?

J.D.: What do you mean by "draw"? To take from the source? To find? To deduce? To induce? To draw consequences? To conclude? As for some philosophy that would be "mine," I have already told you no. I prefer to speak of *experience*, this word that means at the same time traversal, voyage, ordeal, both *mediatized* (culture, reading, interpretation, work, generalities, rules, and concepts) and *singular*—I do not say immediate (untranslatable "affect," language, proper name, and so forth). To take up your word again, what I suggested a moment ago is "drawn" from (without ever pulling free of! [*s'en tirer*]) this experience, more precisely *there where it crosses*, where work and singularity cross, where universality crosses with that *preference* of singularity which it cannot be a question of renouncing, which it would even be immoral to renounce. It is not a preference that I prefer but the preference *in which* I find myself inscribed and that embodies the singular decision or the responsibility without which there would be neither morality, nor right, nor politics. It so happens (with many complications which cannot be gone into here even if we had the time—I have spoken of them elsewhere and most recently in *Du droit à la philosophie, Circumfession,* and *The Other Heading*), it so happens, then, that I was *born,* as we were saying, in the European *preference*, in the preference of the French language, nation, or citizenship, to take but this example, and then in the preference of this time, of those I love, of my family, of my friends—of my enemies also, of course, and so on. These preferences can, and this is everyday experience, contradict and threaten the imperatives of the universal respect of the other, but their neutralization or their disavowal would also be contrary to any ethico-political motive. Everything is "drawn" for me from the (living, daily, naive or reflective, always thrown against the impossible) experience *of* this "preference" that *I have at the same time to affirm and sacrifice.* There is always for me, and I believe there *must be more than one* language, mine and the other (I am simplifying a lot), and I must try to write in such a way that the language of the other does not suffer in mine, suffers me to come without suffering from it, receives the hospitality of mine without getting lost or integrated there. And reciprocally, but reciprocity is not symmetry—and first of all because we have no neutral measure here, no *common measure* given by a third party. This has to be invented at every moment, with every sentence, without assurance, without absolute guardrails. Which is as much as to say that madness, a certain "madness" *must* keep a lookout over every step, and finally watch over thinking, as reason does also.

Q.: Could one also say that between the philosophical work and the work of writing that are yours, on the one hand, and politics, on the other, one should not want to establish links?

J.D.: The links are not immediately identifiable, according to the codes in force. There are links, of course, you have no doubt of that, but here or there they may pass through trajectories that are not plotted on the map of politics. They in turn politicize discursive zones, bodies of work, places of experience that generally are taken as apolitical or politically neutral. There are discourses and gestures whose code and rhetoric are apparently highly political, but whose foreseeable submission to exhausted programs seems to me seriously apolitical or depoliticizing. And vice versa, if you like...

Q.: Some will say that in relation to a certain tradition of philosophy, which always had its moral component, your practice of philosophy is a little disappointing.

J.D.: Well, if that's true, let me place my hope in that "disappointment." What is a disappointment? It urges you at least to ask yourself why you were waiting, why you were waiting for this or that, why you were expecting from this or that, from him or her. It is always the best incitement to questions and reflections. Why do people expect a philosophy there where one has explained that it had to be a matter also of something other on the subject of philosophy? Why have people believed that morality was a part of philosophy? Was it justified, morally justified, for example, to believe that a philosophy had to include a moral "component," region or consequence, the consequence of a philosophical knowledge? As I said a moment ago, there is in fact no philosophy and no philosophy of philosophy that could be called deconstruction and that would deduce from itself a "moral component." But that does not mean that deconstructive experience is not a responsibility, even an ethico-political responsibility, or does not exercise or deploy any responsibility in itself. By questioning philosophy about its treatment of ethics, politics, the concept of responsibility, deconstruction orders itself I will not say on a still *higher* concept of responsibility—because I am also wary, we have all learned to be wary of this value of height or depth (the altitude of the *altus*)—but on an exigency, which I believe is more *inflexible* [intraitable], of response and responsibility. Without this exigency, in my view no ethico-political question has any chance of being opened up or awakened today. I will not go so far as to say that it is a matter there of a hyper-ethical or hyper-political "radicalization," or even ask (this would take us too far afield today) whether the words "ethical" and "political" are still the most appropriate ones to name this other exigency, gentle or inflexible, this exigency of the other that is precisely [*justement*] inflexible...

Counter-Signatures

Q.: For you, Jacques Derrida, what was the revelatory force of Francis Ponge's poetry when you discovered it? What was its novelty? Where did you begin when you wrote your text *Signéponge/Signsponge*?[1] You had some landmarks...

J.D.: The first landmarks, or rather the first guiding threads, went in the direction of the dissemination of all the elements of his proper name in his work. I set out from the first name, from F.R., "francité," the fresco, the value of frankness that is very affirmed in his work. And Ponge: the whole play with "éponge" [sponge]. Moreover, there is a text of Ponge's called: "La serviette éponge" [The terrycloth towel]. All the sponges, therefore, everything one does with a sponge, the thing and the word, the play between the thing (sponge as a thing) and the word ("éponge"). This net of the first name and family name takes in a great number of Ponge's texts. Often in a deliberate way. It is a way of inscribing his signature right on the text. And this develops a logic of the signature that interests me very much. When a proper name is inscribed right on the text, within the text, obviously it is not a signature: it is a way of making the name into a work, of making work of the name, but without this inscription of the proper name having the value of any property rights so to speak. Whence the double relation to the name and to the loss of the name: by inscribing the name in the thing itself (whether one is talking about the poem or the poem become a thing or the thing become a poem), by inscribing the name in the thing, from one angle, I lose the signature, but, from another angle, I monumentalize the name, I transform the name into a thing: like a stone, like a monument. You know how interested Ponge was in engravings, lithographies, sculptures, and inscriptions of names in stone. One has to lose the name in order to make it become a thing, in order to win for it in some way the value of thing, which is to say also a survival. And this double constraint is readable in all of Ponge's texts. The explanation with language: explanation between the proper name and language.[2] Between the Frenchness [*francité*] of the language (one naturally thinks of the *Malherbe*) and the Frenchness or Latin-ness of his proper name, there is a whole genealogy inscribed in these two names. At which point the thing itself becomes the stakes, the thing as place where the proper name must inscribe itself, must in a certain way counter-sign the poem. The thing is no longer, as one used to say from the phenomenological point of view, what has to let itself be unveiled, that has to be, that one must let be what it is. The thing is the Other that one must force to counter-sign the poem in some way. And beginning with this guiding thread, one recognizes a certain number of texts in which this scene of the signature is in play and in which it is a matter of forcing the Other— an animal, a thing, a swallow, a meadow—to counter-sign the poem. I am thinking of that passage from *Pour un Malherbe* where Ponge writes: "Rightly or wrongly and I don't know why, but since childhood I have always considered the only valid texts to be those that could be inscribed in stone. The only texts that I can with dignity accept to sign (or counter-sign)."[3] Texts are already signed in stone; as for him, he counter-signs them, but at the same time he wants to make nature counter-sign his text, "the only texts that I can with dignity accept to sign (or counter-sign) are those that could be unsigned altogether." Thus they are signed to such a degree that they go beyond the limit of the signature. They are so much what they are, independent of any initiative, of the accompaniment by the living poet, that they dispense with a signature.

"Those that would hold up as objects of nature, in the open air, in the sun, under the rain, in the wind, that is exactly the proper character of inscriptions."

A little farther on: "In sum, I approve of nature," I approve of nature, I countersign the work of time.

This approval of nature has a general philosophical sense that Ponge himself often defines as an Epicureanism, a great wisdom. But at the same time this approval of nature is a manner of counter-signing: I prove and I sign, you see, I counter-sign, I say "yes," I say yes to nature, and my work consists in this yes that counter-signs the work, the work of time or the work of nature...

One finds this effect of counter-signature everywhere. He often describes the thing, which may be an animal, a human scene, an anthropomorphic form when he describes them as themselves scenes of writing or signature. For example, in the swallows or in the style of swallows, that is, in the writing of swallows, it is a flight of signatures that he describes. I quote: "Each swallow tirelessly hurls itself—infallibly exercises itself—in the signature, according to its species, of the skies. Steely quill, dipped in blue-black ink, you write *yourself* quickly! If no trace of it remains. . . ." And the "you write *yourself* quickly" (the apostrophe *yourself* in italics) is thus the mark of a reflection, of a self-reference that signals we are talking about a signing writing, one which, while writing, refers to itself; and yet reference has flown away in the airborne traffic, in this putting into orbit of the thing: "each one," says Ponge, "each one, launched headlong into space, spends the better part of its time signing space. . . . They take off from us, and do not take off from us: no illusions!" "They take off from us": that is, they distance themselves from us but at the same time they proceed from us in this moment of signature. And "they do not take off from us," that is, they do not proceed from us but at the same time they do not leave us, and once again there is a double constraint here. It is when they proceed from us, when they take off from us that they leave us without coming back, and it is when they do not take off from us, by not proceeding from us, that they remain most attached to us.

One comes across this scene again in "La guêpe," in "L'avant-printemps," with the Pear Trees, with the Mimosa Trees; it's always the same scene of the signature, but always in a singular fashion, each time in an irreducibly original fashion. I would say that I *take off* from Ponge's proper name: that is why not everything comes back to it, that is why I would not want to lead one to believe that, by concerning myself with his legal proper name, I tried to deduce everything from it. Moreover, in this text I take precautions in this regard: it is not at all a matter of deducing everything from the patronymic proper name, or even of deducing everything from the signature of the proper name. Everything *takes off* from his proper name, that is, it proceeds from it, and at the same time takes its distance from it, detaches itself from it. And it is this detachment that makes the work in some way.

Q.: You are concerned with oracular, definitive inscription. But a poet is someone who has lived the other side of speech, the sketchy beginning, the stammering, the "oral attempt," aphasia.

J.D.: Yes, you are right, "the other side of speech." All great writers are aphasic in a certain manner. Perhaps I am wrong but I have difficulty imagining someone living an explanation with his or her own language, with the intensity that Ponge does, and being at the same time a speaker, an orator, an easy talker. Writing works in a certain difficulty of elocution. And Ponge has kept the record of this work. With the Table, the *Pré* [the Meadow], the Making of the *Pré*,[4] he has left us with all the traces of an explanation, a hand-to-hand confrontation with language. It is something slow, laborious, difficult, and that does not exclude an extraordinary grace. They go together, don't they? When one reads the sketches, the projects, the drafts, we see the slowness, the caution, the circumspection, the difficulty going forward, and then at the same time, in the relation to language, an agility, a suppleness, a knowing-how-to-leap in some way that are inseparable from all that. Yes, that is what I most admire in Ponge, as well as that preparation of the work, that "pré" of the work in some way from which he makes a work. We no longer know how to separate, we no longer know whether we ought to be able to separate a poem like the *Pré* from the Making of the *Pré*, the table from a certain making of the Table. We ought to be able to separate them and yet the fabrication is a work by itself. He has succeeded in incorporating the "pré" of the labor, the preparation of the labor in the work.

Q.: But don't you find that the fabrication devours the *Pré*?

J.D.: No. The *Pré* stands by itself, if I can say that. The poem has an admirable economy, it does not need the Making. Nevertheless reading the Making, which itself, in a certain way, could do without the poem, has an extraordinary value of elucidating the poem itself. And yet they get along very well without each other. In sum, they *take off* from each other. They are two departures and two partitions: dissociable and inseparable. I will say re-quoting this passage "they take off from one another" that they each proceed from the other and at the same time separate from the other very well. They love each other, they separate from each other without ever separating. Among the things I most admire in Ponge, there is the *Pré*, there is the Sun. Obviously there are many other things…

Q.: Throughout history, the philosopher often comes to complement the poet: Hegel and Hölderlin, Jacques Derrida and Francis Ponge.

J.D.: I think your…

Q.: There are other examples: Heidegger and Trakl.

J.D.: … list… here, is impertinent… in so many regards.

Q.: There is nevertheless an indispensable rapprochement like that of the poet and the painter.

J.D.: In all the cases you cited, that of Hölderlin and Hegel and Trakl and Heidegger, the relations are very different. Hegel, it seems to me, does not take into account this latter relation between the philosopher and the poet. Heidegger does, obviously, and precisely in the texts on Trakl, in what he says about the *Dichter* and the *Denker*. He insists on the difference between the two, on the fact that the reading of the thinker cannot be substituted for the poetic reading of the poet. Only a poet can speak of a poet. Heidegger asserts this in a text on Trakl. Only a poet can speak properly of a poet. But what interests me here, what I would bring into proximity with Ponge, with what happens to us with Ponge, is that they have nothing in common, but they are divided along parallels (somewhere Heidegger says that the thinker and the poet are on parallels that cross at some point, they are parallels that cross so as to wound each other, make a certain cut or notch in each other); what they have in parallel, precisely, if not in common, is that for both of them (he does not say the philosopher but rather: the thinker and the poet), for both of them, their business is: the essence of (the) language. And of the French language, for the essence of (the) language is always inscribed in a unique language. Since language cannot be thought in general, we cannot separate the language in question and the French language. This thought is not a theoretical one, it is a poetic thought or a poetic explanation with the French language. And it is not just an unveiling of the French language; it is an *event*: something happens to the French language that reveals in it a power, powers, possibilities, in its lexicon, its syntax, its history, and so forth, and at the same time *does* something to it. I am thinking of the scene in "Le soleil placé en abyme" [The sun placed in abyss] in which something sexual happens, in which something happens to the body of language through the signature of the poet. To do [*Faire*] something to the language and in the name of the language: *faire l'amour, faire la vérité*, make love, make the truth.

Q.: Did the question hurt you?

J.D.: Pardon me? Hurt?

Q.: Yes. You spoke of impertinence.

J.D.: Oh! No, it was a clause... an expression of modesty. You put me in a list with Hegel, Heidegger... I was obliged to say: no. And also because I think: no.

Q.: What are you in relation to Ponge if Ponge is the poet-thinker?

J.D.: I don't know. These schemas, of the poet and the thinker in Heidegger, although they interest me a lot, can only be said one time and in German. It would have been necessary to add: behind Ponge's history there is not only phenomenology, there is also Heidegger, whom he talks about. So things get complicated, they accumulate, they get overdetermined. I don't know what I am... probably what I am trying to do in that text is to try to sign in my turn something right on Ponge's text and make him counter-sign my text. No doubt [laughter]... I am very dissatisfied... I am very worried about what I have just said. I will never be resigned to radio technology. One should never have to sign confessions under the torture of a microphone.

Passages—
from Traumatism to Promise

Q.: In your book on Paul Celan, *Schibboleth*, you say that it is the "indecision" of the limit between literature, poetry, and philosophy that "most provokes" the latter "to think." If philosophy "then finds itself in the vicinity [*les parages*] of the poetic" or of literature, it is because of what you call "the *philosophical experience*," namely, "a certain questioning traversal of limits, the insecurity as to the border of the philosophical field—and especially *the experience of (the) language*, always as poetic, or literary, as it is philosophical."[1] If philosophizing consists in always interrogating once again the insecurity of the limits of philosophy, could one then describe philosophy as "the accepted memory of an unchosen destination," as one later reads in this book?[2] However, for philosophy not to choose its own destination seems to make what is specifically philosophical disappear...

J.D.: Yes, the difficulty of the question or of this swarm of questions that you just set in motion, its difficulty, but also its necessity, has to do with the fact that the indecision as to the limit is not simply between literature and philosophy, poetry and philosophy. This indecision has to do with the very limit that separates for example literature from anything whatsoever or philosophy from anything whatsoever. The same text, the same phrase, can in different situations belong now to the literary field, now to what is called ordinary, everyday language. Consequently, it is not an internal reading of a phenomenon of language that allows one to assign it to this or that field. The same sentence, in different *pragmatic* conditions, given other conventions, may be a simple newspaper sentence here, and then a poetic fragment there, or philosophical example still elsewhere. This has to do with the fact that the determination of these fields is never decidable by an *internal* reading or an *internal* experience of (the) language, or rather linguistic utterances, but on the basis of a situation whose limits are themselves difficult to recognize and in any case very changeable. Hence the difficulty one always has in answering the question: What is literature? or: What is philosophy? These limits are not natural. Not that one has simply to trust the distinction between convention and nature, or to say consequently that, since everything is conventional, there is nothing intrinsically philosophical, or naturally literary. It is perhaps this conceptual criterion that one must interrogate at the moment one attempts to decide between literature, philosophy, and poetry. Now, if we come back to philosophy, literature, or poetry, you mentioned *parages*. Les *parages* means a vicinity; it is a metaphor that comes to us from nautical or maritime language; it names a vicinity at a distance that is difficult to measure: that which is neither near nor far. There is an attraction there, a kinship, a proximity but without the one reaching the other; and what determines here in some way the experience of *parages* you have mentioned, and what made you speak of experience in both cases, is precisely the word *experience*: philosophical experience, experience of language. Experience can be understood in different ways in philosophy and in literature. Experience obviously supposes a meeting, reception, perception, but in perhaps a stricter sense, it indicates the movement of traversing. To experience is to advance by navigating, to walk by traversing. And by traversing consequently a limit or a border. The experience of (the) language should be an experience common to poetry and to philosophy, to literature and to philosophy. In general, even though the philosopher makes wide appeals to experience, even though he interrogates experience or even though the concept of experience may be a problem for him, traditionally he does not thematize the experience of (the) language. That philosophy is written and written in an idiom, was for a long time disavowed by the philosopher, whether because he claimed to transcend his idiom in view of a sort of universal and transparent language, or whether because—and this amounts to the same thing—he considers the natural language in which he speaks to be an empirical accident and not an experience tied to the exercise of thought. But this disavowal is never assured, constant; it is, like every disavowal, caught up in contradiction. The philosopher has indeed to recognize that philosophy does not take place outside of a natural language. The so-called fundamental concepts of philosophy were tied to the history of certain languages, the Greek language, the German language, the Latin language; and there comes a moment in which one can no longer dissociate the concept from the word in some way. Sometimes this link between the concept and the word imports metaphors, tropes, rhetorical figures that, without being assimilable to the philosophical concept, continue nonetheless to haunt it, so that the philosophical critique may often consist in liberating oneself from the rhetorical figure...

Q.: and from the source...

J.D.: ... and from the source in a natural language. But whatever may be the complexity of the work effected by the philosopher in his language, whether he assumes the language, disavows it, or transforms it, the experience of thinking is also an affair of language; it cannot simply pretend that there is no language in play in the philosophical experience. At this point obviously it is sometimes difficult to discern between a philosophical text and a poetic or literary text. To prevent any misunderstanding, I believe that in clear contextual situations, not only you can but *you must* discern between a philosophical discourse, a poetic discourse, a literary discourse, and we have at our disposal, from this point of view, large critical resources, large criteriological apparatuses for distinguishing one from the other. *It is necessary* to do so as far as possible. And I will insist as much on this possibility as on this necessity. But there is perhaps a moment, and this is the difficulty, the one that interests me in particular, where discerning between two experiences becomes more risky; and once one realizes the fact that philosophy inherits a language or is inhabited by a language, the most lucid choice one can make, and the freest, is not to avoid this problem, but to write with this language, to push as far as they can go the philosophical experience *and* the poetic experience of the language.

Q.: In a same text? In the text that one is in the process of writing and working on?

J.D.: It is possible, I believe, only in determined historical situations. One can do it, one must do it. For example—and these are situations in which we often find ourselves and in which I have found myself more than once—when one wants to foreground this resource of (the) language in philosophy, or the fact that philosophy cannot traverse the linguistic element as if it were diaphanous or transparent, at that moment one must write in such a way that the addressee or reader becomes aware of the stakes of language in philosophy and inversely the stakes of thinking or philosophy— perhaps one will be able to distinguish between them—within a poetic discourse. Hence the necessity in fact of making cohabit in a same text or of grafting codes, motifs, registers, voices that are heterogeneous; naturally, one must not do it simply in order to do it or in order to force incompatible things into cohabitation or in order to create confusions—but do it while trying to articulate these different registers, to compose in some way the text so that the articulation of the heterogeneous voices among themselves both causes one to think and causes the language to think, or philosophy in the language.

Q.: So philosophy does not determine in advance its own destination? This would lead us to the second part of my question. For if it accepts to be traversed by different voices that do not belong only to its own domain or what it believes to be its domain, it can be carried off into very different regions. And I think that is what you have effected. This has won you many criticisms.

J.D.: Yes. The singularity of philosophy is that a domain is not given to it in advance. If there is philosophy, it is a mode of questioning or of research that does not let itself be closed up at the outset in a region of discourse or in a region of knowledge. Philosophy is not a science related to a domain of determined objects. Consequently, philosophy is always called upon to transgress the border of the regions of research or knowledge and to ask itself about its own limits, but also about its own destination. Philosophy does not know—from *this point of view* philosophy is a non-knowledge—what its destination is. That is why it can sometimes proceed a little blindly, but also with the greatest possible liberty, toward the encounter with other types of knowledge, discourse, writing. Philosophy is always in the process of displacing its limits. And at bottom, what is called philosophical discussion or exchange between philosophers—whether this exchange takes place in some sort of synchronic, contemporary fashion, in a kind of interview, or whether it takes place in the history of philosophy, when one philosopher responds to another, critiques, quotes, refutes another—it is always a discussion on the subject of these limits of philosophy. All philosophical discussions carry within them the question: What is philosophy? Where does it begin, where does it end? What is the limit? Even if the discussion seems to bear on a determined object, it suffices to pursue it a little to realize that it is the question of the limit of the philosophical that is, each time, in play.

Q.: The poems of Celan often inscribe in them the memory of a *date*. This date marks the poem as the incommunicable, irreducible uniqueness of an event, decipherable only by the witnesses, the initiated and *at the same time*, as a piece of information that is not indispensable for the readability of the poem. The date is thereby both essential and inessential. You go on to describe the date as a "notch" or an "incision that the poem carries in its body, like a memory, sometimes several memories in one, the mark of a source, of a place and a time. Incision or notch, which is as much as to say [...] that the poem there opens itself up [*s'y entame*]: it begins by wounding itself at its date."[3] You later say of the philosophical hermeneutics of the poem that it has "its effaced source" and in some way its condition of possibility in the date, in the singular event that is thereby marked. Is this to say that philosophical reflection also begins "by wounding itself at its date"?

J.D.: Yes, it begins at that rather singular wound that is the date, precisely. Singular wound because it has to do with singularity, this one and no other, with what happens to singularity. But before one gets to that, I will echo what you were saying about the source. A moment ago we were saying, in effect, that a philosophical discourse or discussion always bore in a certain way on the limit of the philosophical, on the border between what is philosophical and what is not. One can say the same thing about the source. Still today, but this is not new, we feel strongly the seriousness of the question of whether philosophy was born in Greece or not, whether it is European or not, whether one can speak of Chinese philosophy, whether one can speak of African philosophy, or whether the destination of philosophy is marked by a singular source, thus by a singular language or a network of singular languages. This question always has serious consequences. And in a certain way, it is philosophy itself. Which means that, at the same time, one feels led to reaffirm that *philosophia* has a Greek or Greco-European source with all the consequences that that entails, and without that necessarily limiting thereby its universality; or, inversely, since philosophy is the question about its own source, and bears the question of its own limit within itself, then at that moment there is not only no reason that precisely the non-European may not accede to philosophy but no reason that the non-European may not be the place of the philosophical question about philosophy. Well, the same logic of this latter fold or ambiguity in the question of the source, one finds it again in some way in the question of the date.

In the texts to which you were alluding, notably on Celan, I try to analyze the disturbing structure of a date and the mark of the wound, precisely, concerning the date. A date marks singularity:

this happened in this place, not only at such a moment but in such a place. In French one says "daté de," dated from, and that also means the place of origination. So the date is the mark of a singularity, of a temporal and spatial "this here." And it is with the date that one wants to keep the trace of this irreplaceable uniqueness. The fact that Celan often inscribes dates in his poems, not only at their borders but sometimes in the body of the poem, is obviously a very interesting thing; but it is interesting insofar as it re-marks what is produced, I would say, in every poem or in every experience, in particular the experience of language, namely, that the reference to the "this here" of the date is always marked in a certain way; the poetic comes along here to re-mark it, but it is already marked. Now, I said that the structure of this mark is paradoxical and wounding because a date is at once what is inscribed so as to preserve the uniqueness of the moment but what, by the same token, loses it. A date inscribes this singularity in a readability, that is, in reference to a calendar, to marks that are in any case repeatable, accessible to everyone. A date cannot be secret, can it? Once it is read, whether it makes reference to the calendar or not, it is immediately repeated and, consequently, in this iterability that makes it readable, it loses the singularity that it keeps. It loses what it wants to keep. It burns what it wants to save. Wherever it happens, the date is the experience of a wound, but this wound does not come about in some way after the experience. Given that all experience is the experience of a singularity and thus is the desire to keep this singularity as such, the "as such" of the singularity, that is, what permits one to keep it as what it is, this is what effaces it right away. And this wound or this pain of the effacing in memory itself, in the gathering-up of memory, is wounding, it is a pain reawakened in itself; the poetic in Paul Celan is also the thing of this pain.

Q.: This is very clear for the poems and for the experience of the poetic no doubt, but it seems to me that in most cases philosophical texts do everything to hide this initial wound, if I can put it like that, or to disavow it. In other words, I think that it is very rare that this wound, if there is a wound, is readable in a philosophical text. And among the rare examples, there are in my opinion the texts of Levinas, but would you say that all philosophical thinking begins by wounding itself precisely at a date? And what would this wound be? Can it be described for philosophical thinking?

J.D.: You are right in any case. The phenomenon confirms you are right if you say that philosophical discourse tends to efface its date more than poetic discourse would do. One would have to nuance things, however: the re-marking inscription, in some way, the one that makes the date explicit, is a rather rare thing even in poetry, is it not? But it is true that wanting to make of the inscription of the date a moment of the text itself, an essential moment of the text, is still more difficult in philosophy than elsewhere. The philosophical gesture consists precisely in trying to render itself universal and thus in considering the date where it is written to be an empirical accident that can be lost, that must be effaced, that even in any case must play no role within the philosophical demonstration. From this point of view, the philosophical as such resembles the effacement of the date. But as we said a moment ago, the effacement of the date is such a paradoxical thing and is so essential to the inscription of the date itself, is it not, that one cannot say of the effacement of the date that it is characteristic of this or to that. The date is always effaced. Even when it is inscribed, it is effaced. The philosophical, in its specificity, is a particular way of effacing the date, and of doing so deliberately. Even in the poems of Celan that mark a singular date, the poem becomes readable only to the extent that it carries off this date, that this date itself no longer signifies this or that date, that the poem is given in some way to any reader whatsoever who must appropriate the date at the point of also effacing it, in a certain way, in any case of effacing the absolute singularity within it. Because of this paradox in the structure of the date, what happens in philosophy also happens in poetry and vice versa. It doesn't happen in the same way. The regimes of dating or of the effacement of the date are not the same, but there is effacement even in a poem of Celan's that inscribes the date, and there are dates even in philosophical discourse. But it's just that they are not read, they are not produced in the same way. If we had the time, we would naturally have to distinguish among several types of philosophical discourses that, each time, have a different relation to the date. It is obvious that the texts of Nietzsche do not have the same relation to the date that the texts of Hegel do, the latter do not have the same relation to the date that the texts of Plato or Plato's letters do, or certain texts of Rousseau, and so forth. Each time, one would have to differentiate the inscription of autobiographical, historical singularity in the so-called philosophical text.

Q.: And do you think that there is a date, a traumatic incision, so to speak, that leads you to philosophize?

J.D.: Me?

Q.: For example...

J.D.: No, the question should be addressed in general, does a philosopher...

Q.: It is to be understood in a general fashion but, obviously, if you could say...

J.D.: By date, do you mean a singular moment or experience?

Q.: Yes, the singular experience of a wound, if I take up again the terms of *Schibboleth*, that sets off this process of philosophical reflection.

For example, the book *Otherwise than Being* by Levinas is dated in its own way.[4] It is dated without being dated explicitly, but it is dated by the inscription of its dedication, a dedication to the victims of National Socialism. This dedication takes the place of a date, it is a wound following which—it is doubtless very simplistic to describe it in these terms, but I do not think it is altogether false—this book was possible.

J.D.: Yes, a text is always destined; what later arrives at its destination is something else again, but in principle it is destined, and this destination can play the role of a dating. In this sense, once a text is addressed to someone, to some one or to several ones, it has, it carries a date in itself. But here I would distinguish among several wounds. To say, as we did a moment ago, that every date is wounding in some way, this is valid even for the dates of happy experiences, the experience of the gift, the experience of gratitude, the experience of joy. I can date a text or a letter, by rooting it in a happy experience or by destining it to someone or to some ones in a gesture that bears no reference to any misfortune: the date will not be any less wounding, perhaps at least just as wounding since it marks by effacing the date of a happy event, or of a gift, of gratitude, and so forth. The reference to the victims of National Socialism marks the date with a wound, yes, but also with another wound, a wound within the wound. Even if Levinas was referring to a blessed event, to a date of benediction, there would be wound. It's a matter of another wound, of a wound that comes to re-mark this date. As for knowing whether a book of philosophy or a discourse of philosophy dates itself by its destination or on the basis of a traumatism, I would say yes, necessarily, yes a priori, even if the thing is not remarked by the philosopher him- or herself, even if it is not underscored and published. As for this traumatism, it is not necessary for it to happen once or just once. When it is alive in some way, when it is not sclerotically enclosed in its mechanics, the philosophical discourse goes from jolt to jolt, from traumatism to traumatism. I would not want to give a too-pathetic turn to this response, but a philosophical discourse that would not be provoked or interrupted by the violence of an appeal from the other, from an experience that cannot be dominated, would not be a very questioning, very interesting philosophical discourse. That said, a discourse can also be destroyed by the traumatism. When the discourse *holds* in some way, it is at once because it has been opened up on the basis of some traumatizing event, by an upsetting question that doesn't let one rest, that no longer lets one sleep, and because it nevertheless resists the destruction begun by this traumatism.

Q.: Which is to say that it forgets...

J.D.: It has to "deal," so to speak, with the traumatism. At the same time discourse repeats it—when one repeats a traumatism, Freud teaches us, one is trying to get control of it—it repeats it as such, without letting itself be annihilated by the traumatism, while keeping speech "alive," without forgetting the traumatism totally and without letting itself be totally annihilated by it. It is between these two perils that the philosophical experience advances.

Q.: In this context, you write that philosophy must forget the very thing without which it would not exist. And it can remember this thing only by forgetting it. The effacement of the wound, of the date, their forgetting would be according to you the source, not to say the origin, for example of philosophy. But you yourself attempt an anamnesis of this forgetting. Must not philosophy be consumed in such an attempt at anamnesis?

J.D.: Yes, if there is anamnesis, it is not just a movement of memory to find again finally what has been forgotten, to restore finally an origin, a moment or a past that will have been present. One would naturally have to distinguish between several kinds of anamnesis. And every philosophy in history has been an interpretation of anamnesis. The Platonic discourse is essentially anabasis or anamnesis, that is, a going back toward the intelligible place of ideas. The conversion in speleology, the Platonic cave, is an anamnesis. The Hegelian discourse is an anamnesis. The Nietzschean genealogy is an anamnesis. Repetition in the Heideggerian style is an anamnesis. Today, to want to remember philosophy is already to enter into an interpretive memory of all that has happened to memory, of all that has happened to anamnesis, of all the anamnesiac temptations of philosophy. It is naturally a very complicated operation since these anamneses are enveloped in each other. But it is also an interminable operation—this is precisely one of the motifs of deconstruction, let us say to go quickly—for if there is anamnesis, it is because the memory in question is not turned toward the past, so to speak, it is not a memory that, at the end of a return across all the other anamneses, would finally reach an originary place of philosophy that would have been forgotten. The relation between forgetting and memory is much more disturbing. Memory is not just the opposite of forgetting. And therefore the anamnesis of the anamneses I just mentioned will never be able to lift an origin out of oblivion. That is not at all its movement. To think memory or to think anamnesis, here, is to think things as paradoxical as the memory of a past that has not been present, the memory of the future—the movement of memory as tied to the future and not only to the past, memory turned toward the promise, toward what is coming, what is arriving, what is happening tomorrow. Consequently, I would not feel, let's say, at ease in a philosophical experience that would simply consist in practicing anamnesis as remembering. It is not just a matter of remembering but also of something altogether other.

Q.: In "How to Avoid Speaking" you write: "There is necessarily some commitment or promise even before speech, in any case before a discursive event as such. . . . As soon as I open my mouth, I have already promised, or rather, earlier, the promise has seized the *I* that promises to speak to the other. . . . This promise is older than me."

I come back to Levinas because one finds in his work the same diachronic structure for responsibility. Levinas also sets out from the fact that Western philosophical discourse is incapable of saying this structure.

J.D.: I would be tempted to take a few preliminary precautions in order to speak of promises. First of all, at a level of immediate, phenomenal appearance, there are promises. There is a language of the promise *next* to other languages. In everyday life, I can from time to time make promises, and from time to time speak otherwise. I can say: I promise to do this or that, and then at another moment I can use a discourse that, evidently, is not that of the promise. There exists—and it's a very lively attempt today—a theory of speech acts which analyzes this performative character of promises. A promissory utterance is an utterance that describes nothing, that states nothing, but by means of which I do something while speaking. When I say: I promise to come tomorrow, I do not say simply: I will come tomorrow or it is true or likely that I will come tomorrow, which are theoretical utterances. Rather, I commit myself to coming tomorrow. This act of promising does something. This is the analysis of certain discursive events among others. Now, I believe one ought to be able to say that, beyond determined promises, all language acts entail a certain structure of the promise, even if they do something else at the same time. All language is addressed to the other in order to promise him or her to speak to him or her in some way. Even if I do it in order to threaten, to insult, to hold forth a scientific discourse, to do anything other than promise, there is in the simple fact that I am speaking to the other a kind of commitment to go to the end of my sentence, to continue, to affirm by making a commitment. This general structure is such that one cannot imagine a language that is not in a certain way caught up in the space of the promise. Before I even decide what I am going to say, I promise to speak to you, I respond to the promise to speak, I respond. I respond to you as soon as I speak and consequently I commit or pledge myself. This is what would lead me to say that precisely I do not master this language, because even if I wanted to do something other than promise, I would promise. I do not master it because it is older than me; language is there before me and, at the moment I commit myself in it, I say *yes to it and to you* in a certain manner. To say *yes* is also to promise, to promise moreover to confirm the *yes*. There is no *yes* that is not a promise to confirm itself. It is before me. As soon as I speak, I am in it. Whatever my discursive mastery may be, I submit at once to language and to the structure of the promise whereby language is addressed and, consequently, responds to the other. And it is there that I am responsible before even choosing my responsibility. From this point of view, responsibility is not the experience of something one chooses freely. Whether we will it or not, we are responsible. We respond to the other, we are responsible for the other, even before any kind of freedom—in the sense of mastery.

This responsibility—before freedom—is perhaps also what gives me my freedom.

Q.: I would like to talk about the paths followed by your writing. During an interview, you once said that you were trying in certain of your texts to produce a new type of writing: "the text produces a language of its own, in itself, which, while continuing to work through translation, emerges at a given moment as a *monster*, a monstrous mutation without tradition or normative precedent."[5] This was referring to *Glas*, but it could also refer to texts like *The Post Card*. There is no doubt that philosophical discourse does violence to language. Does the "monster" mean to indict this violence while augmenting it, would it even like to render it inoffensive? Elsewhere, you have recently said that we are all "powerless." Permit me to quote you again: "Deconstruction, from that point of view, is not a tool or technical device for mastering texts or mastering a situation or mastering anything; it's, on the contrary, the memory of some powerlessness . . . a way of reminding the other and reminding me, myself, of the limits of the power, of the mastery—there is some power in that."[6]

What is the relation between what you call the monsters of your writing and the memory of this absence of power?

J.D.: If there were monsters there, the fact that this writing is prey to monsters or to its own monsters would indicate by the same token powerlessness. One of the meanings of the monstrous is that it leaves us without power, that it is precisely too powerful or in any case too threatening for the powers-that-be. Notice I say: if there were monsters in this writing. But the notion of the monster is rather difficult to deal with, to get a hold on, to stabilize. A monster may be obviously a composite figure of heterogeneous organisms that are grafted onto each other. This graft, this hybridization, this composition that puts heterogeneous bodies together may be called a monster. This in fact happens in certain kinds of writing. At that moment, monstrosity may reveal or make one aware of what normality is. Faced with a monster, one may become aware of what the norm is and when this norm has a history—which is the case with discursive norms, philosophical norms, socio-cultural norms, they have a history—any appearance of monstrosity in this domain allows an analysis of the history of the norms. But to do that, one must conduct not only a theoretical analysis; one must produce what in fact looks like a discursive monster so that the analysis will be a *practical* effect, so that people will be forced to become aware of the history of normality. But a monster is not just that, it is not just this chimerical figure in some way that grafts one animal onto another, one living being onto another. A monster is always alive, let us not forget. Monsters are living beings. The monster is also that which appears for the first time and, consequently, is not yet recognized. A monster is a species for which we do not yet have a name, which does not mean that the species is abnormal, namely, the composition or hybridization of already known species. Simply, it *shows* itself [*elle se* montre]—that is what the word monster means—it shows itself in something that is not yet shown and that therefore looks like a hallucination, it strikes the eye, it frightens precisely because no anticipation had prepared one to identify this figure. One cannot say that things of this type happen here or there. I do not believe for example that this happens purely and simply in certain of my texts, as you said, or else it happens in many texts. The coming of the monster submits to the same law as the one we were talking about concerning the date. But as soon as one perceives a monster in a monster, one begins to domesticate it, one begins, because of the "as such"—it is a monster *as* monster—to compare it to the norms, to analyze it, consequently to master whatever could be terrifying in this figure of the monster. And the movement of accustoming oneself, but also of legitimation and, consequently, of normalization, has already begun. However monstrous events or texts may be, from the moment they enter into culture, the movement of acculturation, precisely, of domestication, of normalization has already begun. One begins to repeat the traumatism that is the perception of the monster. Rather than writing monstrous texts, I think that I have, more than once, used the word monster to describe the situation I am now talking about. I think that somewhere in *Of Grammatology* I said, or perhaps it's at the end of *Writing and Difference*, that the future is necessarily monstrous: the figure of the future, that is, that which can only be surprising, that for which we are not prepared, you see, is heralded by species of monsters. A future that would not be monstrous would not be a future; it would already be a predictable, calculable, and programmable tomorrow. All experience open to the future is prepared or prepares itself to welcome the monstrous *arrivant*,[7] to welcome it, that is, to accord hospitality to that which is absolutely foreign or strange, but also, one must add, to try to domesticate it, that is, to make it part of the household and have it assume the habits, to make us assume new habits. This is the movement of culture. Texts and discourses that provoke at the outset reactions of rejection, that are denounced precisely as anomalies or monstrosities are often texts that, before being in turn appropriated, assimilated, acculturated, transform the nature of the field of reception, transform the nature of social and cultural experience, historical experience. All of history has shown that each time an *event* has been produced, for example in philosophy or in poetry, it took the form of the unacceptable, or even of the intolerable, of the incomprehensible, that is, of a certain monstrosity.

Q.: The scriptor in *The Post Card* at one point writes to his addressee (or to one of his addressees) whom he loves that neither laughter nor song can be sent, "nor can tears." He continues: "At bottom I am only interested in what cannot be sent off, cannot be dispatched in any case."[8] Could one go further and say "what is not readable"? Would there be a relation with the tradition of victims in Walter Benjamin, whose history is not readable either in historiography? Are you engaged in this "obsessed meditation" on writing because not only can it, like letters and tears, *not arrive*, but also because it remains in a certain way unreadable? Do "monsters" demand the right to laugh, to sing, and to weep, but also the right of victims? Do they demand precisely what philosophy cannot demand in its conceptuality?

J.D.: That which the signatory in *The Post Card*—the one whom you call the scriptor—says interests him is what cannot be sent. And the examples chosen are laughter, song, tears. What do laughter, song, and tears have in common? What causes the scriptor to say that one cannot send them (as he also says of the child[9])? Perhaps precisely, to come back to what we were saying a moment ago, what links them to non-repeatable singularity. An organized discourse, one which is articulated (to sentences, for example), can be sent only to the extent that, already readable in the element of universality, it has a consistency and a translatability. When it is sent, whether the sending is postal or not, when it is addressed and it crosses, it changes, in some way, space and time, this permits it to remain up to a certain point what it is precisely because it is detached from the singular and unique moment of its apparition. Whereas laughter, song, and tears are detached with much more difficulty from the uniqueness of that particular moment. First of all, one cannot send tears through the mail, one cannot send a burst of laughter or a song. Song is linked precisely to something in the language that is not easily repeatable, is in any case less repeatable than prose, for example. What cannot be sent is in a certain way what cannot be repeated or at any rate is repeated with much more difficulty. And the signatory of the "Envois" in *The Post Card* says that at bottom he is interested only in what resists the postal mediation in some way, by what takes place only once, what is destined to a single person and what, he then adds in a French locution that is difficult to translate, "ne se dépêche pas."[10] For just like *given time*, what *takes* time and what is *taken by* time can never be sent. Time itself cannot be sent. The uniqueness of the moment is what one cannot explain to a third party, it cannot be put in an envelope, it cannot be sent very quickly ("expédier" in French also means to send very quickly). "Expédier" means to send through the mail, but also to throw together, to do something very quickly and in a calculable amount of time. Whereas neither the time of tears nor the time of laughter or song is calculable or repeatable. And by the same token, obviously, they are not readable. A tear is not readable, if by readability one means an intelligibility that can be transported elsewhere, just as a book becomes readable to the extent to which one can read it elsewhere several times. A sentence is readable once its identity is firmly enough established that one can translate it, transfer it, transport it. It is not as simple as all that because there is a certain readability of tears; but if in the absolutely unique moment of the song, the tears, or the laughter, there is already repetition, this repetition is much less obviously destructive of singularity than it is in a philosophical or journalistic or other kind of discourse. And this difference is a difference within a law of analogy, a law of likeness. Naturally, you are right to associate this category of the unreadable with the value of the victim. One of the meanings of what is called a victim (a victim of anything or anyone whatsoever) is precisely to be erased in its meaning as victim. The absolute victim is a victim who cannot even protest. One cannot even identify the victim *as* victim. He or she cannot even present himself or herself as such. He or she is totally excluded or covered over by language, annihilated by history, a victim one cannot identify. To meditate on writing, which is to say also on effacement—and the production of writing is also the production of a system of effacement, the trace is at once what inscribes and what effaces—is to meditate constantly on what renders unreadable or what is rendered unreadable. This unreadability arrives or happens, like the date, with the first inscription. But there is also the unreadability that stems from the violence of foreclosure, exclusion, all of history being a conflictual field of forces in which it is a matter of making unreadable, excluding, of positing by excluding, of imposing a dominant force by excluding, that is to say, not only by marginalizing, by setting aside the victims, but also by doing so in such a way that no trace remains of the victims, so that no one can testify to the fact that they are victims or so that they cannot even testify to it themselves. The meditation on writing is a meditation on this *absolute weakness*, the weakness of what you are calling the victim.

Q.: Hence the importance of the witness and cinders also in your texts.

J.D.: The absolute misfortune—and it is the misfortune of cinders—is that the witness disappears. Cinders is a destruction of memory, one in which the very sign of destruction is carried off. The name of the victim is effaced. It is also a matter of the paradox of the name, which is the same as the paradox of the date. The name is the appellation of a singularity but also, in the possibility of repeating this appellation, it is the effacement of that singularity. To name and to cause the name to disappear is not necessarily contradictory. Hence the extreme danger and the extreme difficulty there are in talking about the effacement of names. Sometimes the effacement of the name is the best safeguard, sometimes it is the worst "victimization." This double bind to which we are always coming back renders impossible a determined or determinable decision concerning which is better: very often to inscribe the name is to efface the bearer of the name. In this meditation on writing, one must constantly try to make the absolute destruction reappear, which does not necessarily mean to save it or resuscitate it. The name *is necessary* [*Il* faut *le nom*], love consists perhaps in *over-naming* [surnommer; also nicknaming].

Q.: You were saying that cinders testify to the disappearance of memory, even the disappearance of the witness. It is so to speak the trace of the forgetting of forgetting. But in bearing witness to that, you invoke, through your texts and however indirectly it may be, witnesses...

J.D.: As soon as one speaks of cinders, as soon as one writes on cinders, one begins or one continues to incinerate cinders themselves. For example, the text to which you are alluding, *Cinders* [*Feu la cendre*], is not only or first of all a meditation on cinders in general, the concept of cinders, with all that it consumes within it...

Q.: You would call it a concept?

J.D.: Precisely, it is also the memory and the reading of a very singular sentence, for it was unique: "il y a là cendre." This sentence in itself remains untranslatable. The fact that this book was translated into German or English does not mean that the sentence is translatable. "Il y a là cendre" is not translatable in the play in French of the *là* which in some way carries the whole text.[11] Even before translation, moreover, in the writing of the text itself, the singular little sentence may be encrypted; it may have taken place only once and have been meant only for someone in a singular situation; it is thus effaced. It is carried off, incinerated once again in the word itself. The sentence "il y a là cendre," which is part of a dedication, linked to a singular event, should not even have been repeated. But it is repeated in the text and, consequently, it is lost or causes to disappear the witnesses themselves once it becomes a sentence. And it is this incineration that was my concern in those texts which, at a given point, say that the figure or the motif of the cinder is finally more *correct* [juste] for speaking of the trace or the step, that is, of what at the same time inscribes the vestige and carries it off: there, right there where there is the cinder [*là, là même où il y a la cendre*].

Q.: But you would speak of a concept of cinders, you said the concept of cinders. Is it still a matter of a concept?

J.D.: There is a concept of cinders, that is not really debatable. One can analyze it. The cinder is that thing—the cinder is a thing—that remains after a material has burned, the cinders or ashes of a cigarette, of a cigar, of a human body, of a burned town. But from the moment this concept of cinders becomes the figure for everything that precisely loses its figure in incineration and thus in a certain disappearance of the support or of the body whose memory is kept by the cinders, at that moment cinders is no longer a determined concept. It is a trope that comes to take the place of everything that disappears without leaving an identifiable trace. The difference between the trace "cinder" and other traces is that the body of which cinders is the trace has totally disappeared, it has totally lost its contours, its form, its colors, its natural determination. Non-identifiable. And forgetting itself is forgotten. Everything is annihilated in the cinders. Cinders is the figure of that of which not even cinders remains in a certain way. There is nothing that remains of it.

Q.: But the readers of this text, for example *Cinders*, become, even if it is in spite of themselves, the witnesses of this disappearance, even if it is an absolute disappearance. And if there are witnesses of it, the disappearance cannot be absolutely absolute.

J.D.: They are strange witnesses because they are witnesses who do not know what they are witnessing. They keep a secret but without knowing anything about it. They witness an experience in the course of which someone says: "il y a là cendre," but they do not know what that means, finally, or who says it, cinders of what, and so forth. They are witnesses to something they are not witness to. And this situation is not exceptional.

We are witnesses of a secret, we are witnesses of something we cannot testify to, we attend the catastrophe of memory. One could precisely give great examples—collective, historical, political—of witnesses that cannot testify or who do not know what or whom they are witnessing. It is a situation that can take on disproportionate dimensions, immense and on the measureless measure of the most unbearable cataclysms, genocides, or murders, but also of the most trivial everydayness.

Q.: So you are also thinking of historical events of the twentieth century?

J.D.: Yes, this text alludes to them in an altogether direct way. The text names, for example, the crematoria or genocides by fire, but also all the genocides for which the genocide by fire is a figure, all the destructions whose victims are not even identifiable or countable.

Q.: In *Cinders*, several voices make themselves heard. This plurality of voices also characterizes other texts, such as *The Post Card*. Along with many others, there is a place in this text where the tears reminded me of two poets at least: "I no longer cry when you depart, I walk, I walk, on my head of course."[12] Here, Georg Büchner's Lenz, who "sometimes" regrets that he cannot walk on his head, appears in the wings; and then one thinks of Celan's commentary: "a man who walks on his head sees the sky below, as an abyss."[13]

J.D.: One can then follow several threads. There is first of all the plurality of voices as plurivocity—*Mehrdeutigkeit*. Already when a word has several meanings—and this plurality is irreducible—you can hear in it, or it lets you hear even if you don't take the initiative, several meanings and thus several voices. There are several voices already in the word. One can give this plurality of voices in the word itself its freedom, more or less freedom. There is another experience that consists in organizing a text in such a way that several voices take it over. There as well it is not necessarily a question of mastery. I have on occasion deliberately written several texts in several voices—this is the case with *The Truth in Painting*, *Cinders*, "At This Very Moment in This Work Here I Am," "Right of Inspection," and so forth—and each time I did it at a moment in which it was literally impossible for me to maintain a monologic discourse. Interlocution, the plurality of voices imposed itself in some way and I had to let it through. But in those texts I tried nonetheless to organize this multiplicity up to a certain point, to assign places, to distribute the interruptions, the resumptions of speech, and so forth. But there are yet other situations for the plurality of voices: There is that of explicit citation, where one turns speech over to a poet, where one lets the other speak in the text in more or less visible quotation marks, and there is finally— and it is the irreducible loss of mastery in writing—that situation where, without even knowing it, one repeats or lets the other speak. For example, in the sentence that you quoted, there was no explicit reference to Lenz or to Celan, but it happened that they spoke there without my even knowing it. That is also a manner of walking on one's head, of not knowing where one is going when one speaks. One is not sure of one's direction precisely because it is the other who is leading the march or the discourse. To walk on one's head means of course to look at the sky, but also to walk upside down, to do the opposite of what one thought one wanted to do. And to lose one's voice or let the other speak is always in a certain way to walk on one's head.

Q.: The plurality of voices causes to explode in your thought the unique Logos of the West. Thus is put to work what a text from 1986 asserts as follows: "The call of the other is the call to come, and that happens only in multiple voices."[14]

In one of the "Envois" in *The Post Card*, it is said: "You also showed me absolute horror, hatred, injustice, the worst concentration of evil—I was virgin, quite simply, even if I knew everything. Only the song remains, it is reborn each time, nothing can be done against it, and it is only it, within it, that I love. Never will any letter *ever* make it heard."[15] Not even philosophy and not even a writing like yours? Were you never tempted to write on the multiplicity of voices in music?

J.D.: Before trying to answer that question—but I don't know if I could—I will say this: as you know, I write several sorts of texts, sometimes alternatively, sometimes in a stratified fashion in the "same" sentence, so to speak. One of them is always regulated, normed by the philosophical experience as such. But I wonder if philosophy, which is also the birth of prose, has not meant the repression of music or song. Philosophy cannot, as such, let the song *resonate* in some way. Each time that a multiplicity of voices has imposed itself on me in such form that I tried to present it as such, that is, to distribute the voices in some way, to act *as if* I were distributing voices in my text, there were always women's voices or a woman's voice. For me, the first way to turn speech over, in a situation that is first of all mine, consists of recognizing by giving passage to a woman's voice or to women's voices that are *already there* in a certain way at the origin of speech or of my speech. There are women's voices. I do not write *about* these voices—you ask me if I am tempted to write about the multiplicity of voices in music—I never write about them. In a certain way, I try to let them take over—and keep—speech through me, without me, beyond the control that I could have over them. I let them, I try to let them speak. And this music, consequently, if there is any, I cannot say that I sign it. I do not write on it and when it arises, if it arises, I would say of it as I wrote, I think, elsewhere about the poem: a poem, I never sign it. The music of voices, if there is any, I do not sign it. I cannot precisely have it at my disposal or in my control. Music, if there is any and if it happens in the text, mine or that of others, if there is any music, first of all I listen to it. It is the experience itself of impossible appropriation. The most joyous and the most tragic.

Q.: So, let's listen.

J.D.: Let's listen.[16]

Two «Affairs»

Honoris Causa:
«This is *also* extremely funny»

Q.: The proposal by Cambridge University to award you an honorary degree provided the occasion for a controversy that attracted national, and indeed international, attention. Let's begin with the question of the role of the media themselves. The representation of this debate by newspapers and television (at least in Britain) was partly shaped by certain stereotypes of the "intellectual" and of the nature of intellectual work. How would you analyze the operation of these stereotypes?

J.D.: Can one speak of a debate when newspapers and television seem only to have offered a "representation," a stereotyped representation, as you yourself suggest? Did a debate actually take place somewhere, at a given moment, which would have been presented and then *represented* elsewhere, in the media? I doubt it. The "public," "publicity" in the form they assume in the media, seem to me to have been at the center, taking a full and not disinterested part in the said debate right from the beginning. And reciprocally, the legitimate "actors" in the academic debate, the lecturers or professors (some more or less completely than others, some sooner than others), behaved immediately as actor-journalists on the media scene. We come here then to one of the most serious problems of today, in my view, a problem which is at the same time intellectual, political, and ethical. It concerns the whole of society, but

399

particularly all those who like us, intellectuals, researchers, or teachers, retain some hope and want to take some responsibility for what I would call the "Enlightenment" of today and tomorrow (which must not without qualification be reduced or assimilated to the *Aufklärung*, the *Enlightenment*, the *Illuminismo*, or the *Lumières* of the eighteenth century).

The role of the media in their present form seems indeed to have been a determining one, at least with regard to the national and international dimensions given to the recent debates in Cambridge. This was predictable from the outset, particularly for the Vice-Chancellor's office. Informing me, not without embarrassment, that a non-placet[1] had been voiced (for the first time, so I was told, for thirty years), they warned me that there was likely to be quite a stir in the media, and that the Vice-Chancellor's office would do everything in its power not to go along with this. And, in fact, I wish to acknowledge this publicly, the office has been beyond reproach in this respect. As for myself, as you will have noticed, I took no part at all in the debate and made a strict point of having no contact with the press nor of making any public statement before the vote and as long as the discussion in Cambridge lasted, even when I could have considered the public declarations of certain of our colleagues, whether they were from Cambridge or not, English or not, not only as falsifying but as insulting and defamatory. Indeed, I was anxious to show respect, not just for the elementary norms of politeness, but for the rules of what was going to be an internal discussion within Cambridge (rules of democracy, academic freedom, absence of external pressure or of argument based on authority). But it must never be forgotten, and it's this that I want to insist upon: *the stereotypes you speak of do not have their origin in the media.* Most of the distorting, reductive, and ridiculous talk circulating in the newspapers, on the radio, or the television on this occasion was first shaped in the academic arena, through a sort of public opinion transmitted "on the inside," so to speak, of the university. It is true that this "interiority" has been radically transformed by the changing structure of the public space, as it is marked out by the modern media. But it is academics, *certain academics,* who are responsible for these stereotypes, and who then pass them on to journalists who are often just as unscrupulous and just as unqualified for reading difficult texts, just as careless about respecting and patiently reading through work that actually requires time, discipline, and patience, work that requires several readings, new types of reading, too, in a variety of different fields. From this point of view, in spite of all the respect I feel for the fact that there was a debate within Cambridge, I have to say that what I read, after June 11, of a text inviting to vote non-placet, seemed to me in its style (dogmatic, uncomprehending, ignorant, with no evidence of having read me, in every sentence a misreading or an untruth) comparable to the worst excesses of journalistic misrepresentation. And let me not be accused of denouncing errors of falsehood where I am supposed to have deprived myself of any right to such distinctions, as is so frivolously claimed. I have made this clear on several occasions, most recently in an afterword to *Limited Inc*, "Toward an Ethic of Discussion," and I can only refer those who contradict me to this text. They are not obliged to agree with me or to take my word for it, but are they not under an obligation, should they wish to object to or reject what I say here, to read a little, and if this proves difficult, to make the necessary expenditure of time and effort?

What certain academics should be warned against is the *temptation of the media*. What I mean by this is not the normal desire to address a wider public, because there can be in that desire an authentically democratic and legitimate political concern. On the contrary, I call *temptation of the media* the compulsion to misuse the privilege of public declaration in a social space that extends far beyond the normal circuits of intellectual discussion. Such misuse constitutes a *breach of confidence,* an *abuse of authority*—in a word, an *abuse of power*. The temptation of the media actually encourages academics to use the media as an easy and immediate way of obtaining a certain power of seduction, sometimes indeed just power alone. It encourages them to appear in the media simply for the sake of appearing, or to use their professorial authority for purposes which have as little to do with the norms of intellectual research as they have with political responsibility. This temptation of the media encourages these intellectuals to renounce the academic discipline normally required "inside" the university, and to try instead to exert pressure through the press and through public opinion, in order to acquire an influence or a semblance of authority that has no relation to their own work. This is an old problem (it was already a problem in Kant's time, as you know²) but it's getting worse today, when the public space is being transformed by new developments in the structure of the media. As a result, the relation between what is inside and what is outside the university isn't the same anymore. Our responsibility is to redefine rules, to invent others (for journalists as well as for academics), a huge and formidable task, I agree, and by definition an endless one. It is difficult to enter into this debate in any depth here: I am trying to do so elsewhere. But replying to you "live," as it were—and we are implicated here in one of those semi-mediatized situations we have been discussing, even if this review isn't part of the mass media (this is an interview, the space and time are limited, there is an obligation to simplify and so on)—to illustrate what I have been saying, I will restrict myself to *two examples*, selected from the dozens of such interventions, often of the most outrageous sort, made during the affair surrounding the honorary degree in Cambridge. I do this because it is impossible here to single out and to analyze in detail all of the distorting and malicious presentations of my work (or similar work, because were it merely a question of myself alone, none of this would have unfolded in such spectacular fashion), presentations by colleagues whose every sentence proves clearly that they either haven't read or haven't understood one line of the texts they wish to denounce. Likewise it is impossible to refute in a few words their accusations of nihilism, skepticism, or relativism. I have been trying, explicitly and tirelessly, to do this for thirty years (these questions, in particular the question of nihilism, are much more complex than these imperturbable censors seem to believe). Anyone who has read even a little of my work knows this, and it is easy to find out that far from seeking to undermine the university or research in any field, I actively militate for them in ways that, so far as I know, none of my detractors does. But let's leave this to one side, as we haven't the right conditions here for more precise references. Those who are interested will find all this in the book-shops or in the university library.

Here then are the two examples I promised. They are typical and I will use them to ask two questions.

1. First question. *Where is the fallacy?* (See the letter reproduced on pp. 419–21.) First example: for the first time in history, to my knowledge, there has been the spectacle of academics at universities other than Cambridge, not even in England, claiming to protect the institution, that of Cambridge, and of the university in general. They do this not by way of discussion and argument supported by reading and references, as one does in scholarly publications, but through the most powerful organs of the media, in a style reminis-cent of the slogan or manifesto, the denunciatory placard or elec-tion propaganda. Some twenty of them, from some ten countries, addressed a letter to a "great" newspaper, the *Times* (London, May 9, 1992), to intervene in a debate going on in a university of which not one of them is a member, and apropos of a distinction which was honorific. When and where has such an infringement of academic freedom ever been seen? And such violence directed through the media at a colleague who in this particular case hadn't asked for anything and was not a candidate for anything? What would have been said if the State or some other power had tried to bring external pressure to bear on those individuals entitled to vote in Cambridge, thus calling into question their ability to decide for themselves in intellectual matters? Suddenly, one felt as though one were dreaming: on the pretext of saving or immunizing Cambridge against evil, contagion, decadence, on the pretext of coming to the assistance of a university institution, an exemplary and prestigious one, we saw some twenty academics, their titles on show, trying to form a kind of international consortium and treating their Cam-bridge colleagues with contempt, offering them advice such as one would bestow on children or illiterates, pretending to enlighten them, as if they had not reached their intellectual age of consent, or had remained intellectually retarded. What can these people have felt threatened by to lose their self-control in this way?

This wasn't the only betrayal of the very principles this interna-

tional militia was claiming to defend. Just as serious a betrayal, for
example, was their "quotation" of phrases I have never written,
phrases fabricated from I cannot imagine what rumors. I challenge
anyone to find in my writings the expression "logical phallusies,"
by which the signatories of this document, in what is a serious and
dogmatic abuse of their authority in the press, try to discredit me.
Even if they should find these terms in somebody else's work,
nothing can be proved by citing a few words out of context. And
let's not go into the argument according to which the influence of a
philosophy on other disciplines or more generally outside the
profession is held to signify that it can't then be philosophy! Here
are intellectuals who are using the press to put about the idea that
philosophy should only influence professional philosophers and
should not be open to the judgment of scholars of other disciplines!
How many examples could one find of the contrary, to remind
them that philosophy, in its best tradition, has never allowed itself
to be put under house arrest within the limits of its own discipline,
to say nothing of the limits of its profession? Moreover would the
authors of this letter to the *Times* be so worried if the work they
denounce really had no influence on professional philosophers?
And how can they pretend to prove what they so calmly put
forward on this subject, and on the subject of French or international philosophy, in a letter of only a few lines which it is *ipso facto*
impossible to answer effectively (for it is the question of the "right
of reply" which is in fact at issue here, at the center of the debate on
the press[3])? And how can they say that what I write "defies comprehension" when they are denouncing its excessive influence and
end up by saying that they themselves have very well understood
that there is nothing to understand in my work except the false or
the trivial? The fact that this is *also* extremely funny doesn't detract
from the seriousness of the symptom. In the responses that are
called for here, and in spite of the discouragement that can on
occasion take over, we must stay sensitive both to the comedy and
to the seriousness, never give up either the laughter or the seriousness of intellectual and ethico-political responsibility. Each sentence of the letter[4] violates the very principles in whose name these

academics pretend to speak ("reason, truth, and scholarship"). This manifesto, the product of an anxious obscurantism, is thrust into the media arena in an attempt to consolidate a power which is perhaps under threat but which is still very strong within the university institution, as a simple analysis of the status, institutions, and respective careers of the signatories would confirm. Backed up by the strength of a paper like the *Times*, by its national and international distribution, this power is indeed formidable. Against it a discourse which is argued through, which is slow, difficult, rigorous, will have but little purchase. Unfortunately, there is little chance of its being heard by a wider public. Let us not forget that the "Cambridge affair" is part of a whole sequence of events which goes back at least twenty years and which is not an exclusively English concern. One lady signatory of this letter to the *Times*, which a French paper described as an attempted "theoretical lynching,"[5] had written from the United States ten years before to a minister of the French government protesting against what she interpreted as my appointment as Director of the International College of Philosophy, whereas I was in fact, in that case also, *elected (unanimously) by my colleagues.*[6]

2. Second example or symptom, and second question: *where is the poison?* This time it is not a journalist, nor even an English journalist, it is an academic, Sarah Richmond, who first says of my "ideas" that they are "poison for young people," which *then* becomes *Der Spiegel*'s title (*Gift für den Geist*, no. 16, 1992). What needs to be analyzed here is the alliance, surely not accidental, between two dogmatisms: on the one hand certain academics say whatever they like, with no proof and no discussion; on the other hand certain journalists in their turn misuse the formidable powers at their disposal (powers of precipitation, acceleration, reproduction, and diffusion, particular to the modern press) by placing them in the service of these academics and the forces they represent. The same weekly quotes Roger Scruton's accusation that my work is "pure nihilism." Nobody forces this professor at another great English university to read me, but since for several years now he has made numerous allusions of this type in the press, he should

at least begin to find out a little more about my work. If he thinks that it's in vain that I have been protesting for thirty years against nihilism, if he thinks that what I say, literally, quite explicitly, page after page, in favor of *a way of thinking which is affirmative and not nihilist* is not convincing, then let him discuss this using texts and quotations, let him take to argument and stop this throwing around of invective which it is impossible to respond to in the press. I will always judge such behavior as unworthy of the university which this professor, for instance, claims to represent and to wish to save. Nothing means that I am right, or that I should be believed merely because I say so, but let those who want to criticize take the trouble to do so, let them read, quote, demonstrate, and so on. Yet in one day we have publications like the *Times* or *Der Spiegel*, with an international circulation of millions, putting about what I consider to be lamentable and damaging pieces of nonsense. In an infinitely self-reproducing and self-imitating language the same phrases, the same clichés are repeated, translated and echo one other. The *Observer* only has to call me a "computer virus" for my photograph to appear a few days later (as always, the question of the modern media is the question of speed) in *Der Spiegel* with the title "*wie ein Computervirus.*" (There would be a lot to say about these questions of poison and of computer viruses, but this is not the place, and I am not going to encumber you further with references to what I have written on this subject, so let's leave it there.) These accusations, made by irresponsible academics and reproduced by journalists who can't have read, properly read, one line of my books—these accusations, as terrible as they are ridiculous, are always highly revealing. Most important, in one single day they reach so many more people than those who in fact read, patiently or laboriously, my own publications! This is the answer I gave to a journalist who was surprised that I found it difficult to improvise a response to what he was asking me to do, that is to define deconstruction "in a nutshell"! Luckily, naturally, we still have to make this kind of quantitative evaluation more complex. And we continue to hope, perhaps in vain, for a new Enlightenment, and that a small number of clear-minded readers may in the end count for more than millions of the other sort. All of this would be of only limited importance if it weren't so clearly symptomatic of the general situation concerning the relations between the media and intellectual research or academic life. Though it goes back a long way, the problem is taking on new forms today, and all those presently researching the history of university institutions in relation to the press and the public domain in what, with your permission, I will call a more or less "deconstructive" style, are attentive to these changes.[7] It is a question here not only of theoretical research but of praxis, of ethics, or of a deontology aimed at creating new kinds of contract. This doesn't mean such things as for example a signed charter of formal undertakings, but truly inventive research attempting to redefine in specific situations, each of them different, the co-responsibility which should link together intellectuals, scholars, researchers, students, and journalists. Since there are no norms pre-existing or independent of research, of intellectual questioning, of thinking in general, this co-responsibility needs to be reinvented every day and by each of us in particular.

Q.: Do there seem to you to be any significant differences between the nature and the extent of the media's interest in such matters in France and in Britain?

J.D.: There are interesting differences which would deserve analysis if there were the time or space, but they are secondary to the general structure I have just described, I think. Besides, journalists mostly gather information on this type of subject by reading other newspapers. Unfortunately that's the way they measure the importance of or give importance to the material they select, evaluate, or simply publish. In the present case, there are many indications that the French press started off by reacting to the English press. However, if some (and only some) of the French newspapers seemed to oppose the apparent signs of rejection coming from Cambridge, this wasn't in order to ask more crucial or searching questions about my work, "deconstruction," and so on (which were treated by the "popular" French press in more or less the same way, if not even worse, than by the press of other countries), but in order to take these signs of rejection, *wrongly in my view*, as a *simple example* illustrating a general rule (England's isolation, Cambridge's traditionalism, the ancestral hostility between Anglo-Saxon analytical philosophy and Continental philosophy and so on—in short, another demonstration of nationalism, which was sometimes answered on the French side by another nationalism, a little as if we were at the Olympic games, or a philosophical tennis tournament). It is true, and this changes things a little, that in one or two cases there are regular philosophical columns in the French newspapers, in general once a week, which are written by journalists who are also professional philosophers with posts in university institutions. But this regularity and monopoly, this institutional situation creates other problems, which I can't go into here.

Q.: Other differences aside, does the position of the university in the two societies seem to you a crucial part of this contrast, or do you agree with those who see an increasingly common pattern to the role and type of higher education and research in all "developed" societies?

J.D.: To answer this question seriously, one would have to analyze the symbolic position that Cambridge and Oxford occupy, and not only in England. There has never been an "affair" in the case of the honorary doctorates I have been given in past years by other universities outside Europe (Columbia, the New School for Social Research, Williams College), on the Continent (Louvain), or even in England (Essex). Cambridge continues then to play a very particular role for the university consciousness in the world, and this means that what was at stake wasn't merely localizable in Cambridge but also elsewhere (in Paris for example, if you will allow me another allusion, this time rather cryptic, to that letter in the *Times* which was, no doubt, as was said both in private and in the press, more Parisian in its inspiration and in its intended destination than a simple look at the list of signatories would suggest). This exemplary influence of Cambridge, deserved both by its history and by its academic merit, isn't necessarily an object of lament or concern, as long as this tradition does not become paralyzing (and we should never forget that in this case it was ultimately not paralyzing). Having said this, to answer your question, yes I believe the "common pattern" you are describing exists. It explains also to a large extent why the Cambridge affair created such a stir, and why what was at stake could immediately be identified as something common to all European systems of education and research, and more widely, to the so-called developed Western democracies.

Q.: Your work has, to put it mildly, always stimulated a great deal of controversy, but more than this, you have been attacked in exceptionally violent ways, and denounced as undermining the very nature of intellectual inquiry itself. How do you account for the ferocity and exaggeration of these attacks on your work?

J.D.: If it were only a question of "my" work, of the particular or isolated research of one individual, this wouldn't happen. Indeed, the violence of these denunciations derives from the fact that the work accused is part of a whole ongoing process. What is unfolding here, like the resistance it necessarily arouses, can't be limited to a personal "oeuvre," nor to a discipline, nor even to the academic institution. Nor in particular to a generation: it's often the active involvement of students and younger teachers which makes certain of our colleagues nervous to the point that they lose their sense of moderation and of the academic rules they invoke when they attack me and my work. If this work seems so threatening to them, this is because it isn't simply eccentric or strange, incomprehensible or exotic (which would allow them to dispose of it easily), but as I myself hope, and as they believe more than they admit, competent, rigorously argued, and carrying conviction in its re-examination of the fundamental norms and premises of a number of dominant discourses, the principles underlying many of their evaluations, the structures of academic institutions, and the research that goes on within them. What this kind of questioning does is modify the rules of the dominant discourse, it tries to politicize and democratize the university scene. If these blindly passionate and personal attacks are often concentrated on me alone (while sometimes maintaining that it isn't me but those who "follow" or "imitate" me who are being accused—an all too familiar pattern of argument), that's no doubt because "deconstructions" query or put into question a good many divisions and distinctions, for example the distinction between the pretended neutrality of philosophical discourse, on the one hand, and existential passions and drives on the other, between what is public and what is private, and so on. More and more I have tried to submit the singularity that is writing, signature, self-presentation, "autobiographical" engagement (which can also be ethical or political) to the most rigorous—and necessary—philosophical questioning. Not that I intend putting the subject (in the biographical sense) at the center or origin of philosophical discourse (indeed, I would normally be accused of doing the opposite), but I do try in each case to put these questions in their primary terms, to relate them with themes which no doubt must irritate or disturb certain colleagues who would prefer to repress them (for example questions of sexual difference and femininity, the "proper name," literature and psychoanalysis—but it would be necessary here to review so many other themes, scientific, technical, or political). All of this probably explains why my most resolute opponents believe that I am too visible, that I am a little too "personally" "alive," that my name echoes too much in the texts which they nevertheless claim to be inaccessible. In short, to answer your question about the "exceptional violence," the compulsive "ferocity," and the "exaggeration" of the "attacks," I would say that these critics organize and practice in my case a sort of obsessive personality cult which philosophers should know how to question and above all to moderate.

Q.: Your own academic background is in philosophy, and your work has involved a prolonged engagement with the Western metaphysical tradition. Yet, as you know, some of your critics have wished to deny that what you write can really be classified as "philosophy." Can you comment on the role of this kind of intellectual essentialism in general, and particularly on what seems to you at stake in promoting an exclusive definition of "philosophy"?

J.D.: Allow me to be even more brief, as I have replied too often before to this objection. The question of knowing what can be called "philosophy" has always been *the very question* of philosophy, its heart, its origin, its life-principle. Since this gesture, which is originally and constitutively a philosophical gesture, is both repeated and examined in everything I write, since my work would have no sense outside its explicit, recurrent, and systematic references to Plato, Aristotle, Descartes, Kant, Hegel, Nietzsche, Husserl, Heidegger, and several other authors (whether in the canon or not), references made over a period of thirty years, the motives of those who want to deny that my work is "philosophy" must be sought elsewhere. This is their problem, not mine. Most often, I think these inquisitors confuse philosophy with what they have been taught to *reproduce* in the tradition and style of a particular institution, within a more or less well protected—or rather, less and less well protected—social and professional environment. There's nothing new about this: each time a philosopher, ensconced in his or her philosophical niche, doesn't understand another philosopher, another philosophical language, other premises, other rules or other logical or rhetorical procedures, other discursive or pedagogical setups, each time s/he wants to attack them or remove their legitimacy, s/he simply says: this is no longer philosophy. That kind of behavior has always been rather facile, don't you think? The history of philosophy is full of such examples for those who are at all acquainted with it, and it is crucial to have some knowledge of this history. Among the many differences distinguishing my work from those who attack it, there is on my side a taking into account of the historical nature of philosophy, an attempt to be as well informed as possible of this historical dimension. I think that things are getting worse today because of the profound malaise in the profession (this is true for the humanities in general). In all of our so-called developed industrial societies, the teaching and doing of philosophy are being threatened by the State

and by a certain liberal logic of the marketplace (our activities in
the group GREPH and the International College of Philosophy are
a response to this tendency—I refer again to *Du droit à la philosophie* on these points). Paradoxically, many professional philosophers are becoming more defensive and protectionist than ever. In
every new questioning of philosophy (in areas where they cannot,
will not, or no longer wish to read), they see a threat to the
specificity of their discipline or their corporation. So they construct
a phantasm of specificity that they claim to be untouchable, and
they confuse the threats that come from the State or the marketplace with radical questionings which should, on the contrary,
ensure the life and survival of philosophy. Having said this, I would
up to a certain point, and after some essential caveats, be in
agreement with those who "deny that what [I] write can really be
classified as 'philosophy'." That's true: not all of what I write can be
completely "classified as 'philosophy'," and I have spent a good deal
of time and many pages explaining why, how, and for what reasons
that doesn't then mean "non-philosophical" and still less "anti-
philosophical," nor even simply foreign to philosophy. It is necessary to distinguish between several types of texts here. Some are, I
hope, recognizable as being philosophical in a very classical way;
others try to change the norms of philosophical discussion from
inside philosophy; still others bear philosophical traits without
being limited to that. The same goes for the variety of authors and
texts which interest me (there are among them a good number of
great authors from the canon, but there are also others; sometimes
authors who don't belong to the philosophical tradition at all
inspire me more, whether about philosophy, or about questions
bearing on philosophy). These differences do not always separate my
books from each other, sometimes they function within the same
book, and, in certain extreme cases, within the same paragraph. In
any case, whether I practice philosophy or ask questions bearing on
philosophy, on its paradoxical history and on its limits, I always
place myself in relation to philosophy. I will always find it hard
to understand how it can be said of a question *about philosophy* that
it is simply *non-philosophical*. What is more, I am always sur-

prised or amused when I see someone, in the name of a discipline, calmly *classifying* a discourse—for example as philosophical or non-philosophical. I recognize that this can be of use, but what use, and to whom? This introduces a whole set of questions.

Q.: In the United States, and to some extent in Britain, your work has had enormous impact upon literary studies. How far do you think your reputation in these two countries has been shaped by the particular tensions which now characterize the discipline of literary studies and the part it had historically played in the wider culture?

J.D.: In the last two centuries, literary studies, and more widely, the humanities, have played a determining role in the self-awareness of the "great" English and American universities. They consolidated exactly that which had given them their structure: national tradition, the works in the canon, the language, a certain social or ethnic hegemony, and so on. This situation is changing, as is all too clear. What is called "deconstruction" is concerned with (theoretically) and takes part in (practically) a profound historical transformation (technico-scientific, political, socio-economic, demographic) which affects the canons, our relation to language and to translation, the frontiers between literature, literary theory, philosophy, the "hard" sciences, psychoanalysis and politics and so on. Deconstruction therefore finds itself at the heart of what you call "tensions." It is a question of assuming these tensions, of "living" them as much as of "understanding" them. Those who fear and wish to deny the inescapable necessity of these transformations try to see in deconstruction the agent responsible for such changes, when in my eyes it is above all else a question of trying to understand them, of interpreting them, so as to respond to them in the most responsible fashion possible.

Q.: In the case of the Cambridge vote, it was noticeable that quite a few scientists (many of whom, it is probably reasonable to assume, had never read your work) felt that in opposing the award of the degree, they were in some way upholding the standards and procedures which constitute their disciplines. In speaking of philosophy and literary studies, we have raised the question of the cultural role of "disciplines," but do you think the question takes a different form with those who practice the natural sciences?

J.D.: If it were true, as you suggest, that these scientists wanted to protect their discipline against a threat coming from work that *they have not read*, what can one reply to this? I would be content here with a classical answer, the most faithful to what I respect the most in the university: it is better, and it is always more *scientific*, to read and to make a pronouncement on what has been read and understood. The most competent scientists and those most committed to research, inventors and discoverers, are in general, on the contrary, very sensitive to history and to processes which modify the frontiers and established norms of their own discipline, in this way prompting them to ask other questions, other types of question. I have never seen scientists reject in advance what seemed to come from other areas of research or inquiry, other disciplines, even if that encouraged them to modify their ground and to question the fundamental axioms of their discipline. I could quote here the numerous testimonies of scientists in the most diverse disciplines which flatly contradict what the scientists you mention are saying.

Q.: We have been speaking of the attitudes involved in the cultivation and defense of academic "disciplines." It is frequently said that those who practice one of the traditional humanities disciplines, such as philosophy or literature, ought to be able to write in a way that is accessible to the non-specialist reader. Do you agree?

J.D.: That's very difficult. Everything possible must be done to come close to such accessibility, but on several conditions:

1. *Never totally renounce* the demands proper to the discipline (whose complexity is never natural, nor definitively stabilized); "never totally renounce" basically supposes a degree of negotiation and a constant renegotiation of previous compromises, according to the situation, its urgency, and so on. What is essential here in my view is never to lose sight of the rigor of the discipline.

2. As a consequence, we should be aware that there is no imme-diate and perfect solution to this difficulty, which is a recurrent one. Hence the need to account for all kinds of social mediation: the press and publishing, which also have pedagogical respon-sibilities, education at school and outside school. This is why "deconstruction" also takes an active concern in pedagogical re-form, and why I am fighting, with others, for the extension of the teaching of philosophy in secondary schools and at the university.

3. It should not be believed that there is on one side the "special-ist reader" and on the other side the "non-specialist reader." These two categories are riddled with all sorts of internal differences, and in fact have no dependable identity. Some of those one would class as specialists, and sometimes as "important professors," remain incompetent, or from a certain moment become so, seriously incapable of reading certain texts in their "own" discipline (see above; this isn't just the case in philosophy, either). Conversely, "non-specialists" make up a highly differentiated set, constantly evolving and with whom one can attempt a whole range of media-tions, translations, and teaching strategies. Only *certain* journalists and *certain* teachers, again in alliance here, try to give credit to the idea that there are only *two* categories of reader, specialists and non-specialists, and thus only two languages (the difficult, which makes no concessions, and the easy, which is supposed to be immediately intelligible). No doubt we should begin by reworking this set of problems, by calling into question these self-interested and protec-tionist presuppositions. This is all very difficult, I agree.

Q.: It has often been alleged of your work (but not of your work alone) that it is intimately bound up with not only a French, but a distinctively Parisian, intellectual situation, and indeed that it loses its force and some of its intelligibility when removed from this context. There is obviously an implicit charge of parochialism here: how would you respond to this allegation?

J.D.: Here too it's difficult to respond in a few words. It is true that what I'm trying to do, especially back in the 1960s and principally in *Of Grammatology*, will be better understood if aspects of the French, and more narrowly, Parisian university and cultural scene are taken into account, for example, the hegemony of structuralism, of a certain Althusserian Marxism, of Lacanian psychoanalysis, of Blanchot, Lévi-Strauss, Foucault, Barthes, and so on. So you're right, it is better to take account of this French and even Parisian dimension, of all the signals and signs of complicity that can be found in a work like *Of Grammatology*. One never writes just anywhere, out of a context and without trying to aim at or privilege a certain readership, even if one can't and shouldn't limit oneself to this. That is true even for publications whose project is the most philosophical and the most universal. I can no more reject this French or Parisian reference than an English philosopher would dare claim, I think, that s/he owes nothing to the context of intellectual commerce at Oxbridge. Should I remind you, in addition, that I only ever write in French and that I attach great importance to this fact, as to all problems concerning idiom, natural and national language, traditions of thought, their filiations and genealogies? But here again, one must go further and point out that things are much more complicated. Because very quickly, and perhaps even from the beginning, this complicity with the "French" or "Parisian" context also meant conflict, opposition, rupture, estrangement, a certain uprootedness. Not only has the French "context" been less and less determining for me, but there have been more and more instances of antipathy, rejection, or misconception on the part of the French press and the French universities in relation to my work (this is no doubt something separate from the reaction in Cambridge and elsewhere, but not entirely unrelated to it: don't forget that though I was fortunate enough to be assistant lecturer at the Sorbonne, to teach for twenty years in the Ecole Normale Supérieure and now to be Directeur d'études in the Ecole des Hautes Etudes en Sciences Sociales, I have always been refused a university chair. I could give many similar examples to show how very complex, contradictory and—to use the language of the sixties—overdetermined the situation is here).

Because on the other hand, not only the "context," the destination, the reception of my work—and correlatively my own activities—have become internationalized, whether by translation or by teaching, but also the thinkers and writers who interest me are not, for the most part, French. This is all too obvious as concerns the canonical philosophers and their work, but it is also true for Kafka, Joyce, or Celan, for instance, about whom I have written articles or books.

Q.: Media-fed controversies have a short life, but eventually the historians arrive and treat them as symptomatic of larger developments they claim to trace. What significance do you think historians will in the future attribute to "the Derrida affair" at Cambridge in 1992?

J.D.: This little event is symptomatic of a number of things, so more than one type of approach would be needed. Some historians might adopt the classical interpretation of a renewed or displaced conflict between philosophical traditions which go back two or three centuries (English, empiricist, or analytical/Continental, French, or German). They might focus on the conflict between accepted models of the university institution and contemporary historical forces (Cambridge and England, Cambridge and the rest of the world). Other historians might look at the problem of professionalization and the different disciplines, or the relation between philosophy and its "others" (science and technology, literature, painting or drawing, and newer arts, like the cinema, which the authors of the letter to the *Times* seemed to find particularly disturbing). Others still might concentrate on the media (see above), the present evolution of the European community, with the prospect (threatening for some, welcomed by others), of the unification of the European or Western academic system, or on the series of very rare non-placet (most often "political" ones) in the history of Oxford and Cambridge. From this point of view, another historian (that makes a lot of work and a lot of people, doesn't it, but they are necessary and division of labor is necessary, when things are not simple) could emphasize the political dimension, in its most classical and coded form, and ask why, supposing that titles, qualifications, and "scholarship" were comparable—already a very problematic, even fictional hypothesis—why the nomination of an "extremist" doctor *honoris causa* (say a Marxist or a conservative, from the extreme revolutionary left or the extreme right) would not, probably, have aroused to much anger and disquiet. What does that mean for politics today? For my work? For "deconstruction"? One would also have to take account of the present situation of Cambridge in England, its relations with the other universities in the country and in the wider context of the Anglo-American university system (all big questions). A more philosophical historian would see in what has just happened the projection of a disarticulated and overcondensed figure (metaphor, metonymy, or synecdoche), amplified out of all proportion, onto a huge media screen (synoptic, synchronous, in "technicolor," with subtitles or dubbing), a figure representing a crucial philosophical moment. Not a moment of crisis, a critical moment, but (if I may) a moment of "deconstruction." At stake here are precisely those themes deconstructive work addresses, to begin with the theme of crisis or critique, but also—the list is unending—that of science, truth, literature, politics, sexual difference, the democracy to come, the Enlightenment of today and tomorrow. But another historian—or the same one—should insist on what in my eyes is an essential fact: unlike so many universities or European academic institutions (the French ones, for instance—here a ten-volume history at least would be necessary), Cambridge was able to organize a public debate, in full daylight, or almost. Cambridge didn't try to conceal the spectacle of conflict, nor the gestures of rejection or censorship which shook its august body, and finally at the end of a debate and a vote that were as democratic as could be, chose not to close its doors to what is coming. If we had the time and space, I would explain why Cambridge is for me always exemplary, in this respect at least, and needs no lessons, particularly not from the French academic institutions which serve, in the half-light, their inglorious and daily non-placet on so many foreign and French philosophers (thus I am glad to remain, *honoris causa*, a proud and grateful Doctor of the University of Cambridge). Again, other historians could quite as legitimately follow other threads, other causal chains, the analysis of which would be just as necessary. But in that case it would be a question of generalities, of *general conditions* for what I should prefer to call the "Cambridge affair." If there had been a "Derrida affair," and should its micro-history still deserve the attention of the historian of tomorrow, which I doubt, then to approach it one would need to pull on some tenuous and rather peculiar threads, to follow their trajectory through the chain of "general conditions" which I have just referred to. This is a task I do sometimes apply myself to (I have done so a little more intensely or thoughtfully these last few weeks, thanks to Cambridge) but about which it would not be fitting that I engage your attention any longer here.

TRANSLATED BY MARION HOBSON AND
CHRISTOPHER JOHNSON

Appendix

[From the *Times* (London), Saturday, May 9, 1992]

DERRIDA DEGREE A QUESTION OF HONOUR

From Professor Barry Smith and others

Sir, The University of Cambridge is to ballot on May 16 on whether M. Jacques Derrida should be allowed to go forward to receive an honorary degree. As philosophers and others who have taken a scholarly and professional interest in M. Derrida's remarkable career over the years, we believe that the following might throw some needed light on the public debate that has arisen over this issue.

M. Derrida describes himself as a philosopher, and his writings do indeed bear some of the marks of writings in that discipline. Their influence, however, has been to a striking degree almost entirely in fields outside philosophy—in departments of film studies, for example, or of French and English literature.

In the eyes of philosophers, and certainly among those working in leading departments of philosophy throughout the world, M. Derrida's work does not meet accepted standards of clarity and rigour.

We submit that, if the works of a physicist (say) were similarly taken to be of merit primarily by those working in other disciplines, this would in itself be sufficient grounds for casting doubt upon the idea that the physicist in question was a suitable candidate for an honorary degree.

M. Derrida's career had its roots in the heady days of the 1960s and his writings continue to reveal their origins in that period. Many of them seem to consist in no small part of elaborate jokes and the puns "logical phallusies" and the like, and M. Derrida seems to us to have come close to making a career out of what we regard as translating into the academic sphere tricks and gimmicks similar to those of the Dadaists or of the concrete poets.

Certainly he has shown considerable originality in this respect. But again, we submit, such originality does not lend credence to the idea that he is a suitable candidate for an honorary degree.

Many French philosophers see in M. Derrida only cause for silent embarrassment, his antics having contributed significantly to the widespread impression that contemporary French philosophy is little more than an object of ridicule.

M. Derrida's voluminous writings in our view stretch the normal forms of academic scholarship beyond recognition. Above all—as every reader can very easily establish for himself (and for this purpose any page will do)—his works employ a written style that defies comprehension.

Many have been willing to give M. Derrida the benefit of the doubt, insisting that language of such depth and difficulty of interpretation must hide deep and subtle thoughts indeed.

When the effort is made to penetrate it, however, it becomes clear, to us at least, that, where coherent assertions are being made at all, these are either false or trivial.

Academic status based on what seems to us to be little more than semi-intelligible attacks upon the values of reason, truth, and scholarship is not, we submit, sufficient grounds for the awarding of an honorary degree in a distinguished university.

Yours sincerely,

Barry Smith
(Editor, *The Monist*)

Hans Albert (University of Mannheim)
David Armstrong (Sydney)
Ruth Barcan Marcus (Yale)
Keith Campbell (Sydney)
Richard Glauser (Neuchâtel)
Rudolf Haller (Graz)
Massimo Mugnai (Florence)
Kevin Mulligan (Geneva)
Lorenzo Peña (Madrid)
Willard van Orman Quine (Harvard)
Wolfgang Röd (Innsbruck)
Edmund Ruggaldier (Innsbruck)
Karl Schuhmann (Utrecht)
Daniel Schulthess (Neuchâtel)
Peter Simons (Salzburg)
René Thom (Burs-sur-Yvette)
Dallas Willard (Los Angeles)
Jan Wolenski (Cracow)
Internationale Akademie für Philosophie,
Obergass 75, 9494 Schaan, Liechtenstein.
May 6.

The Work of Intellectuals and the Press

(The Bad Example: How the *New York Review of Books* and Company Do Business)

Q.: The interview "Heidegger, the Philosophers' Hell," originally published in 1987 in *Le Nouvel Observateur*, appeared very soon afterward in several other languages, as happens with almost everything you write. In this case, there was apparently the additional motive of the "newsworthiness" of the so-called Heidegger affair, precipitated by the publication of the book by Victor Farías. As you indicate quite clearly in your responses to Didier Eribon, however, there was almost nothing in Farías's book that constituted revelations for those who, like yourself, had for decades been coming to terms in their own writings with the implications of Heidegger's political engagements between 1933–1945 (and beyond).

The French text of "The Philosophers' Hell" has now been reprinted in *Points de suspension* (in its entirety, of course, and without emendation, like all the other interviews in the collection). On the occasion of the English translation of that collection, certain circumstances concerning this particular text need to be made explicit. For, like several other interviews included here, an English translation of "The Philosophers' Hell" has already appeared in a previous publication. It is usual in such cases not to retranslate a text for the purpose of its inclusion in another volume; instead, the translation as it first appeared is merely reprinted (after appropriate permissions are obtained). In the case of "The Philosophers' Hell," however, a new translation was commissioned and appears here. The principal reason is the poor quality of the first translation, a fact you were the first to point out but which anyone may verify. But that is not the sole reason, of course. If Richard Wolin undertook to translate "The Philosophers' Hell," it was in order to include that interview in the volume he himself was editing, *The Heidegger Controversy: A Critical Reader* (Columbia University Press, 1991). This book opened with an introduction by Wolin that sought to be an overview of all the essays collected but that, at least with respect to your interview, tends to repeat the sort of ill-informed or bad-faith understandings that "The Philosophers' Hell" had tried to dispel as concerns the ongoing interest in Heidegger and the effort to think critically about his adherence to Nazism.

Doubtless you resigned yourself long ago to this kind of "misinterpretation." Perhaps Wolin's reproduction of so many unexamined or uncritical assumptions would not have disturbed you unduly if it had not been for the combined circumstances of the very poor translation, but especially the fact that this translation had been published wholly without your knowledge, not to mention your permission. Given these circumstances, you were led to protest the publication of the translation to the publisher, Columbia University Press, and to request that the interview be withdrawn from any subsequent printing or edition of the book.

All of these circumstances have since been made public: first, in a revised edition of Wolin's edited book, published by MIT Press (after Columbia U.P. decided not to reprint the book in its original form), then in a lengthy *New York Review of Books* article by Thomas Sheehan. This was ostensibly a review of Wolin's book and another book on Heidegger, but at least a third of Sheehan's article was devoted to defending Wolin against your complaint and then to attacking you for ever making it in the first place. Finally, the whole "case" was discussed in a series of letters exchanged in the back pages of the *NYRB*, including two letters from you, a letter each from Eribon and Hélène Cixous, a collective letter protesting the procedures of both Wolin and Sheehan signed by twenty-four academics, and, of course, responses to all of the above by Sheehan and Wolin.

Now, no doubt some would be tempted to conclude that this whole "affair" (an "affair" about an "affair") had been sufficiently aired already. And in proposing that we do an interview about the circumstances of this retranslation, I did not intend to invite you to repeat what you have already written about it . . .

J.D.: Indeed, I would not like to repeat once again what I have already said in what is, it seems to me, a clear and public manner and on several occasions. That is why I propose we republish in an appendix the letters I wrote to the *NYRB* on this subject. Since, unlike Wolin, I respect the rule whereby one should not oneself publish anything but one's own texts and never publish those of others without their authorization, I must invite the reader himself or herself to refer, other than to these texts, to the set of texts and letters published by the *NYRB* on this subject, in particular to those of Wolin and Sheehan. I insist on this request: If the reader wishes to be thoroughly informed on this subject, he or she must not be content to read only me. What is more, I find Wolin and Sheehan, in the end, more eloquent than I am. I even believe that, in the eyes of a vigilant reader, they say more or less everything. Almost everything there is to know. They say it, they talk about it, whether they chose to or not.

Q.: But it seems to me that many aspects of the "case" may be more generally instructive about the conditions governing our ethical and critical disputes in the University and in the publishing outlets more or less annexed to it (for example, the *NYRB*). Elsewhere, and as regards another dispute (in which, perhaps not coincidentally, the *NYRB* also figures), you have considered the minimal conditions of what you call an "ethics of discussion" ("Toward an Ethics of Discussion," in *Limited Inc*). In what ways did this more recent dispute fall short, in your opinion, of meeting those minimal conditions?

J.D.: Like you, I think there is nothing fortuitous here. Nor is there anything surprising in the fact that the theater of these operations has once again been furnished and controlled by the *NYRB*. "Not coincidentally," you say correctly. Without going back over what followed on *Limited Inc* in the pages of the *NYRB*, one may always wonder if it is merely a coincidence that, two years before the facts you refer to, a certain Richard Wolin began his book with a sentence that may be compared to what in French is called the "générique" of a film [opening credits]. But perhaps this *incipit* also generously delivers a cast of characters, a rehearsal, a dress rehearsal [*une générale*], or a sneak preview. Wolin writes: "In his marvelously thorough *New York Review of Books* essay on 'Heidegger and the Nazis,' Thomas Sheehan concludes . . ." Everything is already in place, isn't it? All the characters, the programmatic script, the name of the producer, the tone and the score of the accompanying music. That was in 1991.

The *NYRB* is not satisfied merely with furnishing the underwriting capital for this theatrical production. Controlling the space of visibility, active in the wings, this singular magazine is at once the producer, the director, and the principal character of the play. It plays at being the omnipresent mediator. One could call it the hyphen [*trait d'union*] linking these contracts and alliances. I therefore take the journalistic moment of this episode to be the most significant symptom of what we are obliged to talk about once again. The task is all the more imperative today by reason of the (real or imaginary) power that is often granted to such a press. No one dares any longer to say anything against it. It is not enough to underscore that the things that count and endure are in fact happening elsewhere, most often very far out of sight and beyond the scope of such a magazine whose power is exaggerated; it is not enough to recall that this power is amplified by the very credit that people grant it out of weakness. It is more important to specify also that that power consists, paradoxically, in this imaginary and projective exaggeration. It is this credit, this imaginary capitalization and this occult power that must be analyzed and, again and again, criticized. For they put in danger everything that partisans of democracy, in their attachment to the freedom of the press, hold dear.

That is why, you are right, even though all these facts are

accessible for the most part in earlier publications, it is doubtless necessary to recall them. At least for those who did not follow or did not understand the painful, and sometimes comical, polemic into which Messrs. Sheehan and Wolin tried to drag me. To do this, they invested the columns of a magazine that cares little about its professional obligations and that had decided in advance to play their game, to take their side, and to let them have, apparently, the last word. When I say that they invested this magazine, one could also say just as correctly that they were invested by it. For if the behavior of the *NYRB* remains in my view very serious, if it constitutes what is no doubt the most disturbing thing about this "affair," it is because such a series of abuses of power, along with that of Richard Wolin and Thomas Sheehan, sets a disastrous example for all that concerns the ethics of discussion and the honesty of intellectual debates. These three accomplices, the magazine and the two academics, violated in a particularly indecent fashion the principles that should inspire exchanges between the academic or cultural world in general and the mass media.

Let us then review at least briefly this string of symptoms and try to overcome this effect of tedium or repulsion. I do so first of all out of duty, a duty that is at once ethico-political and intellectual, given the determinant place, the growing and, in many respects, new role of the media in the public space. However new it may be, this development is certainly familiar enough and there are many reasons for a democrat to rejoice in it. But its effects are terribly ambiguous; they deserve a new and vigilant analysis concerning the conditions in which the responsibility and freedom of each of us are involved in this development. What are these conditions and why do they produce "ambiguous" effects? Once again, it is not a matter of opposing the media of any kind and any size to academic research or publication. We are not dealing with a homogeneous milieu on either one side or the other. At times there are more differences (in the structure, the specialized themes, the chosen public, and so forth) between two newspapers with relatively large print runs than between one of them and some "scholarly" book or some journal that is considered academic if one takes into account its contributors, its funding, and the sociology of its public. And on both sides one may find, in my opinion, the worst and the best. Allow me to give an example. In many regards, the responsibilities in these two kinds of publications should be basically analogous; in any case, they should be compatible and complementary to the extent that they appear to share the same mission: the task is always *in principle* to *render an account* and to *render reason*. In both cases one should mark—in the *public* space and as rationally as possible—one's respect for the *principle of reason*. This should be done *in principle*, which is what implicitly at least both the academic and the journalist, *the one no less than the other*, promise to do there. Both of them *have a duty* to do so through research, questioning, inquiry that seeks the "true," analysis, presentation of what "is" or exposition of the "facts," historical narrative, discussion, evaluation, interpretation, and putting all these propositions together thanks to what is called language, communication, information, pedagogy, and so forth. I insist on these two motifs, *the public space* and the *principle of reason*, as I have often done.[1] The media and academia have the duty to respect, as their condition, the duty and the right on which they are founded, the principle of reason and the spirit of Enlightenment (*Lumières, Aufklärung, Illuminismo,* and so forth), which is to say among so many other things, their *public* destination, as Kant used to say, their belonging to the public sphere where one is required to give one's reasons, to justify one's discourse, to present an argument, and so on. This is quite obvious. And it implies the mutual respect of those who, on both sides, respect these principles. Without giving in to any rhetorical convention, I say that professional journalists who do everything they can to acquit themselves of this difficult task inspire in me an admiration and gratitude equal to that I feel for colleagues who do the same.

But having offered this reminder, I want to come to the point where this schema begins to get complicated, and complicated in an original way today. We are all familiar with the complaints of scholars and artists about the abuses of journalistic simplification that, in many fields, can have terrible political effects. These effects are on the scale of the demographic field covered by the media and by the almost *instantaneous* type of effect they produce. This complaint or this grievance sometimes motivates, but does not always justify, disdain or condescension toward journalistic language. Well, this is nothing new, as we too well know. What is new, however, and what bears no doubt like a threatening chance the mark of our time is the intersection of two phenomena that are apparently heterogeneous but doubtless profoundly linked:

(a) *on the one hand,* the extraordinary development of the media (first, in their speed; second, in the quantitative extension of their field of production and consumption; and third, in their structure, that is, in the type of inscription and intervention in the public space, in their relations with public debate—political or academic, for example—wherever the old borders are being crossed or displaced between the public and the private, the social and the individual, the communicable and the secret, etc., in the terms in which it was thought that these borders could be identified, in their relative stability, during the Enlightenment);

(b) *on the other hand,* the development of research, in the sciences as much as in the humanities, that also questions these certainties and axioms of Enlightenment. Not necessarily to criticize or contest them (that is even rarely the case), but in order to think them better and especially to translate and transform them better in the light of what should be the Enlightenment of our time, with its new scientific, technical, philosophical, ethical, juridical, political, and other demands. These kinds of research are by definition laborious, erudite, they seem often to go against the current, they pass by way of increasingly subtle languages, codes, modes of writing, which it is the mission of the university but also the media to teach and to learn. These difficult and refined research activities (of a scientific, philosophical, literary, or other type) thus make necessary questions on the subject of these very principles (the history and foundation of the principle of reason, the history and foundation of the value of truth, of the interpreted language as communication or as information, of the structure of public space, and so forth). Risky but indispensable, this work calls for transformations in the modes of writing and argumentation. It gives rise to texts that are more difficult to summarize, to translate, or to teach immediately in the larger public space and sometimes in the academic space itself. The shared obligation of the researcher and the journalist, or even of the professor who fulfills the role of journalist, is to make every effort to explain without betraying, to respect the principles laid out above even when he or she is reviewing the complicated and over-determined questions *on the subject of these very principles and their consequences.* And especially, especially when this task appears impossible or when it is too difficult to acquit oneself of fully within the imposed limits of space and time (which happens in newspapers as well as in the university), the duty, the categorical imperative, I would say, *as much for the academic as for the journalist, and for both of them when they are the same person,* is to mark *humbly and clearly* that things are still more complicated—and that the reader ought to be aware of that. One must tell readers that they are called upon to work, to read the text being discussed and not just the article that is devoted to it or substituted for it, to verify the information that is proposed to them and not to take at its word what they are being told about a text or a fact. One must teach the reader as well as the student that the difficulty of a discourse is not a sin—nor is it the effect of obscurantism or irrationalism. And that it is often the contrary that is true: obscurantism can invade a language of communication that is seemingly direct, simple, straightforward.

The conditions in which these shared responsibilities and missions are exercised remain different, notably as concerns the available time and space, especially as concerns the rhythm. The concept of rhythm is essential and irreducible here; it should be at the center of any consistent reflection about these subjects. Such a difference can only sharpen our reflection on deontological rules, norms, and principles. When we see journalists (or professors who improvise as journalists, thereby accumulating the powers and publics of both) abuse their power and cite, for example, the lack of

time or space to justify outrageous and thus distorting simplification, omission, non-reading, the refusal to render an account of
difficult texts, and so forth, we are within our rights to accuse them
of failing to uphold the principles of this deontology. Such behavior breaks the implicit social contract that founds the press and
publishing, the freedom of the press, the right to information, but
also the possibility of a *democratic* education, teaching, and academic research. Of course, we know that the absolute respect of
these rules is never guaranteed or is not always possible. Of course,
we know that what we are talking about here is something like an
infinite task or a regulating idea. But even when one cannot acquit
oneself of this task, it must always be possible to mark, here and
now, in a readable fashion, that one is conscious of this limit. It
must be possible to warn readers of it and caution them to be
vigilant. (I was greatly and pleasantly surprised when I read recently, in an English newspaper, an article signed by a university
professor who wrote concerning a certain text, which he was asked
to review or announce, that it was written to resist journalistic
simplification, and that this was a good sign, the sign of a position
that was probably correct and even politically wise: it was up to the
readers to go see for themselves and do the work. Bravo!)

I repeat that any reader who may still be interested in this can
consult all the documents already published.[2] So I will do no more
than recall several verifiable, obvious facts, including, among the
most massively obvious, those that seem to me to deserve still today
our attention and a more general reflection.

1. Let's begin with the so-called affair. Speaking of only the
journalistic sequence and staging, we can look first at the word
"affair" that both of us cite in quotation marks. By giving to this
incident the title of "affair" (and even of the "Derrida affair," a title
printed on the cover page of the magazine for visibly and vulgarly
commercial reasons, to make one believe, by associating my name
with it, that a new scandal with a political odor was going to be
inscribed in a series of other notorious "affairs"), the *NYRB* began
by taking sides and breaking unscrupulously with the elementary

rules of fairness and with journalistic ethics in general. Even if one presumes that there was some "affair," why would it be a "Derrida affair"? Why would it bear the name of the plaintiff and not the aggressors? Even if one presumes that there was some "affair," it was first of all, as I myself pointed out in one of my letters (March 25, 1993), the "Wolin/Sheehan affair." By feigning to quote mischievously from a letter of the attorney, Mme Weill-Macé, the magazine in fact indulged in a violent and derisory mystification. In doing that, it was following the example of Thomas Sheehan, who, as he too often does, will have once more given proof of his ignorance—of both French language and culture—even as he pretended to give everyone lessons on the subject with an imperturbable arrogance.[3] What in fact did the letter from the French lawyer do? Contrary to what Thomas Sheehan maintained for page after page, slipping constantly from insinuation to lie, the attorney never instituted the slightest action against anyone. No more than did I myself. She merely reiterated my rights and my intention to claim them *if, and only if, in the future*, a first violation were to be repeated *once again*: if Wolin republished my text in that translation and in a *future* edition *without my authorization*. And she thus did what many French attorneys do to indicate the reference to the file of a case in progress: she wrote "affaire Derrida" in the upper left corner of her letter. This did not have at all the unpleasant or denunciatory connotation that Sheehan-*NYRB* so vulgarly and dishonestly abused when they, from the outset, formed a common front against me. Simply by reading this title, everyone understood that the editors of the magazine had decided to *go on a campaign*, as one says, and to launch (a) *at any price* (b) *an offensive against me*.

(a) *At any price, in fact*: inventions, insinuations, lies, manipulations,[4] massive unbalance in the deadlines and the space accorded to the different parties, the last word always reserved for one of the parties in question, that is, as in so many other newspapers, alas, for the party that has the newspaper's preference, thus for the newspaper itself, for the owners, producers, and sellers of this powerful merchandise. Sheehan and Wolin always were given four to five

times more space than all their interlocutors, and they always had
the last word. And they would have had it *interminably*, which ends
up by discouraging those who might have wanted to add some
piece of information, to share their reflection, or to protest once
more against these maneuvers. The strategy of this obscene abuse
of power allies them to the point that it is no longer possible to
dissociate here Wolin, Sheehan, and the *NYRB*, to the point that
one must say from now on "Wolin-*NYRB*-Sheehan," even if, as I
also do, one maintains a more differentiated opinion concerning
the violence and impudence of each of them, the degree of incompetence or the style of invective of each. Depending on the moment, the issue, and the sentence, one of them is more or less
shocking than the other.

Moreover, there is what the readers do not know, what they
would never know if I did not say it here, but also what so many of
them will never know, in fact, the great majority of them if one
compares the number of potential readers of this book and the
number of readers of such a magazine. (Such a comparison is
decisive here, and well beyond this example, for it gives the measure of the disproportion and characterizes in part the nature of the
specific abuses of power that can be those of the media in general.)[5]
What the great majority of the readers of that magazine will never
know, then, because they will have read the magazine and not this
book, is, for example, the *NYRB*'s refusal to publish a (second) letter of protest from Didier Eribon, my partner in this interview. In
this letter, which was literally censored (the editor, Robert Silvers,
envisioned publishing only the part he judged to be appropriate),
Didier Eribon not only declared his complete solidarity with me,
from the beginning to the end of this debate, but he condemned, as
writer, philosopher, intellectual historian, and also as journalist
(journalist at *Le Nouvel Observateur*!), the professional behavior of
the *NYRB*. He also brought to bear legal arguments of the most
convincing sort, for those who may still have any doubts on this
subject, concerning the necessity to obtain in advance the agreement of an author for the publication and translation of his or her
text.[6] The editor of the *NYRB*, professing himself in a private letter

to be personally not in agreement with these arguments, decided then *arbitrarily* not to publish the letter, thereby indicating that he intended to publish only what he personally approved or what could serve his interest. Even in the case where the author of the letter protested legitimately against the accusation that the magazine (or one of its contributors) had unjustly launched against him!

Faced with the abuses of power that Wolin-*NYRB*-Sheehan have committed, faced with the violence of this asymmetry, which in the final analysis knows only the law of the marketplace, the various laws concerning the "right of response," in most Western democracies, are very insufficient. A magazine can censor more or less whatever it wants when it wants, it can refuse to publish responses, oversee their length and framing, control their date of publication, and so forth. There is here a terrible unilateralness in the occupation of public space by a form of speech that is, finally, private; this violent appropriation will always limit the concrete effectivity, the real functioning of that fundamental right that in principle links democracy to the freedom of the press.[7] This limit will never disappear, to be sure, but just because the task is infinite should not discourage us—quite the contrary—from working to see that this right is respected to an ever greater degree.

(b) *The offensive* launched by Wolin-*NYRB*-Sheehan was in fact unleashed against me only in order to get at my work and everything that can be associated with it, in an ideological campaign that began a long time ago. The archives of the magazine give eloquent testimony to this effect. Its defensive reactivity attempts not only to reduce to silence something threatening for the discourse, axioms, and practices of a publication of this type, something vaguely resembling "deconstruction," as Wolin and Sheehan imply in the mode of disavowal when, one after the other, both of them say they are not "enemies of deconstruction." This allegation is massively contradicted by both editions of Wolin's book, which is a blind and compulsive indictment against my work and against my reading of Heidegger. As for Sheehan, I cannot say anything on this point. I confess to being among those who know next to nothing about his work. No, the stakes that must here be associated with this name "deconstruction," but that go beyond it, are much broader. They concern thinking, research, teaching, the media, the ethical and political responsibilities assumed there, the *res publica*, and the democratic field—not only in this country and not only as a citizen of a nation-State. All the colleagues who wrote to the magazine to express their indignation in the face of the incredible behavior of Wolin-*NYRB*-Sheehan were sensitive to these serious stakes and to the necessity of resisting such a disturbing development. Whoever has some knowledge of the world of research, philosophy, literary theory, law, the theory of art and painting, history, and the epistemology of the social or political sciences, and so forth, knows that the twenty-four American signatories of this letter, not to speak of Hélène Cixous and Didier Eribon, form anything but a homogeneous group or a school. Most of them are known for being neither close to nor even in favor of something like "deconstruction." On occasion they have been opposed to one another in their work. Their agreement to denounce the Wolin-*NYRB*-Sheehan operation and all that it implies is therefore even more significant. It underscores the seriousness of the threats that, in common, they are worried about and that preoccupy so many intellectuals, regardless of their discipline and the direction of their work.

2. Richard Wolin, for whom apparently nothing is a secret and who is so quick to diagnose, has never missed a chance to rush forward with an extravagant hypothesis delivered in the tone of triumphant certainty: my primary motivation in this "affair" would stem, according to him, from the fact that I am embarrassed by this interview and would have preferred not to see it republished! Who did he dream was going to believe him when he spoke so blithely of "Derrida's reluctance to see the text more widely 'disseminated'"? Wolin also speaks of what he describes as being on my part "an act of self-criticism; that is, an attempt to mitigate and distance [myself] from a standpoint that [I myself] in retrospect [view] as problematic. . . ."[8] The first response to such gibberish is very simple: even before being found again *right here*, with the integral reprinting of the interview, this response was already available in all the

countries and in all the languages in which, *for years now*, I have
agreed to see the same text integrally republished and translated
each time I was asked for authorization to do so. Thus, to take up
Wolin's amusing and original word-play, this interview will have
been "disseminated" limitlessly throughout the whole world. With
my permission. What is more, as you have just pointed out, the
same interview was republished in French without the slightest
change in the collection of which the present book is the translation. It has thus always been and will from now on be even more
"disseminated."

What is the significance of these *multiple and always integral*
republications or translations of which Wolin has, or pretends to
have, no knowledge? It is not that I deem this interview to be
indisputable and non-perfectible. I never think any such thing
regarding any of my publications. But it signifies clearly that,
rightly or wrongly, I have never deemed it necessary either to
change or to dissimulate anything whatsoever of this interview, in
particular as regards its philosophico-political content.

3. I must insist on this again, since Wolin seems to have so much
trouble understanding something that is a little bit complicated but
that ought to go without saying for a professor or a scholar worthy
of those titles: By republishing it as is so many times, in so many
languages, I never claimed that this interview, which I have thus
countersigned and confirmed, ought to be spared any criticism.
Such a preposterous idea, which Wolin and Wolin alone will have
gotten into his head, has never occurred to me, either for this text
or for any other I have ever published. A published text is from the
outset offered up to discussion and it is even for this reason that
Wolin was able, in complete freedom, to criticize it or a part of it—
which would have been true even if I had not republished it so
often in so many countries; and, above all, he was able to do so
without having to republish it integrally himself, in his own book
and in *his* translation (more on this later). Where would we be if we
could discuss a text only by republishing it and translating it, well
or badly (more on this later), in our own books? Who would ever

have thought of blaming Wolin if he had said, even while quoting me at length: I read such and such an interview, I don't agree with it, here is why, here is what the interview says, I quote long passages from it, following the most commonly accepted rules and practices, and so forth? My indignation, therefore, had nothing to do with the fact that Wolin did not agree with me. That is, I assure you, a situation I tolerate very easily. In general, but particularly in this case. The very simple question was therefore the following, let us repeat: In order to express his disagreement, did Wolin need to, and above all did he have the right to, publish *all* of my text in *his* book without ever requesting the least authorization from me? And even without ever informing me of it? And this during the two years or more that was required for the preparation, editing, and publication of his book? And this, moreover, when we knew each other personally, so to speak, ever since a lecture I gave at his own university at which he was in attendance? In order to interpret or evaluate it, did he need, did he have the right, not only to republish my whole text without informing me or requesting my authorization, but also to translate it himself in an execrable version (more on this later), which is to say, in a version that I discovered on a trip to New York, not believing my own eyes, almost by chance, in a bookstore? This brings me to the next point.

4. What I have just recalled ought to suffice to ridicule one of the innumerable counter-truths (another word for lie) that Thomas Sheehan will have lavished on this "affair." Even though there is a comical side to this, these outrageous remarks did not, I confess, always make me laugh; they even sent chills up my spine (what would happen in effect if such people—or such newspapers—had *even more* power, if all this ended up in veritable monopolies?). But I did burst out laughing when I read, in Sheehan's hand, the following: "If Wolin had praised Derrida instead of criticizing him, Derrida would have let the book stand as it was, with or without permission from *Le Nouvel Observateur*, with or without translation errors." Really, does this man think that every time a book "criticizes" me or discusses my work, I am ready to

send a protest to its publisher or not to "let the book stand as it was"? Can you imagine the expense I would have to undertake to confront such a situation! I would need armies of lawyers on every continent. Thomas Sheehan doubtless has another way of managing his time and his work, but he cannot seriously imagine that I am prepared to riposte in such a way to whoever does not praise me or whoever criticizes me. When he has recourse to this grotesque argument, he makes me think of someone (surely not me) who, *a contrario*, would have contemplated putting forward the following hypothesis: "If Wolin, you see, had not, first of all, in his book praised so eloquently the article formerly published by Sheehan (precisely in the *NYRB*), the latter would not have gotten into the ring (once again the *NYRB*) to defend at any price Wolin's book, which begins, from its very first words, by praising Sheehan; he would not have done so in the same magazine where he, Sheehan, had earlier published a first article upon which Wolin lavished his praise; he would not, in his turn, in duly reciprocal fashion, have extolled the book that lavishes praise on him; he would not have gone so far as to guarantee Wolin's abilities as a translator, that is, so far as to deny the sad fact. In other words, one might continue, if Sheehan has taken Wolin's side, you see, if he even deemed it necessary to silence or minimize his disagreement with the latter's reading or interpretation,[9] it is because Wolin's book opens, on its very first page, in its very first line, with praise of Sheehan, and (as if by chance or as if to seal the tripartite pact) of a Sheehan who is the author of an article in the *NYRB*."

In other words, when Sheehan suspects me of having reacted as I did to Wolin only because the latter does not praise me, it's as if I were to suspect Sheehan of reacting as he did only because Wolin does praise him. I am sure he will vigorously reject such suspicion; as for me, I find it both unworthy and vulgar.

5. I come *almost* to the central nerve of the argumentation, namely, the issue of the translation. I say *almost* to the nerve, because in my view the principal nerve, in this case, is neither Wolin nor Sheehan nor their recognized incompetence. One would have

to follow the route of this nerve, the trajectory of this nerve (which is also, as one says in French, *le nerf de la guerre*) the whole length of the "*NYRB* symptom" and its mediatic equivalents in our modern democracies. Beyond this example, which is finally rather mediocre, and even well beyond the United States, it is also the relation of these media with work, and notably, in this case, the work of intellectuals, scholars, artists, and teachers. (Permit me to remark in passing that this is one of the major concerns and one of the tasks of the International Parliament of Writers, which has just been instituted.)[10]

This *almost* central problem, then, is that of translation. My interview was really very badly, much too badly translated. It is true, and I admit this willingly, that if the book had been more interesting and, above all, if the translation of my text had been, let's not say perfect, but acceptable, I might perhaps have let it go, "laissé courir" as one says in French. I might perhaps have let it go, at least to save my time and energy, despite my indignation in the face of the arrogance of an attitude that was as abusive and illegal as it was impolite. But there you are, the translation is one of the worst I have ever read. Before showing this, which it was impossible to do in the press (they would never have allotted me the necessary space because it is not in the style of the magazine to do so, but here is an essential aspect of our problem: the scholarly claims of newspapers that do not have the means to accommodate scholarship and do not want to acquire them), I quote Wolin's and Sheehan's blithe allegations on this subject so that we can confront them with the facts. One will thus be able to judge whether or not it is a matter here of just a "red herring," as Wolin so imprudently would like us to believe. The latter writes, in fact: "Finally, there is the matter of the translation, which I've always viewed as a red herring. I stand fully behind the rendering of the text" (*NYRB*, March 25, 1993). We will see in a moment what kind of "rendering of the text" Wolin has the unconscious temerity to "stand fully behind." And I don't know whom he thinks he can convince and what he claims to prove by alleging that, "Moreover, none of the other authors has raised objections akin to M. Derrida's, including

Pierre Bourdieu, whose text was also translated from the French." This proves nothing. I did not take the time to verify *as well* the other translations. What I was able to discover with consternation in the translation of my text was quite enough. As regards the other translations, I have only three hypotheses: (1) There are as many errors in the other translations and my friend Pierre Bourdieu did not notice them, for one reason or another; I won't mention it to him; (2) the other texts were easier to translate than mine, for one reason or another, in any case on certain points that would become apparent were one to read the original or your own fine translation for this book; (3) as the number and seriousness of the errors will show, Wolin did particularly *bad* work on my text, he went at it fiercely and doggedly [*il s'est acharné sur lui*], he hounded it and me, for one reason or another.

The nature of the errors, as we will see, demonstrates rather—and in any case—that Wolin has a very rudimentary knowledge of French in general (vocabulary, grammar, usage). If he's willing to do some more work, he would be well advised to undertake a basic course in this language before attempting to translate anything whatever. If, that is, he still had the courage, for this apprenticeship would take—and, as I will demonstrate, I am choosing my words carefully—years.

The same thing for Sheehan. Before his ignorance of French was so mercilessly made plain in his own translations, before the stinging letters that the magazine received on this subject, and even before the confession he had to resign himself to making, he also had the audacity to defend staunchly Wolin's translation (guilty only, according to him, of "three infelicities"). With the unshakable assurance that he characteristically displays in his evaluations as well as in his insults, Sheehan had in fact decreed, in no uncertain terms, that my judgment on this subject was quite simply "wrong": "Derrida calls Wolin's translation 'execrable.' He is wrong. Whatever infelicities there may be in the translation (there are three, at most, that are even worth talking about) could be easily corrected in a new printing."

Three "infelicities" worth talking about? Let us talk about these infelicities and count only those that are worth talking about. One will see that their quantity and seriousness, the massiveness of these mistakes excluded any partial fix. Nothing here could be "easily corrected." Here is the list of errors that I made after a first reading. I transcribe the letter that I sent on this subject to certain of those who, in conformity with the public offer I made in the *NYRB*, asked me for the complete file of correspondence concerning the "affair." One of these correspondents insisting as well that I include the list of Wolin's translation mistakes, I sent him the following summary, which I ask you to transcribe as such in an English translation. Forgive me for the length of this quotation; I am not the one responsible for it, and I have limited myself to only the most serious errors, such as they appear after a preliminary inventory. How much we all would have been spared if there had been only three "infelicities" as Sheehan so peremptorily stated (a little while before he had to concede publicly his own incompetence)! This statement was not only incredibly peremptory, it was also, as always, imprudent. For, you see, these people show not only an uncommon arrogance and ignorance; they are also very careless, and I find them terribly lacking in foresight. They think everything will be settled forever once they have gotten into print in the first newspaper that comes along. And that no matter how outrageous may be the things they say there, they will be taken at their word once it is "in the newspaper."

Here, as you requested, is a partial list of the errors found in the unauthorized translation of "The Philosophers' Hell" by Mr. Wolin. Since you tell me you are interested in all this, I presume you have access to the French text (*Le Nouvel Observateur*, November 6–12, 1987, reprinted without revision in *Points de suspension* [Paris: Galilée, 1991], pp. 193ff.), as well as to his translation in the first edition of Mr. Wolin's book (Columbia University Press, 1991).

In any case, the list of errors will be published when the translation of *Points de suspension* appears (forthcoming, Stanford University Press). It will include a new translation, this time authorized, of the interview in question.

I indicate only gross errors and pass over all the mistakes that have to do with tone, connotation, or some idiomatic nuance or another. The page numbers refer to Mr. Wolin's translation.

p. 265:

"The essence of the 'facts' " is a poor translation of "L'essentiel des 'faits' "; in what is called idiomatic French, which is clearly the French being spoken in this sentence of the interview, "l'essentiel" most certainly does not mean "the essence" but the major part, the most substantial of the facts. The same mistake is repeated on p. 266.

"Quant au dépouillement d'une certaine archive": totally omitted by the translator or displaced without undue scruple into "as for the availability of materials . . ."

"The most significant" has never meant "les plus solides"

"people have been discussing" has never meant "on discutera" (*future* tense with which I indicate, by emphasizing it, a still necessary task in the future and not a past discussion: "it is important that the discussion remain open," I add).

p. 266:

"the fundamental qualities of National Socialism" is something completely different from "un certain fonds proprement national-socialiste"

"qui certes lui appartiennent" is unrecognizable in "that are clearly appropriate to it"

"justement à comprendre": "justement" in idiomatic French (and obviously in this context for anyone who knows the language) does not have in this sentence the sense of "justly," as Mr. Wolin translates, but rather of "precisely"

"Depuis plus d'un demi-siècle, aucun philosophe rigoureux n'a pu faire l'économie d'une 'explication' avec Heidegger." Wolin has clearly understood nothing of this sentence. Once again, he disfigures it with a total and serious counter-sense: "For more than a half-century no rigorous philosopher has been able to present a simple interpretation of Heidegger's case." No one who knows a little French can read this translation without being startled. The French sentence means that no philosopher has been able to do without (avoid) an *explanation-with* (that is, a debate with) Heidegger—the German word *Auseinander-*

setzung, in its Heideggerian usage, is clearly behind this expression for whoever has some familiarity with the context. Alas . . .

p. 267:

"mais parce qu'elle n'a opposé au nazisme de fait, à sa fraction domi-nante, qu'un nazisme plus 'révolutionnaire' et plus pur!" gives rise once again to a very serious counter-sense: "because it is opposed to actual Nazism, to its dominant fraction, a Nazism that . . ." The "ne . . . que" construction is simply omitted, etc., etc.

"trajets" does not mean "circumstances"

"questions du propre" has almost nothing to do with "questions of what is mine," especially when one compares *propre* and *proche* (*prope* in Latin), as is the case here, and in all my texts. If he claims to want to discuss me, which is his right, does not Mr. Wolin have the obligation to read me a little?

The whole sentence that immediately follows remains uncompre-hended and gives rise to a monstrous construction. There where I speak of "la question du point de départ de *Sein und Zeit*" ("les questions du propre, du proche et de la patrie [*Heimat*], du point de départ de *Sein und Zeit*, de la technique et de la science, de l'animalité ou de la différence sexuelle . . ."), anyone who reads French correctly and knows a little what is being talked about understands quite well that I am speaking (as I have in numerous texts) of the question of the point of departure *of the* book *Sein und Zeit*, *in* the book *Sein und Zeit*, and then also of the question of technology, and then also of the question of science, and then also of the question of animality, etc. Nothing to do with "beginning with *Being and Time*, with technology, etc."

p. 269:

"occurs" cannot translate "se mettre en scène"

"the routes that refuse the simple hiatus" cannot translate "les traits qui interdisent la coupure"

"various analogous diagnoses are often proposed" is very inadequate to translate "On propose des diagnostics souvent analogues": "souvent" modifies, in fact, "analogues" and not "propose"

"always swells up and arises" seriously deforms "s'enfl*ait* alors et s'él*ève* toujours" (these mistakes of tense miss or erase the very thing I am insisting on: that that which swelled up in Heidegger's time *arises once again today!*)

"partages" means also border lines and not only "shared perspectives"

"loi commune" does not mean "law of commonality"

p. 270:

"si possible sans limite" is very badly rendered by this punctuation: "of exhibiting, if possible, without limit"

"dans des schémas bien connus et somme toute rassurants" is translated in an absolutely monstrous fashion by "according to well known schemes and a completely reassuring unity"

"Tirons la conclusion suivante—et l'échelle" gives rise to the translation that is at once the most aberrant and the most comical of the whole piece ("Let's draw the following conclusion and balance"!). The French is playing on the idiomatic expressions: "tirer une conclusion" and "tirer l'échelle," the latter having absolutely nothing to do with "balance."

"effet d'évidence" obviously does not mean "evidential status" (a mistake reproduced three times)

p. 271:

"discourse about method" is not the surest translation for "discours sur le concept de méthode"

"si on ne la leur pose pas" is quite simply omitted

"in each case" is not the best translation of "à chaque livre"

"justifiably," despite appearances (it is what is called a "false friend"), does not correspond to "justement," which, here, means more precisely "precisely."

"is" is not the best translation for "était" [in Eribon's question: "Votre livre sur Joyce était tout de même un peu déroutant."]

p. 272:

"chance" (in "si la chance vient") has the sense of "luck" and not of "opportunity"

"ton" should be translated by "tone" and not by "sound" (three times)

"Undoubtedly" (another "false friend") renders very badly the expression "sans doute" in "je ne suis sans doute ni l'un ni l'autre." "No doubt" would undoubtedly be more appropriate.

"but for the field in which I work" is a pure aberration. My text does not say "mais" but "ou": ". . . pour moi ou dans le champ où je travaille"

"il faut le dire" does not have the meaning of "one must confess," but of, for example, "it should be noted"

"activization" is a pure counter-sense for "potentialisation," which, on the contrary, means the fact of *not* activating or actualizing, but of accumulating potentialities.

p. 273:

"en reste malaisée" means "remains difficult" and not "remains ill at ease"

P.S. Another matter of translation, by the way. Since your interest in all the stakes of translation is linked to Mr. Sheehan's several interventions in the *NYRB*, I call your attention to a symptomatic detail, if one can put it that way. Mr. Sheehan offers guarantees on several occasions for Mr. Wolin's translation, which, according to him, contains only "three mistakes, at most, that are even worth talking about" (last issue of the *NYRB*) and he even wants to give lessons to the translators of some of my books. Now, one has to know even less French than Mr. Wolin to translate, as Mr. Sheehan does, "je poursuivrai mes recherches sur l'aspect juridique de la chose et ne manquerai pas de lui donner les suites les plus appropriées" by "I shall pursue my investigations into the juridical aspect of the case and shall not fail to make Wolin pay the most fitting consequences." Believing (if one accepts the hypothesis of serious *incompetence*) and/or wanting to make others believe (if one accepts the hypothesis of a dishonest *manipulation*) that "lui" referred to a person and not to the "juridical aspect of the case," as anyone who knows a little French understands it, Mr. Sheehan added, but only in a note, after "lui": "[i.e. Wolin]" (incompetence) and without further ado he inscribed "Wolin," as if it were in my text, within his translation (manipulation). All of this can do without any further commentary.

Q.: Your list of errors may itself have erred on the side of generosity to Wolin's translation. A number of other mistakes, some quite as serious as those you have already noted, could be added.[11]

J.D.: Yes, well, let us leave this subject. I'll return now, in conclusion, to what remains in my view the nerve, not to say the brain of this detestable and ridiculous scenario.

6. It is the press, *this* particular press, which occupies a privileged place on the borders of politics and culture, literature, scholarly or academic research in general, this press that evaluates, judges, concludes, rewards, condemns with a power of distribution most often incomparably greater than that of scholarly or academic publications (which, as you know, are undergoing economic difficulties and crisis today), often also greater than many works of art. Whatever one may think of this or that organ of the press, of this or that professional or occasional journalist (and in the press we are talking about, these journalists are often professors whose motivations, talents, tastes, preferences, and competence deserve a very detailed analysis), one must beware any hasty generalization: There are newspapers and journalists—whether professional or not—who set an admirable example of competence and integrity which is not, alas, always followed. In many countries, in an individual or collective fashion, journalists who are justly concerned with their rights, as we are as well, as all democrats must be, but who are also conscious of their duties and their responsibilities, are in ever greater numbers thinking in a systematic manner about the stakes we are talking about. We ought to work with them to analyze and, if possible, combat that which, in the course of an accelerated transformation of the marketplace, of teletechnologies, of the speed of distribution, and so forth, can corrupt from within the very principle of freedom of the press and of opinion that ought to be served by these kinds of progress. The constant paradox is that the threat accompanies the chance and the principle of corruptibility is at the heart of the progress and the perfectibility. One must avoid above all what might limit in any way whatsoever the freedom of the press. On the contrary, it is in the name of that freedom that I am speaking here and that I protest against the appropriations and monopolizations that threaten both democracy in general and public discussion. In the example that concerns us here, notice the sequence *in three stages*. (1) *Prologue*: a professor (W) publishes *without authorization*, in an appalling translation, the text of another professor (D) whom he did not even consult or inform on this subject, a gesture that everyone deems to be a

serious fault in the university and in the world of publishing. (2) *First scene*: The journalistic stage now begins, in the course of which a newspaper alone takes the initiative of a polemic, opens it, installs it, decides what its time and space will be, and above all keeps the last word. This newspaper (the *NYRB*) will have had the first and last word simply because it deemed it interesting (that is, in its interest) to publish the text of a third professor (S), a more or less regular contributor to the newspaper, who vehemently takes the side of the first (W, the same W who had judged S's previous article in the *NYRB* to be "marvelous") and, piling on rude invective against D, decrees, moreover, without proof (which is not surprising), that W's translation is virtually above reproach. (3) *Last scene*: Everything, therefore, that is visible on the stage draws its visibility only from the newspaper in which, since this newspaper is anything but scholarly and academic, it will never be possible for the plaintiff (D) to respond to S and to demonstrate *all* of W's errors, at least the translation errors, which are far too numerous and cannot be analyzed in a publication of this sort. In vain D will have pointed out the wrongs, the lies, and the abuses of W and S, supported in this by proof and by the approval of numerous colleagues, the three accomplices—the newspaper, W, and S—will reserve almost all the space and the last word for themselves. The conclusion—at least the conclusion that, in the immediate, reaches the greatest number of readers—remains therefore the one that the newspaper will have decided, for its own reasons, to stage. In a space of great visibility that remains its private property.

Q.: Do you see or can you imagine some remedy for such abuses, whose possibility remains perhaps even greater on the American scene, where there is not, as in France, the same journalistic tradition established and more or less regulated of a "droit de réponse," as you yourself have noted in *The Other Heading*?[12]

J.D.: We are here in a sensitive and dangerous zone of our political life and of the democratic space that we all hold dear. All the more so in that it cannot be a question, setting aside certain exceptions, of fighting these abuses of power through proliferating legislation, corporative rules, or some kind of constraint. The remedy, as we know too well, would be worse than the disease.

Let us say that for the ethico-philosophical rules, more precisely for the demand for justice that ought to guide us here, there are no legal rules, there are only examples. Good examples must be given that call for a law that is more just. I do not even know (let's leave this for another occasion) whether I would invoke here reflective judgment in the Kantian sense. I don't think so. But my conviction, and you will not be surprised to hear me say this, is that the example given by the *NYRB* and its two professors in my view accumulates all the defects. It is the worst example: incompetence lends a hand there to iniquity. If one were to yield to optimism, one might think that the law of the marketplace must remain the sole and the best judge: readers evaluate, judge, decide, like, or do not like, buy or do not buy, for example, a newspaper that, by continuing to give bad examples, gets a bad reputation. And as far as I can tell, because I hear it said in all quarters, the reputation of the *NYRB*, which does not emerge enhanced from this affair, has gotten in fact worse and worse in many intellectual circles, in the United States and in Europe. But we must, unfortunately, moderate this optimism and take into account the principle of internal corruptibility—I mentioned it a moment ago—which links the freedom of the press to the development of the free market. For the law of the marketplace does not provide this wise regulation. Newspapers that set the worst examples and whose reputation continues to get worse in intellectual, academic, analytical circles—for example, newspapers that feed and feed off of "affairs"—are also those that *do business* [font des affaires]. They are the ones that sell best.

In the final analysis, the good examples are and must of course remain, I repeat, singular in each case, without *determinant* rule, left to what will always be each person's responsibility according to the different contexts. And yet, I believe that a culture and a pedagogy can help to prepare them. For that, one needs a critical discipline of reflection, observation, and analysis. In the university, at least to my knowledge, there is not enough scholarly work (of a socio-historical, politological, and philosophical nature) on the press. Notably on the press that claims in part to reflect or evaluate academic work. The *NYRB* would be, in this regard, an interesting object of study. One would have to retrace the life of this publication over a long period, in its social, political, and ideological history, in its belonging to a certain New York intellectual milieu at a certain moment, in its mechanisms and places of decision, in its economic structure, in its distribution, in the configuration of its collaborators—both regular and other, both academic and non-academic. And if they are professors, one ought to know their sociology, their professional inscription, their desire and ambition: what are their choices and motivations in the ideological, political, theoretical, philosophical debates within and outside the United States, etc., what is their real competence, how were they recruited and treated by the management of the newspaper, what are they able to and what are they unable to understand, what do they know, no longer know, or not yet know how to read, what do they defend and why, to what threats are they reacting, both they and their newspapers, from what and from whom are they protecting themselves, what systems of alliance do they form to this end, whether consciously or not, etc.

If these avenues of research must be developed, in my opinion, it is not only so as to aid journalists (by reminding them on occasion, for example, that their decisions, their culture, and their competence are eminently *evaluable* and evaluated as much as they are evaluating, and if they think they occupy a panoptic observation post from which they imagine themselves speaking of everything to "everybody," they are also seen seeing and they are heard speaking, in other words, they are judged even if most often they don't realize it at all, do not want to realize it or let others realize it); it is also because, far from wishing to withdraw scholarly work from the public space of the written or audio-visual press, we have already considerably entered into a period in which one must, *on the contrary, open and increase the number of passages* between them. With the help of informed, cultivated, vigilant journalists of integrity. One must neither allow the world of research and invention (whether it is academic or not) to withdraw into itself, because the phenomena of appropriation, dogmatism, ignorance, misapprehension, and censoring are just as frequent and just as threatening there, making the alliance with the press I am denouncing all the easier and in truth supplying it with its weapons; nor, inversely or by the same token, must one allow any press whatsoever, once it has acquired great economic or social power, the right to exercise without an opposing counterpart the authoritarian pressure of its incompetent and massively distributed evaluations. To resist this danger (because we are talking about an act of resistance), one must—without limiting anyone's freedom—exercise one's critical judgment, speak, study, respond, *increase the number of examples*, create counter-powers, and above all invent new spaces and new forms, new types of publication and communication—and we must begin now preparing ourselves and students to do this. For example, by discussing the ways of reading—or not reading—the *NYRB*. We shouldn't discourage anyone from doing so; it is also very funny, sometimes. Sometimes.

Appendix

[From the *New York Review of Books*, February 11, 1993]

To the Editors:

In "A Normal Nazi," Mr. Thomas Sheehan has the nerve to speak of "Derrida's legal threats against the very existence of Wolin's book." This is a falsification. Moreover, he himself recognizes that it is and thus contradicts himself in a flagrant manner. He knows very well that no one ever threatened the existence of Mr. Wolin's book. I merely demanded that my interview be withdrawn from any subsequent printings or editions and only from these printings or editions of the book in question. May I recall that this interview was published without my authorization, in an execrable translation, and in a book that, as is my right, I judge to be weak, simplistic, and compulsively aggressive. I emphasize that I

was never informed either of the project of this book or its publication, and this despite the fact that the said book included, in order
to attack it, a long text of mine. Do I not have the right to protest
when a text of mine is published without my authorization, in a
bad translation, and in what I think is a bad book? As I have since
written to him, Mr. Wolin seems to be more eager to give lessons in
political morality than to try to respect the authors he writes about
and publishes, in a greater hurry to accuse than to understand
difficult texts and thinking—not to mention foreign languages (the
reader who wishes to form a judgment of this not unimportant
element of the affair can refer to the translation of my text that Mr.
Wolin had the nerve to publish; it is accessible to the public in the
first edition of his book, as are the crude mistranslations that
characterize it; one may then compare it with my own text as it
appeared in the *Nouvel Observateur*, 1987, and which has just been
republished in its integrity in *Points de suspension*, Paris: Galilée,
1992). The fact that Mr. Wolin's errors are not, alas, only linguistic
gets us to the bottom of things. If Mr. Sheehan deems it worthwhile, for reasons the reader may judge, to devote almost a third of
a very long article to this incident, one can only regret that he did
not say more about what he believes it suffices merely to point out,
as if in passing, namely that "Derrida's position on all this is more
complex than Wolin's brief criticism (correct as far as it goes)
allows . . ."

Jacques Derrida

Ecole des Hautes Etudes en Sciences Sociales
Paris, France

[From the *New York Review of Books*, March 25, 1993]

To the Editors:

I regret that I must ask you once again to publish a response from
me, this time to the letter of Mr. Sheehan. The text of this letter
follows.

I would have preferred not to take up any more space in this column nor any more of the reader's time with what could more correctly be dubbed the "Wolin/Sheehan affair." However, the letter from Mr. Sheehan (11 February 1993) compels me to recall a few stubborn and massive facts and then to pose several questions. The most incredible thing in this "affair," let us note, is that now Mr. Sheehan seems to be demanding that I respond and justify myself in circumstances where it would be more appropriate and in better faith to demand it of Mr. Wolin. Isn't he the one who translated (very badly) then published a text of mine without requesting my authorization and without even informing me of it, not even after the book was published?

1. Mr. Sheehan claims to have a complete file on the matter ("I have documentation for everything," he says). He declares that he called or wrote to everyone (to Columbia University Press and even to France, to *Le Nouvel Observateur*). Why then did he never contact me during the six months that, so it seems, it took him to prepare his article? Is what I know or think about the non-authorized publication of my text or is what I can attest to in this regard so unimportant in his view? Strange, "embarrassing," isn't it? Anyone can see that Mr. Sheehan's behavior resembles Mr. Wolin's. The latter had also informed everyone but me. He informed everyone (his publisher and *Le Nouvel Observateur*) of his intention to publish my text in translation; he then did in fact publish it without my agreement and without my knowledge, thereby carefully avoiding talking to me about it at any time (that is, for months and months), leaving me to discover the thing after the fact. Strange, "embarrassing," isn't it? For whom? Why these oversights, why this avoidance on the part of Mr. Wolin as well as Mr. Sheehan? I will do no more than pose the question, but the hypotheses are not "hard to divine," to take up the expression with which Mr. Sheehan, at least twice, disguises his insinuations. No harder to divine, moreover, than the reasons for which Mr. Wolin had from the first absolutely insisted on publishing a long text of mine, even if he had to do so without my knowledge. After all, he could have easily quoted my text, analyzed long excerpts from it,

referred to it, and so on, without any authorization. No, he wanted
at all costs for me to figure as one of the co-authors of his book. So
why? Is it "hard to divine"? And then the withdrawal of my text
from the second edition becomes, in Mr. Sheehan's view, the most
notable thing about this book. For, when he comes to talk about
the book, he makes almost everything he has to say turn around
this incident, neglecting, in his promotional haste, to explain how
my "position" is, as he nevertheless recognizes in one line, "more
complex" than Mr. Wolin thinks. Why? Is it "hard to divine"?

2. I maintain that *Le Nouvel Observateur* does not have the right
to authorize without my accord the republication of my text in
translation. Any competent lawyer will confirm this to be the case.
No contract was ever signed between this magazine and myself on
the subject of a text of which I remain the sole legal owner. Mme
Valentini acknowledged in a letter to Mr. Wolin (12-11-91) that she
had "forgotten," as had Mr. Wolin, to ask me for authorization
(this "was forgotten," she says calmly, "by you and by us"). If Mme
Valentini has recently claimed the contrary (over the telephone and
in English, as Mr. Sheehan reports), she is mistaken or is mislead-
ing her questioner. If I have not taken legal action against *Le Nouvel
Observateur* ("why doesn't he take it up with the French journal?"
asks Mr. Sheehan), just as I have never taken any legal action (I
reiterate and insist on this point) against Mr. Wolin, it is because I
do not like to assert my rights in this way when I can avoid it. This
ridiculous affair has already made me lose too much time, and I was
thinking especially of the future. Given that this wrong was irreversible, since the book was already published, I thought, let's make
sure at least that it is not repeated, and worry only about the next
printing or edition. If there had been no wrong, by the way, would
Mr. Wolin have offered his apology ("I apologize," letter dated
June 11, 1991 [*sic*: the letter in question is in fact dated November 6,
1991, the date was mistranscribed by the *NYRB*], that is, long after
his book was published and, in particular, after I had become
indignant about it)? Even supposing, *concesso non dato*, that my
legal agreement were not necessary, how can one justify that Mr.
Wolin "forgot," for months and months, to ask me, at least out of

courtesy, for my authorization to include a long text of mine in his book? Did he think I was dead? How can one justify that, even afterward, he left me in the dark so that I had to discover his book in a store during a trip to New York? How is one to understand the fact that Mr. Sheehan, who claims to have conducted an exhaustive and impeccable inquiry on this question, vehemently takes the side of Mr. Wolin but "forgets" as well, for months and months, to get in touch with me? What is the most "embarrassing" here, "to say the very least" (I am deliberately employing the words that are so abused by Mr. Sheehan's rhetoric as to render them immediately suspect)? And "embarrassing" for whom? Is it "hard to divine"?

3. As I have already said, the serious translation deficiencies, which I consider "not unimportant," were not my first concern. But I nevertheless continue to find this translation "execrable." There are many more mistakes than "three, at most, that are even worth talking about" as Mr. Sheehan claims. Counting only the most serious ones, I have found at least two per page and the text has nine pages! If Mr. Sheehan disagrees with this or if, in good faith, he is not aware of it, then I must conclude that his knowledge of language (at least the French language) and the demands he makes of a translator are as lax as those of Mr. Wolin.

4. Naturally I will make the list of these mistakes available to whoever may wish to consult it. And since Mr. Sheehan seems to think he is intimidating heaven knows who by this proposition, I declare that I am ready, for my part and from the outset, to communicate to whoever asks me all the correspondence I have on the subject (in particular the letters exchanged between Mr. Wolin and myself). If moreover it is possible to publish all these documents, including Mr. Wolin's unpublished preface, in fair conditions, I accept to do so and would see only an advantage in it. One would then know for whom this is in fact "embarrassing," whom it "embarrasses" the most, and who, as one says in French, *ne s'est pas embarrassé de scrupules*, that is, was not bothered by scruples throughout this whole episode.

5. But I do not make any commitment to explain publicly and in detail why my evaluation of Mr. Wolin's work is, I repeat,

"negative." First of all because I do not have the time and there are more urgent things to do. Next because I would never have offered a public evaluation of Mr. Wolin's behavior or work if Mr. Sheehan had not compelled me to do so when he took the initiative to quote from my letters while all the time piling up counter-truths and bad faith arguments. Does Mr. Sheehan really believe one should be obliged to explain oneself publicly and in the press each time one judges a book to be bad, when one prefers not to share the responsibility for it, especially to the point of figuring in spite of oneself as author, and still less when one has not been previously alerted to that fact? Does he want to call on me from now on to justify myself in public and in the press each time I disagree with what I read? Or each time what I read bores me or doesn't interest me? Or each time I refuse to write, speak, or publish here or there? Not to mention the practical consequences of such a constraint, I wonder about the political regime and quite simply the public space in which one would then have us live.

Jacques Derrida

Ecole des Hautes Etudes en Sciences Sociales
Paris, France

Reference Matter

Notes

Introduction: Upside-Down Writing

1. Jacques Derrida, "How to Avoid Speaking," pp. 14–15. "Promise of memory, memory of promise . . ." one reads as inverted echo in "Number of Yes," p. 131.

2. For this translation, two interviews have been added to the original selection: "*Honoris Causa*: 'This is *also* extremely funny'" and "The Work of Intellectuals and the Press (The Bad Example: How the *New York Review of Books* and Company Do Business."—Trans.

3. "Number of Yes," p. 131.

4. *The Post Card*, pp. 128, 194. The "Envois," which literally and in many respects prefigures *Given Time*, accumulates "praise" of the voice and of so-called living speech, of improvisation, of the word and voices that "touch" and "touch each other," of what seems made "in order to give us again the time to touch each other with words" (p. 56). In a televised interview with Didier Eribon (see Bibliography, p. 499), Derrida declared: "I do not like to improvise, but I like to write by preparing a speech act that will be exhausted at the same time as [. . .] the session. I am often associated with a theory of writing, but I am more a man of speech, of a certain type of speech, of a certain writing of speech."

5. "Psyche: Invention of the Other," p. 62.

6. Derrida has often explained this necessity, including here: cf. in particular the end of "Choreographies" and "Voice II."

7. Among these texts in the form of conversation (more than one voice, and sometimes more than one feminine voice), one can include "Pas," first published in 1976 and later collected in *Parages*, "Restitu-

457

tions—of the Truth in Pointing," in *The Truth in Painting*, "At This Very Moment in This Work Here I Am," first published in 1980 and collected in *Psyché, Inventions de l'autre, Feu la cendre*, first published in 1981, "Droit de regards" (1985), "Post-Scriptum: Aporias, Ways and Voices," trans. John P. Leavey, Jr., in *Derrida and Negative Theology*, ed. Harold Coward and Toby Foshay (Albany, N.Y.: SUNY Press, 1992). On this "more than one voice/no more one voice," on the plurality or differance that marks from within, thereby opening it, the very singularity of the appeal as uniqueness of the "come," cf. for example "Of an Apocalyptic Tone Recently Adopted in Philosophy" (1981). More than one voice or "more than one language": "If I had to risk, God forbid, a single definition of deconstruction, one as brief, elliptical, and economical as a password, I would say simply and without overstatement: *plus d'une langue*—both more than one language and no more of one language. In fact it does not make a statement or a sentence. It is sententious but it has no sense if, at least as Austin would have it, by themselves words have no meaning. What does have meaning is the sentence. How many sentences can one make with 'deconstruction'?" (*Mémoires for Paul de Man*, p. 15; translation modified).

8. On the expression "points de suspension," see the Foreword.—Trans.

9. " 'Etre juste avec Freud', L'histoire de la folie à l'âge de la psychanalyse," in *Penser la folie, Essais sur Michel Foucault* (Paris: Editions Galilée, 1992), p. 180.

10. A wide bibliographic selection of all published interviews may be found at the end of the volume, pp. 495–99.

Between Brackets I

NOTE: An interview with D. Kambouchner, J. Ristat, and D. Sallenave, published in *Digraphe* 8 (1976). The editor's note stated: "The interview we are publishing here took place in early September 1975. There was another session in late October, a transcript of which will be published in the next issue of *Digraphe*. The prepared questions were further elaborated, in the course of the interview, by brief interventions."

1. First published in *Poétique* 21 (1975); later included in *The Post Card*.

2. Cf. diverse texts reprinted in *Du droit à la philosophie*.

3. First version published in *Derrière le miroir* 214 (May 1975); later included in *The Truth in Painting*.

4. For reasons that will become obvious, any insertions in the translation will be indicated in curly brackets, the square brackets being reserved for Derrida's own use.—Trans.

5. Imre Hermann, *L'instinct filial* (Paris: Denoël, 1972).

6. *Glas*, pp. 216–17.

7. Ibid., p. 142.

8. Ibid., p. 160.

9. Nicolas Abraham, "Introduction to Hermann," in *L'instinct filial*, p. 14.

10. "Ça décramponne": As in *Glas*, the use of the impersonal pronoun "ça" is overdetermined; its grammatical antecedent is always written over or undermined by the unconscious agency of the id—the *ça*.—Trans.

11. Ibid., pp. 11ff.

12. Cf. *Digraphe* 5 (1975). Written by the editorial committee of the journal, this text sets out a program of theoretical, political practice and analysis of fiction.—Trans.

13. The only other interview Derrida had given until this time was published as *Positions* in 1972.—Trans.

14. *Glas*, pp. 184–86.

15. Cf. J. Derrida, "L'âge de Hegel," in *Du droit à la philosophie*, pp. 181ff.

16. "Pas," reprinted in *Parages*, pp. 19ff.

17. *Glas*, p. 65.

18. *Reste*: both a noun (remainder, residue, remnant, the rest) and the second-person singular imperative form of the verb "rester" that means to stay, to remain. Derrida has also pointed out and exploited the anagrammatic relation between the verbs "rester" and "être," to be.—Trans.

19. An abbreviation in *Glas* for absolute knowledge (*savoir absolu*). It is also a standard abbreviation in French for the signifier, as opposed to the signified (*Sé*). *Sa* is, finally, a homonym of *ça*, the id.—Trans.

20. *The Truth in Painting*, p. 154.

21. Ibid., pp. 157–62.

22. Cf. the epigraph to *Speech and Phenomena*.

23. See *Speech and Phenomena*, pp. 96–97.

24. *Glas*, pp. 149–50.

25. Ibid., p. 79.

26. In *Margins—of Philosophy*, p. 295.

27. *Positions*, p. 96.

28. Abraham, "Introduction" to *L'instinct filial*, pp. 30ff.

29. *Signéponge/Signsponge* and "Pas."
30. *Glas*, p. 140.

Ja, or the *faux-bond* II

NOTE: Published in *Digraphe* 11 (1977). See above, "Between Brackets,"
NOTE.

1. Besides its use to mean recording tape, *bande* has several other
meanings, in particular: (1) band, group, or gang; (2) strip, as in comic
strip or strip of land; and (3) as a form of the verb *bander*, to bandage, to
strain, to tighten, hence to have an erection. The word has a central
importance in *Glas*, where the two columns are also called "bandes," and
thus the double-band effect coordinates with a double-bind effect. Derrida takes advantage of this semantic ambiguity in ways that cannot be
rendered adequately. Each time, therefore, the translation will have to
make a different compromise.—Trans.

2. Jonathan Swift, *Gulliver's Travels and Other Writings* (New York:
Bantam Books, 1981), pp. 218–59.

3. See above, "Between Brackets," n. 10.

4. *Faire faux bond à quelqu'un* means to stand somebody up; literally
"un faux-bond" would be a false leap.—Trans.

5. "A combien d'orthographes, comptez, sa phonie fait faux-bond! A
combien d'orthodoxies prises au mot il lui faut bien faire défaut, défauts
multiples!" These two sentences reduce to near minimum the differences
among the phonetic, semantic, grammatical, and rhetorical axes of
meaning, even as they insist on the irreducible gap that prevents any final
coming together in a meaningful encounter. Meaning is stood up by the
faux-bond, which, to the ear, has a number of possible homonyms in
French, among them: *faux-bon*, a false welldoer, or a fraudulent bond, or
a worthless title; *faut bond*, on the other hand, suggests both the necessity
of a leap and its default, failure, or shortcoming. Also, in the word *défauts*
one may hear *des faux*, forgeries.—Trans.

6. In *Gramma* 3/4. *Pas de désir*: *pas* is both a noun meaning step and
the adverbial particle of negation, not. Thus the phrase induces a double
movement—an affirmative step forward, a negative withdrawal back.—
Trans.

7. On this term, see *Glas*, p. 130.—Trans.

8. See Jacques Derrida, "Scribble (pouvoir/écrire)."—Trans.

9. The allusion here is to the legal corporation, which in France is known as a *Société anonyme à responsabilité limitée*, or by its acronym Sarl.—Trans.

10. See *Glas*, p. 199; a *potence* is a gallows, but it also retains links to potency, potential, and *Potenz*. On the latter term in Hegel, see also *Glas*, pp. 104–5.—Trans.

11. "*Où il faut (de faillir)*". The verb *faillir* (to fail, as in to fail to keep a promise, or to be lacking) forms a homonym in the third-person singular with the verb *falloir* (to be necessary). "Il faut" thus can mean either it is necessary, one must, or it fails.—Trans.

12. Cf. "Fors."

13. The "good again," or the rebound (of the good).—Trans.

14. Cf. *Glas*, pp. 86 and 97.

15. Parts of this seminar have since been included in "To Speculate—on 'Freud'," in *The Post Card*.—Trans.

16. Op. cit., see for example p. 133.

17. Cf. for example, *Glas*, p. 205 and passim; "Pas," pp. 210–11; *Signsponge*, pp. 114–16; "Fors." The topos of the signature, one which is structurally multiple and which cannot be reduced simply to the order of the patronymic, guided me through a reading of Heidegger's *Nietzsche* during a seminar last year. The scene of the signature in *Ecce Homo*, for example, was identified as the very thing that a Heideggerian type of reading had to bury. The deconstruction of the *word* and more precisely of the *name*, singularly of the *proper*, of all that tends to reassume itself there in a single vocable, this deconstruction is no doubt the most continuous motif of that which, as you put it, makes me "write and speak." These are my "own motifs," in a certain way, and one can find explicit formulations of them beginning with *Of Grammatology* or "Différance," which ended, already so long ago, on the question of the "finally proper name" in Heidegger.—J.D.

18. In *Dissemination*, pp. 175ff.

19. "The Parergon" and "+R" in *The Truth in Painting*.

20. *Glas*, pp. 94–95.—Trans.

21. *Glas*, pp. 86–98.

22. "Trente-huit réponses sur l'avant-garde," *Digraphe* 6, p. 153.—Trans.

23. *The Truth in Painting*, pp. 151–52; see Walter Benjamin's "Der Autor als Produzent," in *Gesammelte Schriften*, 2, 2 (Frankfurt am Main: Suhrkamp, 1977), pp. 683–701.

24. The emphasis here on *-cline* suggests that we should read this movement as that of the *clinamen*: both a decline or a fall and an inclination toward something, a deviation from a "proper" path.—Trans.

25. The allusion here is to the fact that Derrida had changed publishers several times.—Trans.

26. An "affair" that had stirred up the milieu of philosophy in 1976: The philosopher Pierre Boutang had been barred from teaching in the aftermath of the Second World War for reason of collaboration with the Nazi occupation. He had also authored numerous patently anti-Semitic books. After being officially reinstated in the ranks of the national education system in the early 1970s, Boutang was promoted in 1976 by the government commission on university appointments to a chair in philosophy at the Sorbonne, ahead of other candidates whom the philosophy department there had ranked higher. This anomaly provoked the "blunder" to which Derrida refers in the interview: the letter, initiated by members of the Collège de Philosophie and signed by many university professors to protest the unprecedented reversal of the rankings, had also referred to Boutang's collaborationist past. Counter-protests then arose from across the political spectrum which accused the letter's signatories of conducting a witch-hunt. Derrida's indignant reply to this charge was printed in *Le Monde* under the title "Où sont les chasseurs de sorcières?" (Where are the witch-hunters?), July 1, 1976.—Trans.

27. The acronym stands for Groupe de Recherche sur l'enseignement de la philosophie (Research Group on the Teaching of Philosophy). Derrida was one of its founders.—Trans.

28. On the relations between deconstruction, the onto-encyclopedic project of *universitas*, and the university today, see in particular "Où commence et comment finit un corps enseignant."—J.D.

29. Derrida later reported the same anecdote in more detail in *The Post Card*, pp. 266–68.—Trans.

30. Cf. *Positions.*—J.D.

"The Almost Nothing of the Unpresentable"

NOTE: Interview with Christian Descamps published under the title "Jacques Derrida sur les traces de la philosophie," in *Le Monde*, January 31, 1982, and in *Entretiens avec Le Monde*, vol. 1, *Philosophies* (Paris: La Découverte, 1984).

1. Paris, 1951.   2. In *The Post Card.*—Trans.
3. *Of Grammatology*, pp. 101ff.   4. Paris: Gallimard, 1970.

Choreographies

NOTE: Correspondence with Christie V. McDonald published in *Diacritics* 12, no. 2 (Summer 1982). It was presented by this note: "The following text is the result of a written exchange carried on during the fall of 1981. Jacques Derrida wrote his responses in French, and I then translated them into English for publication. It should be noted that I do not ask the following questions in the name of any specific feminist group or ideology. I do nevertheless owe a debt to long-standing conversations on the subject of 'Woman' and 'Women' with, among others, A. Jardine, C. Lévesque, N. Miller, N. Schor, and especially J. McDonald."

1. *Spurs*, p. 43.
2. Ibid., p. 89.
3. On August 26, 1970, a group of women calling themselves the Emma Goldman Brigade marched down Fifth Avenue in New York City with many other feminists, chanting: "Emma said it in 1910/Now we're going to say it again."—Trans.
4. See Rodolphe Gasché, "The Internal Border," and the response by Jacques Derrida in *The Ear of the Other.*—Trans.
5. In *Dissemination.*
6. Jacques Derrida refers here to the text "At This Very Moment in This Work Here I Am." He interprets there two texts in particular by Levinas ("Le judaïsme et le féminin" in *Difficile liberté*, and "Et Dieu créa la femme" in *Du sacré au saint*). In order to clarify this part of the discussion, I am translating the following passage from Derrida's text in which he quotes from and then comments upon Levinas's commentary: "The sense of the feminine will be found clarified by taking as a point of departure the human essence, the *Ischa* following the *Isch*: not the feminine following the masculine, but the partition—the dichotomy—between masculine and feminine following the human. . . . Beyond the personal relationship which establishes itself between these two beings issued from two creative acts, the particularity of the feminine is a secondary matter. It isn't woman who is secondary, it is the relation to woman *qua* woman that doesn't belong to the primordial human plan. What is primary are the tasks accomplished by man as a human being,

and by woman as a human being. . . . The problem, in each of these lines we are commenting upon at this moment, consists in reconciling the humanity of men and women with the hypothesis of a spirituality of the masculine, the feminine being not his correlative but his corollary; feminine specificity or the difference of the sexes that it announces is not straightaway situated at the height of the oppositions constitutive of Spirit. Audacious question: How can the equality of the sexes proceed from the property of the masculine? . . . There had to be a difference that would not compromise equity, a sexual difference; and consequently, a certain pre-eminence of man, as woman arrived later and *qua* woman as an appendix to the human. Now we understand the lesson: Humanity cannot be thought beginning from two entirely different principles. There must be some *sameness* common to these *others*: woman was taken from man, but has come after him: *the very femininity of woman consists in this initial afterwards* [après-coup]" ("Et Dieu créa la femme"). And Derrida follows up, commenting: "Strange logic, that of the 'audacious' question. It would be necessary to comment upon each step and verify that each time the secondary status of sexual difference signifies the secondary status of the feminine (but why is this so?) and that the initial status of the pre-differential is each time marked by this masculinity that should, however, have come only afterwards, like every other sexual mark. It would be necessary to comment, but I prefer, under the heading of a protocol, to underline the following: he is commenting himself, and says that he is commenting; it must be taken into account that this discourse is not literally that of E.L. While holding discourse, he says that he is commenting upon the doctors *at this very moment* ('the lines we are commenting upon at this moment,' and further on: 'I am not taking sides; today, I am commenting'). But the distance of the commentary is not neutral. What he comments upon is consonant with a whole network of affirmations which are his, or those of him, 'he'" (pp. 41–42).—Trans.

7. M. Heidegger, "Metaphysische Anfangsgründe der Logik im Ausgang vom Leibniz," ed. K. Held, in *Gesamtausgabe* (Frankfurt am Main: Klostermann, 1978), 26: 171ff.

8. See "*Geschlecht*: Sexual Difference, Ontological Difference" and "*Geschlecht* II: Heidegger's Hand."

9. This is an allusion to, among other things, all the passages on the so-called argument of the *gaine* ("sheath," "girdle") in *Glas*, on the

reversals of the "gaine" and the "vagina," in particular pp. 211ff. and 226ff. Furthermore, the word "invagination" is always taken within the syntax of the expression "double chiasmatic invagination of the borders" in "Living On/Borderlines" and "The Law of Genre" (in *Glyph* 7).—Trans.

10. Allusion to "Pas," *The Truth in Painting,* "At This Very Moment in This Work Here I Am," and *Cinders.*—Trans.

Of a Certain Collège International de Philosophie Still to Come

NOTE: An interview with Jean-Loup Thébaut, published with the title "Derrida, philosophe au Collège," in *Libération,* August 11, 1983. The introduction specified: "May '82, Jacques Derrida, François Châtelet, Jean-Pierre Faye, and Dominique Lecourt were given the responsibility by [Jean-Pierre] Chevènement [then Minister of Education] to establish the charter of a Collège International de Philosophie. The kickoff took place in July 1983. Derrida explains here the rules of the game."

1. "Hautes Etudes" refers to the Ecole Pratique des Hautes Etudes, and "EHESS" to the Ecole des Hautes Etudes en Sciences Sociales, both prestigious public institutions primarily for post-graduate education and separate from the French university; "CNRS" refers to the Centre National de Recherches Scientifiques, which is a publicly funded, non-teaching research foundation.—Trans.

2. GREPH is an acronym for Groupe de Recherche sur l'enseignement de la philosophie (Research Group on the Teaching of Philosophy), of which Derrida was one of the founders. The Estates General of Philosophy was a large meeting organized by the GREPH. It assembled many philosophy teachers opposed to a government reform that would have curtailed significantly the teaching of philosophy in secondary schools.—Trans.

3. This is a reference to an article that had recently appeared in the newspaper *Le Monde.* It was signed by Max Gallo, a historian with close ties to the new Socialist government. Gallo deplored there the failure of his fellow "leftist intellectuals" to support more publicly the efforts of the Socialist majority. The article provoked considerable controversy of a sort Derrida characterizes in his reply.—Trans.

4. Allusion to Montesquieu's well-known novel of social and political

commentary, *The Persian Letters.* It described French customs from the perspective of a Persian visiting Paris in the eighteenth century.—Trans.

5. The date of François Mitterrand's first election in 1981, which marked the beginning of the first stable leftist government in France since the 1930s.—Trans.

Unsealing ("the old new language")

NOTE: Interview with Catherine David published under the title "Derrida l'insoumis" (Derrida the unsubdued) in *Le Nouvel Observateur*, 983, September 9–15, 1983. We reproduce here the introduction to the interview: "If philosophy, which was threatened even in the *lycées* during Giscard's term, is today honored in the form that is most welcoming to the future of intelligence, it is thanks to Jacques Derrida, the principal instigator of the Collège International de Philosophie that has just been created under the aegis of three ministerial offices. And yet, this fifty-three-year-old thinker-writer is, in France, at once famous and unknown, respected and ignored. Not well-liked by the universities that act as guardians of stagnant knowledge, he is also exceptionally discreet on the public stage. Jacques Derrida does not play the game. An explorer of the margins, he causes the limits of philosophy, psychoanalysis, literature to vacillate in his multiform work. This thinker who travels willingly through the works of others—Husserl, Kant, Freud, Nietzsche, Genet, Jabès, Levinas, Leiris—has often been reproached for the difficulty of his style. While making every effort to keep things simple, he explained to Catherine David what are, in his opinion, the misunderstandings and traps that today threaten thinking."

1. Allusion to *Glas* and *The Post Card,* among other texts.

2. The first of two post-*baccalauréat* classes that prepare students for the competitive examination required for entry into the Ecole Normale Supérieure, one of the most prestigious *grandes écoles* in France, dedicated primarily to the formation of teachers and professors. Derrida spent a year in *hypokhâgne* in Algiers before coming to Paris, where he continued his preparatory studies in *khâgne* before entering the Ecole Normale.—Trans.

3. An allusion to Sartre's celebrated remark that communism is "the unsurpassable horizon of our age."—Trans.

4. On the *khâgne* and the Ecole Normale, see n. 2 above. The *agréga-*

tion is a national, competitive examination given in each academic discipline. Those who pass it are assured a teaching position either in the secondary schools, the university, or one of the *grandes écoles.*—Trans.

5. That is, Gallimard.—Trans.

6. See above, "Of a Certain Collège International de Philosophie Still to Come," n. 2.—Trans.

7. A proposal by the then Minister of National Education under the government of Valéry Giscard d'Estaing that would have curtailed the teaching of philosophy in the *lycées* and universities in various ways.—Trans.

8. "Of an Apocalyptic Tone Recently Adopted in Philosophy."

"Dialanguages"

NOTE: Interview with Anne Berger, published in *Fruits* 1 (December 1983). Here is how the interview was presented: "This conversation took place on September 27, 1983. It was understood that Jacques Derrida would improvise. Nothing was prepared and nothing has been reworked. We wanted to leave untouched what was a present of friendship."

1. See above, "Unsealing ('the old new language')," pp. 115–31.—Trans.

2. See "Racism's Last Word" and "The Laws of Reflection: Nelson Mandela, in Admiration."

3. See "Of an Apocalyptic Tone Recently Adopted in Philosophy," p. 14.

4. Ibid., p. 24.

Voice II

NOTE: Correspondence with Verena Andermatt Conley, published in bilingual edition in *boundary 2* (Winter 1984).

1. See above, "Choreographies," pp. 107–8.

Language (*Le Monde* on the Telephone)

NOTE: First published in *Le Monde Dimanche*, June 20, 1982, inaugurating thereby, with the title "Language," a series of "lessons"; reprinted in *Douze leçons de philosophie*, ed. Christian Delacampagne (Paris: La Découverte/Le Monde, 1985).

1. Programs of study in the *lycées* are distinguished among sections with different orientations. The "terminale" is the last year of pre-*baccalauréat* training. Formerly, philosophy was the principal subject studied in the "terminale" (which was thus often referred to as "Philo"), but the proliferation of "sections," especially in the last twenty years, has significantly displaced philosophy's centrality.—Trans.

2. The remarks attributed to Christian Delacampagne are obviously fictive, and since certain commentators at the time thought otherwise, it is better to make clear that their author is Jacques Derrida.

Heidegger, the Philosophers' Hell

NOTE: Interview with Didier Eribon published in *Le Nouvel Observateur*, November 6–12, 1987. The interview was preceded by this note: "Victor Farías's book, *Heidegger et le nazisme*, published last month by Verdier, has suddenly relaunched the polemic over the political past of the great German thinker. The evidence gathered is overwhelming. Some are wondering whether one can still read Heidegger, still comment on his work. This week two books by Jacques Derrida will be published by Galilée: *De l'esprit, Heidegger et la question* and *Psyché, Inventions de l'autre*. In the first of these, he shows that Nazism is inscribed at the very heart of the philosophy of the author of *Being and Time*. Nevertheless, we must not give up reading this disturbing work, he declares in the interview he gave to Didier Eribon. For we must continue to think what Nazism was. And we must continue to think, period."

1. Victor Farías, *Heidegger and Nazism*, trans. Paul Burrell and Gabriel R. Ricci (Philadelphia: Temple University Press, 1989).

2. In the American translation of *Heidegger and Nazism* from the French (which is itself a translation from Farías's original Spanish), the passage Derrida refers to reads as follows: "we ourselves could not really understand his later development without taking account of his evident loyalty to a certain principle that rightly belongs to National Socialism and is conveyed in a manner and style that also belong to it" (p. 7). The translators, thereby, bring an added zeal to their task, since even Farías apparently did not go so far as to suggest that Heidegger's "manner and style" "belonged" to National Socialism.—Trans.

3. *Heidegger, Questions ouvertes* (Paris: Osiris, 1988).

4. Christian Jambet, "Preface" to *Heidegger and Nazism*, op. cit., p. 14.

5. "The Laws of Reflection" and "Racism's Last Word."

Comment donner raison? "How to Concede, with Reasons?"

NOTE: These several pages connect quite naturally to the preceding interview. They were published in *Diacritics* 19, nos. 3–4 (1989) and were presented as follows: "The principal destination, the form, and the brevity of this note call for some explanations. Its context was very determining. It was autumn 1987. At the same time as the publication of my book *Of Spirit: Heidegger and the Question*, Farías's *Heidegger et le nazisme* had just appeared in France. Whatever the difference between the two books, the question of Nazism was central to them. In certain newspapers and through a kind of rumor, one became aware of the violence of a condemnation. This condemnation claimed to reach, well beyond Nazism and Heidegger, the very reading of Heidegger, the readers of Heidegger, those who had referred to him—even if they had asked deconstructive questions about him—still more those who were likely to take a continued interest in him, even if it might be in order to judge and think, as rigorously as possible, Nazism and Heidegger's relation to Nazism. The gravest and most obscurantist confusions were being maintained, sometimes naively, sometimes deliberately. It was, not only but also, rather evidently, a question of banning the reading of Heidegger and of exploiting what was believed to be a strategic advantage, in France, in France above all, against all thought that took Heidegger seriously, even if in a critical or deconstructive mode.

Catherine David, who was preparing a dossier on this subject for *Le Nouvel Observateur* (the main part of which is now published in the United States in *Critical Inquiry* 15, no. 2 [1989]), asked me for a brief text on that occasion. Since Didier Eribon had in the meantime also proposed that I do an interview for the same magazine, it is the interview, much longer and more detailed, that was published" (see above, "Heidegger, the Philosophers' Hell," NOTE).

1. "Correspondence between Max Kommerell and Martin Heidegger," *Philosophie* 16 (Fall 1987).

"There is No *One* Narcissism" (Autobiophotographies)

NOTE: An interview broadcast during the radio program prepared by Didier Cahen for France-Culture, "Le bon plaisir de Jacques Derrida," on March 22, 1986, later published with the title "Entretien avec Jacques Derrida" in *Digraphe* 42 (December 1987).

1. Reading of *Droit de regards* by M.-F. Plissart; translated as "Right of Inspection."

2. A common nickname for the French citizens of Algeria, many of whom were "repatriated" to France when Algeria's independence was declared in 1962.—Trans.

3. I.e., "rester" and "être." Derrida's displacement of "être" by "rester" takes advantage of the anagrammatic relation between the two verbs and the visual pun possible in the third-person singular present indicative forms: "est" and "reste."—Trans.

4. The Parc de la Villette is a large, multi-use site in the north of Paris on the grounds of a former slaughterhouse. Derrida had been commissioned, along with Peter Eisenman, to design one of the gardens in the park but this part of the project was never built.—Trans.

5. "Point de folie—maintenant l'architecture," first published in a bilingual edition in Bernard Tschumi, *La case vide* (London: Architectural Association, 1986); reprinted in *Psyché*, pp. 477ff.

Is There a Philosophical Language?

NOTE: Published in *Autrement* 102 (November 1988), "A quoi pensent les philosophes?" (What are the philosophers thinking about?), edited by J. Roman and E. Tassin. The text was introduced as follows: "In rethinking the texts that have constituted it as a tradition, philosophy discovers its alliance with writing. What of the limits, what of the closure of philosophical discourse? Jacques Derrida wrote four replies to this question."

1. *The Philosophical Discourse of Modernity: Twelve Lectures*, trans. Frederick Lawrence (Cambridge, Mass.: MIT Press, 1987).

2. All the terms in quotation marks figure in titles of texts by Derrida.—Trans.

3. In *Margins—of Philosophy*.

4. The CNU is the Conseil National des Universités. Appointed by the government for each discipline, it has the power of final approval over nominations to a full professorship. When Philippe Lacoue-Labarthe and Jean-Luc Nancy were recommended for professorships in philosophy by the University of Strasbourg, the CNU preferred another candidate each time. These decisions, as well as many others in philosophy and other disciplines, were publicly contested and drew much criticism of the sectarian, partisan procedures of the CNU. Both Lacoue-Labarthe

and Nancy have since been named professors of philosophy at Strasbourg.—Trans.

The Rhetoric of Drugs

NOTE: Published in *Autrement* 106 (April 1989), an issue titled "L'esprit des drogues" and edited by J.-M. Hervieu.

1. The word is roughly equivalent to the English slang "rush."—Trans.

2. Derrida refers to the legislation adopted by the French parliament in 1970 under the title "law concerning health measures for the struggle against toxicomania and the repression of trafficking and illicit use of poisonous substances." The provisions of this law have remained substantially unchanged.—Trans.

3. Article L. 626: "A penalty of two months to two years imprisonment, or of a fine of 2,000 F to 10,000 F, or of both these penalties together is established for any person who will have contravened the provisions of those regulations of public administration concerning the production, conveyance, importation, exportation, holding, tender, transfer, acquisition, and *use* of substances or plants, or the cultivation of plants classified by statutory decree as harmful, *as well as any act relating to these operations*" (emphasis added).

4. *Phaedrus*, 275a.—Trans.

5. Le Grand Jeu (The big game) was a literary movement in France contemporary with the surrealists that included among its numerous members Georges Gilbert Lecomte.—Trans.

6. *Gesammelte Schriften*, 4, 1 (Frankfurt am Main: Suhrkamp, 1972), pp. 409ff.

7. "One of the first adventures of the *nostos* proper reaches much further back. The story of the Lotus-eaters goes back well beyond the barbaric age of demonic caricatures and magic deities. Whoever browses on the lotus succumbs, in the same way as anyone who heeds the Sirens' song or is touched by Circe's wand. But the victim does not die: 'Yet the Lotus-eaters did not harm the men of our company.' The only threats are oblivion and the surrender of will. The curse condemns them to no more than the primitive state without work and struggle in the 'fertile land': 'All who ate the lotus, sweeter than honey, thought no more of reporting to us, or of returning. Instead they wished to stay there in the company of the Lotus-eater, picking the lotus and forgetting their homeland.' "

Obliteration of the will, unproductivity (a society of foragers), non-work, oblivion as the forgetting of the city. Adorno and Horkheimer correctly tie all these motifs tightly together, and, by contrast, tie them to the history of truth or of Western rationality. Moreover, they propose a modern political reading: "This kind of idyll, which recalls the happiness of narcotic drug addicts reduced to the lowest level in obdurate social orders, who use their drugs to help them endure the unendurable, is impermissible for the adherents of the rationale of self-preservation. It is actually the mere illusion of happiness, a dull vegetation, as meager as an animal's bare existence, and at best only the absence of the awareness of misfortune. But happiness holds truth, and is of its nature a result, revealing itself with the abrogation of misery. Therefore the sufferer who cannot bear to stay with the Lotus-eaters is justified. He opposes their illusion with that which is like yet unlike: the realization of utopia through historical labor . . ." (Theodor W. Adorno and Max Hork-heimer, *The Dialectic of Enlightenment*, trans. John Cumming [London: Verso, 1979], pp. 62–63). I find this reading convincing, at least within the general perspective of the book. But this would raise other types of questions which I cannot go into here.

8. Ibid., p. 63.

9. I propose the word *telerhetoric* or *metatelerhetoric* to designate that general and more than general space in which these matters would be treated. For example: in the case of computers, is the use of the word "virus" simply a metaphor? And we might pose the same question for the use of the word "parasite." The *prerequisite* to this sort of problematic would have to concern rhetoric itself, as a parasitic or viral structure: originally and in general. Whether viewed from up close or from far away, does not everything that comes to affect the proper or the literal have the form of a virus (neither alive nor dead, neither human nor "reappropriable by the proper of man," nor generally subjectivable)? And doesn't rhetoric always obey a logic of parasitism? Or rather, doesn't the parasite logically and normally disrupt logic? If rhetoric is viral or parasitic (without being the AIDS of language it at least opens up the possibility of such an affection) how could we wonder about the rhetorical drift of words like "virus," "parasite," and so forth? And furthermore, the computer virus, just like its "literal" counterpart, attacks, in this case telephonically, something like the "genetic code" of the computer (cf. Fabien Gruhier, "Votre ordinateur a la vérole" ["Your infected computer"], *Le Nouvel Observateur*, November 18–24, 1988. The author notes

that computer viruses are "contagious" and "travel through telephone lines at the speed of an electron. . . . One need only be equipped with a modem to be contaminated by a virus from Asia, America, or a nearby suburb"). Even now "software vaccines" are being developed. Once again we have the question of the *pharmakon* as the familial scene and the question of paternity: last year it was a student at Cornell, the son of an official responsible for electronic security, who sent out the virus "guilty" of spreading this "infection" (and will we put quotation marks everywhere, these speech act condoms, to protect our language from contamination?). This so-called computer infection, spliced onto the AIDS virus itself grafted onto drugs, is more than a modern, worldwide figure of the plague; we know that it mobilizes the entire network of American security forces, including the FBI—and the DST (Direction de la Surveillance du Territoire) and the DGSE (Direction Générale de la Sécurité Extérieure). . . . I bring this up to revive our initial exchange concerning the delimitation of competence. Who will determine the pertinence of these questions? By what authority? According to what criteria? These questions should in return affect everything that we have up to now said about drug addiction. I take the liberty of mentioning the many places where I have attempted to treat the *alogic* of the parasite (for example: *Of Grammatology*, "Plato's Pharmacy" in *Dissemination*, "Signature Event Context" in *Margins—of Philosophy*, *Limited Inc*, *abc* . . . and passim).

"Eating Well," or the Calculation of the Subject

NOTE: Interview with Jean-Luc Nancy published in *Cahiers Confrontation* 20 (Winter 1989), an issue titled "Après le sujet qui vient" (After the subject who comes). The note presenting the interview read as follows: "Jacques Derrida was unable to write a text in time for *Topoi* (the journal in which this interview was initially published in English translation in October 1988 [vol. 7, no. 2]; the issue has since been re-edited as a book: *Who Comes After the Subject?* ed. Eduardo Cadava, Peter Connor, and Jean-Luc Nancy [New York: Routledge, 1991]). He proposed that we do an interview instead. The latter, however, took place too late to be integrally transcribed and translated in *Topoi*, which was able to publish only about half of it. It appears here almost in its entirety (although not without the omission of certain developments whose themes were announced in *Topoi*: the whole would have been both too long and occasionally too far afield from the main theme)."

1. Cf. *Spurs: Nietzsche's Styles, Parages,* "Préjugés" in *La faculté de juger* (Paris: Editions de Minuit, 1984), "Ulysses Gramophone," *Of Spirit,* "Number of Yes" in *Psyché,* and passim.

2. See for example *Speech and Phenomena,* p. 84, n. 1. This long note develops the implications of Husserl's sentence: "We can only say that this flux is something which we name in conformity with what is constituted, but is nothing temporally 'objective.' It is absolute subjectivity and has the absolute properties of something to be denoted metaphorically as 'flux,' as a point of actuality, primal source-point, that from which springs the 'now,' and so on. In the lived experience of actuality, we have the primal source-point and a continuity of moments of reverberation. For all this, names are lacking." The rest of the note describes that being-outside-the-self of time as spacing, and I conclude: "There is no constituting subjectivity. The very concept of constitution must be deconstructed."

3. See Jean-Luc Nancy, *Ego Sum* (Paris: Flammarion, 1975).—Trans.

4. See Derrida, "Forcener le subjectile" in *Antonin Artaud: Portraits et Dessins* (Paris: Gallimard, 1986).

5. Cf. *Of Spirit,* and "Heidegger's Hand," passim.

6. See Derrida, "Désistance," preface to American translation of Philippe Lacoue-Labarthe's *Typography,* trans. Christopher Fynsk (Cambridge, Mass.: Harvard University Press, 1989).—Trans.

7. "My Chances," trans. Irene Harvey and Avital Ronell, in *Taking Chances: Derrida, Psychoanalysis, and Literature,* ed. Joseph H. Smith and William Kerrigan (Baltimore, Md.: Johns Hopkins University Press, 1984).

8. Jean-Luc Nancy, *The Experience of Freedom,* trans. Bridget McDonald (Stanford, Calif.: Stanford University Press, 1993).

9. Cf. also, for example, *The Truth in Painting,* p. 286: "Unless Heidegger ignores (excludes? forecloses? denies? leaves implicit? unthought?) an *other* problematic of the subject, for example in a displacement or development of the value 'fetish.' Unless, therefore, this question of the *subjectum* is displaced *otherwise,* outside the problematic of truth and speech which governs *The Origin.*"—Trans.

10. On the question, see *Of Spirit,* passim; on the "yes, yes," see "Otobiographies," trans. A. Ronell, in *The Ear of the Other,* and "Number of Yes"; on "viens," see "Psyche: Invention of the Other."—Trans.

11. "The Politics of Friendship."

12. Maurice Blanchot, *L'amitié* (Paris: Gallimard, 1971), p. 328; see also Jean-Luc Nancy, *The Inoperative Community,* trans. Peter Connor et

al. (Minneapolis: University of Minnesota Press, 1992), and Maurice Blanchot, *The Unavowable Community*, trans. P. Joris (New York: Station Hill Press, 1988).

13. Cf. above, n. 11.

14. Even Hitler did not propose his vegetarianism as an example. This fascinating exception, moreover, can be integrated in the hypothesis I am evoking here. A certain reactive and compulsive vegetarianism is always inscribed, in the name of denegation, inversion, or repression, in the history of cannibalism. What is the limit between coprophagy and Hitler's notorious coprophilia? (See Helm Stierlin, *Adolf Hitler, Psychologie du groupe familial* [Paris: Presses Universitaires de France, 1975], p. 41.) I refer the reader to René Major's valuable contribution (*De l'élection* [Paris: Aubier, 1986], p. 166, n. 1).

15. The phrase in play here, "Il faut bien manger" (which is also the original title of this interview), can be read in at least two ways: "one must eat well" or "everyone has to eat." In addition, when the adverb "bien" is nominalized as "le Bien," there results the sense of "eating the Good." It is this multivalent sense that Derrida explores in the succeeding sentences.—Trans.

Che cos'è la poesia?

NOTE: First published in *Poesia* 1, no. 11 (November 1988); republished in *Poésie* 50 (Autumn 1989), where it was preceded by the following note: "The Italian journal *Poesia*, where this text appeared in November 1988 (translated by Maurizio Ferraris), begins each of its issues with the attempt at or the simulacrum of a response, in a few lines, to the question 'Che cos'è la poesia?' It is asked of a living person, while the question 'Che cos'era la poesia?' is addressed to the dead, this time to the 'Odradek' by Kafka. At the moment he or she is writing, the living respondent does not know the answer given by the dead one: it appears at the end of the issue and is the choice of the editors. Destined to appear in Italian, this 'response' exposes itself in passing, sometimes literally, in letters and syllables, the word and the thing ISTRICE (pronounced IZ-TRRI-TCHAY), which, in a French connection, will have yielded the 'hérisson' [and in English, the hedgehog]."

Throughout the text, the *str*-sound is stressed. One may hear in it the distress of the beast caught in the strictures of this translation. For that reason, the text is published also in the original French.

Istrice 2: Ick bünn all hier

NOTE: Interview with Maurizio Ferraris, published in *Aut Aut* 235 (January–February 1990), following the publication of "*Che cos'è la poesia?*" (see above).

1. "*Che cos'è la poesia?*" see above, p. 297.
2. *The Origin of the Work of Art*, in *Poetry, Language, Thought*, trans. Albert Hofstadter (New York: Harper & Row, 1971), pp. 72–73.
3. "The Self-Assertion of the German University," trans. William S. Lewis, in *The Heidegger Controversy: A Critical Reader*, ed. Richard Wolin (Cambridge, Mass.: MIT Press, 1993), p. 33.
4. Lacoue-Labarthe and Nancy, *The Literary Absolute*, trans. Philip Barnard and Cheryl Lester (Albany, N.Y.: SUNY Press, 1987).
5. *L'absolu littéraire* (Paris: Seuil, 1978), p. 126.
6. *The Literary Absolute*, pp. 44, 43.
7. *Identität und Differenz* (Pfullingen: Neske, 1967), p. 60; *Identity and Difference*, trans. Joan Stambaugh (New York: Harper & Row, 1969). I don't know whether the hedgehog of Nietzsche's *Ecce Homo* belongs to the same family as Schlegel's, or the one Heidegger talks about, or especially my humble *istrice*. I doubt it, despite a certain family resemblance, in fact, despite the taste of the "yes" and the "yes" to taste, and in spite of its Italian origins. Its coming into the text is heralded by a discourse on the choice of food, of place, and of climate, on the instinct of conservation (*Selbsterhaltung*) that tends toward self-defense (*Selbstverteidigung*). One has to know how not to say, how not to hear a lot of things (*Vieles nicht sehn, nicht hören*), one has to know how not to let them get to you (*nicht an sich herankommen lassen*). That is wisdom, that is also "taste," the proof that it is not "chance" but a "necessity." It commands not only that one say "no," when the "yes" would be a mark of altruistic disinterest or abnegation (*Selbstlosigkeit*), but that one say "no" as infrequently as possible. In order to save one's strength, one must separate from what compels one to say "no" and wastes energy. Nietzsche writes then *from Turin*, he describes, names, and finally dates *his hedgehog* from Turin: "Suppose I stepped out of my house and found, instead of quiet, aristocratic Turin, a small German town: my instinct would have to cast up a barrier to push back everything that would assail it from this pinched and flattened, cowardly world. Or I found a German big city—this built-up vice where nothing grows, where everything, good or bad, is

imported. Wouldn't this compel me to become a *hedgehog*? [Nietzsche's emphasis: *Müsste ich nicht darüber zum* Igel *werden?*] But having quills is a waste, even a double luxury when one can choose not to have quills but *open* hands" ("Why I Am So Clever," in *Ecce Homo*, trans. Walter Kaufmann [New York: Vintage, 1969], p. 253).

A response to Maurizio Ferraris, after the interview, in *aparte*, in place of a thank-you, and in memory of our Italian encounters—in Turin, where the question of "Che cos'è la poesia?" first arose and where he has so often put me on Nietzsche's trail, in Naples as well, more than once, in Palermo, in Lerici, and elsewhere. J.D. July 15, 1992.

8. German edition, p. 60; trans., pp. 62–63.

9. See "Language," in *Poetry, Language, Thought,* op. cit., p. 194.

10. *The Origin of the Work of Art,* op. cit., p. 62.

11. German edition, p. 70; trans., p. 72.

12. *Philosophie* 16 (Fall 1987), p. 16.

13. Op. cit., pp. 62–63.

14. *Letter on Humanism,* trans. Frank A. Capuzzi, in Martin Heidegger, *Basic Writings*, ed. David Farrell Krell (New York: Harper & Row, 1977), p. 219.

15. M. Heidegger, *Gesamtausgabe,* 2, 4: *Erläuterungen zu Hölderlins Dichtung* (Frankfurt am Main: Klostermann, 1981), p. 127.

16. Paul de Man, "Sign and Symbol in Hegel's *Aesthetics,*" *Critical Inquiry* 8, no. 4 (Summer 1982); see *Mémoires for Paul de Man.*

17. Pascal, *Pensées* (Paris: Hachette, 1912), § 282.

18. "I have more memories than if I were a thousand years old . . . my sad brain. It's a pyramid, an immense vault, that contains more dead than a common grave. . . . From now on you are nothing more, o living matter! than granite surrounded by a vague dread, crouching somewhere deep in the misty Sahara; an old sphinx unknown to a carefree world, forgotten on the map. . . ."—Trans.

19. *Mémoires for Paul de Man,* pp. 28–29.

20. *Sein und Zeit,* p. 240.

21. *Hölderlins Hymnen "Germanien" und "Der Rhein,"* in Heidegger, *Gesamtausgabe,* 39.

22. The translations of the noun *reste* and the verb *rester* are awkward: "the rest" is sometimes possible, but more often one must translate with the noun "remainder" and the verb "to remain." See also above, "There is No *One* Narcissism," n. 3.—Trans.

Once Again from the Top: Of the Right
to Philosophy

NOTE: Interview with Robert Maggiori published with the title "Le programme philosophique de Derrida" in *Libération*, November 15, 1990. The subheading introduced the article in these terms: "Submitted to Lionel Jospin in 1989, the report by Jacques Derrida and Jacques Bouveresse on the content of philosophical teaching has provoked numerous debates and polemics. The author of *Du droit à la philosophie* [*Of the Right to Philosophy*] explains his intentions." Lionel Jospin was the then Minister of National Education; *Du droit à la philosophie* (Paris: Editions Galilée, 1990) is a collection of Derrida's writings on the educational institution and in particular the teaching of philosophy. The title may also be translated: From Law to Philosophy.—Trans.

1. The last year of the *lycée* for those students preparing to take the *baccalauréat* exam. Traditionally, this year was devoted primarily to philosophy and was known simply as the year of "Philo." Successive reforms since 1968 have introduced other options of specialized study for this final year and have considerably reduced the importance of philosophy in the *lycée*.—Trans.

2. Cf. *Du droit à la philosophie*, pp. 146ff.

3. Ibid., pp. 619ff.

4. The body charged with oversight of the performance of teachers and administrators throughout the French national primary and secondary educational system.—Trans.

5. The year before the *classe terminale* in the *lycée*; see above, n. 1.—Trans.

6. *Du droit à la philosophie*, p. 628.

7. On this notion of democracy to come, see J. Derrida, *The Other Heading*.—Trans.

8. A highly normalized form of argument on a philosophical topic. It is a traditional component of the *baccalauréat* examination in philosophy.—Trans.

"A 'Madness' Must Watch Over Thinking"

NOTE: Interview with François Ewald that appeared in an issue of *Le Magazine littéraire* devoted to Jacques Derrida (286, March 1991). A subtitle introduced the interview in these terms: "Refusing to build a philosophical system, Derrida privileges experience and writes out of 'compulsion.' A dialogue concerning traces and deconstructions."

1. I.e., "je suis né," which has the value of the past tense, "I was born," but literally it says "I am born."—Trans.

2. Louis-le-Grand, one of the oldest and most prestigious *lycées* in France, is where Derrida spent several years in a post-secondary, preparatory class, known as *khâgne*, before entrance into the Ecole Normale Supérieure.—Trans.

3. The Métropole was the term for France among the francophone and colonial populations in Algeria, the latter also calling themselves and known as *pieds-noirs*.—Trans.

4. The first level of post-secondary, preparatory training for entrance into the Ecole Normale Supérieure. The next level is called *khâgne*.—Trans.

5. A reference to the entrance examination for the Ecole Normale and the *agrégation*, also a national competitive exam.—Trans.

Counter-Signatures

NOTE: Interview with Jean Daive published in *Fig. 5* (1991). It is in fact an extract from a radio interview broadcast earlier.

1. *Signéponge/Signsponge*. The French text was initially published in 1976.—Trans.

2. "Explication avec la langue": the idiomatic sense is "to have it out with," a discussion or an argument. In Derrida's frequent uses of the expression, it echoes the German term *Auseinandersetzung*.—Trans.

3. *Pour un Malherbe* (Paris: Gallimard, 1965).

4. *La Fabrique du pré* (Paris: Skira, 1971); *The Making of the "Pré,"* trans. Lee Fahnestock (Columbia: University of Missouri Press, 1979).—Trans.

Passages—from Traumatism to Promise

NOTE: Interview with Elisabeth Weber, broadcast in German translation—intercut with musical excerpts—in a radio program on Jacques Derrida in Hesse, by Hessischer Rundfunk, May 22, 1990; subsequently published in *Spuren in Kunst und Gesellschaft* 34–35 (October–December 1990).

1. *Schibboleth, pour Paul Celan* (Paris: Editions Galilée, 1987), p. 80.

2. Ibid., p. 90.

3. Ibid., p. 36.

4. *Otherwise than Being, or Beyond Essence*, trans. Alphonso Lingis (The Hague: Martinus Nijhoff, 1981).

5. "Jacques Derrida: Deconstruction and the Other," in *Dialogues with Contemporary Continental Thinkers: The Phenomenological Heritage*, ed. Richard Kearney (Manchester, Eng.: Manchester University Press, 1984), p. 123.

6. "A Discussion with Jacques Derrida," in *Writing Instructor* 9, nos. 1–2 (Fall 1989–Winter 1990), p. 18.

7. I.e., that which or the one who arrives.—Trans.

8. *The Post Card*, pp. 14–15.

9. Ibid., pp. 24–25, 143–44, 163, 166–67, 219, 229, 248, 253–54, and passim.

10. Both "does not dispatch itself" and "does not hurry."—Trans.

11. The play is between "là" and the homonym "la," which allows one to hear either "There are cinders there [*là*]," or "There is the cinder."—Trans.

12. *The Post Card*, p. 43.

13. Paul Celan, "The Meridian," in *Collected Prose*, trans. Rosemarie Waldrop (Riverdale-on-Hudson, N.Y.: Sheep Meadow Press, 1986), p. 46.

14. "Psyche: Invention of the Other," p. 62.

15. *The Post Card*, p. 43.

16. There follows a selection from "Le mystère des voix bulgares," Bulgarian women's chorus; see above, NOTE.

Honoris Causa: "This is *also* extremely funny"

NOTE: In the spring of 1992, a vote took place among the fellows of Cambridge University to decide whether or not to award an honorary degree (doctorate *honoris causa*) to Jacques Derrida. This almost unprecedented vote had been precipitated by the opposition to the award that manifested itself soon after the proposal was made and, over the course of the next several months, found outlets throughout the national and international press. The vote went largely in favor of approving the award, and on June 11, 1992, Cambridge bestowed the honorary doctorate on Jacques Derrida. For its October issue that year, the *Cambridge*

Review chose to devote most of its pages to what had come to be called "the Derrida affair" and their invitation to Derrida to contribute resulted in the following pages. Here is how the editors introduced the text they titled simply "An 'Interview' with Jacques Derrida": "M. Derrida preferred not to contribute to our symposium by writing an article, but asked if we could send him some questions to which he could reply. The questions naturally reflect the themes that were prominent in the recent debate."

1. I.e., a negative vote: "it does not please."—Trans.

2. Given the restrictions on space and time, for a discussion of such questions I refer you to *Du droit à la philosophie*, in particular to the chapters "*Mochlos*—or the Conflict of the Faculties" and "The Principle of Reason: The University in the Eyes of Its Pupils."—J.D.

3. To refer to my most recent publications only, allow me to indicate that I have discussed this question of the right of reply, of democracy, and of culture in "Democracy Adjourned" in *The Other Heading.*—J.D.

4. I would be very grateful if you would agree to reproduce the letter here [see "Derrida degree a question of honour"]. It has to be given the necessary publicity so that your readers can verify everything themselves and study this extraordinary document in detail, in ways that I have neither the time nor inclination to do here today. And with respect to intellectual and democratic rigor, to the future of universities, and to the level of public discussion, one ought to ask the authors of this letter to justify with texts and precise references each of their assertions, in open forum. The same request ought to be addressed to all the authors of the "fly sheets" after republishing them.—J.D.

5. Robert Maggiori, in *Libération*, May 16–17, 1992.—J.D.

6. I am alluding here to the "Ruth Barcan Marcus" affair, Barcan Marcus being the author of this letter to the French government in 1983. For details of this other (or rather, the same) affair, of this kind of "academic Interpol," as I described it, and what goes on "with chains of repressive practices, and with the police in its basest form, on the border between alleged academic freedom, the press, and state power," allow me to refer again to "Toward an Ethic of Discussion" in *Limited Inc*, pp. 158–59, n. 12.—J.D.

7. Besides *Du droit à la philosophie*, to which you will excuse me for referring again—in particular on the subject of the GREPH—I mention among other things a volume which will be appearing in the next few

weeks and in which I have collaborated with several colleagues, mostly English and American: *Logomachia: The Conflict of the Faculties*, ed. Richard Rand (Lincoln: University of Nebraska Press, 1992).—J.D.

The Work of Intellectuals and the Press
(The Bad Example: How the *New York Review of Books* and Company Do Business)

NOTE: This interview, with Peggy Kamuf, was conducted in writing and was commissioned for the present volume.

1. Especially in *Du droit à la philosophie* and notably in "The Principle of Reason: The University in the Eyes of Its Pupils."—J.D.

2. In particular, my book on Heidegger, *Of Spirit: Heidegger and the Question*, trans. Geoffrey Bennington and Rachel Bowlby (Chicago: University of Chicago Press, 1989); my interview in its original version (*Le Nouvel Observateur*, December 6, 1987), reprinted in *Points de suspension* (Paris: Editions Galilée, 1991); the two editions of Wolin's book, *The Heidegger Controversy: A Critical Reader*; and all the issues of the *NYRB*, from February to April 1993.—J.D.

3. See on this subject the April 22nd issue of the *NYRB* where his gross errors of translation are mercilessly analyzed by a good number of French and American colleagues, and my letter quoted below, p. 453.—J.D.

4. Upon rereading this interview, I feel it is necessary to justify once again the choice of these four words whose tone might seem, quite rightly, violent. I cannot address here directly the major question of the *tone* of academic or journalistic discussions. (What does "good form" or, as we say in French, "bon ton" prescribe or prohibit as regards tone, sincerely or hypocritically? When is "bon ton" the sign of respect for the interlocutor, of the seriousness of the discussion and what is at stake in it? When is it the sign of the opposite? Are there rules for polemics? Who makes them? Who questions them? I think I have at least approached these questions in *Limited Inc*, in the article and then in the book with that title, and so forth.) I will say merely this: these four words recall first of all the aggressive accusations launched against me in the *NYRB* in a tone whose violence is, in my view, without precedent (I mean there has never been a grosser insult made publicly against me). Readers can refer to the texts of Sheehan and Wolin: they will see in what manner I am accused there, *without the slightest grounds*, of inventing, insinuating,

lying, and so forth. *Inventing, insinuating, lying* (no other words can say it more correctly or more frankly), that is what Sheehan and Wolin are doing, and they know, as does everyone, that it is *false* when they accuse me of having brought proceedings against Wolin and forbidden or limited, in the slightest way whatsoever, the publication or republication of his book. They have done so in a repeated manner, before and after all the proof and explanations that were given to them in public. As for "manipulation," see below, p. 444.—J.D.

5. Of course, it is difficult to measure this disproportion. It cannot be instantaneous and its quantitative measure must be carefully calculated. One might be tempted to devote a new discipline to it, or at least a whole book. But, by definition, what I will call a force of the future will always prevent such a discipline and such a book from closing and from formalizing the laws of a calculation. For one must take into account (and in advance, which is what is impossible since every work invents in this respect a new law!) differences of rhythm, quality, force, and effective influence of the texts in question. Let us put it concretely: for example, an article in a newspaper that prints 500,000 copies may be sold to—and even read by!—all its purchasers the day after it is written, and then it may be forgotten the next day, along with the name of its author. This is even what happens most of the time. At the other extreme, another article or book, whose initial printing, sales, or even readership may be very small, sometimes next to nothing, can make its way over the years or the centuries, mark succeeding generations through reprintings and relays that are so numerous they become incalculable. There would be so many examples of this! It gives one something to think about and it leaves room for hope. Here is a domain of predictability (to know *whom* and *what* people will still be reading tomorrow) in which there is still an irreducible margin of wager, even if one can, to a certain degree, reasonably calculate based on reliable signs. One must also say "let's wager." There is no writing without calculation, but there is also no writing without such a wager.—J.D.

6. As is confirmed in particular by the texts and the experts cited by Didier Eribon, French law clearly stipulates that the author of a text published in a newspaper remains the absolute owner of it so long as a contract does not bind him or her to the newspaper. This is indeed the situation we are talking about: no contract bound me to *Le Nouvel Observateur* and the director of their permissions department explicitly acknowledged, in a quoted letter, that she should have asked for my

authorization and that she forgot to do so. That this law is thus ignored in certain cases does not mean that it doesn't exist, except for those who think that a law is not a law from the moment they do not respect it or others do not take it into acount. In any case, the legal aspect remains secondary here, as I have often said, even when speaking of my rights. The legalism of which Wolin had the gall to accuse me was the cause for much laughter, which I can attest to. Was it not he who thought he could get by with a legal, mechanical (and insufficient!) procedure addressed to *Le Nouvel Observateur*, while neglecting every other sign of politeness? As is often the case, the *appearance* of literal legalism (to be "en règle," to be straight with the authorities, to put the police on one's side) is accompanied by the non-respect of the law, of its letter as well as its spirit. If, instead of being satisfied with this façade of legalism, he had had the courtesy to write me a note at some point during the several years it took to edit his book, none of any of this would have happened. So the question remains: Why did he not dare to do so? Why did he deem it prudent not to do so?—J.D.

7. On this point, I refer to *The Other Heading*, pp. 98ff, esp. pp. 106–7, and to *Specters of Marx: The State of the Debt, the Work of Mourning, and the New International*, trans. Peggy Kamuf (New York: Routledge, 1994), pp. 53ff, 68ff, 78ff, 185n5, and passim. To be sure, there are differences among national legal systems. For example, there exists in France a "right of response" that obligates newspapers to publish, in certain conditions, the responses of persons whose reputations have been put in question. I point this out and analyze also the inadequacies of this right in *The Other Heading*. In a general fashion, one may say that wherever this right is not effectively assured, as it should be, democracy is inadequate to its idea. Since these violations of the right of response are the most widespread thing in the world, to different degrees and in different forms, this is an indispensable site for reflection on the real state of democracy—today more than ever, for the reasons we mentioned in speaking of the Enlightenment of our time and of techno-mediatic mutation. And of course, all of this in a certain way has just begun. The transformation of the so-called interactive media (on-line TV, newspapers, and so forth) now under way will have to call for new analyses, new legislation, and be met by the most vigilant hospitality.—J.D.

8. Richard Wolin, Preface, *The Heidegger Controversy*, rev. ed. (Boston: MIT Press, 1993), pp. xv and xii. This second edition proves clearly that the existence of Wolin's book was never either threatened or compro-

mised. The most novel thing here seems to me to be in the nature of publicity. The publisher, MIT Press, therefore advertised the book commercially by using once again my name in order, in effect, to recommend to potential buyers a book whose only interest lay, if one were to believe the advertisement, in the fact that a text by Derrida was missing from it!! Has anyone ever seen such a thing? I don't think so. The strength and the interest of a book, even its commercialization, would here reside in the very "absence" of the text that is not included in it. What dissemination! What power of absence! This absence ("the absence from this edition of an interview with Jacques Derrida," is what one reads) is even defined on the book cover as a "springboard" for Wolin. What is he complaining about? All at once I started to daydream. Was this not the first time a book had been urged on the buying public on the strength of a text that it does not include or comprise and in the name of an author who is absent from it? Would not Wolin have been better advised to use this "springboard," namely, my absence, beginning with the first edition of his book at Columbia University Press? That would have saved us some time and energy (although it is true that it would not have worked as well for his book; for this book, it was necessary not that I be absent but that I disappear from it even as I came back, like a ghost, in some way, in order to provide him with a "springboard"). But I go on dreaming: and what if now this practice of advertising academic books were to spread? And wouldn't it be a stroke of genius if all of a sudden people started citing my name in order to recommend all the books that include no text of mine? I mean to recommend them *principally* on the basis of this absence, for the "missing text" as Wolin puts it in his note. "Buy this book, even read it, it doesn't have any text by Derrida!" Just imagine the career I could have!

But this passage from Wolin contains another incongruity. Basing himself on an allegation whose absurdity I have just demonstrated once again, Wolin adds in a note an insinuation meant to show that I really did not want this interview to be "disseminated": "It may be of interest to note that the interview failed to appear in the overseas edition of the November 6–12 issue of *Le Nouvel Observateur*. It would therefore be unavailable in almost all North American libraries" (p. xx, n. 11). Is Wolin trying to suggest that I had something to do, even minimally, with this well-known practice of abridging all overseas editions, which are generally in smaller format and on lighter paper, of so many daily newspapers and magazines? My interview was unusually long and I imagine (having no information on this subject and no familiarity of any sort with the magazine) that it made the decision, as is often the case, to sacrifice the "cultural" sections rather than others. Wolin's remark, once again, is all the more extravagant in that he has to add immediately afterward: "There is, however, a German translation of the text. It appears in . . ." If I had wanted the interview not to be "disseminated," why would it have appeared so quickly in translation? And not only in Germany: in a number of languages the list of which it would be immodest to cite here. And each time, I insist, with my authorization.—J.D.

9. See in this regard the conclusion of my letter dated February 11, 1993.—J.D.

10. Planned and instituted at Strasbourg in November 1993, this International Parliament of Writers is currently under the presidency of Salman Rushdie. Adonis, Breyten Breytenbach, Pierre Bourdieu, Jacques Derrida, Carlos Fuentes, Edouard Glissant, and Toni Morrison together form its World Council. Its second public and ceremonial meeting will take place in Lisbon, in September 1994.

11. P. 266: Derrida writes "et le nazisme et le silence de Heidegger après la guerre" and Wolin translates simply "Heidegger's silence after the war."

P. 267: Derrida writes "au moment où l'on s'explique avec" and Wolin once again mistranslates this "explaining-with" as "interprets": "from the moment one interprets Heidegger . . ."

P. 268: Derrida writes "J'étudie avec le même souci d'autres motifs connexes," meaning "I have a similar concern when I study other related motifs"; Wolin, however, translates "With the same degree of care I study related motifs."

P. 269: Derrida writes "sur la crise, sur la décadence ou la 'destitution' de l'esprit" and Wolin translates as if it were a parallel series: "about the crisis, about decadence, or about the 'destitution' of spirit."

P. 271: Eribon's question reads in part "On dit souvent que pour lire Derrida il faut avoir lu tout Derrida. En l'occurrence, il faut avoir lu aussi Heidegger, Husserl, Nietzsche . . . ," which Wolin shortens to "One often says that in order to read Derrida, one must have read Heidegger, Husserl, Nietzsche . . ." Derrida responds to this question in part by saying "C'est une question d'économie," which Wolin renders nonsensically as "It's a question of economics" ("économie" here clearly means economizing one's time, effort, and so forth, and there is no reference to "economics" in the ordinary English sense). He continues his response: "Elle se pose, si on ne la leur pose pas, à tous les chercheurs scientifiques.

Pourquoi la poser seulement aux philosophes?" Wolin once again truncates the response to read merely "It is one that confronts all scientific researchers." Moreover, here "scientifiques" has the sense of "scholarly" in general and not of "scientific," which in English is more discipline-specific. In response to the remark that *Ulysse gramophone* is rather disconcerting, Derrida replies: "Il s'agissait de Joyce," meaning it was a matter of Joyce, I was writing about Joyce; Wolin translates: "That has to do with Joyce."

P. 272: Derrida writes "de la scène qu'on peut faire, qu'on se laisse faire" and Wolin translates "of the scene one makes if one allows oneself." Derrida writes "cela tient aussi à la façon dont ces textes sont écrits," referring clearly to the several texts of his that are then being discussed. Wolin, however, translates "it also has to do with the way in which texts are written."

12. See above, note 7.

Works Cited

Frequently cited works by Jacques Derrida are listed below alphabetically. If a published translation exists, the English title is listed first, followed by the original title.

BOOKS AND COLLECTIONS

Cinders. Translated with an introduction by Ned Luckacher. Lincoln: University of Nebraska Press, 1992. *Feu la cendre.* Paris: "Bibliothèque des voix," editions des femmes, 1987.

Dissemination. Translated by Barbara Johnson. Chicago: University of Chicago Press, 1981. *La dissémination.* Paris: Editions du Seuil, 1972.

Du droit à la philosophie. Paris: Editions Galilée, 1990.

D'un ton apocalyptique adopté naguère en philosophie. Paris: Editions Galilée, 1983. (For English translation, see "Of an Apocalyptic Tone Recently Adopted in Philosophy.")

The Ear of the Other: Otobiography, Transference, Translation. Translated by Peggy Kamuf and Avital Ronell. Edited by Christie McDonald. Lincoln: University of Nebraska Press, 1985. *L'oreille de l'autre, Oto-biographies, Transferts, Traductions.* Edited by Claude Lévesque and Christie V. McDonald. Montréal: VLB Éditeur, 1982.

Edmund Husserl's "Origin of Geometry": An Introduction. Translated by John P. Leavey, Jr. Lincoln: University of Nebraska Press, 1989 (rev. ed). *Introduction à "L'origine de la géométrie" par Edmund Husserl.* Paris: Presses Universitaires de France, 1962.

Given Time I: Counterfeit Money. Translated by Peggy Kamuf. Chicago: University of Chicago Press, 1992. *Donner le temps I, La Fausse monnaie.* Paris: Editions Galilée, 1991.

Glas. Translated by John P. Leavey, Jr. and Richard Rand. Lincoln: University of Nebraska Press, 1986. *Glas.* Paris: Editions Galilée, 1974 (reprinted, in two volumes, by Denoël/Gonthier, 1981).

Limited Inc. Translated by Samuel Weber. Evanston, Ill.: Northwestern University Press, 1988. *Limited Inc.* Edited by Elisabeth Weber. Paris: Editions Galilée, 1990.

Margins—of Philosophy. Translated by Alan Bass. Chicago: University of Chicago Press, 1982. *Marges—de la philosophie.* Paris: Editions de Minuit, 1972.

Mémoires for Paul de Man. Translated by Cecile Lindsay, Jonathan Culler, Eduardo Cadava, and Peggy Kamuf. New York: Columbia University Press, 1989 (rev. ed.). *Mémoires pour Paul de Man.* Paris: Editions Galilée, 1988.

Of Grammatology. Translated by Gayatri Chakravorty Spivak. Baltimore, Md.: Johns Hopkins University Press, 1976. *De la grammatologie.* Paris: Editions de Minuit, 1967.

Of Spirit: Heidegger and the Question. Translated by Geoffrey Bennington and Rachel Bowlby. Chicago: University of Chicago Press, 1989. *De l'esprit, Heidegger et la question.* Paris: Editions Galilée, 1987.

The Other Heading: Reflections on Today's Europe. Translated by Pascale-Anne Brault and Michael Naas. Bloomington: Indiana University Press, 1992. *L'autre cap.* Paris: Editions de Minuit, 1991.

Parages. Paris: Editions Galilée, 1986.

Positions. Translated by Alan Bass. Chicago: University of Chicago Press, 1981. *Positions.* Paris: Editions de Minuit, 1972.

The Post Card: From Socrates to Freud and Beyond. Translated by Alan Bass. Chicago: University of Chicago Press, 1987. *La carte postale, De Socrate à Freud et au-delà.* Paris: Aubier-Flammarion, 1980.

Le problème de la genèse dans la philosophie de Husserl. Paris: Presses Universitaires de France, 1990.

Psyché, Inventions de l'autre. Paris: Editions Galilée, 1987.

Schibboleth, pour Paul Celan. Paris: Editions Galilée, 1986. (For English translation, see "Shibboleth.")

Signéponge/Signsponge. Bilingual edition. Translated by Richard Rand. New York: Columbia University Press, 1984. *Signéponge.* Paris: Editions du Seuil, 1988.

Speech and Phenomena and Other Essays on Husserl's Theory of Signs. Edited and translated by David B. Allison. Evanston, Ill.: Northwestern University Press, 1973. *La voix et le phénomène, Introduction au problème du signe dans la phénoménologie de Husserl.* Paris: Presses Universitaires de France, 1967.

Spurs: Nietzsche's Styles. Translated by Barbara Harlow. Chicago: University of Chicago Press, 1979. *Eperons, Les styles de Nietzsche.* Paris: Aubier-Flammarion, 1978.

The Truth in Painting. Translated by Geoffrey Bennington and Ian McLeod. Chicago: University of Chicago Press, 1987. *La vérité en peinture.* Paris: Aubier-Flammarion, 1978.

Ulysse Gramophone, Deux mots pour Joyce. Paris: Editions Galilée, 1987. (For English translation, see "Ulysses Gramophone.")

Writing and Difference. Translated by Alan Bass. Chicago: University of Chicago Press, 1978. *L'écriture et la différence.* Paris: Editions du Seuil, 1967.

ESSAYS AND PARTS OF BOOKS

"L'âge de Hegel." In *Du droit à la philosophie.*

"At This Very Moment in This Work Here I Am." Translated by Ruben Berezdivin. In *Re-Reading Levinas*, edited by Robert Bernasconi and Simon Critchley. Bloomington: Indiana University Press, 1992. "En ce moment même dans cet ouvrage me voici." In *Psyché.*

Circumfession. Translated by Geoffrey Bennington. In Geoffrey Bennington and Jacques Derrida, *Jacques Derrida.* Chicago: University of Chicago Press, 1993. *Circonfession.* In Geoffrey Bennington and Jacques Derrida, *Jacques Derrida.* Paris: Editions du Seuil, 1991.

"Economimesis." Translated by Richard Klein. *Diacritics* 11, 2 (1981). French text in *Mimesis, Des articulations*, edited by Sylviane Agacinski et al. Paris: Aubier-Flammarion, 1975.

"Fors: The Anglish Words of Nicolas Abraham and Maria Torok." Translated by Barbara Johnson. Foreword to Nicolas Abraham and Maria Torok, *The Wolf Man's Magic Word: A Cryptonomy.* Minneapolis: University of Minnesota Press, 1986. "Fors, Les mots anglés de Nicolas Abraham et Maria Torok." Foreword to Nicolas Abraham and Maria Torok, *Cryptonomie, Le verbier de l'homme aux loups.* Paris: Aubier-Flammarion, 1976.

"*Geschlecht*: Sexual Difference, Ontological Difference." Translated by

John P. Leavey, Jr. *Research in Phenomenology* 13 (1983). "*Geschlecht*, Différence sexuelle, différence ontologique." In *Psyché.*

"*Geschlecht* II: Heidegger's Hand." Translated by John P. Leavey, Jr. In *Deconstruction and Philosophy: The Texts of Jacques Derrida*, edited by John Sallis. Chicago: University of Chicago Press, 1987. "La main de Heidegger (*Geschlecht* II)." In *Psyché.*

"How to Avoid Speaking: Denials." Translated by Ken Frieden. In *Languages of the Unsayable: The Play of Negativity in Literature and Literary Theory*, edited by Sanford Budick and Wolfgang Iser. New York: Columbia University Press, 1989. "Comment ne pas parler, Dénégations." In *Psyché.*

"The Laws of Reflection: Nelson Mandela, in Admiration." Translated by Mary Ann Caws and Isabelle Lorenz. In *For Nelson Mandela*, edited by Jacques Derrida and Mustapha Tlili. New York: Seaver Books, 1987. "Admiration de Nelson Mandela, ou les lois de la réflexion." In *Psyché.*

"Living On/Borderlines." In *Deconstruction and Criticism*, edited by Harold Bloom et al. New York: Seabury Press, 1979. "Survivre/Journal de bord." In *Parages.*

"*Mochlos*—or the Conflict of the Faculties." Translated by Richard Rand and Amy Wygant. In *Logomachia: The Conflict of the Faculties*, edited by Richard Rand. Lincoln: University of Nebraska Press, 1992. "*Mochlos*—ou le conflit des facultés." In *Du droit à la philosophie.*

"Number of Yes." Translated by Brian Holmes. *Qui Parle* 2, no. 2 (Fall 1988). "Nombre de oui." In *Psyché.*

"Of an Apocalyptic Tone Recently Adopted in Philosophy." Translated by John P. Leavey, Jr. *Oxford Literary Review* 6, no. 2 (1984). (For French edition, see *D'un ton apocalyptique adopté naguère en philosophie.*)

"Où commence et comment finit un corps enseignant." In *Du droit à la philosophie.*

"Pas." In *Parages.*

"+R (Into the Bargain)." In *The Truth in Painting.*

"The Politics of Friendship." Translated by Gabriel Motzkin and Michael Syrotinski. *American Imago* 50, no. 3 (Fall 1993). (No published French version.)

"The Principle of Reason: The University in the Eyes of Its Pupils." Translated by Catherine Porter and Edward P. Morris. *Diacritics* 13, no. 3 (1983). "Les pupilles de l'Université, Le principe de raison et l'idée de l'université." In *Du droit à la philosophie.*

"Psyche: Invention of the Other." Translated by Catherine Porter and

Philip Lewis. In *Reading de Man Reading*, edited by Wlad Godzich and Lindsay Waters. Minneapolis: University of Minnesota Press, 1989. "Psyché, Invention de l'autre." In *Psyché*.

"Racism's Last Word." Translated by Peggy Kamuf. *Critical Inquiry* 12 (1985). "Le dernier mot du racisme." In *Psyché*.

"Right of Inspection." Translated by David Wills. *Art & Text* 32 (Autumn 1989). "Droit de regards." In Marie-Françoise Plissart, *Droit de regards*. Paris: Editions de Minuit, 1985.

"Scribble (writing-power)." Abbreviated translation by Cary Plotkin. *Yale French Studies* 58 (1979). "Scribble (pouvoir / écrire)." Preface to translation of Bishop Warburton's *The Divine Legation of Moses Demonstrated: Essay on the Hieroglyphs of the Egyptians*. Paris: Aubier-Flammarion, 1977.

"Shibboleth." Translated by Joshua Wilner. In *Midrash and Literature*, edited by Geoffrey Hartman and Sanford Budick. New Haven, Conn.: Yale University Press, 1986. (For French edition, see *Schibboleth*.)

"Toward an Ethic of Discussion." Translated by Samuel Weber. In *Limited Inc*.

"Ulysses Gramophone: Hear say yes in Joyce." Translated by Tina Kendall and Shari Benstock. In *James Joyce: The Augmented Ninth*, edited by Bernard Benstock. Syracuse, N.Y.: Syracuse University Press, 1988. (For French edition, see *Ulysse Gramophone*.)

Bibliography of Other Interviews with Jacques Derrida

This selection lists only those interviews that have not been published in either two earlier collections, *Positions* and *Du droit à la philosophie*, or the present volume. [Some entries listed here are not included in the French edition. Several of these have been obtained from *Jacques Derrida: An Annotated and Secondary Bibliography*, ed. William R. Schultz and Lewis L. B. Fried (New York: Garland, 1992).]

PUBLISHED INTERVIEWS

"Culture et écriture, La prolifération des livres et la fin du livre." *Noroît* 132 (Nov. 1968).

"Avoir l'oreille de la philosophie," with Lucette Finas. *La Quinzaine Littéraire* 152 (Nov. 16–30, 1972). Reprinted in *Ecarts, Quatre essais à propos de Jacques Derrida*. Paris: Fayard, 1973.

"Philosophie et communication," discussion with Paul Ricoeur. In *La Communication, Actes du XVe Congrès de l'Association des sociétés de philosophie de langue française*. Montréal: Editions Montmorency, 1973.

"Jacques Derrida" (interview). *Almanach de Shakespeare and Company* 2 (1975).

"Littéraire, philosophique et politique sont inséparables," with S. Agacinski, S. Kofman, P. Lacoue-Labarthe, J.-L. Nancy, B. Pautrat. Article prepared by C. Delacampagne. *Le Monde*, Nov. 30, 1976.

"An Interview with Jacques Derrida," with J. Kearns and K. Newton. *Literary Review* 14 (Apr.–May 1980).

"Jacques Derrida, Europas 'svazarte' filosof," with Horace Engdahl. *Expressen*, Apr. 23, 1981 (Sweden).

"Jacques Derrida sur les traces de la philosophie," with Christian Descamps. *Le Monde*, Jan. 31, 1982. Reprinted in *Entretiens avec Le Monde*, vol. 1. Paris: La Découverte, 1984.

Discussions of *The Post Card* with Marie Moscovici, Jean-Claude Sempe, Didier Cahen et al. In *Affranchissement du transfert et de la lettre*, edited by René Major. Paris: Editions Confrontations, 1982.

"Je n'écris pas sans lumière artificielle," with André Rollin. *Le fou parle*, Nov. 21–22, 1982.

"Derrida, philosophie au Collège," with J.-L. Thébaut. *Libération*, Aug. 11, 1983.

"La visite de Jacques Derrida," *VU!* 38–39 (Jan. 1984) (Japan).

"Questions à Jacques Derrida: *Eidos* et *télé-vision*," with Bernard Stiegler. *Digraphe* 33 (May 1984).

"Les philosophes et la parole, Passage du témoin de François Georges à Jacques Derrida" (a series of radio programs on France-Culture). *Le Monde*, Oct. 21–22, 1984.

"Plaidoyer pour la métaphysique," with Jean-François Lyotard. *Le Monde*, Oct. 28, 1984.

"Jacques Derrida: Deconstruction and the Other," with R. Kearney. In *Dialogues with Contemporary Continental Thinkers: The Phenomenological Heritage*. Manchester, Eng.: Manchester University Press, 1984.

"Artists, Philosophers, and Institutions." *Rampike* 3:3 and 4:1.

"Deconstruction in America: An Interview with Jacques Derrida," with James Creech, Peggy Kamuf, and Jane Todd. *Critical Exchange* 17 (Winter 1985).

"The Crisis in Knowledge: Poststructuralism, Postmodernism, Postmodernity," with R. Cheatham and J. Cullum. *Arts Papers* 10, no. 1 (Jan.–Feb. 1986).

"Jacques Derrida on the University," with Imre Salusinszky. *Southern Review* 19, no. 1 (Mar. 1986) (Australia). Reprinted in *Criticism in Society*, edited by Salusinszky. London: Methuen, 1987.

"Une carte postale de l'Amérique," with V. Vasterling. *Krisis: Tijdschrift voor filosofie*, Mar. 22, 1986 (Amsterdam).

"Entrevista: Del materialismo no dialectico," with K. Jihad. *Culturas* 69 (Aug. 1986).

"Deconstruction: A Trialogue in Jerusalem," with G. Hartman and W. Iser. *Mishkenot Sha'ananim Newsletter* 7 (Dec. 1986) (Israel).

"Architecture et philosophie," with Eva Meyer. Translated in *Beseda: Revue de philosophie et de religion* 4 (1986) (Leningrad-Paris).

"Gespräch," with Florian Rötzer. In *Französische Philosophen im Gespräch*. München: Klaus Boer Verlag, 1986.

"Jacques Derrida: Leer lo ilegible, deporte y modernidad," with C. Conzales-Marin. *Revista de Occidente* 62–63 (1986) (Spain).

"On Colleges and Philosophy," with G. Bennington. *ICA Documents* 4–5, 1986. Reprinted in *Postmodernism: ICA Documents*, edited by Lisa Appignanesi. London: Free Association Books, 1989.

"Artaud et ses doubles," with J.-M. Olivier. *Scènes Magazines*, Feb. 5, 1987 (Geneva).

"Ma l'ideologia non è azione," with Lidia Breda. *Panorama*, Nov. 8, 1987 (Milan).

"Labyrinth und Archi-Textur," with E. Meyer. In *Das Abenteuer der Ideen*. Berlin: Internationale Bauausstellung, 1987.

" 'Les mots' auto-biographiques—pourquoi pas (why not) Sartre," with Minatomichi (in Japanese). *Revue de la pensée aujourd'hui* 15, no. 8 (1987).

"Some Questions and Responses." In *The Linguistics of Writing: Arguments Between Language and Literature*, edited by N. Fabb, D. Attridge, A. Durant, and C. MacCabe. Manchester, Eng.: Manchester University Press, 1987.

"A Conversation with Jacques Derrida," with G. Vergani, P. Shinoda, and D. Kesler. *Precis* 6 (1987).

"Philosophie, s'ouvrir aux provocations de la modernité," with P. Chastener. *Sud-Ouest Dimanche*, June 19, 1988.

"Le philosophe et les architectes," with Hélène Viale. *Diagonal* 73 (Aug. 1988).

"Controverse sur la possibilité d'une science de la philosophie," debate with F. Laruelle. *La décision philosophique* 5 (1988).

"The Derridean View," with E. Marx. *BM 04* 2, no. 1 (Sept. 1988).

"Abus de pouvoir à la Sorbonne," with H. Guirchoun. *Le Nouvel Observateur* 1255 (Nov. 24–30, 1988).

"Conversation with Jacques Derrida (1), L'école a été un enfer pour moi," with B. Defrance. *Cahiers pédagogiques* 270 (Jan. 1989).

"Conversation with Jacques Derrida (2), Libérer la curiosité, susciter du désir," with B. Defrance. *Cahiers pédagogiques* 272 (Mar. 1989).

"Jacques Derrida in Conversation with Christopher Norris." *Architectural Design* 58, nos. 1–2 (1989). Reprinted in *Deconstruction: Omnibus*

Volume, edited by Andreas Papadakis, Catherine Cooke, and Andrew Benjamin. New York: Rizzoli, 1989.

"Entrevista con Jacques Derrida," with C. de Peretti. *Politica y Sociedad* 3 (Spring 1989) (Madrid).

"Jacques Derrida, autor de la teoria de la 'deconstrucción': La Amistad esta siempre por venir, y solo llegara con el superhombre," with Cristina de Peretti. *El Independiente* 12 (Dec. 24, 1989) (Madrid).

"Un penseur dans la cité, Jacques Derrida," with Yves Roucaute. *L'événement du jeudi* 284 (Apr. 1990).

"Accecato di fronte al disegno," with Luciana Mottola Colban. *Il Giornale dell'Arte* 82 (Oct. 1990) (Italy).

"Jacques Derrida, ici et ailleurs," with Roger-Pol Droit. *Le Monde*, Nov. 16, 1990.

"La democrazia come pensiero e promessa," with Manlio Iofrida. *L'Unità*, Nov. 17, 1990.

"A Discussion with Jacques Derrida," with Peggy Kamuf et al. *Writing Instructor* 9, nos. 1–2 (Fall 1989–Winter 1990).

"Le dessein du philosophe," with J. Coignard. *Beaux-Arts* 85 (Dec. 1990).

"Jacques Derrida on Rhetoric and Composition: A Conversation," with Gary A. Olson. *Journal of Advanced Composition* 10, no. 1 (1990).

"Feminismo y de(s)construcción," with C. de Peretti. *Debate Feminista* 2 (1990) (Mexico).

Interview with Derrida, conducted by Raoul Mortley. In *French Philosophers in Conversation*. London: Routledge, 1990.

"Socrate, raccontaci una storia: Intervista con Jacques Derrida sullo stato della filosofia contemporanea," with C. Dignola. *Avvenira*, Jan. 17, 1991 (Milan).

"Entretien avec Jacques Derrida," with F. Bilbaut-Faillant. *La Sept* 13 (program broadcast Mar. 23–29, 1991).

"Conversation," with Raoul Mortley. In *French Philosophers in Conversation*. London: Routledge, 1991.

"Otazky se nikdy nelze vzdat" (One must never give up asking questions), with Karel Thein. *Pritomnost* 3 (1991) (Prague).

"Summary of Impromptu Remarks." In *Anyone,* edited by C. Davidson and J. Kipnis. New York: Rizzoli, 1991.

"Guai ai nuovi domatismi," with Vincenzo Vitiello. *Il Mattino*, Mar. 2, 1991 (Naples).

"This Strange Institution Called Literature," with Derek Attridge. In *Acts of Literature*, edited by Attridge. New York: Routledge, 1992.

"L'atelier de Valerio Adami, Le tableau est avant tout un système de mémoire," text edited by Armelle Auris. *Rue Descartes* 4 (1992).

"Autour de Paul de Man," with Michel Deguy, Elisabeth de Fontenay, Alexander García Düttmann, and Marie-Louise Mallet. *Les Papiers du Collège International de Philosophie* 11 (1992).

"Conversazione," with Maurizio Ferraris. *Aut Aut* 248–49 (Mar.–June 1992).

"Le frontiere di Derrida," with Fabio Gambaro. *La Repubblica,* July 8, 1992 (Italy).

"Canons and Metonymies," with Richard Rand. In *Logomachia: The Conflict of the Faculties,* edited by Rand. Lincoln: University of Nebraska Press, 1992.

"Invitation to a Discussion," with Mark Wigley. *Columbia Documents,* 1992.

"Répliques" (on Francis Ponge), with G. Farasse. *Revue des Sciences Humaines* 228, no. 4 (1992).

VIDEO AND TELEVISION INTERVIEWS

"Réflexions faites: Jacques Derrida," film by Didier Eribon, directed by Philippe Collin, GMT Productions (with Geoff Bennington, Hélène Cixous, René Major, Gérard Titus-Carmel, Gianni Vattimo). *La Sept en cassettes.* Paris: Scherzo, 1990.

"Les Grands Entretiens: Jacques Derrida," by A. Spire, with M. Field and P. Pachet. Paris: Socam Video, 1991.

"Architecture et déconstruction," with Asada A. and Isosaki A. Tokyo: NH4, 1992.

"Interview," with Alan Montefiore (Oxford Amnesty Lectures, Feb. 13, 1992). Broadcast by Channel Four.

MERIDIAN

Crossing Aesthetics

Jacques Derrida, *Points . . . (Interviews, 1974–1994)*

J. Hillis Miller, *Topographies*

Philippe Lacoue-Labarthe, *Musica Ficta (Figures of Wagner)*

Jacques Derrida, *Aporias*

Emmanuel Levinas, *Outside the Subject*

Jean-François Lyotard, *On the Analytic of the Sublime*

Peter Fenves, *"Chatter": Language and History in Kierkegaard*

Jean-Luc Nancy, *The Experience of Freedom*

Jean-Joseph Goux, *Oedipus, Philosopher*

Haun Saussy, *The Problem of a Chinese Aesthetic*

Jean-Luc Nancy, *The Birth to Presence*

Library of Congress
Cataloging-in-Publication Data

Derrida, Jacques.
[Points de suspension. English]
Points . . . : interviews, 1974–1994 /
Jacques Derrida ; edited by Elisabeth Weber ;
translated by Peggy Kamuf & others.
p.   cm. — (Meridian : crossing aesthetics)
Also includes two articles not in the original French ed.:
Honoris Causa; The work of intellectuals and the press.
Includes bibliographical references.
ISBN 0-8047-2395-8 (cl.)
ISBN 0-8047-2488-1 (pbk.)
1. Philosophy.   I. Weber, Elisabeth, 1959–   .   II. Title.
III. Series: Meridian (Stanford, Calif.)
B2430.D483P6513   1995
194—dc20
94-26823
CIP
Rev.

⊛ This book is printed on acid-free, recycled paper.
It was typeset in Adobe Garamond and Lithos by
Keystone Typesetting, Inc.